She Is Everywhere! Vol. 2

The Circle at Brescia

1285 Western Road

London, Ontario, Canada

N6G 1H2

"Dance of the Serpent" by Tricia Grame
10.5" X 8" lead, and coffee liquid, 40 works on watercolor paper

She Is Everywhere! Vol. 2

An anthology of writings in womanist/ feminist spirituality

gathered by Annette Lyn Williams, M.A., Karen Nelson Villanueva, M.A., and Lucia Chiavola Birnbaum, Ph.D.

Chandra Alexandre, Victoria Batraski, Laura Scaccia Beagle, Kim Bella, Lucia Birnbaum, Joan Beth Clair, Jayne DeMente, Ida J. Dunson, May Elawar, Maria Fama, Elinor Gadon, China Galland, Heide Goettner-Abendroth, Tricia Grame, Deborah Grenn, Dianne Jenett, Pairin Jotisakulratana, Mara Keller, Malgorzata (Margaret) Kruszewska, Jamie Kuehnl, Willow LaMonte, Naomi Lombardi, Jodi MacMillan, Jan Marijaq, Tommi Mecca, Jen Miller-Hogg, Rainbow Mooon, Louise Pare, Arisika Razak, Dorotea Reyna, Mary Ann Robinson, Francesca Roccaforte, Genevieve Vaughan, Karen Nelson Villanueva, Claudia von Werlhof, Addae Watson, Annette Williams, Gina Wilson, Lynne Wilson

iUniverse, Inc.
New York   Bloomington

She Is Everywhere Vol. 2
An anthology of writing in womanist/feminist sprituality

The gatherers of this anthology have kept in mind that we do not want to define an author or define an author's work by trying to make the text of this anthology consistent in style, grammar, punctuation, et al.

iUniverse books may be ordered through booksellers or by contacting:

iUniverse
1663 Liberty Drive
Bloomington, IN 47403
www.iuniverse.com
1-800-Authors (1-800-288-4677)

ISBN: 978-0-595-46668-9 (pbk)
ISBN: 978-0-595-49518-4(cloth)
ISBN: 978-0-595-90963-6 (ebk)

Printed in the United States of America

iUniverse rev. 12/18/2008

to her

All royalties from this volume of She is Everywhere! are donated to the Women's Spirituality program of the California Institute of Integral Studies to help fund diversity scholarships.

"My hypothesis is that primordial and continuing migrations from Africa, as well as return migrations of ultimately african semites from west Asia into the region greeks called Europe, left a cellular and/or cultural memory that has persisted in descendants of african migrants."

-- Lucia Chiavola Birnbaum

"It is humbling to think that we matter so much to our creator that, in the complexities of one small life, so much love could be bestowed on us by spiritual beings 'disguised' as animals; in spite of the deep lack of understanding that their life forms may inspire in others."

-- Joan Beth Clair

"Feminism is not just a question of countering sexism, of allowing more women into academic, government or business positions but it is a question of revising all our thinking and economic behavior to create our humanity in a different way, through free and liberated gift giving."

-- Genevieve Vaughan

"There is no question that Mary is the female figure to whom the greatest attention is given in the *Qur'an*."

-- May Elawar

"How is the Creator Woman of South Africa, the caring Mother and also the life-giving Mother--as well as the rageful, independent, rebellious woman--embodied in the Semitic goddesses Lilith, Ishtar, Tanit, and in us?"

-- Deborah Grenn

"Perhaps the appeal of Juliana is that she can be whatever the pilgrim needs her to be."

-- Jen Miller-Hogg

"Annapurna Ma is a gracious, attractive woman in her mid-forties who lives with her husband and family in an ample thatched-roof house by the side of the shrine of the Goddess Sarangei whom she serves. ... Annapurna Ma serves her goddess, Sarangei, as a priestess and her devotees as a healer."

-- Elinor Gadon

"…all of her forms and manifestations are rooted in the power of the primordial mother, the Mother of all creatures."

-- Pairin Jotisakulratana

"With the Eve-Jezebel-accursed female mythos firmly entrenched in our collective psyches and a cornerstone of major world religions, it is little wonder that the area of women's sexual rights and freedom is one of rancorous political struggle…The struggle is not a modern phenomenon. It is a struggle that is at the very heart of Jezebel's story."

-- Annette Williams

"I am hopeful that as we move further into this new millennium, psychic women will continue to come out of the closets, the kitchens, the gardens, wherever we're hiding, and tell the delectable, passionate mysteries or mist-stories of the love between body and spirit."

-- Jodi MacMillan

"As we live through the opening years of a new millennium, we need to question whether we will perpetuate the evils of times that have gone before."

-- Jan I. Marijaq

"I believe these long-lived cultural images of *sacred African women* have the power to nurture and heal our bruised embattled psyches, awakening us to the many possibilities of our inherent divinity, creativity, and beauty."

-- Arisika Razak

"In order for me to embrace intrinsic movement as my spiritual practice I had to cultivate a faith and trust in the wisdom of my moving body."

-- Louise M. Paré

"Woman's love---a mother's, wife's, sister's or a daughter's, any woman's---by its own law fosters and sustains life, but the male always assails with his pride, ambition, self-righteousness, and the woman pays, hapless mankind pays, the entire commonwealth pays; but woman pays most of all."

-- Rainbow Mooon

"The Fall" from biblical Genesis is a powerful, sublime passage that has dictated doctrine, impassioned souls, and mobilized the masses, for better or for worse.

-- Jamie Kuehnl

"A woman to emulate, to walk with on my journey: for me she is there in Mary and Eve, hand in hand, the serpent binding them into one woman, a woman of earth and sky and sea, a woman of the day and of the night—a VIRGIN—a WOMAN—EVA and AVE."

-- Mary Ann Robinson

"Perhaps it is a faith and belief in the feminine Divine, like Mari, God the Mother of the Basque, who promises our most success as a species, through her, we are all her children, and this is our only home."

-- Karen Nelson Villanueva

"For me, this event was a way of following Black Elk's teaching, which tells us that: in order to have the power of one's vision, one has to perform it on the earth for all the people to see."

-- China Galland

"With the acceptance of the Goddess across cultures, and with Her followers taking on roles of leadership, I firmly believe that a more fully integrated ecofeminism of Tantra, in which theory and praxis come together for both participatory discourse and action, will facilitate a new paradigm."

-- Chandra Alexandre

'At the two *World Congresses on Matriarchal Studies* which took place in 2003 in Luxembourg/Europe and in 2005 in San Marcos/Texas, the speakers and scholars who presented their international research there have introduced the term "matriarchy" for all non-patriarchal societies worldwide.'

-- Heide Goettner-Abendroth

Contents

List of Illustrations xix

Note on Style for *She is Everywhere! Vol. 2* xxi

Prefaces xxiii

Untitled 1

Addae Watson, M.Div.

Jezebel. Whore? 5

Annette Williams, M.A.

"I Found God in Myself": Sacred Images of African and

African-American Women 21

Arisika Razak, R.N., C.N.M., M.P.H.

Exploring a Cross-Cultural Women's Spirituality:

Inspirations from India 41

Chandra Alexandre, Ph.D.

Awakening the Energy for Change: The Black Madonna

and the Womb of God 57

China Galland, M.A.

Self-appointed Saviors Propagate Globalization 71

Claudia von Werlhof, Ph.D.

Creator Woman 81

    Deborah J. Grenn, Ph.D.

As If There Were A Goddess 95

    Dianne E. Jenett, Ph.D.

One Day 111

    Dorotea Reyna, M.A.

Annapurna Ma: Priestess and Healer 113

    Elinor Gadon, Ph.D.

Beyond the Wooden Spoon 125

    Francesca Roccaforte, poet and painter

Hot Tomatoes 129

    Francesca Roccaforte, poet and painter

She is in the words we speak and in the better world we seek. .131

    Genevieve Vaughan, Gift Economy theorist

Untitled 143

    Gina Wilson, M.A.

Matriarchal Society - Definition and Theory 145

    Heide Goettner-Abendroth, Ph.D.

A color blind society? A big affirmative action scam! 155

    Ida J. Dunson, poet

Falling for Knowledge: New Interpretations of "The Fall"

    in Genesis 157

    Jamie Logsdon Kuehnl, M.A.

Soul and Soullessness 169

    Jan I. Marijaq , Ph.D.

The Trinity of the Hebrew Goddess 181

    Jayne Marie DeMente, M.A.

Looking for Saint Juliana 199

    Jen Miller-Hogg, M.A.

The Spirit of Moon: A Journey of Love. 207

    Joan Beth Clair, M.A., M.Div.

"The Caul". .217

    Jodi MacMillan, M.A.

Mari: God the Mother of the Basque 223

    Karen Nelson Villanueva, M.P.A., M.A.

Rags to Riches: The Inner Road to Gypsyhood 237

    Kim Bella, M.A.

Ancient Ache 253

    Laura Scaccia Beagle, poet and novelist

Moving Between the Worlds 255

    Louise M. Paré, Ph.D.

The Future Has An Ancient Heart 269

    Lucia Chiavola Birnbaum, Ph.D.

Sardegna. 285

    Lynne Wilson, poet

Krolow Polski: Black Queen-Mothers of Poland 287

   Małgorzata (Margaret) Kruszewska, M.A.

Goddess-God Creation Myth 305

   Mara Lynn Keller , Ph.D.

I Am Not White 309

   Maria Fama, poet

A Beautiful Mother, A Sister to Walk with Us 311

   Mary Ann Robinson , M.A.

Mary in Islam 325

   May Elawar, M.A.

Dancing in the Underworld 337

   Naomi Lombardi, M.A.

Primordial Mothers in My Chinese Family 349

   Pairin Jotisakulratana, M.A.

Sita: Perfect Wife or Glorified Sex Object in K. R. Srinivasa

Iyengar's Sitayana 361

   Rainbow Mooon, M.A.

La Madre Nera 375

   Tommi Avicolli Mecca, poet

The Symbol: A Source of Empowerment 381

   Tricia Grame, Ph.D.

In honor…in remembrance….of Love's Voice 393

   Victoria M. Batraski, M.A.

Perhaps I'll Find Her? .397

Willow LaMonte, founder of "Goddessing" journal

Biographies 401

List of Illustrations

Cover sculpture: "Creator Woman" by Meshack Raphalalani, "Creator Woman" is shown reaching out to children, offering them safe haven in her womb during the 1980s, when apartheid was still legally sanctioned in South Africa.

Cover image: Marc Babin, Dragonhart Studios ©

Cover photo: Deborah J. Grenn, The Lilith Institute ©

"Dance of the Serpent" by Tricia Grame ii

Tanit, ancient African deity of Carthage 3

Ochumare, Goddess of the Rainbow, by Asungi 32

Dunham's Life Song, by Asungi. 32

The Teacher by Earthlyn Manuel 34

The Lover by Earthlyn Manuel 34

Kāmākhyā Mandir during Ambubāchī Mela 54

Anti-war poster inside the sanctuary of the Black Madonna of Monserrat . . 130

Mural inside the sanctuary of the Black Madonna of Monserrat, Spain . . . 221

Sunflower by Latonia Dixon 251

Menhirs, markers of African migration paths, Place of Silence, Sardinia . . . 268

The Goddess Has A Thousand Faces Mandala, banner by Lydia Ruyle 282

Nuestra Senora La Virgen de Guadalupe, banner by Lydia Ruyle 283

The Great Mother of Catalhoyuk, banner by Lydia Ruyle 284

Black Madonna – Ausros Vartai (Vilnius, Lithuania) 302

Black Madonna – Matka Boza Loretanska (Glogowek, Poland) 303

"Beyond the Symbol" series by Tricia Grame 378

"Beyond the Symbol" series by Tricia Grame 379

"Beyond the Symbol" series by Tricia Grame 380

Owl painted by Stella Kimura 392

Contemporary sculpture that recalls the ancient African black mother and child. . . 399

"Beyond the Symbol" series by Tricia Grame 409

Back cover: "The Madonna of the Rosary in the Woods" by Sculptor Bill Dilley. St. John Vianney Catholic Church, Vashon Island, Washington.

This peaceful Madonna stands in the center of a circle of stones which form a rosary in the woods of Vashon Island. Her organic form, lined with the rich grain of the dark wood, rises over ten feet tall and is crowned with stars. Bill Dilley, the Native American artist who carved this Madonna, wanted his sculpture of Her to have a more universal representation. The Madonna's indigenous features do indeed seem to reflect many cultures. Like the surrounding tall trees that shelter her, this Madonna is rooted in the earth, and washed by the Northwest rains. Her temple is in Nature, accessible to all. She is truly everywhere.

Back cover photo: Mary Beth Moser

Note on Style for *She is Everywhere! Vol. 2*

This anthology, like volume one of *She is Everywhere!* offers
visions, values, tones, and images of women across the ages from
the beginning of time. This is suggested in the many styles and
the kaleidoscope of illustrations. Contributions to this anthology
are "unedited" in the sense that nobody modified anyone's vision,
an open-endedness that also extends to style. Examples of this are
Lucia's habit of downcasing, and Karen's recommendation to order
writings in alphabetical order by the author's first name.

Historically, contributors to volume two of *She is Everywhere!* are
writing in what may be the end times of violent western male elite
patriarchies. These dominant western patriarchies are comprised
of individuals who, according to Lucia, "mistakenly think they are
white because in reality all human life evolved just once in Africa."

More scholarly, perhaps, than contemporary purveyors of
masculinist epistemologics, we acknowledge (in the best
understanding of science) that the variable of perception conditions
all knowledge; and consider that, far from being a flaw, empathy
may open a scholar to deeper knowledge. We hope readers will
glimpse in this sampling some of the hopeful possibilities that
await our nurturance to help them unfold.

Prefaces

I am writing this in 2006 on January 6, date of the church celebration of epiphany, a celebration personified as La Befana in popular latin cultures. For the catholic church, the date marks the holy day of epiphany when the "three kings of the Orient" reached the infant Jesus with gifts of gold, frankincense, and myrrh, an epiphany that signifies that Jesus was the divine son of god.   The vernacular version of this church story in latin countries, notably Italy, is the festa of La Befana, when an old lady called a witch, brings gifts to children on January 6.

In the Women's Spirituality program of California Institute of Integral Studies my classes emphasize appreciation, with a critical perspective, of the differing wisdoms conveyed by doctrines of church and state - - and folklore, or the wisdom of submerged cultures.   In the dominant version of epiphany, all three kings are identified with the "Orient" although one of the kings is from Ethiopia, the ancient term for Africa. The encapsulation of Africa into west Asia has been persistent misinformation conveyed by church and state and by courtier historians, for two millennia.

Church doctrine and authoritative knowledge purveyed by the state have, for two millennia, been considered "true" while everyday and celebratory ways of knowing of subaltern cultures have been ignored or denigrated as "superstition." Knowledge considered threatening to dominant elites has, historically, been branded heresy, and its carriers burned. In the west in the first half of the twentieth century in the thrust toward secularism, for something to be considered "true" it had to be identified with science. Subsequently a half century of deconstruction has led to a consensus of scientists and other scholars by 2006 that objectivity is an illusion - - although the goal remains, for all scholars - - for example in my discipline of feminist cultural history- - to research and tell a story that is as true as possible, which, in my view, means a story informed by as many ways of knowing as possible, not only to deepen our understanding but by checking and balancing differing ways of knowing.

In the enterprise that may historically characterize our time - - the recovery of the submerged story of humankind - - everyone is a researcher in the rescue of suppressed wisdoms, notably the recovery of submerged ways of knowing that informed our grandparents' everyday and celebratory rituals. Folklore, rather than a dilettante amusement, becomes indispensable to this large endeavor of bringing to everyone's awareness the suppressed whole story of humanity. . . a first step in healing the lives of people on our unjust and violent planet.

The folk story of La Befana is a case in point. The story of the witch grandmother (who ultimately refers to the black mother of Africa; see my article in this anthology) recounts that Balthazar, Melchior, and Caspar on their journey to honor the Jesus child, stopped by La Befana's house and invited her to come along with them. In what may be interpreted as a feminist parable, she responded, first she had to sweep her house and then she would take her own journey.

The celebration of La Befana in subaltern cultures reveals a wisdom different from that of the church story. Kings of the known world brought gold, frankincense, and myrrh to Jesus, signifying that he was the christ. La Befana, in a continuing memory (often played out in festive rituals) recalls the black mother of Africa who gave the gift of life to all humans. On January 6, La Befana, an old woman who has historically been persecuted as a witch, brings gifts - - not to one child - - but to *all* children- - signifying, perhaps, that all children are divine. The grandmotherly old witch (strega nonna in italian) gives every child sweets. . . perhaps connoting african wisdom (and the wisdom that can be found on african migration paths throughout the world) as to how a good life is lived. . . working not for individual salvation nor for the state purposes of one's nation,   nor for a utopia reached by violence, but for communities of justice with healing, equality, and nonviolent transformation.

O

This volume of *She is Everywhere!* has three editors, more precisely gatherers, in which Lucia may be regarded as an older gatherer and Annette and Karen as younger gatherers of scholarly and creative work in this enterprise of recovering many ways of knowing. The volume's contributors are particularly indebted to Annette Williams who did all the tedious work of preparing the manuscript for publication. We hope that this anthology will sustain the reader on her or his chosen path toward the nonviolent cultural and political revolution of our time . . . greening the earth with the values of La Befana.

Lucia Chiavola Birnbaum, Ph.D.
Berkeley, California
January 10, 2006

I am dedicating this second volume of *She is Everywhere!* to my toddler *great-grand daughter*, Josephine Lucia Landreth, who is named for my sicilian *grandmothers*, Guiseppina and Lucia.

A womanist/feminist anthology is a delicious concept. It is a place where one can savor multiple flavors and manifestations of SHE – a place where contributors can share their awakening to SHE and their journey to her bosom, a place where being ripped out of her motherly arms can be mourned, a place where death delivering anger at subjugation can be unleashed, and a place where maiden innocence and joy can be found as we rediscover and explore the sensual richness of SHE!

In my ongoing pilgrimage back to SHE, I have recognized my wounding in that which has been stolen from me as well as ascribed to me. I mourn. I have lashed out with scathing diatribe, dagger-tipped pen, and sword-sharp tongue. I kill. I have felt her presence as I dive within my psyche and expunge the radioactive waste that is patriarchal conditioning. I rejoice.

Realization of the complex and nefarious nature of patriarchal conditioning is an area of particular focus. That is in my interest in digging to the root of personal expressions of this contamination in one's life, just as it is my interest to look at the historical roots of various patriarchal aspects and assumptions. Under the millennia of encrusted dominator values and conditioning is the bedrock of Her values. These values encompass mutual love and support between the sexes not subjugation or abuse of one gender by the other.

Excavating my past has also brought me an appreciation of the Afro-Caribbean relationship to SHE as seen through traditional beliefs and practices. Based on ancient tradition, the West African Yoruba continue to honor the *mother* as powerful life-giver and life-taker. Her role in the creation and maintenance of our world is central, and there is acknowledgement that it is through Her power and blessing that kings rule.

More personally, I look at family – my grandmother the Rosicrucian; my grandfather the babalawo in Matanza, Cuba; my eldest sister, omo Yemaya, initiated into Santeria. As I witness their questioning and rejection of the dominant religious paradigms, I feel I have inherited this thirst to quest beyond the status quo of accepted dogma.

In the *She is Everywhere!* anthologies, is found a community of individuals who also quest beyond the status quo of accepted dogma to find SHE who moves in a realm beyond the dogmatic and profane. What is revealed and shared with the reader is SHE in many of her profound and personal, delightful, death-wielding,

and delicious manifestations.
Enjoy the banquet.

Annette Lyn Williams, M.A.
Doctoral Student in Women's Spirituality
At the California Institute of Integral Studies
San Francisco
January 2006

Postscript
It was our hope that the second volume of *She is Everywhere!* would follow closely on the heels of the publication of volume one in 2005. For better or worse the realization of this project has been intimately linked to my own life over the past two years.

The process of gathering submissions for the present volume began in late 2005. In March of 2006, a few weeks before my birthday, I lost my father. I experienced my grief as numbness as I attempted to *get on with life*. This suppression of pain, sadness, and loss only served to prolong the passage through grief. One result of this was that for a good while work on *She is Everywhere! Volume 2* progressed only haltingly. For this I apologize to the volume's contributors who have waited patiently to see their works in print. Thank you for your kindness and understanding.

In this season of remembering our ancestors, I say *Iba'se egun* – homage to the ancestors. On a personal note I say *Mojuba*, daddy. I send you love.

Annette Williams
San Francisco
October 29, 2007

It is through a diversity of voices that She speaks more clearly. For surely it is the spaces in between where She dwells because She is the web, our interconnectedness and interrelatedness to all beings. This is the reason why She is Everywhere!

This volume is an attempt to continue the dialogue that began with the publication of *She is Everywhere! Volume 1*. It includes the essays, poems, and works of art from the growing community of women and men who recognize Her and feel Her call to expression in many forms. Only the page limitations of publishing kept us from including more. With that said, I hope that others will keep the momentum going and continue where we leave off with *She is Everywhere! Volume 3*.

Anthologies of this sort do not come into existence without a tremendous amount of effort. Much of the ground was already broken by our predecessors at Belladonna in presenting *She is Everywhere! Volume 1*, particularly Jodi Macmillan and Andrew Fitzpatrick. In the creation of Volume 2, the support of the degree programs in Women's Spirituality at the California Institute of Integral Studies (CIIS) was immeasurable. This includes program director Mara Lynn Keller, PhD and core faculty Arisika Razak, MPH, and Charlene Spretnak, MA.

Nothing would have been accomplished without the terrific organizational skills of Annette Lyn Williams, co-editor and program assistant at CIIS. She worked tirelessly to enter documents, coordinate with the publisher, and communicate with this volume's contributors. Additionally, none of these volumes would have been conceived without the foresight, vision, and courage to speak Her truth as evinced in the life and work of Lucia Chiavola Birnbaum, PhD core faculty in the Women's Spirituality program at CIIS and author of such courageous and honest works as *Liberazione della Donna: feminism in Italy, Black Madonnas: feminism, religion, and politics in Italy, Dark Mother: Godmothers and African origins*; and her forthcoming *The Future has an Ancient Heart*. I am honored to be included in the effort along with these two remarkable women to speak Her wisdom and let it be heard by the world.

Were it not for the encouragement and support from my husband

and hero Max, I would not be able to be a part of any of the dreams that I have realized. My support system also includes my family on this earth: Encarnacion, Nicole, Kelley, Tracy, and Lauren. Also, I draw support from my family that blesses me from beyond: Mignon, Seigmond, Mamerto, Ethel, June, Harold, and Matilda. To all my ancestors, thank you.

To all of the fabulous people who contributed to this volume, thank you, too. We placed all the works alphabetically according to first name.

May this book be a blessing to all who read it.

Karen Nelson Villanueva, MPA, MA
Doctoral Student in Women's Spirituality
At the California Institute of Integral Studies
San Francisco, California
February 1, 2006

Untitled

Addae Watson, M.Div.

Women, beautiful, women
Grandmothers, mothers,
big bosomed women with
hands that gently stroke my face
and
braid my hair women

Hush baby don't cry
come here,
let big mamma wipe the tears from your eyes

Women, fearless, women
Grandmothers, mothers, daughters
Hands folded in prayer,
scripture reading, faith filled women

Baby
God is good
on time, all the time

Women, busy, Women
Grandmothers, mothers, sisters,
Creative, prize winning
Hands that bake, quilt and sew women

Baby
I made your favorite chocalate cake

Women, bold, women
Grandmothers, mothers, aunties
ebony hued,head turning,
hands on hips audacious women

Ooh child
you're wearing that dress

Women, circles of women
Great grandmothers, grandmothers,
mothers, aunties, sisters, friends
gathering
laying on hands
healing
ordaining
Loving,
women

Addae
copyright Nov.2005

Tanit, ancient African deity of Carthage
who has become an international symbolof world feminism and other
movements of transformation.
Museo Nazionale, G.A., Sassari, Sardinia
Photograph by Wallace Birnbaum 2004

Jezebel. Whore?

Annette Williams, M.A.

My name is Jezebel Mort: you know the thing that that means;
If ever one comes into Court, they call us pleasure-machines.
Aye, for men we were made, and men were made for our sex.
-- from the poem *Jezebel Mort*
by Arthur Symons

The archetypical Jezebel is commonly portrayed as a woman of carnal lust. Listening to the preachers of my youth it was clear that this Jezebel could trace her lineage to the biblical Jezebel of the Old Testament, who was characterized as a whore and a harlot. I knew that if a woman was referred to as "a Jezebel" it meant she was sexually wicked.

Who was this original Jezebel whose name has become an accusation? To be called a Jezebel is to be stigmatized a harlot as clearly as the punishment of wearing *the scarlet letter* branded a woman adulteress. Here, I will visit the life and times of the Jezebel portrayed in the Bible. Was Jezebel a notorious whore? If not, and there seems to be no evidence that she was,[1] why was she so branded? Why, more intriguingly, has the legacy ascribed to her endured over the millennia?

Visiting the life and times of Jezebel is to situate her within her historical and socio-cultural context. The importance of contextualizing biblical accounts is becoming increasingly recognized. Elisabeth Schüssler Fiorenza, scholar of biblical hermeneutics and feminist theology, states:

> Studies of the social world of Israel and early Christianity are in the process of developing heuristic models...that comprehend more fully the social-historical context of the biblical texts. Similarly, feminist theory insists that all texts are products of an androcentric patriarchal culture and history.[2]

The story of Jezebel is no exception.

This paper leans heavily on the work of Janet Howe Gaines. <u>Music in the Old Bones, Jezebel Through the Ages</u> shows Jezebel's maligned portrayal in literature, poetry, music, plays and cinema. However, more importantly, it is Gaines' narrative analysis that masterfully deconstructs each element of Jezebel's story pointing out the inconsistencies and imaginative leaps required to accept it as written. She discusses possible motivations for the biblical compilers to have constructed the story as given and injects feminist rationality into the story of Jezebel.

Gaines states the importance of keeping in mind that the traditional reading of Jezebel's tale "upholds a particular religious, cultural, and political view."[3] The deconstructionist vantage point is echoed by Merlin Stone who states, "it seems quite likely that the biblical Levite reports of the 'pagan' religion in Canaan were presented from the point of view that was most advantageous and acceptable to the Levite theology, rather than as a totally objective historical record."[4]

Sjoo and Mor are more pointed, stating that the Old Testament "prophets were leaders of a holy political war against the people who worshipped the Goddess."[5] The story of the animosity between Jezebel and the prophet Elijah is an account of one battle in that war. One outcome of revisiting the Jezebel story is reevaluation of the fundamental patriarchal assumptions about what personality traits and behaviors constitute wicked women.[6] With the rise of patriarchy women were scripted a role into which they were systematically and often brutally encased. Deviation was met with censure, even death.

Personal interest in Jezebel stems from my re-acquaintance with her portrayal while looking at the influence of childhood sexual abuse on one's self-construction. Historically, "Black women were often portrayed as innately promiscuous, even predatory. This depiction of Black women is signified by the name Jezebel."[7] Sadly, but not surprisingly, children were also viewed as Jezebels. "An analysis of Jezebel images reveals that Black female children are sexually objectified,"[8] often portrayed as seductive, physically precocious, and sexually active as well as sexually irresponsible.

Early experiences profoundly shape our psyches, influencing how we interact with and respond to the world.[9] Suffering childhood sexual abuse can lead the female child to label herself as a sexually wicked being – a seducer of men.[10] This taking of direct responsibility for the predatory sexual behavior of abusive males is possible because at a young age the Eve-Jezebel-accursed female mythos of woman's sexuality being the downfall of man is inculcated into our beings.

With this mythos firmly entrenched in our collective psyches and a cornerstone of major world religions, it is little wonder that the area of women's sexual rights and freedom is one of rancorous political struggle. It is an area of contention that becomes particularly evident within systems of political leadership closely linked to religion. The struggle is not a modern phenomenon. It is a struggle that is at the very heart of Jezebel's story.

Socio-historical Context

Jezebel was ninth century BC Phoenician royalty, Princess of Tyre and Princess of Sidon, her resident city.[11] Her notoriety was formed during her marriage to Ahab, king of Israel between 869 – 850 BC.[12] Gaines states:

> Jezebel is not the first foreign woman to wed a Jewish leader, nor even the first to turn her husband's heart away from God…and later kings would stray from the monotheistic path, but no female threat as great as Jezebel, follower of the Phoenician goddess Astarte would again rule in the Promised Land.[13]

What did Jezebel threaten, and how?

The marriage between Ahab and Jezebel was a political alliance arranged by Ahab's father, King Omri. Phoenicia, a loose confederation of cooperating city-states, was located in the northern coastal region of Canaan. Stretching approximately 380 miles with a width of only 12 to 15 miles, its major coastal city-states were Byblos, Beirut, Sidon, and Tyre. Jezebel's father, Ethbaal (891 – 859 BC), was king of the two major maritime trading centers of Tyre and Sidon.

Phoenicia was an agriculturally bountiful coastal region that established wide trading partnerships throughout the Mediterranean. The Phoenicians were noted for the exceptional quality of their textiles and their highly skilled artisans' work in gold and silver jewelry as well as pottery. The prized cedars of Lebanon are from this region, and King Solomon employed Phoenician craftspeople in the erection of his palaces and famed temple in Jerusalem.[14]

The Phoenicians were a rich commercial power, but they were not warriors as were the people of Israel. The covetous eyes of the neighboring Assyrians were a constant threat, and the Phoenicians "bought the Assyrians off each time they could, fighting only when there was no recourse".[15] The marital alliance of Israel and Phoenicia benefited both countries, with Israel gaining access to Phoenician ports and Phoenicia obtaining access to inland trading routes as well as acquiring military deterrence.

Hebrew Incursion into Canaan

Eight books of the Old Testament comprise the *Deuteronomistic history* – Deuteronomy, Joshua, Judges, Ruth, 1 Samuel, 2 Samuel, 1 Kings, 2 Kings. Within these biblical passages is the story of the Hebrew incursion into and settlement of the land of Canaan. Deuteronomy 1:7-8 reads: "Turn you, and take your journey, and go to…the land of the Canaanites… Behold, I have set the land before you: go in and possess the land which the Lord sware unto your fathers, Abraham, Isaac, and Jacob, to give unto them and to their seed after them."[16] Thus begins possession of the land.

When the Hebrews entered Canaan from the Sinai desert at about 1300-1250 BC,[17] they found flourishing cities. Scouts returned laden with produce from the land and reported that the land flowed "with milk and honey," as told in Numbers 13:28. The Hebrews advanced into Canaan with siege after bloody siege as recounted in the Bible by the Levite chroniclers with chilling matter-of-factness. Going to biblical sources used by Gaines, one reads: "So the Lord our God delivered into our hands Og also, the king of Bashan, and all his people; and we smote him until none was left to him remaining…there was not a city which we took not from them, threescore cities…utterly destroying the men, women, and children, of every city."[18]

The famous battle of Jericho, where the walls tumbled miraculously at the blowing of rams-horns trumpets, was the first led by Joshua after Moses and Aaron died in the desert. Joshua 6:21 recounts that while salvaging all the silver, gold and other valuable items, "they utterly destroyed all that was in the city, both man and woman, young and old…with the edge of the sword."[19]

Why such wanton annihilation of human life? "So Joshua smote all the country of the hills, and of the south, and of the vale, and of the springs, and all their kings: he left none remaining, but utterly destroyed all that breathed, as the Lord God of Israel commanded."[20] The smiting *sic* massacre does not end here. Chapter, after chapter, after chapter tells of bloody sieges. Again, why this utter disregard for life?

Apparently, there was fear of contagion from alien beliefs. For earlier in Deuteronomy 7:2-5 we read:

> And when the Lord thy God shall deliver them before thee; thou shalt smite them, and utterly destroy them…Neither shalt thou make marriages with them;…For they will turn away thy son from following me, that they may serve other gods…But thus shall ye deal with them; ye shall destroy their altars, and break down their images, and cut down their groves, and burn their graven images with fire.[21]

This order to completely annihilate the worship of other gods is evidenced in several Old Testament bible passages. For example in Deuteronomy 12:2-3 we find almost *verbatim* to the above: "Ye shall utterly destroy all the places wherein the nations which ye shall possess served their gods…And ye shall overthrow their altars, and break their pillars, and burn their groves with fire; and ye shall hew down the graven images of their gods, and destroy the names of them out of that place."[22] This extreme and violent xenophobia, justified as the will of God, is the basis of holy war according to Sjoo and Mor. "The Father God not only justified but commanded the slaughter of religious enemies, i.e. of people who believed differently."[23]

Clash of Cosmologies

Who were the deities of Canaan that the Hebrews encountered? Merlin Stone states that "in exploring the influence and importance of the worship of the Goddess in Canaan in biblical times, we find that as Ashtoreth, Asherah, Astarte, Attoret, Anath or simply Elat or Baalat (both defined as Goddess) She was the principal deity of such great Canaanite cites as Tyre, Sidon, Ascalon, Beth Anath, Aphaca, Byblos and Ashtoreth Karnaim."[24] Baal and the plural Baalim are mentioned throughout the Old Testament, in which Baal is specified as the highest Canaanite deity. Note that it is to the male divinity that the biblical chroniclers give this designation. However, Gaines finds that Baal "is actually a neutral term meaning 'lord' or 'husband,' and each village probably had its own baal who husbanded the land, fertilized it, and provided abundant rain and sun for crops."[25]

Comparison is often drawn between divinities of inhospitable terrain such as steppes and desert contrasted with divinities of settled agricultural areas. The encounter of the Hebrews and Canaanites represents such a classic clash of cosmologies. Within the Hebrew system, nature gives its rewards based on how closely laws of social behavior are observed.[26] These laws are prescribed by Yahweh and transmitted to the people by the priests. The rites and rituals of fertility and participation in the mystery of the cycle of life, death, and regeneration are absent.[27]

However, the difference in cosmological orientation should not be overstated. Before, during, and after the time that the Hebrews were in Egypt they were exposed to the worship of the goddess. Although patriarchy was in bloom, worship of the goddess with attendant rites and rituals, was the dominant cultural paradigm of the region.[28] "In fact, the complex of altar, tree, hill, and megalith that characterized this worship was an ancient and integral part of Israel's religious life, and the 'reforms' of Hezekiah and Josiah that destroyed this complex were a radical innovation rather than a return to some pristine purity."[29]

Polytheism existed throughout Canaan (including Israel and Judah) in biblical times. Why else the prophets' continuing laments, condemnations, and threats against *backsliders* and the Israelites who practiced polytheism? In 1 Kings 18:21 we read: "And Elijah came unto all the people, and said, How long halt ye between two opinions? If the Lord be God, follow him:

but if Baal, then follow him. And the people answered him not a word."[30]
That the goddess in the form of Asherah as Yahweh's counterpart was
worshipped among the Jews is evidenced by excavated material found at
Kuntillet in the Sinai. [31]

There were particular aspects related to worship of the goddess that
the Levite priests[32] found most appalling, an assessment based on their
biblical tirades. For a description of these aspects of worship, we have the
following:

> While Canaanites worshipped their gods with sacrifice, prayers,
> hymns, processions, votive offerings, and annual festivals, one of
> the most common methods of supplication was through sexual
> acts that would today be considered licentious. Prostitution of
> women and men was considered a way to honor a fertility deity.
> In some places, including Phoenicia of Jezebel, it was customary
> that a maiden before her marriage prostitute herself in the temple
> or give herself to a foreign guest, thus enacting the fertile earth
> receiving newly planted seeds.[33]

The acknowledgement and honoring of sexual power has endured
into modern times within some traditional societies. For example among
Native Americans, one reads that "ritual sexual intercourse as a means of
acquiring and transferring power was present among some groups on the
Northern Plains."[34]

However, free sexuality is equated with betrayal of Yahweh in the
Bible where the metaphor of husband and wife is used to describe the
relationship between God and Israel. "Failure to maintain exclusive loyalty
to God is called 'wantonness' or promiscuity and God's reaction is to this
faithfulness in his 'jealously'... this 'jealously' is the reaction of a husband
who suspects that his wife has committed adultery."[35]

Sjoo and Mor ask then answer the question "What was Yahweh jealous
of? Of the Goddess, and her lover, of their sacred-sexual relationship itself,
and of its domination over the minds and hearts and bodies of generations
of Neolithic people...Sex – the source of life and pleasure of love – becomes
the enemy of God."[36]

In the realm of human interaction during the Biblical era, it is stated
that "this fear of women's sexual license arises in part from the male's fear
of losing control over his wife. It is not sexuality that is the problem, but
the fact that it is not directed towards the husband."[37] This human male
mind-set mirrors God's response. "How strange the Hebrew God must
have seemed to Jezebel. He forbade some types of sexual expression that
her people regarded as essential to the continuance of life."[38]

Woman was in fact viewed as economic property,[39] spelled out clearly in the tenth commandment: "Thou shalt not covet thy neighbor's house, thou shalt not covet thy neighbor's wife, nor his manservant, nor his maidservant, nor his ox, nor his ass, nor any thing that is thy neighbor's."[40] Here the woman as wife is listed among that which belongs to the male. How different from the religion of the goddess in which women's power was honored rather than feared. "In this ancient religion, knowledge, power and property passed down through the mother. It was a matrilineal system in which women had social, political, legal and economic independence."[41]

Merlin Stone underscores the point made above in stating that the reason for Levite attack on women's sexual autonomy and the reason they devised the concept of sexual morality was the need to establish "certain knowledge of paternity."[42] Of course this sexual morality, comprising premarital virginity and marital fidelity, was imposed and enforced rigorously for women. Stone goes on to point out that this Levite law promulgated as *morality* is "the antithesis of attitudes toward female sexuality held in the religion of the Goddess... (Further) once having invented this concept of 'morality,' they flung accusations of 'immorality' at women *whose behavior and lives, in accordance with their own most ancient beliefs, were of the highest and most sacred nature*"[43] (my emphasis).

The Levite laws were designed for the total sexual control of Hebrew women. Deviations from the laws of *moral* sexual conduct could result in death. And "though these laws appear in the books of Leviticus and Deuteronomy, said to have been written at the time of Moses, Bible scholars generally date their writings to between 1000 and 600 BC."[44] The antagonism between Jezebel and the Levite prophet, Elijah, occurred during the mid-900's BC, early in the campaign to codify this new morality.

Historical Precedence for Levite/Hebrew Actions

The laws imposed by the Levite priests as the will of God reflected the continuing shift to patriarchy and suppression of matriarchal traditions that had long been underway.

> Archeological findings indicate that in some Kurgan camps the bulk of the female population was not Kurgan but rather of the Neolithic Old European population. What this suggests, as Gimbutas notes, is that the Kurgans massacred most of the local men and children but spared some of the girls and women, whom they took for themselves as concubines, wives, and/or slaves – a practice of warlike pastoralists also documented in biblical accounts of how, during the invasions of Canaan by his pastoralist

worshipers, Yahweh ordered that all the inhabitants of conquered cities be slaughtered except for virgin girls.[45]

Accounts of this practice can be found at Numbers 31:35 and Deuteronomy 21:10-13. This apparent contradiction of Yahweh's command calling for the total slaughter of invaded peoples likely brought Hebrews direct experience of goddess worship.

Although captured and subjugated young women were undoubtedly coerced into worship of Yahweh, it is unreasonable to expect that in their hearts they accepted the god responsible for their enslavement as well as the murder of friends and family. Customs associated with the goddess could have been passed on to succeeding generations, even if in modified or hidden variants. This process might have been similar to the vestiges of African traditions New World slaves were able to maintain.

As further evidence to the early press of patriarchal values, "Sumerologist Samuel Noah Kramer reports that under Sumerian law, if a wife was childless because she refused her husband conjugal relations, she could be thrown into the water and drowned."[46] In the Babylonian code of Hamurabi[47] "still generally hailed by scholars as a major advance in civilization ... are laws prescribing that 'a flagrantly careless and uneconomical wife' was to be drowned and that 'a worthless wife' could be made 'a slave in her own house if her husband took another wife.'"[48]

Although the status of women deteriorated with the shift to patriarchy, women were not abruptly stripped of their power and status. In Sumer "for example, women continued in their priestly roles. But gradually even these roles changed. Thus by the time of the Third Dynasty of Ur (2278-2170 B.C.E.), reflecting radical changes in how sexual relations were viewed, priestesses were described as concubines of the male gods and prostitutes in the temple."[49]

Jezebel's Actions

Two major accusations are made against Queen Jezebel. One is promoting the worship of *false gods*, the other is orchestrating the execution of an innocent man to secure his land. Gaines (1999) speaks of many inconsistencies in the stories concerning Jezebel's actions such as illogical sequencing of events. "On many occasions it seems possible that the writer's moral purpose far outweighs his sense of historical accuracy."[50]

When Jezebel goes to Israel and marries Ahab, she does not renounce her gods nor does she relinquish her beliefs and practices. "Jezebel flouts patriarchal authority and threatens monotheism by continuing to worship Phoenician gods."[51] Here is Jezebel's great threat. Through her independent agency Jezebel is a threat to monotheism and patriarchal authority.

"She organizes and supports guilds for hundreds of prophets of Baal and Asherah; 1 Kings 18.19 says that there are 'prophets of Baal four hundred and fifty, and the prophets of Asherah four hundred, that eat at Jezebel's table.'"[52] Also, Jezebel is said to have ordered the murder of Yahweh's prophets just as her biblical antagonist, the prophet Elijah, murdered hundreds of Baal's priests at Mt. Carmel.[53] Of course, the former is heavily condemned in the bible while the latter is lauded as virtuous.

The second major accusation against Jezebel involves a vineyard owned by Naboth that lay adjacent to the palace at Jezreel. King Ahab desired this land. When Naboth declines to sell or trade the land, the story told[54] is that Jezebel masterminded a plot to have Naboth falsely accused of treason thus ensuring his execution and the loss of heritage rights to his descendents. Here Jezebel is shown to violate the laws of Israel, "defying Israelite limitations on her royal power."[55] Under Mosaic law it is Naboth's sacred right and responsibility to keep his land for his family.

The intricate coordination of this Machiavellian plot gives Gaines cause to wonder at the story's veracity. "If Jezebel is able to orchestrate a judicial murder while following the letter of Hebrew law, she is indeed a remarkably astute woman, well ahead of her time. She is also lucky. To involve so many elders, nobles, and perjurers and to trust them not to expose her hostile plan stretches readers' credulity."[56]   Gaines speculates that if Jezebel is innocent, then this story was "used by the ethnocentric and sexist Deuteronomist to teach lessons about the evil influences of foreign pagan women."[57]

In her native Phoenicia strong female rulers were not uncommon. Dido, the legendary founder of Carthage in 814 BC, was Phoenician and reportedly the great-niece of Jezebel.[58] Therefore, "when Jezebel advises Ahab, acts in his stead, or handles domestic problems as she sees fit, her behavior is not outrageous."[59] Her Phoenician education as to the role and style of rulership appropriate to a queen were in definite conflict with Israelite law and custom and their marginalization of women. "She now breaks not only God's religious laws but society's code of moral conduct as well."[60]

Jezebel as Whore

Gaines (1999) makes the observation that "never in biblical stories is she caught in an adulterous act; in fact, she is a loyal wife to King Ahab."[61] As spoken to earlier, being unfaithful to Yahweh by worshipping other deities was equated with adultery or *whoring after false gods*. "For example, the prophet Hosea is commanded, 'Go take unto thee a wife of harlotry and children of harlotry for the land doth commit great harlotry, departing from the Lord' (Hosea 1.2). A country desiring false gods is symbolically represented by a woman lusting after additional sexual partners."[62]

Although the Bible makes reference to the worship of "false gods" as harlotry, "Jezebel's harlotry has not been identified as mere idolatry."[63] However, on only one occasion in the Bible is the accusation of harlotry made in connection with Jezebel. Unbeknownst to King Joram that he is facing his would be assassin in the person of his military commander, General Jehu, Joram calls out: "'Is all well, Jehu?' Jehu responds: 'How can all be well as long as your mother Jezebel carries on her countless harlotries and sorceries?' (2 Kings 9:22) ... For these words alone – uttered by a man who is about to kill Jezebel's son – stems Jezebel's long-standing reputation as a witch and a whore."[64]

False gods, the goddess, and sexual rites celebrating fecundity were an abomination to the Levites. The sexual license accorded to women under this system of worship ran directly counter to the patrilineal need to control women's sexuality. Associating Jezebel with a sexuality they reviled might have seemed to the Levite chroniclers to be the ultimate insult and act of derision.

Jezebel came from a land in which the goddess and her rites were venerated. "According to first-century CE historian Josephus, who drew on a Greek translation of the now-lost Annals of Tyre, Ethbaal served as a priest of Astarte, the primary Phoenician goddess."[65] Merlin Stone indicates that the Phoenician king and queen served as high priest and priestess to Ashtoreth and Baal.[66] Virginia DeBolt states that in the role of high priestess and priest Jezebel's parents "represented the goddess and god of an ancient pagan system."[67] As a king's daughter it is highly probable that Jezebel would have served in the temple as a priestess.

We have the following description of the complex Mesopotamian temple hierarchy ca. third millennium:

> In the Mesopotamian temple system there apparently were a high priestess and associated priestesses of elevated rank who only married under certain conditions; there was a second rank of virgin priestesses, the Naditu, and several ranks of women performing

special services. One of these services was 'temple prostitution.' In Babylonia, as in Egypt and Phoenicia, the concept of rendering sexual services on a public basis evidently first developed in connection with temples, and intercourse with temple women was considered an act of worship.[68]

Although "the women who provided the services were often of the middle and upper classes,"[69] they were not officially priestesses.

Jezebel worshipped Baal and Asherah, who constituted the male and female aspects of the great god of Canaan. As such, "Jezebel's threat is not just to monotheism in general but also to the Father-God representing masculine authority. Exponents of the jealous male Yahweh therefore are hostile to Jezebel because they are universally antagonistic to goddesses."[70]

Conclusion

My intention has not been to claim that Jezebel was a woman of saintly virtues.

She was as zealous in adherence to her religion as Elijah was to his religion. She was threatening to the Levite priests because she was not intimidated by their god or their brutality but meted out brutality for brutality. It is said that Jezebel and Elijah were "equally determined to eliminate one another's followers, even if it means murdering them. The difference is that the Deuteronomist decries Jezebel's killing of God's servants (at 1 Kings 18:4) but sanctions Elijah's decision to massacre hundreds of Jezebel's prophets."[71]

It is Jezebel's strength and integrity with regard to her religion that enrages the Levites. It is their story of her that we have inherited in the Bible. Levite xenophobia and religious absolutism as expressed in their hostility to the goddess and to women's free sexual expression and autonomy heavily color Levite portrayal of any woman who runs counter to their prescriptions for moral behavior. These are by-and-large the same prescriptions in place today. Hence, Jezebel's enduring legacy.

Queen Jezebel represents female autonomy. "She lives her life according to her own convictions, steadfastly maintains her religious independence, exercises what authority she possesses, and dies bravely. Yet Jezebel is almost universally hated."[72] Jezebel is defamed by biblical writers because she was indeed "a threat to patriarchal prerogative and monotheism."[73]

Attention to the socio-historical context emphasizes the antipathic relationship the Levites had toward female sexuality. This antipathy helps explain the historical connection between Jezebel's purported evil and sexuality. The exploration has also enhanced my personal understanding regarding society's schizophrenic relationship to sexuality. A cellular memory of sexual sacredness is submerged beneath the conceptual moralizing and fear of punishment connected with Levitic laws of moral sexual conduct.

Jezebel is not a whore as the term is commonly used today to describe a woman who has multiple sex partners outside of marriage. However, in Jezebel's time as today to be decried a harlot or a whore is considered a defamatory affront. Also, as Luisah Teish has pointed out the term has come to be virtually synonymous with being female:

> The word '**whore**' carries an incredible amount of power, most of it negatively directed toward women. Ministers condemn women from the pulpit, and Rap artists degrade their sisters with this word. Innocent little girls have been accused of instigating incest; and women have been murdered by serial killers trying to rid the world of whores. Women may be regarded as whores irrespective of their age, their race, their income, or their conduct. So what does it really mean?[74]

To be a whore/harlot, as conventionally conceived, can be viewed as a challenge to the prescribed absolute right of male authority over female sexuality. Unfortunately, the sacred aspect of sexuality so important to the goddess is sorely missing from the equation. The contemporary whore often lacks a sacred connection to her sexuality and a sacred connection to herself that would engender loving self-respect. Additionally, in bitter irony, sexual license has become a tool of patriarchy primarily through the commercialization of sex.

Investigating the woman who was Jezebel reminds me, yet again, of the importance of psychological deprogramming from patriarchal brainwashing. The research stimulates my thirst to imbibe a spirituality in which women and the goddess are sacred, in which women's sexual and economic autonomy are not perceived as threatening to men, and in which men and women form equal, complementary partners enacting *hieros gamos* – sacred union – in our everyday lives.

Notes

1 Janet Howe Gaines, Music in the Old Bones – Jezebel through the Ages (Carbondale, IL: Southern Illinois University Press, 1999).

2 Elisabeth Schüssler Fiorenza, "In Search of Women's Heritage," in Judith Plaskow and Carol P. Christ (Eds). Weaving the Visions: New Patterns in Feminist Spirituality (San Francisco: Harper San Francisco, 1989), 31.

3 Gaines (1999), op. cit., 28.

4 Merlin Stone, When God was a Woman (NY: Harcourt Brace & Co., 1976), 167.

5 Monica Sjoo and Barbara Mor, The Great Cosmic Mother, Rediscovering the Religion of the Earth (San Francisco: HarperSanFrancisco, 1987), 267.

6 Gaines (1999) op. cit.

7 David Pilgrim, Ph.D., Jezebel Stereotype, 2002, http://www.ferris.edu/news/jimcrow/jezebel, Accessed 18 April 2005.

8 Ibid., 3.

9 John W. Santrock, Life-span Development (Madison, WI: Brown & Benchmark Publications, 1997).

10 Ellen Bass and Laura Davis, The Courage to Heal: A Guide for Women Survivors of Child Sexual Abuse (NY: HarperCollins, 1994).

11 Virginia DeBolt, Jezebel, 1997, http://www.vdebolt.com/jezebel/text.html, Accessed 18 April 2005.

12 Kathryn Capoccia, "Jezebel," Women of the Bible, 2000, http://www.biblebb.com/files/KSS/kss-jezebel.htm, Accessed 7 May 2005.

13 Gaines (1999), op. cit., 6.

14 Gaines (1999), op. cit.

15 Elise Boulding, The Underside of History – A View of Women Through Time (Boulder, CO: Westview Press, 1976), 240.

16 King James Version of the Holy Bible.

17 Stone, op. cit., 168.

18 Deuteronomy 3:3-6 KJV.

19 King James Version.

20 Joshua 10:40 KJV.

21 Karen Elizabeth Ray, "Asherah," Topical Bible Studies, 1997-2007, http://www.topical-bible-studies.org/37-0036.htm, Accessed 7 May 2005.

22 King James Version.

23 Sjoo and Mor, op. cit., 269.

24 Stone, op. cit., 164.

25 Gaines (1999), op. cit., 32.

26 Tikva Frymer-Kensky, In the Wake of the Goddess: Women, Culture and the Biblical Transformation of Pagan Myth (NY: The Free Press, 1992).

27 Ibid.

28 Sjoo and Mor, op. cit.

29 Frymer-Kensky, op. cit., 153.

30 King James Version.

31 William G. Denver, "Kuntillet 'Ajrud and the History of Israelite Religion," in John R. Bartlett (Ed.) Archaeology and Biblical Interpretation (NY: Routledge, 1997).

32 Stone (op. cit.) states speculation that the Levite priests were in fact of Indo-European Aryan origin and not Semites as were the Hebrews who they governed through religious laws.

33 Gaines (1999), op. cit., 32.

34 Howard I. Harrod, The Animals Came Dancing, (Tucson, AZ: University of Arizona Press, 2000), 76-77.

35 Frymer-Kensky, op. cit., 146 and 263 footnote 8.

36 Sjoo and Mor, op. cit., 270.

37 Frymer-Kensky, op. cit., 151.

38 Gaines (1999), op. cit., 33.

39 For example see Stone, op. cit.

40 Exodus 20:17 KJV.

41 DeBolt, op. cit., 1.

42 Stone, op. cit., 161.

43 Ibid., 182.

44 Ibid., 190.

45 Riane Eisler, Sacred Pleasure (San Francisco, Harper San Francisco, 1996), 90-91.

46 Ibid., 114.

47 © 1700 BC

48 Eisler, op. cit., 115.

49 Ibid., 116.

50 Gaines (1999), op. cit., 92.

51 Ibid., 23.

52 Ibid., 35.

53 1 Kings 18:40 KJV.

54 1 Kings 21:2-16 KJV.

55 Frymer-Kensky, op. cit., 123.

56 Gaines (1999), op. cit. 69.

57 Ibid.

58 Ibid., 40.

59 Ibid., 15.

60 Ibid., 69.

61 Ibid., 28.

62 Ibid., 14.

63 Gaines (2000), op. cit., 5.

64 Ibid.

65 Gaines (2000), op. cit.

66 Stone, op. cit., 177.

67 DeBolt, op. cit.

68 Boulding, op. cit., 220.

69 Ibid.

70 Gaines (1999) op. cit., 36.

71 Gaines (2000), op. cit., 3.

72 Gaines (1999), op. cit., 29.

73 Ibid., 93.

74 Luisah Teish, "The Stained Glass Whore and Other Virgins," In She Is Everywhere! An Anthology of Writings in Womanist/Feminist Spirituality (Lincoln, NE: iUniverse, 2005), 34.

Bibliography

Bass, Ellen and Laura Davis. The Courage to Heal: A Guide for Women Survivors of Child Sexual Abuse. NY. HarperCollins, 1994.

Boulding, Elise. The Underside of History – A View of Women Through Time. Boulder, CO: Westview Press, 1976.

Capoccia, Kathryn. "Jezebel." Women of the Bible, 2000. http://www.biblebb.com/files/KSS/kss- jezebel.htm. Accessed 7 May 2005

Christ, Carol P. Rebirth of the Goddess: Finding Meaning in Feminist Spirituality. NY: Routledge, 1997.

DeBolt, Virginia. Jezebel, 1997. http://www.vdebolt.com/jezebel/text.html. Accessed 18 April 2005.

Denver, William G. "Kuntillet 'Ajrud and the History of Israelite Religion." In John R. Bartlett (Ed.) Archaeology and Biblical Interpretation. NY: Routledge, 1997.

Eisler, Riane. Sacred Pleasure. San Francisco: HarperSanFrancisco, 1996.

Frymer-Kensky, Tikva. In the Wake of the Goddess: Women, Culture and the Biblical Transformation of Pagan Myth. NY: The Free Press, 1992.

Gaines, Janet Howe. "How Bad was Jezebel?" Bible Review, October 2000. http://fontes.Istc.edu/~rklein/Documents/how_bad_was_jezebel.htm. Accessed 7 May 2005.

Gaines, Janet Howe. Music in the Old Bones – Jezebel through the Ages. Carbondale, IL: Southern Illinois University Press, 1999.

Harrod, Howard I. The Animals Came Dancing, Native American Sacred Ecology and
Animal Kinship. Tucson, AZ: The University of Arizona Press, 2000.

Pilgrim, Ph.D., David. Jezebel Stereotype, 2002. http://www.ferris.edu/news/jimcrow/jezebel. Accessed 18 April 2005.

Ray, Karen Elizabeth (compiler). "Asherah." Topical Bible Studies, 1997-2007. http://www.topical-bible-studies.org/37-0036.htm. Accessed 7 May 2005.

Reilly, Patricia Lynn. A God Who Looks Like Me, Discovering a Woman-Affirming Spirituality. NY: Ballantine Books, 1995

Santrock, John W. Life-span Development (6th edition). Madison, WI: Brown & Benchmark Publications, 1997.

Schüssler Fiorenza, Elisabeth. "In Search of Women's Heritage." In Judith Plaskow and Carol P. Christ (Eds). Weaving the Visions: New Patterns in Feminist Spirituality. SF: Harper San Francisco, 1989.

Sjoo, Monica and Barbara Mor. The Great Cosmic Mother, Rediscovering the Religion of the Earth. San Francisco: HarperSanFrancisco, 1987.

Stone, Merlin. When God was a Woman. NY: Harcourt Brace & Co., 1976.

Symons, Arthur. Jezebel Mort, and Other Poems. London: W. Heinemann Ltd, 1931.

Teish, Luisah. "The Stained Glass Whore and Other Virgins," In She Is Everywhere! An Anthology of Writings in Womanist/Feminist Spirituality. Lincoln, NE: iUniverse, 2005.

Sacred Images of African and African-American Women

Arisika Razak

Like many young Black women in America, my soul sang when I first read Ntozake Shange's famous lines: "i found God in myself/and i loved her/i loved her fiercely" (63). Growing up as a young Black feminist in America during the 1960's, I experienced the "cultural humiliation" that Cheryl Gilkes documents in If It Wasn't for the Women, a groundbreaking text on African-American women in the Afro-Christian church (181). Many activists and scholars of color have explored the enormous impact that racism and oppression have had on the bodies, lives, and culture/s of African-American women – whether that oppression is internalized by African-Americans, or imposed by the greater society (Ani; Collins; Davis; hooks; Lee).

According to Gilkes, "(s)elf-hatred may be one of the deepest sources of conflict and turmoil within the African-American community. This may be especially true concerning women and their bodies" (181). Contemporary African-American women are inundated by images implying that our bodies are still socially and culturally unacceptable. The absence of *large, dark, natural-haired, full featured* African Diasporan women in popular media; the disproportionate use of Black people's bodies to illustrate social and cultural deviance in scientific and academic discourse; and the lack of our likeness in mainstream religious iconography all contribute to our perceptions of imperfection and marginalization. Living in a culture that usually defines 'femininity' as small, fair, delicate, and dependent, we find ourselves to be large, dark, independent women – women who are too large, too loud, too Black, too nappy-headed! Openly or covertly, our parents, partners, religious leaders, health providers and teachers all remind us that our natural bodies are somehow flawed.

For some Black women, pressure to succumb to these negative constructs is over-whelming. Marimba Ani writes:

A continual pressure exerts itself upon the psyche of a 'nonwhite' person living within the ubiquitous confines of the West to 'remold', 'refashion', 'paint', 'refine' herself in conformity with this European aesthetical image of what a human being should be. The pressures begin at birth and out live the person, often breaking her spirit long before her physical demise. . . . So deep is the wound it inflicts that in Senegal, West Africa, women, some of the most beautiful in the world, burn and disfigure their rich smooth, melanic, ebony skin with lye in the attempt to make it white (221).

These negative images of Black women's bodies are a relatively new phenomenon. Historically, our bodies were viewed as the seat of the Divine, the body of the Beloved, and the very incarnation of what is feminine and beautiful. Schwartz-Bart and Brown and Toussaint offer the following translations of Black women's names which attest to the respect and reverence accorded Black women and their bodies:

The one who is loved like the Nile
The Bright one
Intoxication
The Moon's abode
Queen of eternity
    (Schwartz-Bart 55).
Aisha (Life Bringer)
Precious Beauty   (Azisa)
Sent by God   (Manzili)
Dignity   (Ola)
Star of my Life (Thuraia)
    (Brown and Toussaint 215-219).

Visionary African artists have produced spiritual images of African women for over ten thousand years. Their work subverts the modern paradigm by placing the bodies of Black women front and center as representatives of a God who is Black and female, embodied and divine. I believe these long-lived cultural images of *sacred African women* have the power to nurture and heal our bruised, embattled psyches, awakening us to the many possibilities of our inherent divinity, creativity, and beauty.

While modern society has moved away from degrading stereotypes of Black women as servile, self-effacing mammies, lascivious jezebels, and tragic mulattos (Collins 69-92; Bogle 3-18), it has replaced these figures with hyper-sexualized, Euro-centric images of Black women and their bodies. These images place our eroticism under the control and definition of corporate media conglomerates and patriarchal male projections. They limit our ability to construct self-referenced, multi-dimensional sexualities, and obscure the fact that we are all *embodiments of the sacred*. Our eroticism, creative powers, beauty and transformative energies are *our own* divine gifts – and their sharing and dispersal must be under our control.

Many practitioners of women's spirituality (Christ; Goboldte; Noble; Teish) suggest that women need *embodied, female* images of Spirit in order to claim first class spiritual citizenship. Rachel Bagby's spirited memoir, *Divine Daughters*, explored the repercussions of the lack of a divine female presence in the Black Christianity of her youth; while Carol Christ's essay, "Why Women Need the Goddess" suggested that:

> Religious symbol systems focused around exclusively male images of divinity create the impression that female power can never be fully legitimate or wholly beneficent. . . . A woman . . . can never have the experience that is freely available to every man and boy in her culture, of having her full sexual identity affirmed as being in the image and likeness of God (25).

In a similar fashion, I believe that *some* African-American women need a Black or African Goddess if they are to find wholeness and meaning at the heart of the world/s in which they live. These images are currently more available to women and men who want them because modern artists, activists, spiritual practitioners and healers have resurrected or re-created African or Afro-centric pantheons which include: traditional African *spirits*, *orishas*, and *loas*; African goddesses and sacred queens; Black Marys; and deified Diasporan ancestors, community activists and soul mothers.

In this article I explore a few of the images created by traditional and modern African Diasporan artists who seek to transmit positive, life affirming images of African and African-American women.

Our African Heritage

African cultural history begins millennia before the slave trade, readily antedating the racism and "racialized slavery" (Drake 1990) of the last five hundred years. Our African foremothers were: ". . . senior sisters, revered mothers, farmers, textile workers, merchants, healers and religious leaders" (Rushing 124). Most African cultures were spiritually based embodied cultures that valued the roles, spirits and physicality of men *and* women. The power and authority of male social roles were *balanced* by the power and authority of female social roles, for the moral, physical and spiritual power/s of women *complemented* the moral, physical and spiritual power/s of men, including in some instances, the power/s of the king (Badejo; Rushing; Stoeltje). Dance and music supported personal and community spirituality and healing; sexuality and fertility were *spiritual* qualities; and the material and spiritual worlds were not separate realms. Our full figured bodies were honored as embodiments of the awesome energies of fertility, power, nurturance, and change – foundational qualities of the physical *and* spiritual worlds.

In West Africa among the Yoruba, the term, 'mother', was a title of power that linked women to the awesome *spiritual* energies of "fertility, power and cosmic harmony" (Badejo 80). Used within the family lineage, it was a term of respect; used outside of it, as in the Yoruba term, *'iyalode'*, 'mother of the outside' it acknowledged women's ability to hold roles of authority beyond the domestic sphere (Badejo 181). These powerful female roles were suppressed in slavery, but they were never forgotten. They live within the psyches of individual African-Americans, and within the complex web of cultural traditions that we have inherited and transformed.

Sacred Women of the Tassili Frescoes

The ancient rock paintings of Tassili-n-Ajjer in Algeria in the central Sahara were discovered in 1956 by Henri Lhote and his associates. Some images are seven to ten thousand years old; others date from 2000 BCE when a wet green Sahara supported lakes, fishes, and herds of animals. Lhote's group copied approximately eight hundred of the fifteen thousand rock paintings found in the caves (Yarbrough 94). Some images of naked, elongated "bird-headed goddesses" with cobra headdresses appeared linked to Egypt (Lhote 71-73; 96-97); other figures wore tunics resembling those of the local modern day Peul women (Lhote Fig. 34). Lhote found drawings of pregnant and nursing women, women with hunting bows, and figures he believed were goddesses, queens or priestesses (Lhote 81).

One of Lhote's most famous pictures depicts a horned woman running (Lhote Fig 35). White dots resembling scarification marks ornament her leg, torso, breasts and arms, and a fringed skirt covers her hips. Her extremities are decorated with fringed arm bands, anklets, and leg bands. Her bare-breasted body is colored with yellow ochre, and outlined in white, while "(f)rom either side of the head and above two horns . . . was an extensive dotted area resembling a cloud of grain falling from a wheat field . . . "(Lhote 80).

We can only speculate about what these pictures meant for they are not accompanied by any known texts. For many of us, these ancient images of Black women are extremely beautiful. The women's breasts are usually uncovered; their limbs are symmetrical and smooth; stylized patterns adorn their bodies. Lhote and Jeffries believe these images were connected to agricultural or fertility cults and rituals, and Lhote suggested that their remote placement was an indication of their spiritual nature:

> It is . . . strange that we should have discovered so many splendid paintings in a massif so difficult of access and so little suited for human habitation. . . . we may well ask ourselves in view of the character of their art whether they did not make Aouanrhet a high place for religious initiation and for secret mysterious cults (83- 84).

Sacred Women of Egypt

Egyptian art presents us with many images of historic African women who were revered as goddesses and sacred queens. Deciphered hieroglyphic writing frequently accompanies these images. Lesko indicates that by 4000 B.C.E., agriculture was established in Egypt, and people of the Badarian culture had begun to lay out their dead in well conceived graves (7).There is evidence that women's graves in the pre-dynastic period were generally larger than men's graves – and artifacts found in grave sites and on pottery allude to the high status and authority of women. Lesko writes: "The independence and leadership roles of ancient Egyptian women may be part of an African cultural pattern that began millennia ago and continued into recent times" (13).

Adult women of authority in Egypt were typically depicted wearing a semi-transparent garment of linen and jewelry that symbolized power, life and health. Sometimes an open work bead dress surmounted this gossamer sheath which was held in place by strap/s over the breasts (Hawass 112). A close fitting vulture crown with wings enfolding the ears was frequently worn by Egyptian queens, for Nekbhet, the vulture goddess, represented the lands of the south, and Wadjet, the cobra goddess symbolized the north. Royal women wore jewelry made of semi-precious stones, while less wealthy women wore multi-colored beads similar to the jewelry of the nobility. The many-stranded *wesekh* collar was linked to the goddess Hathor and worn by royal and non-royal women alike. Egyptian women's elegantly dressed hair appears resembles the braids and dread locks of contemporary African Diaspora women.

Female imagery from Egypt includes a myriad of goddesses. Some goddesses combined depictions of power and death with functions of compassion and protection. For example, Selket, the scorpion goddess was the protectress of birthing and nursing mothers. A golden sculpted image found in King Tut's tomb, portrays her as a beautiful woman wearing a scorpion on her head. The swelling contours of her breasts and belly are delicately outlined beneath her linen dress; her hands reach out to guard; and her dark-kohl-rimmed eyes are fixed and far-seeing, as befits a spiritual teacher and protectress of the dead.

Queen Nofretari's tomb at Abu Simbel depicts the goddess Isis leading Nofretari to the underworld. Dressed in linen overlaid with beads, Isis wears the solar disk and horns of Hathor. Nofretari wears the vulture crown and white tunic of the New Kingdom. The two women are radiant; powerful, beautiful, and slim, they walk hand in hand, fearlessly moving forward.

The historic queen Ahmose-Nofretari reigned during the 18th Dynasty. According to Schwartz-Bart this ruler, priestess, and protectress of the poor (40) is the first Egyptian queen named as a wife of the god Amon. Schwartz-Bart makes the following comments on the intimacy of images of the god Amon's wives:

Among the most beautiful and carnal of all feminine representations, the god's wives are frequently depicted in the company of Amon, during the Ethiopian period. Often facing his wife, the god presents the ankh, the sign of life, while expressing his bliss to 'the one who fills the shrine with the scent of her perfume'. Moreover, these love scenes include captions . . . etched by the god himself: 'she who delights the god's flesh, who makes love with the god, she who is fulfilled when she sees Amon' (32).

Writing of Ahmose Nofretari, Schwartz-Bart adds:

People say that the god Amon visits her regularly, that he lives in her body and strokes her breasts, and never tires of contemplating her face; and those who come near her at the temple in Thebes whisper that a spark of peaceful, blissful, truly divine sensuality shows in her gaze (39). . . . (T)he veneration which surrounds Ahmose-Nofretari has left her image intact . . . . 'black skin, beautiful face, elegant, her hair crowned with feathers' (34).

Sacred Women of Historic Sub-Saharan Africa

Traditional African art depicts women as powerful members of African society. Even when living under patriarchy, they were recognized as powerful beings. Maulana Karenga (1999) in his translation of "*Odu Ifa*", the sacred oracle of the Yoruba people of West Africa, offers this rendition of *Osa Meji:*

> This is the teaching of *Ifa* for Odu,
> Obarisa and Ogun,
> When they were coming from heaven to earth.
> Odu asked 'O Olodumare, this earth where we are going,
> Ogun has the power to wage war.
> And Obarisa has the *ase* (power) to do anything
> he wishes to do.
> What is my power?'
> Olodumare said: 'you will be their mother forever.
> And you will also sustain the world'.
> Olodumare, then, gave her the power.
> And when he gave her power, he gave her
> the *spirit* power of the bird.
> It was then that he gave women the power
> and authority so that anything men
> wished to do,
> They could not dare to do it successfully
> without women.
> Odu said that everything that people would
> want to do,
> If they do not include women,
> It will not be possible (72-73).

Beliefs about the world-sustaining power of African women's spirituality (as above) are linked to women's fertility. Women's spirituality scholar, Hallie Austen, writes in The Heart of the Goddess:

> In Africa . . . artistic images of mother and child are wide spread. Unlike many depictions of Euro-Western Madonnas, however, the emphasis is on the mother, rather than the child. Traditional African societies consider children divine gifts and value women as the mothers of culture, as well as for their equally miraculous ability to conceive, give birth and feed their physical children. . . . The Mande . . . believe that one derives one's character, capabilities and destiny from one's mother (22).

Sub-Saharan African Images

A sculpted *Gwandusu* figure from sub-Saharan Africa is one of many images of female African divinity depicted in *The Heart of The Goddess* (Austen 23). The figure is from the Bamana culture of Mali, and Austen quotes Kate Exra as saying that the name *Gwandusu* "

> . . .implies a character that embodies extraordinary strength, ardent courage, intense passion and conviction, and the ability to accomplish great deeds" (22). The image's headdress is highly ornamented; her waist beads rest on softly rounded thighs; and the child she holds embraces her elongated torso. Her large breasts shield her child, providing nurturance *and* shelter. Her gaze is lowered and inwardly focused; her posture erect and aware. Like Thompson's description of another mother-child figure in <u>African Art in Motion</u>, she is ". . . relaxed but proud, powerfully emphasized breasts telling of . . . womanly force, and ancestrally based fertility" (51).

<u>The Heart of the Goddess</u> includes pictures of several open legged images that depict a sacred woman, clan mother, or female deity displaying her sacred vulva, which represents the "gateway to life" (118). A 19th century African image from Gabon shows a being with closed eyes whose open arms and legs simultaneously suggest spiritual power and inner peace. The figure is radiant with grace, self-contained and confident. Absorbed in spiritual work, her layered hair, diamond glyph markings, and slightly rounded belly all carry ritual or social significance (121)

Noting that the beautiful and elaborate hair designs depicted by Africans are markers of social status, occupation, or material and spiritual power, Rushing writes:

> Neatly arranged hair is much more than a matter of personal choice for the Yoruba, to whom tousled hair is a sign of chaos, rather than free-spirit sexiness. It is the special province of the powerful, elegant female *orisa* deity Osun – one of whose *oriki* praise names is 'owner of the beaded comb'(130).

Among the Yoruba ". . . where the head is the site of one's spirit/soul/destiny" (Rushing 129), it is the beaded comb of Osun that parts the pathways of destiny (Badejo 7). Commenting on the social implications of the hair styling of a Bamana image, Thompson writes

> The elegance of her coiffure is a cryptic statement on a life lived well, for such an elaborate crest could only be made through the cooperation of others, sympathetic sisters or co-wives or friends (<u>Art in Motion</u> 51).

Images of Sacred African Women by Contemporary Diasporan Artists

I have chosen to review contemporary art by two modern-day African American artists, Earthlyn Manuel and AfraShe Asungi. Each of these artists works outside of the Christian tradition, creating visionary images of sacred African and African-American women. In accordance with African artistic traditions, their images may be based on mythic or historic ancestral figures or emerge spontaneously from dreams and visions. Many contemporary African-Americans follow Afro-centric spiritual paths, honoring Afro-centric divinities in personal rituals or community celebrations. AfraShe and Earthlyn have shared their visions with the larger community, marketing their images in the form of cards, paintings, candles and textile images.

The term "Afro-centric" is a contested term with many meanings. I am using it to define attempts by African-Americans to locate their current experiences and history within a perspective serving the individual and collective needs of peoples of the African Diaspora. Writing on rituals of the Imani Temple Church of Philadelphia, which was formed in response to the racism of the Catholic Church, Catharine Goboldte declares:

> For African Americans, the reclamation of African-centered cultural perspectives and ethos is liberatory praxis. To determine ourselves Afro-centrically is to 'literally place African ideas at the center of any analysis that involves African culture and behavior' ... (242).

When an Afro-centric aesthetic joins a women-centered world-view explicitly celebratingBlack women's power, agency, creativity, and leadership, it becomes a *womanist* world view. Alice Walker's In Search of Our Mother's Gardens introduced the term "womanist" to define "a Black feminist or feminist of color" (xi). Her four part definition praised Black women's historic ability to take leadership in liberation struggles benefiting the *entire* African American community; validated our right to love, support and nurture other women "sexually and/or non-sexually" (xi); honored our physical beauty, curvaceousness, and diversity; and proclaimed the importance of self-love, spirituality, rest, resistance, healing, music, dance, food and nature. This is the tradition in which I situate the work of Earthlyn Manuel.

The term "Afro-centric" is not acceptable to AfraShe Asungi, the other contemporary artist whose work I am reviewing. In an interview in

Woman of Power, Asungi states:

> . . . (It) has been a personal goal of mine . . .(to) transform what I consider the co-opted matriarchy in Afrika and in Afrikan tradition, and to actually intuit, pull out and retrieve the essential elements of the unconquered female, or feminist spirituality. I do not completely agree with what is known as Afrocentric theology because it is very male based. . . . A word that I had developed in 1985 was 'Afracentrik', meaning that we are going one step beyond feminist and one step beyond patriarchal Afrikan analysis to look for that particular vision where the Black female has been revered as norm, as a healthy image in the culture (Asungi, *Afracentric Visions* 42-43).

Each of these two artists utilizes a very different aesthetic and liberatory framework for her visual depiction of Black women's bodies. Asungi's "Afracentrik" images depict our spiritual and cultural past in the lost matriarchies of ancient Africa (Asungi, *Afracentric Visions* 42). Her images show Black women as empowered spiritual creators, whose idealized forms reflect Diasporan women's embodied spiritual power/s linking us to art, culture, nature, and civilization.

Earthlyn Manuel's work defiantly embraces aspects of Black women's bodies which have been defined as negative by the dominant society. By depicting them as 'worthy', she demands that the observer reframe and reject the racist lens through which Black women are viewed. In this strategy, the *natural* bodies of Black women are emphasized, and the artist celebrates our full features, largeness, nappy hair and irregular contours. The inner strength, moral character, and womanly gifts of ordinary women are emphasized. This artist's work refutes oppressive paradigms which create idealized and unattainable *universal* beauty standards.

Images of AfraShe Asungi

AfraShe Asungi is a visionary artist, writer, priestess and healer. She founded **MAMAROOTS: AJAMA-JEBI** an "AfraGoddess sistahoood dedicated to Afracentric spirituality and cultural awareness" (Asungi, *Afracentric Visions* 42). She has been producing art that celebrates Black women for over thirty years, and writes in a note card depicting her art:

> I needed to see strong, self-contained and focused Black wimmin, so I reached into our tales, myths, goddesses and other spiritual realities and thus created this series as my visual song, in praise of the wonders of the feminine spirits I found there . . . .(1982)

In her pastel painting, *Dunham's Life Song*, Asungi depicts a dark, radiant bare-breasted Black woman holding a snake in one hand and a unicorn in the other. A large pair of wings emerges from her back, and another set covers her eyes like a ritual mask. The orange, blue and soft magenta colors of her wings are in strong contrast to the starry night in which a dark moon dances. Her colors and symbols indicate a woman of authority, and Asungi writes this about her piece which is one of a series of "Amazons":

> Katherine Dunham is a great choreographer, anthropologist and priestess of the Haitian religion. She is represented by the snake, also symbol for Damballah, the Haitian god. But she has also been represented by the unicorn, symbol of the mysterious positive life forces and ultimate power of the universe. Other symbols are her golden arm bands – which give her the blessings of Ochun, the river Goddess, the navel guard which is the symbol of Isis, and the moon Goddess, Yemaya (Note card 1982).

Asungi's image of Ochumare, Goddess of the Rainbow, presents a nude Black woman wearing a winged mask who sits in lotus position on a pad created from the starry night. The spinning earth, with the African continent foremost, sits at her navel; she wears golden armbands, and balances the rainbow between her outstretched arms. Behind her, two pyramids rise, and a crescent moon sits at her left shoulder. Her hair is an extension of the night sky. Asungi writes:

> Ochumare as the rainbow moves the sea waters between the heavens and the earth. I see her as the cosmic channel amongst the goddesses of the universe and the earth. Here she rests in the beauty of self awareness . . . . she sits upon the universal waters and the cosmic lily pads symbolizing her ever presence. She is nude, symbolizing her purity and ultimate pride of self. Her mask is a sign of strength and mystery. The Earth in her lap is spinning from the absolute energy that she provides from her navel which is a source of cosmic power. (Note card 1982).

Asungi's images are situated in our spiritual past in ancient '*Kamaat*', the term she uses to name our lost pre-Egyptian matriarchy. This term:

> . . . integrates several ancient root words: 'Ka' which means 'black-faced' or 'Sun-kissed', and 'Maat' the name of the Mama of Righteous Truth . . . which means 'sacred temple and lands' of 'Genuine Truth' and much more. . . The interpretation loosely means . . . Sacred Sun-kissed lands where the Black faced Mama of Genuine Righteous Truth dwells . . . (Asungi, *Afracentric Visions* 44).

Asungi's images depict Black women as mythic goddesses, historic queens, and spiritual warriors who are embedded in nature, and supported by cosmic reflections of the Divine Feminine. Asungi reminds us that the dark and the night are sacred, and she uses clothing, jewelry and adornment to indicate spiritual empowerment, freedom, and woman-centeredness. The lush roundness of the women's bodies, and their radiant, powerful nudity, freedom and ease of posture connect us to an ancient African past in which women and their sexualities were honored and revered.

Ochumare, Goddess of   Dunham's Life Song, by Asungi
the Rainbow, by Asungi

Earthlyn Manuel

Earthlyn Manuel's Black Angel cards illustrate Black women's history in the modern Diaspora. She creates images of ordinary Black women, and human-nature hybrids who symbolize the psychic and spiritual powers of everyday women. Manuel celebrates the ordinary and extraordinary acts of love, courage and perseverance that working class Black women bring to the task of survival. She writes: "The Black Angel Cards have been divined as a gift to black women . . . seeking to rejuvenate their lives. They are for black women (who) have felt stifled by an inability to transform the limitations of blackness and womanness. . . (7).

Earthlyn rejects idealized images of Afro-centric beauty. She emphasizes the full lips, wildly explosive hair, and irregular contours of real Diasporan women's bodies. Her stark, simply drawn, multi-colored images are a radical revisioning that reflects African beliefs emphasizing the pre-eminence of inner character over the impermanence of outer form and appearance.

Following African tradition, she highlights spiritual function rather than 'natural' form (Thompson). 'The Teacher', for example, is a hybridized tree-woman wearing a red necklace. Her roots reach into the ground while her upwardly flowing locks, encased in leaves and branches, erupt into a dawn or twilight sky. Her broad nose and wide mouth are indisputably African and her closed eyes and serene expression evoke the remoteness of African masks. 'The Lover' is depicted nude; she is an ordinary looking black woman who rests against a cushion; her short hair is nappy; her thighs wide; her belly wrinkled. Her erotic power lies in self love and knowledge of her own self worth, as indicated by her relaxed stance, and joyful singing, rather than idealized outer beauty.

Manuel's images of spiritual Black women validate the ordinary woman's body, and the very features that white racism would most condemn. This artist honors and reclaims the soul sustaining activities utilized by our ancestors to create and nurture generations of our people. She has consciously designed her work to represent spiritual revival and awakening, and she writes:

> When I look closely at the artwork on the surface, I see the hairstyles and hats as natural halos. Our wings, representing the ability to rise are in our spirit, lying unseen to the ordinary eye. The chairs and large pillows are thrones on which an angel can rest from the work of unveiling souls. The vibrant colors represent the process of awakening and revival. Revival is light and light is not always white; it can be bright yellow, orange, green, fuchsia or even black. In the art of these symbols, light becomes a feeling expressed in many colors. Even the color of our skin in the cards, going from yellow to purple to blue is an expression of the various essences of our souls. (15-16)

The Teacher by Earthlyn Manuel   The Lover by Earthlyn Manuel

Affirming Ourselves

In closing, I'd like to remind us of the importance of continuing to resist social assaults upon Black women's bodies. Our female bodies are our first point of entry into the world, and it is through the body that we experience life. Rejection and hatred of the female body, and personal and social dissociation from it have produced a wide variety of personal, social and cultural ills (Chernin; Northrup; Wolf; Griffin; Shepherd; Spretnak). Conversely, acceptance and love of the body may be linked both to individual and personal health, *and* to ecological sustainability and planetary well being. (Allen; Christ; Starhawk; Walker). Our emotional health as Black women may depend on our ability to generate authentic, embodied, spiritual re-visionings of our bodies, even as we reject the voices of internalized oppression which are the crippling legacy of racism and color prejudice.

African American women are the daughters of Africa. Our skin is black, brown, ivory; caramel, cinnamon, and honey. We reflect the rich colors of the earth and all the world's peoples. Our large hips embody the strength of trees; the curves of our thighs echo the shapes of hills. Our broad noses declare our strength of character, and our hair is a wilderness holding sunlight, rain, and the spiral patterns of galaxies.

We are the spiritual daughters and great grand-daughters many times removed of powerful African women who became enslaved. We honor and remember them as we unearth their histories, recreate their world views, and salute their spirits which live again in us. I offer my gratitude to all the

Diasporan artists, scholars, theologians, teachers, and healers who work to re-discover and re-create womanist culture for Diasporan women.

In closing, I offer words from twentieth century poet Mari Evans:

I
am a black woman
tall as a cypress
strong
beyond all definition still
defying place
and time
and circumstance
assailed
impervious
indestructible
Look
on me and be
renewed
(Evans 70-71)

Bibliography

Allen, Paula Gunn. Off the Reservation. Boston: Beacon, 1998

Ani, Marimba. Yurugo: An African-Centered Critique of European Cultural Thought and Behavior. 10th ed. Trenton: Africa World P, 2000

Austin, Hallie. The Heart of the Goddess: Art Myth and Meditations of the World's Sacred Feminine. Berkeley: Wingbow, 1990.

Asungi, AfraShe. "Afracentrik Visions". Woman of Power. 21 (1991): 42-45.

- - - . Dunham's Life Song. Notecard. 1982.

- - - . Ochumare. Notecard 1982.

Bagby, Rachel. Divine Daughters: Liberating the Power and Passion of Women's Voices New York: HarperSanFrancisco, 1999.

Badejo, Diedre. Osun Seegesi: The Elegant Deity of Wealth Power and Femininity. Trenton: Africa World P 1996.

Bogle, Donald. Toms, Coons, Mulattoes, Mammies, & Bucks: An Interpretive History of Blacksin American Films 3ʳᵈ ed. New York: Continuum, 1994.

Brown, Dennis, M.D. and Pamela A. Toussaint. Mama's Little Baby. New York: Plume, 1998

Chernin, Kim. The Obsession: Reflections on the Tyranny of Slenderness. New York: Harper Colophon, 1981.

Christ, Carol. Rebirth of the Goddess. New York: Routledge, 1997.- - - . "Why Women Need the Goddess: Phenomenological, Psychological, and Political Reflections". Womanspirit Rising: A Feminist Reader in Religion Eds. Carol P. Christ and Judith Plaskow. New York: Harper & Row, 1979.

Collins, Patricia Hill. Black Feminist Thought: Knowledge, Consciousness, and the Politics of Empowerment. 2ⁿᵈ ed. New York: Routledge, 2000.

Davis, Angela. Women, Race & Class. New York: Random House 1981.

Drake, St. Clair. Black Folk Here and There: 2 vols. Los Angeles: Center for Afro-American Studies, UC, 1990-91.

Evans, Mari. "I am a Black Woman". 1983. The Woman That I Am: The Literature and Culture of Contemporary Women of Color. Ed. D. S. Madison New York: St. Martin's Griffin, 1994. 70-71.

Gilkes, Carol Townsend. If It Wasn't For the Women . . . "Black Women's Experience and Womanist Culture in Church and Community New York: Orbis, 2001.

Goboldte, Catharine. "Laying on Hands: Women in Imani Faith Temple". Ed. Gloria Wade-

Gayles. My Soul is A Witness. Boston: Beacon, 1995. 241-252.

Green, Doris. "Traditional Dance in Africa" African Dance: An Artistic, Historical and Philosophical Inquiry. Ed. Kariamu Welsh Asante. Trenton: African World P. 1996. 13-28.

Griffin, Susan. Woman and Nature: The Roaring Inside Her. Sierra Club, 2000.

hooks, bell. Talking Back: Thinking Feminist Thinking Black Boston: South End, 1989.

Hawass, Zahi. Silent Images: Women in Pharaonic Egypt. New York: Harry Abrams, 2000

Hurston, Zora Neale. Their Eyes Were Watching God. Urbana: University Illinois P. 1978.

Jeffries, Rosalind. "The Image of Woman in African Cave Art". Black Women in Antiquity.

Ed. Ivan Van Sertima. 7th ed. New Brunswick: Transaction, 1992. 98-119.

Karenga, Maulana. Odu Ifa: The Ethical Teachings. Los Angeles: University of Sankore P, 1999.

Lee, Valerie. Granny Midwives and Black Women Writers. New York: Routledge, 1996.

Lesko, Barbara S. The Great Goddesses of Egypt Norman: U of Oklahoma P, 1999.

Lhote, Henri. The Search for the Tassili Frescoes: The Story of the Prehistoric Rock-Paintings of the Sahara. Trans. Alan Houghton Brodrick. New York: E.P. Dutton, 1959.

Lorde, Audre. Sister Outsider: Essays and Speeches. 11th printing. Freedom: Crossing P, 1996.

Manuel, Earthlyn. Black Angel Cards: A Soul Revival Guide for Black Women. San Francisco: HarperSanFrancisco, 1999.

Miller, Alice. <u>For Your Own Good: Hidden Cruelty in Child Rearing and the Roots of Violence</u>. 3rd ed. New York: Farrar, Straus and Giroux, 1990.

Morrison, Toni <u>Beloved: A Novel</u>. New York: Knopf, 1987.

Noble, Vicki. <u>Shakti Woman: Feeling Our Fire, Healing Our World</u>. NewYork:HarperSanFrancisco, 1991.

Northrup, Christiane <u>Women's Bodies, Women's Wisdom: Creating Physical and Emotional Health and Healing</u>. New Bantam ed. New York: Bantam, 2002.

Reagon, Bernice Johnson. <u>The Songs Are Free with Bill Moyers.</u> Prod. Public Affairs Television. Mystic Fire Video.1991.

Robins, Gay. <u>Women in Ancient Egypt</u>. 3rd ed. Cambridge: Harvard UP, 1998.

Rushing, Andrea. "On Becoming a Feminist: Learning From Africa". <u>Women in Africa</u>

<u>and the African Diaspora</u>. Eds. Rosalyn Terborg-Penn and Andrea B. Rushing. 2nd ed. Washington: Howard UP, 1996.

Schwarz-Bart, Simone with Andre Schwartz-Bart. <u>In Praise of Black Women: Ancient African Queens.</u> Trans. Rose-Myriam Rejouis and Val Vinokurov. Madison: U of Wisconsin P, 2001.

Shange, Ntozake. <u>for colored girls who have considered suicide/when the rainbow is enuf</u> New York: McMillan, 1976.

Shepherd, Linda Jean PhD. <u>Lifting the Veil: The Feminine Face of Science.</u> Portland: FireWord, 1993.

Sojourner, Sabrina. "In the House of Yemanja: The Goddess Heritage of Black Women". <u>My Soul is A Witness.</u> Ed. Gloria Wade-Gayles. Boston: Beacon, 1995. 272-277.

Spretnak, Charlene. <u>States of Grace: The Recovery of Meaning in the Postmodern Age</u> New York: HarperSanFrancisco, 1991.

Starhawk. <u>Dreaming the Dark: Magic, Sex and Politics</u>. Boston: Beacon, 1988.

Stoeltje, Beverly J. "Asante Queen Mothers: A Study in Female Authority" <u>Queens, Queen Mothers, Priestesses and Power: Case Studies in African Gender</u> Ed. Flora Edouwaye S. Kaplan. New York: N.Y. Academy of Sciences, 1997.

Teish, Luisah <u>Jambalaya: The Natural Woman's Book of Personal Charms and Practical Rituals</u>. New York: HarperSanFrancisco, 1998.

Thompson, Robert Farris. <u>Flash of the Spirit</u>. New York: Vintage Books 1984.

- - - . <u>African Art in Motion</u>. 2nd ed. Berkeley: UC P, 1979.

Walker, Alice. <u>Anything We Love Can Be Saved: A Writer's Activism</u>. New York: Random, 1997.

- - - . <u>The Color Purple</u> New York: Washington Square,1982.

- - - . <u>In Search of Our Mother's Gardens: Womanist Prose by Alice Walker</u> San Diego: Harvest HBJ, 1983.

Wolfe, Naomi. <u>The Beauty Myth: How Images of Beauty are Used Against Women</u> 1st Perennial ed. New York: Perennial, 2002.

Yarbrough, Camille. "Female Style and Beauty in Ancient Africa" 7th Printing. <u>Black Women in Antiquity</u>. Ed. Ivan Van Sertima. New Brunswick: Transaction, 1992. 89-97.

Exploring a Cross-Cultural Women's Spirituality: Inspirations from India

Chandra Alexandre, Ph.D.

Introduction

One counter-force to manipulative patriarchal identity branding and hierarchical control is the relatively recent development in the modern west of an articulated and engaged Goddess-centered spirituality. Within "Women's Spirituality," as the movement is sometimes called, are contained subversive tactics and stances that define spiritual, womanist/feminist, and woman-honoring spaces from inside as well as outside the mainstream. Many are subversive (if not antinomian) because they serve to undermine pathological systems and/or move experience or consciousness beyond specific patriarchal, national, political and religio-cultural boundaries.

Women's Spirituality as we know it in the west is therefore a paradigm-shifting force. We witness and also participate in the mystery as the face of God changes and She becomes one of us, acting, speaking and being from places more deeply and powerfully connected to our truth, beauty and embodied wisdom. In fact, the Divine Female so central to Women's Spirituality has never been contained by geographic borders or other boundaries—She has only been suppressed and repressed. Today, she is enlivened through art, music, scholarship, ritual and the simple fact of women's breath upon her ancient names. Names such as Isis, Hecate, Lilith, Cerridwen, Macha, and Asherah (to name just a few), join alongside the living and re-claimed or newly-created traditions honoring Mary, Oya, Tara, and Kali (among others) to find deep resonance within individuals regardless of demographic particulars.

41

Syncretism East & West: An Ecofeminism of Tantra

Whether a movement for (r)evolution toward psycho-spiritual wholeness, healing of the planet, social justice or simply a practice in accordance with ancient as well as living traditions that honor God in Her female form, Women's Spirituality embraces many different hearts and minds. Adherents find empowerment through the resacralization of matter and the acknowledgement of women's process, not as analogous to that of the hero touted in western myth, but rather rooted in the phases of life, death and rebirth/initiation extant in creation at all levels: individual, collective, planetary, and cosmic.

Like Women's Spirituality, Indian philosophy and theology has long embraced *prakṛti*—the Feminine principle. Defined as the entirety of nature, inclusive of the ability to create, sustain, and destroy, understanding prakriti can help achieve a more balanced worldview while promoting environmental sustainability and the well being of diverse, autonomous communities.[1]

Because the living, goddess-centered, embodied spirituality of India, known as Śākta Tantra, embraces the fullness of prakriti, it can also be employed to depotentiate patriarchal toxicity and create new spaces for life-affirming and fuller expressions of humanity within physical, emotional and psycho-spiritual realms. Śākta Tantra provides ritualized as well as lived practices in which the body acts as, and becomes substance for, the divine. It considers Female/Feminine energy to be fundamental and activating—the source of all creation without which gods and humanity would perish. There are distinct paths within Tantra; however, it is Devī as pre-eminent, fundamental reality who engages the heart, mind and soul of Śākta devotees.[2]

Garnering impetus for a shift out of the patriarchal paradigm benefits not only from an ecofeminist deconstruction of pathological western worldviews, but also from a Śākta Tantrick embodied spirituality that reinforces the articulated assertions of contemporary Women's Spirituality with extant goddess traditions and their millennia-old rituals, practices and traditions of veneration, devotion, honor and respect for the Divine Female (and in some instances, actual women). Sensing the importance of this alliance, academic writers have already produced an ecofeminism of Tantra.[3]

Empowering for women and woman-occupied spaces, an ecofeminism of Tantra: i) engages feminism across divides; ii) demystifies Devī (as the goddess is called in Sanskrit) for westerners, especially bringing an understanding of Devī worship and the roles of women in such worship to light; and iii) deepens a conversation about women and goddesses. Both generally and within Hinduism specifically, an ecofeminism of Tantra helps to articulate some of the ways in which Śakta Tantrick worship poses a real understanding of the relatedness of women's and goddesses' power (even given that in societies the world over, there is no inherent correlation between the worship of a goddess and a favorable status for women). Articulating an ecofeminism of Tantra can potentiate new paradigms.

Yet, do the innovations of Women's Spirituality appropriate spiritual traditions and deities? Is there contextual understanding and reciprocity when working with divine energies and inspirations across cultures? Can Women's Spirituality open a space within itself to include all women, all continents and all genders? If so, what does that inclusiveness look like, particularly for peoples across differences of race, age, ethnicity, class, religion, culture and other distinctions when Goddess is said to embrace all, yet patriarchy knows marginalization even within its sites of resistance?

Striving for a cross-cultural Women's Spirituality, I argue that a globalized ecofeminist position can be endeavored—one that includes sensitivity to the particulars while also allowing for universal truth claims to ultimately serve in the fight for an emancipatory discourse. Working within a global Women's Spirituality, I believe that a developed ecofeminism of Tantra can heal peoples and the planet, in part because it brings together embodied and cosmological consciousness within a framework of interrelatedness that is mindful of individuals (especially those previously voiceless), heeding of the past, respectful of differences and intent upon sustainability.

The nature of this paper is not only to further a general conversation, but also to enact viable approaches to a cross-cultural embodied spirituality— a cross-cultural Women's Spirituality—that utilizes an ecofeminism of Tantra as methodology to consciously alter systems and practices while maintaining a self-reflective stance. Here, I seek a deepening of theory and ask for a promise of engagement in the issues of today by those committed to Women's Spirituality. Finally, my hope is that this paper offers inspiration and calls readers to action.

Women and Goddesses

Goddesses are helping us reclaim the power of womanhood and the Feminine. However, often in academic literature as well as in actual life, the relationship between women and goddesses is conflated—either ignored or glorified to an extreme—usually to the detriment of actual women.

Indeed, women and goddesses are often simultaneously feared, revered, honored, and expunged, with many of the roles assigned to women by societal dictates, codified laws, or superstitious beliefs—and to goddesses by the scriptures—determined by patriarchal controls that arise particularly out of male fears of essential femaleness; i.e., H/her biology.

It is the fundamental organ of womanhood, the *yoni* (womb/vulva), that is the original site of instigation for patriarchal control; for men can neither bleed fertile blood in accord with the natural cycles nor bear children (though they often attempt to replicate these processes through symbolic and literal means). Of course, the controls arising from male fears may be maintained through any number of patriarchal agencies and agents, including women themselves.

Fear-based responses to women and goddesses have particular context-specific manifestations. In India where Devī is a living, active agent in both religion and popular culture, it is still the case that having powerful goddesses does not necessarily mean acknowledging, promoting, or providing spaces for the creation of powerful women. The establishment of women's identity, largely defined through relationships to men (as wife, mother, or consort), translates equally well to the celestial sphere where myths and stories of the goddesses teach particularly about proper behavior, duty and honor. Within the bounds of H/her roles and with relatively few exceptions, woman/goddess is subservient to gods and men (or both).

The purity or impurity of women, for example, is deemed important, judged by patriarchal means, validated through the written word, manipulated by sanctioned interpreters (usually men), and reinforced with laws as well as religio-cultural structures. The reality of women's marginal status within Hindu society is codified within the *Manu Samhita* (Laws of Manu), a document utilized since the 7th century BCE to validate and reinforce the subjugation of women in addition to defining their societal roles. The categories of subjugation under which women are placed and the related socio-cultural controls have generated, *et alia*, the patriarchal practices of suttee, dowry, and child marriage—all of which are still in force in many parts of India despite efforts (including legal measures) to abolish them.

Interestingly, while most of the systems and structures put in place according to patriarchal mandates are certainly an effort to perpetuate male dominance, some are nevertheless believed to be protection against the *śakti*, or inherent power of woman nature. However, despite myriad methods for, on the one hand, subjugating women or defending against them on the other, there are some spheres (as will be discussed), in which śakti as the feminine principle contained within Devī and/or women is honored. (Who does this honoring and who benefits from it are important points to consider.)

Because of a greater global awareness created through the strides of feminism, activism and communication networks, the impact of Goddess today is not only more discernable, but also more powerful. In both economically and spiritually poor countries, the extent to which those in various positions of power control the relationship of women to the Divine is slowly beginning to crumble or at least be drawn into question. Women are increasingly becoming *svatantrya* (independent or free) because they are empowered to break the bonds and limits of patriarchal imaginings. No amount of religio-cultural sweetening can hide or control the raw potency Goddess can offer, and many women are, in many spheres (work, home, place of worship), demanding as well as radiating the fullest expression of their human natures.

Chandra Mohanty's critique of Northern (First World) feminists who totalize Southern (Third World) women and ignore the differences among them is relevant in a conversation where women, feminism and spirit come together.[4] And a beginning point for discussion is suggested by one western feminist, Carol Lee Flinders, by asking western women to enter into dialogue with Indian feminists so that each can learn from the other, particularly given the living goddess traditions of Hindu India and the ways in which these traditions inform some Indian feminisms.[5] For Hindus as well as for Indian women generally, such a discussion can help facilitate understanding of Devī as an empowering force (rather than relegating Her to the dustbin of patriarchal religion); for westerners it can help bring to light the position of women in contemporary India, as well as their particular concerns and spiritual traditions.

Women and Śākta Tantra

Based upon my own experience and research in the west, many are finding that the Śakta Tantrick path can help strengthen an understanding of the Divine Feminine (or Divine Female). Working with some of Hinduism's most fierce goddesses (e.g., Kali, Chamunda, Durga, Tara) can also lead to an appreciation of the context in which Devī and her human sisters in India live today. If engaging cross-cultural dialogue under the rubric of Women's Spirituality (or within a conversation dedicated to furthering an ecofeminism of Tantra), looking at feminist concerns about the treatment and status of women within contexts of the sacred is necessary. Within Śākta Tantra, for example, the literal position of women tends to pale in comparison to the status afforded the goddess relative to Her male counterparts; i.e., the gods. While women may occupy a metaphysically high position in Śākta Tantra (they may, in some cases, be said to be a small part of Devī's śakti and thereby have some occasional real-world benefits), they are still generally treated as marginal. On the one hand, the Śākta tradition has been said to be:

> suited to all constitutions and to all stations of life. It is for the prince as for the peasant, for the poor as for the rich, for the man of business as for the man of leisure. It makes no distinction of caste, colour, creed, or nationality, welcoming one and all who will bow to the lotus-feet of the Divine Mother. [6]

Yet, it is still a tradition where many interpreters and practitioners often avoid discussing the role and status of women. For example, Barada Kanta Majumdar just quoted, seems to have left at least one distinction off his list—gender. And on the other hand, as David Gordon White notes:

> ...it would be hasty to conclude, on the basis of the general Tantric exaltation of feminine energy, that female practitioners have ever dominated the religious or political Tantric sphere. Even in her transformative initiatory role, the Tantric consort has remained instrumental to the requirements of the male practitioners she transforms. [7]

Other recent attempts to discuss women's place in Śākta Tantra have, while not exhaustive or entirely feminist, at least opened a door to this critical conversation. Some scholars, in agreement with White, recognize that in many interpretations of Tantra, women within the Śākta tradition have not generally served as anything other than the ritual instruments of men's *sādhanā* (spiritual practice). But other writers, perhaps attempting to legitimate a feminist Śākta Tantra, are claiming women to have a significant role to play in the formal worship rites, primarily as initiators. [8]

Taken with a feminist critique in mind, Śākta Tantra can provide a welcome model, I believe, not only to help facilitate the elevation of women's status in Hindu society generally, but also to further the reclamation of goddesses and women's empowerment the world over. The timing could not be better; for combined with women in actual positions of power, the decline of male initiators in the Śakta tradition (many of whom are refusing to continue the lineage because of a lack of sustainable livelihood therein, as well as a commonplace desire for a more typically western and economically successful adulthood for their sons, i.e., an "office job"), [9] is opening doors to the goddess in new and increasingly meaningful ways for women in both east and west. Women are now fulfilling multiple levels of engagement and the taking on of increased responsibility in affirmed positions of power within Śakta Tantra as practiced in both India and abroad. My own experience working in the United States as a priestess of Kalī and initiate of the Śakta tradition (I received *diksha* in India in 1998 and again in 2002) offers one example of what is possible.[10]

While for some Indian feminists (as is true for many western feminists) spirituality is not an important focus, for others it is tremendously important. Particularly given some of the more antinomian practices and devotional traditions associated with Devī and Her worship, utilizing the convergence of ecofeminism and Tantra as an east-west platform for continuing the unfoldment of Women's Spirituality, She may evolve in unison with women the world over into a much more readily embraced agent of change—even for those feminists loathe to embrace spirituality because of the ways in which religion has particularly kept women as subordinated objects in many contexts.

With the acceptance of the Goddess across cultures, and with Her followers taking on roles of leadership, I firmly believe that a more fully integrated ecofeminism of Tantra, in which theory and praxis come together for both participatory discourse and action, will facilitate a new paradigm. Such work will help not only to create a cross-cultural Women's Spirituality, but also it will develop practical approaches to implementing and sustaining new procedures and practices that will catalyze the attainment of health, wholeness, and peace on multiple levels of reality.

Introduction to Kāmākhyā

Kāmākhyā is a famous pilgrimage site located outside of Guwahati in Assam, in the northeast region of India. Primarily important to Hindu Śāktas, or believers in the preeminence of Devī, the site is "regarded as a living center of her [the goddess'] immeasurable power"[11] and functions as the most important Śakta *pītha*, or sacred "seat" of the goddess for devotees. Fifty-one sacred pilgrimage sites exist on the Indian sub-continent; the most sacred for Śāktas is Kāmākhyā.

The *mandir*, or sacred temple, to which pilgrims and devotees come to worship, is situated on a beautiful hill overlooking the Brahmaputra river and the green lushness of Assam's tea plantations and jungles. It is here, the purāṇas tell us, that the yoni of Devī fell to Earth. The story goes that in ancient times, one of Her manifestations, Satī, killed herself in shame over her husband Śiva's not being invited to a great *yagna* (ritual sacrifice) offered by Satī's father. In Śiva's grief over her death, he began his *tandava*, or cosmic dance of destruction, with her body upon his shoulders. It was left to Viṣṇu to stop the tirade and thus save the world by cutting up Satī's body with his *chakra* (discus). These pieces then fell to Earth, giving

Śāktas their most holy pilgrimage sites.

Today, as has been true for millennia, Her presence is deeply felt; for She is everywhere, honored as the sexual, procreative, maternal and devouring force. As noted by N.N. Bhattacharyya, the *Kālikā Purāṇa* describes Devī as a supreme being, "as the supramental Prakṛti, the material cause of the phenomenal world, and the embodiment of all energy, consciousness and bliss. The world owes its origin to her, while she does not owe her origin to anything."[12] She is made immanently manifest through matter in the bodies of the earth and all beings; and She is made apparent as transcendent Divine through devotees' direct experience.

Worship at Kāmākhyā is deeply connected with esoteric Śakta Tantrick rites and practices, some of which involve the honoring of women as embodiments of the goddess, the worship of the *yoni*, and, at least for the ritual's duration, the actual veneration of a particular woman. By contrast within the Indian context, worship of the god Śiva's *lingam* (phallus) is common and exoteric, generally not translating to an honoring of male sexuality or to the worship of the phallus as sacred in actual men.[13] Perhaps this is because patriarchal tradition is phallocentric already—and for the west, the fact that the Abrahamic God is not portrayed, nor generally understood, as a sexual being has ramifications of its own, including a suppression of the richness of the male life force, which might otherwise have many life-affirming manifestations. This, however, is beyond the scope of the present discussion.

Nevertheless, most worshippers disconnect the lingam they honor from the sexual organ of men and God, more specifically regarding it as the symbolic essence of God.[14] And as Wendy Doniger notes (although allowing that there are some extant ambiguities), the depictions of Śiva as ithyphallic are in themselves "accepted as representative of chastity."[15]

This is not at all the case with the rites of the goddess; and it is important to note not only that Śākta Tantra explicitly resonates with the wisdom that validates the mysteries of the body, but also that it does so particularly in relationship to women's bodies and menstruation, for these are recognized as natural expressions of the sacred within this tradition. Most generally, the conception of Goddess defined by the literature of Women's Spirituality also asserts the sacred nature of bodies and sexuality (in direct contrast to mainstream Christianity of both the Catholic and Protestant varieties), often providing examples from European and Near Eastern pre-Christian traditions to do so.[16] Working with Devī, therefore, easily resonates with some western women; yet also it helps to expand western women's relatedness to cross-cultural expressions of the Divine.

Menstruation is specifically central to understanding Devī and women in Śākta Tantra because it plays an instrumental part in the formation of Śākta Tantrick psycho-cosmic reality:

> the menstrual cycle in the female body corresponds to, and represents, the cyclical change of the seasons, and the orderliness in the universe...[further, it serves to] interrelate humans to their environment and to the socio-cultural reality in which their rites and rituals attain fruition...[it is an] episode that provides us with a choreography in which collective acts and events of theological/philosophical and cosmological significance attain fruition.[17]

The menstrual rhythms tap into an ontological, universal ebb and flow resonant at individual, planetary and cosmic/divine levels. At Kāmākhyā, this reality is magnified and its truth heightened for devotees by the actual presence of the goddess' yoni on Earth. Her yoni is believed to share menstrual blood once during the equivalent of our solar calendar year, during the dark moon phase *mela* (festival) known as *Ambubāchī*, a festival at which the forces of life and death co-join and Her blood coincides with the transitional time of the soil, when monsoon rains release the tension in the air and help in turn to realize the coming bounty of Earth's harvest.

Annually drawing over 40,000 devotees primarily from eastern India, Ambubāchī, is at once a spiritual gathering and a celebration highlighting not only people's devotion to the goddess but the potential, I believe, for universal empowerment through Devī and connection to the fundamental life mysteries. At this auspicious time, no pilgrims are allowed to enter Her temple sanctuary for three days; but orthodox dictates are of no relevance to Her ardent devotees. Her potency is so wild and intense that one only has to follow the throngs of red-wrapped *tāntrikas* (female Tantrick practitioners) around the outside of the main shrine to absorb the energy issuing from within it, as well as within each individual enraptured in self-induced trance in Her name.

At Kāmākhyā during Ambubāchī, despite the prevalence of Tantrick practitioners, orthodox practice is observed at the temples. This means that all of Her sacred sites upon the hillside (there are temples dedicated to each of the ten Mahāvidyas at Kāmākhyā) are closed for the three days that make up the duration of Maa Kāmākhyā's menses. (Mā Kāmākhyā is the local name for Mahādevī, the Great Goddess.) In India specifically, it is understood by Śākta Tantricks that women hold within their own individual bodies intimate knowledge of Devī's power through ties to menstruation. Women, especially during their moon time, are considered auspicious.[18] In this there lies a disparity between orthodox and Tantrick traditions—a belief in the power of menstrual blood is directly antithetical to normative Hindu teachings, which hold menstrual blood as a polluting substance.

Thus, during this time and according to Brahmanical dictates, the goddess' presence—her yoni is a cleft in the rock situated in a natural spring within the temple sanctum sanctorum—is bathed by blindfolded priests. She is never looked upon directly, thus maintaining the honor and dignity befitting a deity and especially a female. On the fourth day, the temple doors are opened to the throngs of devotees who wish to receive *darśan* (blessings through viewing—Her form is seen only through draped red cloth), *prasad* (blessed food), and if lucky or somehow deemed particularly worthy on that day, a piece of the red cloth from her sari, which symbolizes fecundity and the bounty of Her creation.

Whether regarded as taboo or celebrated, feared or revered, women's menstruation is nevertheless a site of power. As Ajit Mookerjee describes the meaning of women's blood for the Śākta Tantricks specifically:

> The monthly efflorescence of woman in her cycle in rhythm with the lunar cycle creates a body-consciousness which is related to the processes of the universe. Since, according to tantra, the body is the link between the terrestrial world and the cosmos, the body is, as it were, the theatre in which the psycho-drama is enacted... Woman's body is both a unity and an organism directed towards oneness, wholeness.[19]

It is for this reason that pilgrims during Ambubāchī will drink the *rtu* (menstrual blood) of the goddess with great humility and belief in its healing powers. It is through menstrual blood that women may be equated with the power of the transpersonal Divine Female who infuses matter with spirit in all the worlds, She whose blood is holy, reality-altering, wish-fulfilling and supremely powerful. By utilizing the Śākta Tantrick worldview, it is easy to come to an understanding of women as physical agents of the Goddess who heal through their actual bodies and blood the split between the realms of matter and spirit, ultimately fostering a shift out of patriarchy from both consciousness and engaged perspectives.

Theory in Action

How then to begin implementing an ecofeminism of Tantra across divides of difference, doing work that is both spiritually-based and an effective agent of woman-affirming change? How then to effectuate a cross-cultural Women's Spirituality that takes responsibility for maintaining the integrity of those who claim to be empowered by it? Working at the grassroots level, I believe, is one way to be effective and to also come to greater compassion and understanding across divides of difference.

Because I argue that society and its constructs, along with religious spheres, need to take heed of indigenous traditions, rites, rituals and practices that honor women and nature as sacred—that honor the symbols of our power, such as menstruation—Kāmākhyā provides an answer as to where to begin: we can start by acknowledging the essential fact of menstruation and by finding ways to honor the important transition that takes a girl into womanhood. Penelope Washbourn writes regarding the importance of marking menarche:

> The ritual marks an understanding that the girl needs a symbolic, interpretive framework as she negotiates her first life crisis and redefines herself as a mature female. These rituals also express an understanding that discovering our identity as women is not to be a solitary struggle but is to be worked out within the context of the community. In each primitive ritual a form of self-transformation is expressed through trials, symbolic acts, and words which promote healing and integrate the forces at play. The girls and the community move into a new identity *through* the crisis.[20]

Cultures where there is such a recognition of connectedness to the fullness of the natural world, to its cycles and to the quest for wholeness marked through initiatory rites, possess something we in the west have long forgotten or generally ignored—our immediate tie to the sacredness of our bodies and the Earth.

The realities of women's lives in both east and west show that when no sacred or communal space in which to learn about and honor the mysteries and realities inherent in the transformative process of becoming an adult woman is to be found; or when the rite of passage experienced is a psychologically painful or physically brutal process, girls on the verge of inheriting the responsibilities as well as the blessings of womanhood are often thrust into crisis—the kind of crisis from which many never emerge:

> To emerge enriched from the life crisis of menstruation implies finally trusting and liking one's body...It gives pride and status rather than shame and mistrust...It can be creative for [the woman] and the community. Her trust of her body depends on her seeing it in context of the whole. In that sense, it is part of the very goodness of life and of the creative structures of all living organisms.[21]

The ideas and beliefs that surround women's blood, whether social, political or religious, shape not only the individual woman's sense of self, but also the relationships in which she finds herself throughout life. Women are not naturally ashamed of their monthly course—they are taught to be so by patriarchal constructs in society and within many of the world's religions.

When extant, rites of passage in many parts of the globe are often only brutal reinforcements of patriarchal biases and attitudes that promote girls' self-hatred and the denigration of women's power. Within eastern as well as western contexts, girls are most often taught by cultural, societal, and religious norms (as well as by the dictates of advertising and peer pressure), to be ashamed of their monthly cycle and to associate women's status with subjugation. This of course, translates to easily-controlled and malleable women. Therefore, re-thinking and re-teaching menstruation as a natural, special, and powerful aspect of women's unique culture can mean that women move into a greater sense of empowerment in all areas of their lives.

Integration of a vibrant and respected womanhood into once patriarchal systems would transform those systems completely. Engaging a powerful understanding of womanhood in the world on larger levels will require tremendous effort. Yet it is exactly the coming together of eastern and western disciplines and worldviews that can effectuate change via this understanding. Imagine the global consequences of operating centers that, for example, provide educational materials and help younger women deal with the socio-cultural realities of becoming a woman in today's world, perhaps by providing elder guidance and mentorship in conjunction with rites of passage ceremonies at menarche. This vision offers a vehicle for the transformation of related issues and concerns affecting women and girls, such as the onset of eating disorders which, as is the case with anorexia nervosa, often have a direct correlation to the onset of menstruation.

Conclusion

Specifically of interest to me in furthering Women's Spirituality and with it developing what might be called an integral ecofeminism of Tantra are the contexts in which women, Hindu spirituality, and feminism exist and overlap. Both ecofeminist and Śākta Tantrick philosophies and practices foster the unfolding and dynamic spiraling of life, and these systems are paradigm-altering partners.

A spiritually-articulated and engaged ecofeminism of Tantra within a cross-cultural Women's Spirituality can foster the development of a community supportive of life-affirming struggles rather than those of continuing domination. It can become a rooted category of challenge to the dominant culture—what catalyzes the (r)evolution of change upon our planet through life-affirming radical action in which women, men and nature co-create positive and flexibly sustainable outcomes. Through the Female Divine and Her agents empowered, subordinated communities and individuals will find ways to reclaim marginalized ideological and literal spaces, including those of women's bodies. No matter where in the world, the creation and reclamation of such spaces can act on multiple counts to empower people and institutions in new ways—in ways that ultimately mean the health of our planet's people and resources. It can: i) help build self-worth and positive identity frameworks; ii) foster the development of an "earth family"; iii) foster a participatory and sustainable environment; and iv) develop an ethic where exploitation is not conceivable in any context.

Lastly, such a spirituality can help promote specific action and provide the tools for the unpathologizing or healing of relationships—between men and women, God and Goddess, between a dominant and subordinate, and between our human species and the rest of the planet. Much of the work is already being done. Let us continue to be creative and find empowerment with and through each other and our various visions of the Divine in order to effectuate the kinds of lasting change we wish to achieve for future generations.

Figure 1: Kāmākhyā Mandir during Ambubāchī Mela - June 26, 2003.
Photo by Chandra Alexandre.

Notes

1 Shiva, Vandana, Staying Alive: Women, Ecology, and Development (London: Zed Books, 1989).

2 Although the Śākta and Tantrick traditions are often conflated because of the importance of the goddess within Tantra generally, the followers of Tantra are not all primarily worshippers of Goddess.

3 See, for example: Rita DasGupta Sherma, "Sacred Immanence: Reflections of Ecofeminism in Hindu Tantra," Purifying the Earthly Body of God: Religion and Ecology in Hindu India, ed., Lance E. Nelson, (Albany: SUNY, 1998); Lina Gupta, "Ganga: Purity, Pollution, and Hinduism," Ecofeminism and the Sacred, Carol J. Adams, ed., (New York: Continuum, 1993). Also of note is Christopher Key Chapple's article, "Hindu Environmentalism: Traditional and Contemporary Resources," Worldviews and Ecology: Religion, Philosophy, and the Environment, Mary Evelyn Tucker and John A. Grim, eds., (New York: Orbis Books, 1994).

4 Chandra Talpade Mohanty, "Under Western Eyes: Feminist Scholarship and Colonial Discourse," Colonial Discourse and Post Colonial Theory, eds., Laura Chrisman and Patrick Williams, (New York: Columbia University Press, 1994), 196-220.

5 Carol Lee Flinders, At the Root of this Longing: Reconciling a Spiritual Hunger and a Feminist Thirst, (San Francisco: Harper, 1998), see especially pp. 235-273.

6 Barada Kanta Majumdar, "Introduction: Vaidik and Tantrik Systems of Spiritual Culture Compared," Principles of Tantra, Sir John Woodroffe, (Madras, India: Ganesh & Company, 1991), 153.

7 David Gordon White, ed., Tantra in Practice (New Jersey: Princeton University Press, 2000), 18.

8 See, for example, Georg Feuerstein, Tantra: The Path of Ecstasy (Boston: Shambhala, 1998), especially pp. 102 and 136; and Rita DasGupta Sherma "Sacred Immanence: Reflections of Ecofeminism in Hindu Tantra," 93

9 June McDaniel, "Interviews with a Tantric Kālī Priest: Feeding Skulls in the Town of Sacrifice," Tantra in Practice, 79.

10 For more information, visit www.sharanya.org. a 501(c)3 devi mandir (goddess temple) operating in San Francisco.

11 Ajit Mookerjee and Madhu Khanna, The Tantric Way: Art, Science, Ritual, (London: Thames & Hudson, 1993), 13.

12 N.N. Bhattacharyya, History of the Śākta Religion, (New Delhi: Munshiram Manoharlal Publishers, 1996), 164.

13 Thomas, P. Secrets of Sorcery, Spells and Pleasure Cults of India, (Bombay: D.B. Taraporevala Sons & Co. Pvt. Ltd., 1966).

14 Thomas, P. Secrets of Sorcery, Spells and Pleasure Cults of India, 80.

15 Wendy Doniger O'Flaherty, "The Interpretation of Hindu Mythology," Transformations of Myth Through Time: An Anthology of Readings, (New York: Harcourt Brace Jovanovich, 1990), 183.

16 See, for example, Anne Baring and Jules Cashford, The Myth of the Goddess: Evolution of an Image (London: Arkana/Penguin, 1991); or Monica Sjoo and Barbara Mor, The Great Cosmic Mother: Rediscovering the Religion of the Earth, (San Francisco: Harper, 1991).

17 Kartikeya C. Patel, "Women, Earth and the Goddess: A Shakta-Hindu Interpretation of Embodied Religion," Hypatia IX:4 (fall 1994), 73-74.

18 David Gordon White, The Alchemical Body: Siddha Traditions in Medieval India, (Chicago: University of Chicago Press, 1996), 136.

19 Ajit Mookerjee, Kālī: The Feminine Force, (London: Thames & Hudson, 1998), 35.

20 Penelope Washbourn, "Becoming Woman: Menstruation as Spiritual Challenge," Womanspirit Rising: A Feminist Reader in Religion, Carol P. Christ and Judith Plaskow, eds., (San Francisco: Harper & Row, 1979), pp. 256-7.

21 Ibid. Penelope Washbourn, "Becoming Woman: Menstruation as Spiritual Challenge," p. 257.

Awakening the Energy for Change: The Black Madonna and the Womb of God

China Galland

A report by conference creator and director, China Galland, author of *Longing for Darkness, Tara and The Black Madonna; The Bond Between Women, a Journey to Fierce Compassion*, and the forthcoming non-fiction work, *The Keepers of Love* (2007). Galland is a Professor-in-Residence at the Center for the Arts, Religion, and Education (CARE) at the Graduate Theological Union in Berkeley.

***

The conference took place in Berkeley, CA on Saturday, June 18th, 2005 at the Graduate Theological Union's Pacific School of Religion.

Sunlight streamed through the stained glass windows as the church foyer filled with over two hundred and fifty people by 8:30 that Saturday morning. The conference was sold out and people had to be turned away at the door. The Pacific School of Religion chapel was packed.

Banners of the divine feminine from around the world hung from the rafters and in front of the glass windows, staining the glass with their colors. Images of the divine feminine were everywhere. As the presenters gathered and the last few participants finished registering, so much spirit was filling the air that people began to dance in the aisles.

Then a conch shell pierced the air and focused our attention. Rev Sandy Gess repeated the conch's call to the four directions, opening the space to the female divinities we were calling in from traditions around the world. One at a time, conference presenters each evoked a particular divinity—singing, chanting, praying, playing rattles and gourds. Their heartfelt prayers brought a tangible sense of Mexico's *Guadalupe-Tonantzin*, Africa's

57

Yemanja, Mary, the Mother of Jesus, the Grandmothers, the Ancestors, the *Shekinah*; *Prajnaparamita*; *Pele*; and *Bhagavati*—into the room. Linda Tillery's drum and Lisa Rafel's crystal singing bowls welcomed them all.

Those of us who presented that day—more than twenty of us—sat facing those who had come to participate, Quaker style. Behind us, on the altar, stood five ten-foot high figures created by Annie Hallatt: the Black Madonna of Einseideln (Switzerland), the Black Madonna of Le Puy (France), the Black Madonna of Loreto (Italy), Saint Sara-Kali (the Patron of the Romani people, the Gypsies), and the *Shekinah*, God's Bride in the Jewish tradition, forming an awe-inspiring backdrop.

Then eight Black Madonnas processed in from the back and up onto the main altar, eight giant figures of the great Black Madonnas worn by eight of our presenters and volunteers. The women wearing the figures disappeared underneath the black net that draped the armature on which the Madonna's heads were set. Worn by Women in Black during peace protests throughout San Francisco, it was amazing to see them in this setting, as if the Black Madonna had stepped down from their altars and out of the churches, into the streets with the people.   Women in Black have given us a great gift. These women demonstrate throughout the world, silent witnesses for peace. The chapel was hushed; you could hear every step they took as they slowly walked to the front where they gathered around the altar.

In order to allow all the participants to meet all the presenters, most of whom would be presenting in smaller, overlapping break-out sessions during the day, I had invited each presenter to spend a few minutes in front of the whole gathering, giving us a taste of the work which they would be exploring more deeply in the afternoon.

As each woman spoke to the group, it was clear that we were tapping a rich multiplicity of perspectives on the Dark Mother—some traditional, some non-traditional, some academic, some artistic, some experiential, some musical, and some that defied categorization.

By the time I rose to give the keynote address on the reclamation of the Black Madonna/Dark Mother, the energy in the room told me that what I was talking about was actually occurring right there in the PSR chapel. In the center of one of the country's most important interdenominational Protestant seminaries, images of Dark Madonnas, Goddesses, crones, warrior queens, female Buddhas, were being evoked and honored.

On one hand, the figure of Mary, in the healing form of the Dark Madonna, of the "mother of the Excluded" was being given a place in a mainstream Christian seminary, and on the other, she was being *liberated* from the Church, where, for centuries, she had been relegated to often marginal status. For me, this event was a way of following Black Elk's teaching, which tells us that: *in order to have the power of one's vision, one has to perform it on the earth for all the people to see.*

In this context, I spoke of the many stories in the various traditions of the divine feminine ultimately being the only force that can save the world from destruction. The story of Durga from the Devi Mahatmya is one of the most vivid examples. What's important to remember is that Durga comes to our rescue only when she has been remembered (or re-membered), evoked, called upon. Only when the Gods themselves realize their own limitations in defeating the demons that are threatening the world and call on Durga does she manifest herself.

I believe we are in a similar position today. Or, to put it another way, drawing from our own Western imagery, the Black Madonna/Dark Mother is "the stone the builders rejected," which appears in both the old and new testaments as the one that will become "the chief cornerstone." The cornerstone of a new foundation, I would like to hope, for healing the wounds of racism, oppression and environmental destruction.

Rosemary Radford Ruether, Ph.D., one of our country's foremost feminist theologians, gave a second keynote address titled "Why Do Men Need the Goddess: Male Creation of Female Religious Symbols." With her delicious, deadpan humor, Rosemary immediately began to challenge some of our own feminist beliefs:

> *It has become a kind of dogma among many contemporary feminists interested in religious history that patriarchal religions, such as Judaism and Christianity, suppress all female symbols for the divine. Therefore if any female personified symbols for divinity exist in such religions, they must be "remnants" of some earlier, pre-patriarchal women-centered religion. It is also assumed that female religious symbols must have been created primarily by women and are intrinsically empowering to women. But these are questionable assumptions. A recent collection of essays by feminist scholars of Hinduism has challenged these views. A collection of essays entitled Is the Goddess a Feminist? (Alf Hiltebeitel and Kathleen Erndl, eds. New York University Press, 2000) concludes that most of the Hindu Goddesses were created by men to empower men and to keep women in their place.*

The full text of her talk is being published on www.imagesofdivinity. org, along with a selection of other writings by conference presenters.

In the afternoon, we split up into dozens of small groups to participate in presentations that ranged from spoken-work poetry by young African-American poet, Danielle Drake-Burnette, to the Italian Black Madonnas by one of our greatest scholars on that subject, Lucia Chiavola Birnbaum.

The full list of presenters and topics follows, below.

When I was first asked to create this conference by the GTU, I turned to my Images of Divinity Advisory Circle and together we decided that rather than invite only a few women scholars working in this area, we would open up the day to a multiplicity of women working on the Dark Mother from a variety of perspectives. We opted for a wide mix of entry points into this world of the Divine Dark Feminine. We wanted to draw participants from a broad range of audiences. We were testing the waters.

For this first conference, I invited only women whose work I respected and knew personally, hence the particular shape and flavor of this day and also its limitation. We needed more women scholars from Islam—Mary is mentioned more times in the Koran than she is in the New Testament of Christianity. We needed more Latina scholars and artists. There are a wealth of women here in the Bay Area alone. There are women in the Hindu tradition that need to be here, the Buddhist tradition, the list is endless. We hope to address the concerns, and others, as we plan our next conference, tentatively scheduled for spring, 2007, again, at PSR/GTU.

When midwifing and giving birth to events like this one, one always hopes that its life will continue beyond the actual day or two of the conference itself. It's gratifying to report that two of the presenters, Linda Tillery, musicologist, singer and Bay Area treasure, and Ann Jefferson director of worship at Pacific School of Religion, music director at St. Andrew's Presbyterian Church in Marin City and Images of Divinity advisor who met for the first time at the conference, have been co-teaching a class, called, "From Slave Ships to Sanctuary: A Survey of African American Spirituals." I've been a delighted student in the class which reveals how the Spirituals are really a container for the deep spirit of liberation and freedom that every soul longs for.

Also, several ongoing "Circles of Love" have grown out of the conference. These are small groups meeting to take up the theme of reconciliation using the structure known as "council" or "circle." More information can be found atwww.imagesofdivinity.org/circle. A good and reliable guide for circle work is Christina Baldwin's book, *Calling the Circle, the First and Future Culture,* (Bantam), and the pamphlet that's been produced from her book about guidelines for circles.   You can get a copy from her organization, PeerSpirit, Box 550, Langley, WA 98260 or online at: http:www.peerspirit.com/.

List of Presenters/Contributing Artists:

(in alphabetical order. Italicized, quoted material indicates work published in the Conference Reader. Papers submitted for the Conference

Reader are published on www.imagesofdivinity.org)

Evelyn Avgiola – Musician and composer, conference presenter with Rev. Sandy Gess on music, chants, and how to compose your own. *"Seven Lyrics with Personal Reflections"*

Jessica Batha, M.A., MFCC – conference coordinating committee, builder of main altar with cross-cultural images of female divinities. *"Female Icons"*

Lucia Birnbaum, Ph.D. – Presenter, lecture and slides. Feminist and cultural historian, Professor, California Institute for Integral Studies. Images of Divinity Advisory Circle.
"Black madonnas, and other dark women divinities, and the change of paradigm. Prehistoric african migration paths to the future."

Danielle Burnette, M.F.A. – Award-winning spoken word artist, 2003 Oakland Poetry Slam Champion; MFA in Creative Writing from SFSU. Images of Divinity Advisory Circle.
"Five Poems"

Sandy Butler, M.A. – Presenter. "Praying with our Feet," Women in Black and demonstrating for peace with giant, wearable Black Mother/Madonna figures made by Annie Hallitt, mask-maker extraordinaire. Also assisted China Galland in presentation on forming Circles of Love to explore the theme of reconciliation, with the earth, the community, within ourselves and each other. *"Teaching Our Feet to Pray"*

Jennifer Colby, Ph.D. – Presenter. Artist, curator and lecturer at CSU, Monterey Bay. Coordinated the contemporary art program at the Bade Museum at PSR for nine years, and owns Galeria Tonantzin in San Juan Bautista, CA, where "The Images of the Virgin" exhibition and conference is held annually since 1992. Images of Divinity Advisory Circle *"Transforming Tonantzin"*

Catlyn Fendler, M.A., M.F.A. – Indoor labyrinth walk with Cindy Pavlinac's slides of labyrinths from Chartres Cathedral and other sites. A trained labyrinth facilitator, educator and writer. Holds an MFA from the University of Iowa Writer's Workshop and an M.A. in Interdisciplinary Consciousness Studies, from JFK University. Images of Divinity Advisory Circle. *"The Black Madonna and the Labyrinth"*

China Galland, M.A. – Keynote speaker, "The Power of Vision: Female Divinities and the Black Madonnas around the World," author, conference convener, director, and producer at the request of PSR/GTU; Director, Images of Divinity project at CARE/GTU.
"In Memory of Elizabeth Lloyd Mayer;" "A Note of Gratitude and Acknowledgements;" and, *"Excerpts from The Bond Between Women, A Journey to Fierce Compassion"*

Rev. Sandy Gess, Ph.D. – Presenter. Minister, musician, core conference coordinating committee. Co-founder and leader of Weave of Faith-Christian Feminist Community in Oakland, CA. Presented on the labyrinth as a spiritual and peace-making tool at the Parliament of World Religions in Barcelona, Spain, July 2005. Images of Divinity Advisory Circle. *"Rituals Are Pathways to the Divine"*

Annie Hallatt – Conference coordinating committee, producer of community pageants, ceremony, and rituals with art. Maker of the eight giant wearable figures used in the opening procession and on the altar in the PSR Chapel as well as the ten-foot high stationary Black Madonnas, Shekinah, and Sara-Kali cross-cultural figures that formed the backdrop for the altar. Hallitt's figures were first created from China Galland's Images of Divinity slide collection for the California Revels 2000 production of "The Man Who Juggled for God." Galland and Elizabeth Lloyd Mayer collaborated in the narrative for the Revels play inspired by the tellings of that famous medieval legend. *"Through the Eyes of an Artist"*

Rev. Ann Jefferson, M.A., M.Div. – Welcome, Introduction of keynote speakers and piano and song. Music and ministry Coordinator of Ministry and Liturgy at PSR. Images of Divinity Advisory Circle.

Dianne Jenett, M.A., Ph.D. – Presenter. Core faculty and co-director of the Women's Spirituality Program at New College of California, she has a Ph.D. in Integral Studies with a concentration in Women's Spirituality and an M.A. in Transpersonal Psychology. Her research has been published in the U.S., Europe and India. Images of Divinity Advisory Circle. *"Red Rice for Bhagavati Pongala Ritual at Attukal Temple in Kerala, India"*

Elizabeth Kelley – Presenter. Independent scholar, researcher, writer, dancer, she was ordained into the Holy Order of Mary Magdalene by Tau Rosamonde Miller in 1996. Images of Divinity Advisory Circle. *"Mary Magdalene, Priestess of the Resurrection"*

Ann Grace McCoy, M.A., LL.D. – Presenter. "Spirit on the Energetic Level," calling in the Dark Mother with rattles and drums, transformation and the body. Core conference committee, assistant conference director and producer. Practitioner of Transformational Body Work. She teaches introduction to Cranial Sacral Therapy at the Pacific School of Massage. Images of Divinity Advisory Circle.

Mary Beth Moser, M.A. – Presenter. A presenter and lecturer on the Black Madonnas of Italy, she has been a guest on KPFA public radio in Berkeley. Her thesis, "Honoring Darkness: Exploring the Power of the Black Madonna in Italy" has recently been translated into Italian. *"A Pilgrimage to the Black Madonna of Oropa"*

Cindy Pavlinac, M.F.A. – Fine art photographs – "Labyrinths and

Ancient Goddesses," slide show for the interior labyrinth walk. Exhibiting artist since 1974, she has received numerous awards and appeared in over 300 publications. Principal Photography for the books, *Labyrinths* and *Sanctuaries of the Goddess*. Images of Divinity Advisory Circle, Circles of Love blog, www.imagesofdivinity.org/circles, contributor.

Reda Rackley, M.A. – Presenter. Holds a Masters in Mythology with an Emphasis in Depth Psychology from Pacifica Graduate Institute. Mythologist, storyteller, dancer, and an initiated shamanic diviner by the Dagara Tribe of Burkina Faso. Images of Divinity Advisory Circle.

Lisa Rafel – Tibetan bowls and sounding. Main chapel convocation. Internationally known chantress, sound and energy healer and spiritual teacher. She has sung in sacred sites all over the world, including Chartres Cathedral in France, Sakya Monastery in Tibet, the Great Pyramid in Egypt and the World Festival of Sacred Music in honor of His Holiness, the Dalai Lama.

Rosemary Radford Ruether, M.A., Ph.D. – The Georgia Harkness Professor of Applied Theology at the Garrett Theological Seminary and Northwestern University for 27 years; currently the Carpenter Professor of Feminist Theology at the GTU in Berkeley. She is the author of 27 books and editor of 12 book collections in the areas of feminist theology, women and religion and social justice issues. *"Why Do Men Need the Goddess? Male Creation of Female Religious Symbols"*

Lydia Ruyle, M.A. – Art banners throughout the conference building and PSR chapel.

On the Visual Arts faculty of the University of Northern Colorado. Her Goddess Icon Spirit Banners have flown internationally in over 25 countries. A book about her work, *Goddess Icons Spirit Banners of the Divine Feminine* was published in 2002. *"Goddess Icons of the Dark Mother Around the Globe"*

Anne Scott – Presenter, dream circle. Trained in dreamwork in the Naqshbandi Sufi tradition since 1990, she is the founder of DreamWeather Foundation, a nonprofit organization that provides seminars, retreats and conferences for women. Author of two books, *Serving Fire: Food for Thought, Body and Soul*, and *The Laughing Baby*. *"The Power of Dreaming"*

Luisah Teish – Presenter. "Carnival of the Spirit, dream catchers and sand dancers."

Singer, dancer, storyteller; Yoruban priestess. She is on the faculty of the University of Creation Spirituality and a board member of the Association of Transpersonal Psychology. Author of *Jambalaya* and *Carnival of the Spirit*.

Linda Tillery – Presenter. "The Historical Tradition of Call and

Response Music." Percussionist, leader of music and song. Founder, the Cultural Heritage Choir, and scholar of African American spiritual music.

Judith Tripp, M.A., M.F. T. – Outdoor Labyrinth facilitator and presenter.

A transpersonal psychotherapist and Labyrinth Facilitator, she leads the women's Dream Quest at Grace Cathedral and around the country. Author of *A Dream Quest Companion* and *Poems from a Spring at Chartres*. Images of Divinity Advisory Circle. *"About the Chartres Labyrinth"*

Maria Teresa Valenzuela - Presenter of stories and slides of Guadalupe devotion from the Indigenous and Mexican perspective with Patrice Wynne. A Guadalupana of Mexican and Indian heritage, she has trained with shamans in Mexico, Peru, Ecuador and with indigenous elders from the Mayan cultures of Guatemala. *"Guadalupe, La Morenita Reina de Las America"*

Karen Nelson Villanueva, M.A., Ph.D. candidate – Presenter. A doctoral student at CIIS in Women's Spirituality, she holds degrees from the University of Michigan, George Washington and Holy Names University and teaches Humanities in San Francisco.

Images of Divinity Advisory Circle. *"Multicolored Momma: Toward the Decolonization of Our Denied Dark Mother"*

Meggan Jane Watterson, MTS, M.Div. – Presenter with Danielle Drake Burnette.

Holds a Masters of Theological Studies with a concentration on world religions from Harvard Divinity School. She has a published piece in Sumi Loundon's edited book titled, *The Blue Jean Buddha*. Images of Divinity Advisory Circle. *"Three Poems"*

Comma Williams, M.A. – A Training and Organizational Development Consultant, she has been in the training field for over 20 years. For the past ten years, she has been studying and practicing shamanic healing.

Patrice Wynne – Presenter. Co-presenter of stories, slides, and photographs of Guadalupe devotions from the Indigenous and Mexican perspective with Maria Teresa Vallenzuela.

Former founder/owner of GAIA Bookstore and Cultural Center, the first bookstore in the U.S. devoted to women's spirituality. Author of *The Womanspirit Sourcebook.* *"Global Guadalupe ... But Surely, You Believe?"*

Images of Divinity's *"Awakening the Energy for Change, the Black Madonna and the Womb of God"* was sponsored by the Center for the Arts, Religion, and Education (CARE) at the Graduate Theological Union

(GTU) in Berkeley, CA., on June 18th, 2005. Cosponsors were PSR, the Pacific School of Religion and CIIS, the California Institute of Integral Studies in San Francisco. The conference was dedicated to the memory of Elizabeth Lloyd Mayer, Ph.D., author, psychologist, and founder of the **California Revels**, the annual December Bay area cross-cultural community celebration and play celebrating Winter Solstice at Oakland's Scottish Rite memorial theater.

The sold-out conference of 250 people and presenters will be convened for a second time in the spring of 2007, in celebration of China Galland's forthcoming non-fiction book, *The Keepers of Love*, by Harper San Francisco, on Love Cemetery, an African American burial ground in East Texas.

See the Images of Divinity and Keepers of Love websites for the announcement of dates. Also, subscribe to our periodic, free on-line newsletter for Images of Divinity through www.imagesofdivinity.org, "join us," for notification of the conference and events within our cirlce.

See www.imagesofdivinity.org/circle for our on-going blog and news of our "Circles of Love," local small groups forming to provide spiritual support for the challenges of "putting spirit into action" today and to sit with the question, "what do we need to do to be reconciled with one another?"

Go to the website and circle blog for more information. Also, see www.thekeepersoflove.com

Background on Images of Divinity

Images of Divinity was formed in 1987 when China Galland, in recognition of her work as an independent scholar in the area of the divine feminine in world religions, was invited to become a Research Associate at the Graduate Theological Union. In 1991, the relationship was formalized when the GTU became fiscal agent for the project, first through its Center for Women and Religion, and later, in 2000, through its Center for Art, Religion and Education (CARE).

The book, *Longing for Darkness, Tara and the Black Madonna*, (Viking 1990, Penguin Paperback, 1991) was the first publication to come out of Images of Divinity's research work. The book chronicles Galland's ten year journey in search of the connections between Tara, the female Buddha in the Tibetan tradition, the Black Madonnas of European Catholicism and other forms of dark feminine divinity. It was critically acclaimed in publications as diverse as *The New York Times Book Review* and the *Buddhist*

Peace Fellowship Newsletter. It was cited in the November/December 1994 issue of *Psychology Today* as one of the books signaling, "…a whole paradigm shift in society with the power to heal the mind-body split… [and] the new spiritual awakening that promises to remake the political landscape as well. German and Chinese translations followed.

Next, came *The Bond Between Women*, (Riverhead/Putnam 1998), bearing the fruits of more years of research, this time into the lives of women who were actively changing the world. As the Kirkus Review wrote, "We meet women activists who are battling the increasing traffic of child prostitution in Nepal and India, where girls as young as six are forced into sexual slavery. Across the world in Argentina, Galland interviews women whose children 'disappeared' during the repressive military regime of the late 1970s and early 1980s. These women still demonstrate weekly in the Plaza de Mayo in Buenos Aires, committed to airing the truth of the murders of their loved ones. Other women battle injustice more quietly, but no less dramatically, as with Sister Jessie, who campaigns to increase literacy among poor women and children in India, or an American woman who is crusading to de-pollute the sacred Ganges River there. These are unforgettable stories of courage, and Galland recounts them with admiration but also with the complex anger and helplessness she feels in the face of these insurmountable problems." *The Bond Between Women* was chosen as one of the five best spiritual books of 1998 by "Books for a Better Life," a project of the publishing industry and was a selection of the Book of the Month Club.

In addition to these two major works, China Galland's writing has appeared in a number of anthologies and periodicals such as, *Being Bodies*, *The Moonlit Path*, *Zig Zag Zen*, *Tricycle* Magazine, *Mothering* Magazine, *Inquiring Mind* among others.

True to its name, Images of Divinity as assembled a unique collection of images from around the world that attest to the enormous range of ways humankind has sought to picture a divine feminine presence. These include a comprehensive survey of the Black Madonnas of Europe and the Americas, various forms of Tara, a sampling of dark Hindu Goddesses, contemporary artists' interpretations of traditional figures and photographs of sites in which images of the divine feminine are celebrated and worshipped. IOD is in the process of digitizing its entire collection. Parts of the collection have been shown in exhibitions at the GTU's Badé Museum, at the University of San Francisco's Thatcher Gallery and in conjunction with various conferences presented by IOD.

To date, IOD has presented four major conferences on various aspects of the dark, divine feminine:

1966. University of California at Berkeley;
1999. University of California at Santa Cruz
2001. University of San Francisco
2005   Graduate Theological Union

IOD has sponsored courses by China Galland and associate scholar Rev. Francis Tiso, Ph.D., among others, at the GTU; it has also sponsored research projects like that of Meggan Watterson on the Black Madonna sites of France and Switzerland. The work of IOD has been highlighted in of several documentary films including *On the Road Home* by Christina Lundberg and *Women of Wisdom and Power*, a PBS special. China Galland also appears on the BBC-produced DVD, *Stabat Mater*.

Current Project: 2006-2007

The Keepers of Love began in 2000 as a research project in East Texas initiated by author China Galland. The initial impulse for this undertaking grew out of Galland's research into an untold, hidden, repressed, African-American version of history that runs, sometimes parallel, sometimes in opposition to, the accepted, "official," white narrative. Research into county historical records and interviews with local residents in Harrison County—at one time the largest slave-owning county in Texas—led Galland to the discovery of Love Cemetery, an African-American communal burial ground that the local community had been locked out of for forty years. Research became activism as Galland, at the request of the community, organized a grassroots, interracial committee, made up of local religious leaders and lay people, to work on restoring community access to Love. The work of this committee—both its internal struggles with the assumptions and hidden prejudices that can sabotage even the most well-intentioned groups, and the outer work overcoming the obstacles to reopening and rededicating the cemetery—stands as a model for the kind of compassionate action that is the beginning of reconciliation.

Metaphorically, Love Cemetery stands at the center of a much larger body of unearthed history that Galland has been excavating since 1985. In some cases the material reaches back to the time of slavery and post-Civil War reconstruction. In particular, Galland has researched stories of "landtakings," the theft of land from African-Americans, and forms of slavery, such as debt peonage, that continued well into the 20th century and, in some forms, continues even up to the present day. Unlike South Africa, the United States has no officially sanctioned effort toward "Truth and Reconciliation." If racial healing is to occur, it must begin with efforts like The Keepers of Love.

Galland is now transforming her East Texas experiences into a book that will be published by HarperSanFrancisco in early 2007. The book unpacks the tangled black and white historical narratives that meander through this region like the sloughs and bayous that give the land its character. It chronicles the work of reconciliation that underlies the reclamation of Love Cemetery. (Love includes Native American burials). Ultimately it offers a model for healing the deep racial wounds that prevent democracy from achieving its full flowering in the United States. *The Keepers of Love* is being directed to the widest possible national readership and being offered as a replicable model of grassroots racial reconciliation.

In addition to the book, video and audio projects documenting Galland's work in East Texas are currently in progress. Over forty hours of tape of the Love Cemetery Committee meetings, the clean-up and restoration of the cemetery by a multi-racial group of Boy Scouts and community members, interviews with the descendants of those buried at Love, are being logged and transcribed in preparation for editing. Additional footage is being shot of the unfolding story of the reclamation of Love as it happens. These audio-visual components will have a wide range of applications. The most obvious is broadcast on public and community-based radio and television stations. Additional applications can include educational programs that can be used as part of history curricula. Finally, the Internet's importance in the distribution of this kind of media is growing rapidly and must not be underestimated. The audio-visual elements will also support the public presentations that are a third component of the Keepers of Love Project.

After the initial publication of the book early in 2007, China Galland will undertake a series of public presentations that will take advantage of the existing, grassroots networks of local historical societies, churches, and burial societies, both African-American and white, that exist throughout the country, especially in the rural south. Whenever possible, white and African-American groups will be encouraged to co-sponsor events as a way of ensuring interracial participation. Using people's fascination with family history as a point of entry, Galland will present stories and images from The Keepers of Love as a way to create a "safe place" in which the first steps of truth-telling and reconciliation might occur. In the same way that Galland created the interracial committee that succeeded in restoring Love Cemetery, we hope, through these presentations, to plant seeds that might grow into ongoing groups that will continue to explore the possibility of communal healing throughout the United States.

Telling the story of a small, nearly forgotten, Black cemetery in a part of the world that receives little attention, is a way to give voice to an element of the rich diversity of American life that is rarely heard. We believe that their differences can bring people together just as much as they can keep them apart. But as long as groups are excluded and silenced because of racial, religious, ethnic, economic or sexual difference, our society will never be whole. The interracial, interfaith, intergenerational re-consecration of Love Cemetery in August 2005 was a large step toward restoring the dignity of a severely marginalized community. The cemetery had once been part of a thriving African-American farming community that had been pulled apart by a centuries-old heritage of racism and inequality. Like the biblical "stone that the builders rejected," Love Cemetery can become the cornerstone of a new foundation of reconciliation, tolerance, and unity.

The Keepers of Love Project is sponsored by the Center for Art, Religion and Education, a non-profit, 501 [c] [3] organization in Berkeley, California

Self-appointed Saviors Propagate Globalization

Claudia von Werlhof
o. Univ. Prof. Dr., Institute of Political Sciences, University of
Innsbruck, Austria

Discussion between opponents of globalization and members of the
WEF, World Economic Forum
Salzburg, July 2, 2001

In the first public confrontation between proponents and opponents
of globalization in Austria, I participated on the side of opponents. In
the following, I would like to reflect briefly on this experience with the
following notes:

1. The arguments of opponents and proponents, once presented, were
left largely un-discussed. The main reason for this was that the proponents
did not relate criticisms to themselves in any way at all.

2. Instead, the proponents tried to co-opt the criticisms by presenting
themselves as critics in their own right, according to the motto, "We see
problems too, but we're working at solutions". From this side, obviously,
there was no questioning of globalization **as such**. One proponent, the
"global player" Percy Barnevik, actually went so far as to claim that the
problems related to globalization arise from the fact that instead of there
being too much of it, there is too little.

What disturbed me particularly about this discussion were the lily-
white consciences of the proponents of globalization.
How is it possible for one Percy Barnevik to say that he makes no
apologies for being entirely profit-oriented, and for defining globalization

as "the freedom for my group of companies ..., to invest where and when it wants to, to produce whatever it wants to, to buy and sell wherever it wants to and to support the lowest possible restrictions resulting from labor laws and social contracts"[1] – without regarding this as scandalous, like everyone else did?

Barnevik's answer is that globalization has purportedly rescued around one thousand million people, one third of them Chinese, from absolute poverty. What is a claim of this nature based on? It rests entirely on one measurement alone: that of money. The moment, someone has access to money, even if the tiniest amounts, he or she is no longer regarded as living in "absolute poverty." The problem with this type of calculation is that the flip side of the coin is ignored: the fact that monetarization almost always entails the loss (of control) of the means of production and of subsistence in general that have hitherto made these people's existence possible. Barnevik would thus have to explain why he regards a relatively moneyless life as "absolute poverty" and the miniscule income of someone robbed of their means of production and subsistence as the liberation from such poverty. If questioned, the answers of those affected would be quite clear. But Barnevik isn't interested in them, since he only thinks about money. Whatever else happens as a consequence of introducing money is meaningless for him.

But that doesn't let him off the hook. Because only when people lose (control of) their means of production and subsistence can Barnevik & Co. use them or have them used for their own interests – for the re-implementation of large-scale land-holdings, for the spread of commodity production and to ensure "the market" is a world market, everywhere. Barnevik sees no harm in this, since only in this way can he make money himself, lots of it. And in any case the people can now (allegedly) buy on the market what they used to produce themselves – or else whatever Barnevik & Co. are offering them instead.

There is only one snag: it isn't true. Susan George, who was also on the side opposed to globalization, pointed out that a growing number of people are unable to participate in market activities at all. Now it is already 50% (and in 20 years' time 70% of people) says George, are excluded from the market: not "still," but "**already.**" In other words, absolute poverty is created by globalization in the first place. It is the situation, in which people have neither the means of production, nor of subsistence, nor else a money income that is anywhere near sufficient. Their money income is so limited, that they are in no position to really have "demands" on the market.

What would Barnevik say if confronted with these conditions, which he bracketed out? Presumably he would say that **in the long run**, globalization will raise income and employment levels. Not that he could prove this. On the contrary, at present the global players' corporations employ only 1-2% of all waged employees, whilst constantly destroying millions of small and medium-sized enterprises – precisely those which have up to now provided the most employment opportunities. And it is the plantations, sweatshops, brothels, and "free production zones" that produce for the big corporations that pay wages of less than 1-2 US$ a day; not "still," but rather, they *no longer* pay more than this. This means that not only in the countries of the South, but in others – e.g. in the USA itself – one can speak of a "new slavery", affecting hundreds of millions of people throughout the world[2]. This is where Barnevik's argument ends; after all, he is himself in favor of "the lowest possible restrictions resulting from labor laws and social contracts." This means that he sees to it himself that things won't be able to get any better in the future. On the contrary, the globalizers went to the South first, to exploit the low labor costs there – the only remaining "comparative cost benefits" world-wide – subsequently achieving a gradual but drastic reduction of labor costs in the North too.

The empirically observable **simultaneity** of globalization on the one hand and impoverishment, war, and destruction of democracy on the other can thus be explained. Mr. Barnevik's "argumentation" and his good conscience are based on the fact that he does not take cognizance of the actual causes and effects. As a result, he can also behave as if he were completely "un-ideological" – unlike the critics of globalization, naturally. He puts his faith completely and utterly in money, in "the market." Only, there is a theory behind this faith – monetarism. The monetarism of Milton Friedman, Friedrich von Hayek, and the "Chicago Boys," whose first act in ushering in global neo-liberalism in the 70s was to install the dictator Augusto Pinochet in Chile. This economic theory underlies globalization policies. With the violence with which it is carried through politically, its totalitarian character, and its effects (in the form of its creation of wealth for some and poverty for nearly everyone else), it is of benefit to the global players, but not to the majority of human beings, also not in the long run. Of this there can no longer be any doubt. And so Mr. Barnevik has to act as if he didn't have any theory at all, so as not to be confronted with the preconditions for and consequences of his thinking. That, incidentally, includes deliberately leaving out historical comparisons, so making it possible not to recognize how closely globalization, colonialism, and imperialism resemble one another, except to the extent that globalization, this world economy, doesn't leave out anything or anyone anymore – not even its own inventors, the Western/Northern industrial countries. They too become "colonies of the corporations," because globalization means exactly what Mr. Barnevik understands it to be.

One basis for removing the premises on which this argumentation is built, together with this "good conscience," would therefore be knowledge and information. At the same time, proof of the deliberate ill-intent of the globalization project could be provided. For example, it was no coincidence that the notorious MAI, Multilateral Agreement on Investment was negotiated in secret and not supposed to reach the public eye at all. This happened because the MAI (which subsequently failed as a result of a veto from France and protests from the world-wide, civil-society based, anti-globalization movement, then in its infancy) in fact provided for the legalization of a campaign of exploitation conducted throughout the world by the big corporations. In addition, it would have been a kind of "authorization" in the form of a totalitarian world constitution[4]. Nor can the policies of the OECD, WTO, IMF, and World Bank, which have led to the collapse of entire national economies and to millions of deaths – especially those of children, as UNICEF has established – through poverty, hunger, and war throughout the world, be attributed to naivety or error[5]. Besides, the long-term planning and conduct of armed conflicts throughout the world, or the destruction of Yugoslavia and the war in the Balkans, a new war in the middle of Europe, cannot be seen as being for the good of humanity, although (or for which reason) they were presented as exactly that: as "humanitarian interventions."[6] Business hand in hand with militarism and speculation instead of investment - "investment" is really just more fusion – cannot really be regarded as "economic activity" in any positive sense. In addition, there are the increasingly open attacks on those democracies that still exist. It is not new that the Americans for example are not necessarily among the friends of democracy in countries of the South. Lately, democracy in the North has also been called "outmoded" by the WTO for example; and Margaret Thatcher's chief advisor, John Gray, stated that "global free trade and democracy are like fire and water." [7] In Austria too, in the context of neo-liberal University reform, which belongs to the domain of the privatization of services related to the GATS negotiations of the WTO, there is now talk of democracy in the universities hampering their "business potential."[8] The foreign affairs advisor to the American government in the post-war era, George Kennan, warned as early as 1948 against spreading illusions about growing wealth and democracy[9]. In a TV broadcast approximately two years ago, a member of the EU Commission of that time said: "If people knew what we really negotiate about, they would chase us away!" (Censorship evidently wasn't working normally in this case.)

It is possible to show by now when this project known as globalization will necessarily come to an end; at the latest when the non-renewable resources of the planet have been used up...that Western lifestyles are utterly impossible to impose on a global scale. Ecological collapse would be the immediate result. **Why, in that case, do people continue to pretend that there is "no alternative" to the spread of the Western way of life?** We need to ask what a desirable society would be like, and whether the Western society, even in its centers, would have a place in it at all? Are we happy, are we healthy, do we relate to one another in caring ways, are we free enough not to have to worry about money and power for once? Are we people capable of deep feeling, do we have a good relationship to plants and animals, are we wise, open-hearted, and tolerant, do we know what friendship is, have we managed to defeat crime, violence, and poverty?

On the back cover of the journal "The Ecologist"[10] there is a photograph of a girl of the Jarava people, who have lived on a group of islands in the Indian Ocean for thousands of years. The Jarava are now to be resettled by the Indian government. The girl in the picture is laughing gaily, still covered in water droplets after bathing in the ocean, and her hair is decorated with skillfully arranged shells. The text to the picture runs:

"What choice does she have in civilization?" The answer is: She will become
- "untouchable
- prostitute
- beggar
- servant
- addict or
- corpse".

Who has the right to inflict Western "civilization" on this girl?

Pamela Hartigan, my counterpart in the debate with the WEF, manager of the Schwab Foundation, which founded the WEF in the 70s, began her contribution with the following words:

"The birth of a new world is upon us!" What she meant was the globalized world, and she spoke with pathos. How can she do so, in spite of what we (could) know? And how can Mr. Barnevik still say, "They need our technology!"?

However, to put an end to the good consciences of the culprits, we need to take something more than just information, thinking in terms of cause and effect, and the leaving out of consequences into account. We need to consider **belief**. Because, the nihilism of the globalization project is clearly accompanied by a message of salvation, as well. **Could it not be said that the constant, worldwide large-scale assemblies of representatives of**

corporations and heads of government are in fact propaganda meetings of self-appointed saviors, whose mission it is to convince the public that what is good for capital is also good for humankind? – as, incidentally, was done in the Nazi period. Are smooth global players like Barnevik a "better alternative" to elected politicians, and is the WEF summit in fact conceived as an alternative to democracy? The brainwashing only works as long as people believe in it. After all, we **know**

- that violence and war cannot be good deeds;
- that it was a lie to say that the neo-liberal policy of globalization would bring more wealth and democracy for all;
- that measures to reduce public spending are fraudulent; just like Structural

Adjustment Programs (SAPs) in the South, all they mean is a redistribution from bottom to top, and they serve only speculators and the military arms buildup;

- that reactionary policies are not "reforms";
- that the "privatization" of public assets represents uncompensated expropriation and theft from the population;
- that it is a travesty when what is labeled "racism" and "xenophobia" are no longer worldwide neocolonialism or deaths as a result of deportation practices, but instead criticism of the piracy of large global corporations;
- that opponents of globalization are condemned as being adherents of "protectionism," while the corporations themselves are products of subsidies and of protectionism in their own interests;
- and not least, that opponents of globalization are now being systematically   criminalized, or called "terrorists"; because they heretically refuse to believe in the "good" (and godly?) of globalization; with the result that, right in the middle of Europe, one of them has quite deliberately been shot at (Goeteborg, Genoa) - as if not just economically but also politically banana-republic methods were a feature of the most progressive achievements of global modernization.

The total turn-around of the hitherto (purportedly) valid view of the world is indicated by the macabre cynicism of the globalizers. Their propaganda of salvation however stands and falls with the idea of mission. What was promised in earlier times by Western Christianity is now promised by the "free market," even if it has disappeared behind monopolies by now – if it ever existed at all.

The idea of mission, like Pamela Hartigan's fantasy about the birth of a new world, is the core of the problem of the good conscience. What it means today is that where there is no McDonald's, there is nothing to eat. Away with the roadside food vendor! Today's missionary assumes that McDonald's is the best for everyone, and he wouldn't dream of asking those concerned what they think. If he notices that someone has a different opinion, then he "educates" him – if need be, by the force of the facts that he fabricates. The puzzle about the secret of the good conscience is this: **the demolition of what already exists is not regarded as violence or destruction, but merely as a necessary prerequisite to the brave new world of Western lifestyles, or to be more precise: the American way of life**[11]. For Percy Barnevik and Pamela Hartigan it is inconceivable that anyone could have anything against this. Or if they do, this is interpreted as being way behind the times, and just too inflexible.

The central question to Barnevik and Hartigan and the other proponents of globalization is thus: **how is it that they have no respect for that which other people have made; that they can in fact destroy it - and at the same time view this as legitimate, even as a good thing?** That is the only question which they would, in the final analysis, not have been able to answer. The thinking of pro-globalizationists assumes a common religion, with a quasi-god (the market and money), in which scenario they themselves are a team of cleaners sent to cleanse the world of non-conformists and heretics. They are the heroes who sweep away the filth and set up shiny, clean McDonald's, full of light and air, everywhere. But anyone who talks about "them" needing our technology has failed to even recognize that "they" already have their own, and that it usually works a lot better for them. These shiny, happy global prophets of a clean new world would probably be nauseated if they even tried a roadside vendor's food. On an emotional level, too, they wouldn't know what to do with food that wasn't from McDonald's. Apparently, it seems dangerous to them, maybe even deadly. And since they regard food prepared at the roadside as a threat to life, they impose their own McDonald's on those who have been eating roadside food up to now, without dying from it in the slightest; except that McDonald's really is a threat to life. Without the roadside food vendor, but with McDonald's, many people will starve, and many already have. Not only because McDonald's food is bad, but also because most people can't afford it, and now have no alternative. McDonald's creates a void – and so does modern technology and money, which is oriented towards the world market and profit – not only at the scene of the crime, but also elsewhere, for example in the Amazon rainforests, where deforestation takes place for McDonald's: so that cattle can graze there for a few years and then be made into hamburgers, before the grazing lands turn in due course into barren steppes and deserts. This is what moved José Bové, a French farmer, to "dismantle" a branch of McDonald's under construction in his neighborhood[12].

The religion of progress embraced by the proponents of globalization is a belief in miracles and alchemy; according to this faith, the constant annihilation of life, the dramatic destruction of nature and the ever-faster devastation of other cultures (or what remains of them) are not crimes, indeed, they don't even matter; they should be greeted with jubilation by those affected, because what has been destroyed will be replaced with a wonderful new world of technical and other kinds of progress. This superstition is still found everywhere, even amongst opponents of globalization. After all, it is several hundred years old and, since colonial times, has evidently been the essence of our Western identity[13]. The difference to earlier times is only that now, at last, an end will be made once and for all to the last remnants of non-Western civilization and any impertinent attempts at revival on their part.

The Salzburg dispute in fact brought to light the actual dilemma of the globalization debate, even if it could not be formulated there and then. I doubt whether there are many people here in the West who can really prove that their "civilization" is the "better" one. Nevertheless, most people probably believe that it is. And as long as that is the case, the proponents' "charm offensive" and their strategy of "embracing" certain groups in critical civil society may lead to a rift in the latter, instead of the contra movement embarking **together** on the desperately needed discussion of fundamental alternatives[14] - these being possible alternatives to Western civilization itself.

My conclusion from the Salzburg experience is that the critique of globalization will only be safe from co-option and resistant to being turned into its opposite if it is not conducted under the premise of unreserved faith in Western civilization and its mission to play benefactor to the world.

The way forward is clear. It is also based on a feeling, only a completely different one. It is a feeling of responsibility for and empathy with those people negatively affected by colonization and globalization, and for all other creatures worldwide, and for the planet itself. This feeling tells us that what we want at last, for the whole world, is a non-violent, caring, egalitarian, cooperative civilization, and this is what we will probably need to survive globalization, possibly the last and most radical phase of Western civilization, at all. Because there is one thing that both opponents and proponents of globalization can be assumed to know, or that they could know if they wanted to: the globalization project is not one of long duration. It is already coming up against the material, intellectual, spiritual limits of the world. It is already in a crisis, and will inevitably fail. Neo-liberalism is the capitalist world system's answer to the crisis of profitable capital valorization, i.e. that of supposedly endless growth in the face of the finiteness of the world and its resources.

If the MAI was to last 20 years, then that is presumably the kind of time-span global players think in. But we, the other 99.9% of the world's population, cannot afford to have this kind of "then it's someone else's problem" mentality. We have to become oriented to life once more, and begin to think and act in ways that are both long-term and free of dominance.

(English translation by Patricia Skorge)

Notes

1 Susan George: at the debate, as well as Tagesanzeiger, 15.1.2001

2 Bales, Kevin: Die neue Sklaverei, Munich: Kunstmann 2001; english original: Disposable People, New Slavery in the Global Economy, California University Press 2000;

3 Arlacchi, Pino: Ware Mensch. Der Skandal des modernen Sklavenhandels, Munich: Piper 2000.

4 Mies, Maria/von Werlhof, Claudia (eds.) Lizenz zum Plündern. Das multilaterale Abkommen über Investitionen, MAI- Globalisierung der Konzernherrschaft und was wir dagegen tun können, Hamburg: Rotbuch 1998

5 Chossudovsky, Michel: The Globalization of Poverty, London: Zed Books 1998; Netzwerk gegen Konzernherrschaft und neoliberale Politik, German edition of: The International Forum on Globalization (IFG): Die Welthandelsorganisation (WTO): Unsichtbare Regierung für die Welt des neuen Jahrtausends? Eine Einführung, Analyse und Kritik, Cologne 2001; Soros, George: Die Krise des globalen Kapitalismus. Offene Gesellschaft in Gefahr, Berlin: Alexander Fest 1998; english original: The Crisis of Global Capitalism. Open Society Endangered, New York: public affairs, 1998

6 Chossudovsky, Michel: see 5 above, as well as, by the same author, Washington hinter den terroristischen Anschlägen in Mazedonien, 23.7.2001 (English original: http://emperors-clothes.com/articles/choss/behind.htm); Federici, Silvia: War, Globalization and Reproduction in: Bennholdt-Thomsen, V./Faraclas, N./von Werlhof, C. (eds.): There is an Alternative. Subsistence and Worldwide Resistance to Corporate Globalization, London: Zed Books 2001, pp. 133-145

7 Gray, John. Die falsche Verheißung. Der globale Kapitalismus und seine Folgen, Berlin: Alexander Fest 1999; english original: False Dawn. The Delusions of Global Capitalism, London: Granta Books, 1998

8 cf. von Werlhof, Claudia: Hochschulreform als neoliberaler "Putsch?", paper presented at the 29th German Evangelischen Kirchentag 2001 in Frankfurt/Main

9 cf. Chomsky, Noam: Profit over People. Neoliberalismus und globale Weltordnung, Hamburg/Vienna: Europaverlag 1999, p. 24; english original: Profit over People. Neoliberalism and Global Order, New York: Seven Stories Press, 1999

10 The Ecologist, Vol 31, No. 6, July/August 2001

11 Galtung, Johan: Die Welt in der Krise, in: Galtung et al.: Die Gewalt des Zusammenhangs. Neoliberalismus-Militarismus-Rechtsextremismus, Vienna: Promedia 2001, pp. 53-82

12 Bové, José/Dufour, Francois: Die Welt ist keine Ware. Bauern gegen Agromultis, Zürich: Rotpunkt 2001

13 Lapham, Lewis: Die Agonie des Mammon. Die Herrscher des Geldes tagen in Davos und erklären sich die Welt, Hamburg: EVA 1999

14 Mies, Maria: Globalisierung von unten. Die Kampf gegen die Herrschaft der Konzerne, Hamburg: Rotpunkt 2001; Bennholdt-Thomsen, Veronika/Faraclas, Nick/von Werlhof, Claudia (eds.): .): There is an Alternative. Subsistence and Worldwide Resistance to Corporate Globalization, London: Zed Books 2001

Creator Woman

Deity, Snake and Life-Giving Waters: The Active Female Principle
In the Fertile Crescent and Africa

Deborah J. Grenn, Ph.D.
© 2007
Founding Priestess, Mishkan Shekhinah
Co-Director and Core Faculty, Women's Spirituality MA Program
Institute of Transpersonal Psychology
Palo Alto, California

"She is Creator of the Universe, and of Mankind...She is the Creator Woman," said artist Meshack Raphalalani to me one day. He was describing the magnificent mahogany figure he had sculpted, She Who stands proudly with outstretched arm in rural Ditike (and on the cover of this volume,) a powerful woman emanating both immanent and transcendent divinity. A Venda man living in the Northern Province of South Africa, Meshack and I were happy to finally meet in August 2001, after communicating through one of his art dealers for a year. The Creator Woman, sculpted from the time of apartheid, holds out hope, strength, wisdom and sanctuary to past and future generations, her womb "a place for children to hide during apartheid," Meshack said. In a more recent conversation, he noted, "She's the mark of the nation; she's also the caring Mother and also the life-giving Mother."[75]

It is this Mother – and all my ancestral mothers – who called me to write my dissertation in 2002, "For She Is A Tree Of Life: Shared Roots Connecting Women To Deity." It is as a continuation of that work and out of a continuing belief in the power of the Sacred Feminine that this paper emerges.

My dissertation, an "Organic/Theological Inquiry Into Identities, Beliefs And Practices Among South African Lemba And European-American Jewish Women"[76] began in 1999. At that time, I learned of the Lemba, a nation of 250,000-300,000 indigenous Africans of Jewish descent who migrated from Africa to Judea to Yemen, then back to Africa. Professor Matshaya Mathivha, of blessed memory, head of the Lemba Seremane clan in the Northern Province, writes that after the Lemba migrated into Africa, one group went westwards, eventually settling in Ethiopia. The other group, he says, migrated south, establishing communities in Mozambique, the East coast of Southern Africa, Malawi, Zimbabwe (c. 300 BCE), and South Africa (c. mid-18th Century), where the largest population lives today (Mathivha, 1992).

I first went to Johannesburg, South Africa in the summer of 2000 to learn more about Lemba women's customs; there I worked with Dr. Rudo Mathivha, the primary co-researcher in this project and Professor Mathivha, her father. It was Rudo who first pointed out Meshack's powerful sculpture to me.

I became curious to learn how this Creator Woman, Mother of the Universe—a figure described as the original divine mother by Lucia Chiavola Birnbaum[77]--was embodied in the Semitic and other African goddesses, including Lilith-Ishtar, Tanit and Anat. Birnbaum, a cultural historian, believes that "the oldest veneration we know is of a dark mother of central and south Africa, whose signs—red ochre and the pubic V—were taken by african migrants after 50,000 BCE to caves and cliffs of all continents."[78] This would certainly apply to Tanit, of whom we see traces from Tunisia and Sardinia up through Phoenicia/Canaan, and to Anat, who we can trace from Egypt to Syria.

In this essay, I hope to prompt curiosities and to expand the limited discourse on some of the mytho-religious beliefs and stories inscribed in our cellular memories by this lineage of divine ancestors. One question to be considered is why—if these female deities or essences represent one divine energy—we construct so many separations and barriers to understanding them, and each other, by focusing on their cultural differences?

For example, contemporary women see in Lilith the embodiment of the goddess of life and death, of love and war, transformation and change; these are designations she shares with the Sumerian goddess Inanna, the Semitic Ishtar, the Canaanite-Hebrew goddesses Asherah and Anat, the African-Semitic-Phoenician Tanit, and Egypt's Isis. As a goddess of love, beauty and things erotic Lilith is akin to the African Oshun and Greek Aphrodite.

Where Her various names and descriptions lead to an appreciation of difference and pride in one's cultural identity, we see a positive force for change; however, all too often we fall into the "my god/dess is better than your god/dess" syndrome. Is this not a continuing catalyst to war.

What other lessons can be learned from religious myth and history? How can we incorporate the values of the Sacred Feminine, as we re-learn them, back into our own lives? Perhaps we can start to understand this divine female energy as we examine and begin to comprehend our own hearts and spirits; we can learn what the ancestors and the Creator Woman have to teach us by trusting ourselves enough to follow Snake[79] as a guiding female principle, being willing to live in the unknown as we swim in this sea of myth and inquiry. To understand the female aspects of immanent divinity, we must inquire into the power of our own lifeforce and blood, into the creative, imaginative, sexual and spiritual energies held in our own bodies. To understand Her as both immanent and transcendent, we can look to our rituals, and to the bodies of the ocean, earth and sacred tree.

Attempting To Describe The Sacred Feminine

Whether as a result of geographic dispersion, the need to hide evidence of Her power or because of cultural or religious differences, the female divine, Goddess/Godde has gone by many names. Though She may have been omitted from canon and ignored in the external religious practices of the elite, She remains vibrantly alive in folk religion, and in the daily domestic practices of millions. Her image continually reappears, emerging as many aspects and emanations, with many faces—a strong, steadfast, inspiring presence for those who can see Her. The impact She has on us is visceral, at times hidden, at times unmistakable, whether we think of Her as Iahu-Anat—the original Great Goddess of the Semitic people,[80] Yahweh's predecessor—or as Inanna-Ishtar, Lilith, Shekhinah, Yemaya, Bhadrakali, Tanit, Oya, Olokun, Bhagavathi, Durga, Mami Wata, Isis, Mary, Tara, Qwan Yin, Asherah, Atargatis, Haumea, Amaterasu, Guadelupe, Nyaminyami or by any of her other 10,000 names.

"She is powerful," said Meshack, agreeing with my observation over the phone as I looked at a photo of the Creator Woman, longing to be reunited with Her and with the rich red soil, the *adamah* or bloody clay of Mother Africa. "When people look at her their life is renewed. When they are weak they feel strong; when they are sad, they feel happy when they see her."

He told me was inspired to create Her when he started thinking about all the things our mothers do for us. "I started to think about everything that the ancestors do for the living people. "Because they're creators, the ancestors, and they're also the ones who taught each and every tribe how to speak and how to eat...all the things needed for life. They are the first teachers."

A focus on the importance of the womb is a consistent theme in Meshack's art. The Creator Woman holds open her womb to offer safety to children during apartheid; his eight-foot-tall wood sculpture of a Venda *domba* initiate stands with an empty calabash (representing her virginal womb in this case) atop her head and a large python wrapped around her ankles winding its way to her vulva and belly. She has a beautifully-grained belly, a prominent feature in many of his sculptures including the strong, proud figure he calls "Gender Equity," a woman with arms upraised in a way that recalls ancient priestesses' prayer posture. When I asked about this feature in one of his sculptures he said, very matter-of-factly, "Everything is done by the womb."

Meshack made this statement to me in his studio in 2001. It came to mind again later when I heard Dr. Asha Pillai speak on a "Diverse Dialogues" panel.[81] Dr. Pillai, a pediatric oncologist at Stanford University spoke about how the values of the Sacred Feminine are carried out in her own work: "For me the Sacred Feminine, the feminine force is essentially the womb of the Universe. The smallest point of Creation... that needs complete sustenance and complete protection from all the forces working against it in the world [finds this in] the womb. The small spark grows, then exits the womb and is able to do its work. And for me that is what the feminine really is...the universal energy, spirituality in our daily practices, [it is] in the work we do in the world..."

I find the concept of us living in the womb of the Universe breathtaking each time I hear it expressed. Certainly it is a more compelling image than coming to consciousness in a male-designed construct ruled by male forces, Eden, especially as this was a place from which one could be evicted for bad behavior at any time. Of course, this origin story is viewed quite differently if one imagines Adam, Lilith and Eve living in a Garden of Asherah, where a Serpent of Wisdom taught people how to become immortal like the gods.[82] Cultural theorist Judy Grahn offers another version; in a refreshing female-oriented origin story grounded in her metaformic theory, she posits the first moment of human consciousness as tied to humans' recognition that they, like the moon, went through monthly cycles of dark and light, seclusion and emergence (Grahn, 1993.)

It is not surprising that male theologians clearly understand the connection between constructing deity as male and the male hegemony evidenced in Genesis. In a recent talk feminist theologian Rosemary

Radford Ruether noted, "Patriarchal theologians will immediately accuse ecofeminist theologians of immanentism, of a concept of God that lacks transcendence. But here we need to rethink the whole concept of transcendence, freeing it from its captivity in the dualistic mind-body, male-female split that aligns God with split off male rationality and females with mindless matter. We need transcendence in ecofeminist theology, not as a concept of a God who is male disembodied mind outside the universe, but as a renewing divine Spirit radically free from our systems of domination and distortion."

"The patriarchal God, who rules from outside the universe, is not transcendent in this sense, but is the ultimate captive justification of patriarchal domination and delusion... An ecofeminist understanding of divine Wisdom both sustains daily life processes and also grounds the creative transformations by which we free ourselves from such distortions to rediscover the real nexus of just relations."[83]

"Just relations" would include neither racism nor patriarchy, nor would they leave room for misogyny or other forms of injustice. Mamaissii Vivian Hunter-Hindrew, Vodoun priestess and author of *Mami Wata: Africa's Ancient God/dess Unveiled*, points out: "It never occurred to most modern scholars that [their] demeaning attitude toward the "God" who had given the African and early Mediterranean peoples the best of everything, might be rooted in the same misogynistic crucible from which patriarchy and racism was born." Hunter-Hindrew also says that if we are to get history "even half-way right" it is most important "to (especially) male African clergy, and others…to relearn to respect the Divine African Mother within themselves…" (Hunter-Hindrew, 2004.)

Lucia Birnbaum adds another dimension to defining the Sacred Feminine when she writes that she finds the dark mother's values— justice with compassion, equality, and transformation—in everyday and celebratory rituals of the world's marginalized cultures—and suggests that the image and values are in the submerged memories of everyone.[84]

Why do we need to study our own divinity in the year 2007, to be reminded that Her image and values are inside us all, that women and the Earth are sacred, that living in a male-erected system of domination and hierarchy is not our natural state? Because for four thousand years women have too often been unnamed, erased from much—written perhaps less than oral[85]—history; suppressed, demonized or made silent. "Every time a girl reads a womanless history she learns she is worth less," note Myra and David Sadker.[86]   As we re-create liturgy and rituals invoking our ancient ancestors, calling forth the spirit and energies embodied in divine womanhood and female divinity, the ocean, the earth, and ourselves, we bring these energies back to the surface of contemporary consciousness— more often, and in more places.

Lilith and Tanit – Two Expressions of the Active Female Principle

A prime example of one who has long lived in our consciousness, but rarely as her fullest self, is Lilith. The belief in Lilith-- known to us today as the first woman, the first Eve, Adam's first wife--has persisted throughout many cultures in one form or another for at least 5000 years, in mythology, art, iconography and oral and written traditions.   She has alternately been revered and rejected as goddess, protective deity and evil spirit. Rather than thinking of Her as evil incarnate, I propose that She may only be projected this way as a demonization of Inanna-Ishtar, Queen of Heaven and Earth, who would have both peaceful and warlike characteristics, like any male god we have accepted; that she may well be the same energy. Perhaps we confuse or conflate her identity and persona because of a long line of political manipulations. If the dominant agenda was to control human, especially women's behavior, as it seemed to become circa 2300-2000 BCE, what better way than by changing Lilith from a protective goddess to a demon, or by later tarnishing the supreme power of a female deity by claiming she demanded child sacrifice, as many say of Tanit?

Lilith is said to have been created from the same earth as Adam, as stated earlier, yet he expected her to submit to him sexually, intellectually and presumably in every other way as well. Lucia Birnbaum, in her landmark work *Black Madonnas* (1993), calls Adam's treatment of Lilith "the first violence done to women." If one reads this as rape, as some writers do (Philips, 1984; Ostriker, 1993), one begins to view the Garden of Eden as more prison than paradise.[87] No wonder, then, that Lilith left Adam and Eden for the freedom of a cave by the sea, perhaps choosing "loneliness over subservience," as Aviva Cantor wrote in the first issue of LILITH Magazine (1972:5).

Myths about Lilith doubtless began with oral tradition; visual evidence of her is first seen as a pictograph thought to be Lilith residing in the Huluppu Tree, which Betty De Shong Meador, author of *Inanna, Lady of Largest Heart* (2000) [88] dates back to c. 3300 BCE. The oral stories and visual images were followed by statuary and writings; the first written piece mentioning Lilith is thought to be the ancient epic of *Gilgamesh and the Huluppu Tree* (Johnson, 1988), dated somewhere between 2400-2000 BCE.

Evidence of apotropaic or protective amulets and incantations against Lilith date as far back as 1894 BCE (Scurlock, 1991) and probably earlier, as in the famous Burley plaque, a terracotta relief of a figure often identified as Lilith (now thought by many scholars to be Inanna-Ishtar,) circa 2300-2000 BCE. The only actual Biblical reference to Lilith or 'the liliths' (male *or* female demons) is in the Hebrew Bible (Isaiah 34:14, noted above.) Lilith also lives in Aramaic incantation texts found in bowls around 600 CE in Nippur, Babylonia (Iraq), Arslan Tash (Syria) and Persia; in Talmudic references written around 400-500 CE and additional Rabbinic literature, *midrashim* and folklore from the 7th to the 12th Centuries CE, in 15th and 16th Century European sculpture and woodcuts. The Zohar, the "Book of Enlightenment" from which late 13th Century Spanish-Jewish Kabbalistic teachings emanated, repeatedly links Lilith and Eve in their 'sinfulness,' according to Barbara Black Koltuv in *The Book of Lilith* (1986:68). We also find Lilith in Kabbalistic sources through the 17th Century CE, at which time she was said to come from 'filth and sediment'—no longer just earth—and in contemporary feminist literature, in which her image is quite improved, where she is a symbol of independence, rightful rage in pursuit of justice and proud sexuality.

Interestingly, although many speak disparagingly of "superstitions," as if these are the sole property of the uneducated, ignorant "Other," protective amulets warding off Lilith or comparable "evil" female spirits are still given to pregnant women, placed near the beds of women about to give birth or hung in or near the crib of newborn babies in a number of Middle Eastern and North African countries, including Israel/Palestine, Morocco, Tunisia, Ethiopia, Iran, Kurdistan and Yemen.

Why are we so afraid of Lilith's aspect as a bringer of death or illness? Can we not view her as we do the male god, as one who 'giveth and taketh away', who ends human life as He/She, divine ruler, deems necessary to maintain the balance of the Universe, as an undeniable part of the cycle of life? Why do the qualities we admire in a male god seem abhorrent to us in a female deity? Why is she so threatening that we kill or demonize her, or attempt to erase any sign she ever existed? Lilith has been written about as a threat to our very lives, not seen, as Elinor Gadon (Gadon, 1989:125,) Vicki Noble (Noble 1991:164-65) and others have suggested, as Creatrix/protector.

Tanit, serpent goddess, a Carthaginian deity of formidable power, is known to us, as previously noted, primarily as one who demanded child sacrifice, a practice which preceded her by thousands of years; we read about Abraham's willingness to sacrifice his son Isaac in the Hebrew Bible. Rather it seems Tanit, like Lilith, may have been invoked for support and comfort by women who had stillborn children, miscarried or had abortions. In *Carthage*, David Soren and his colleagues suggest that these circumstances may have accounted for many of the findings at Tanit's *tophet*. (Soren et al, 1990:136), a place where remains of the dead are deposited. In the *tophet* in Carthage, first excavated in 1817, hundreds of urns and stelae, engraved stones have been recovered. Many of these stelae are inscribed with dedications to Tanit and Baal. Urns contained the cremated bones of infants, and there is now controversy, Soren says, over whether these were sacrifices or simply graves. Might the stories of Tanit as bloodthirsty goddess have started as misogynistic or anti-Carthaginian Roman propaganda accusing the people of performing child sacrifice to propitiate her, when they were simply burying their dead?

The Sacred Vulva, and Knowing The Womb As Sanctuary

Neither a female creator, nor the womb of any Creator Woman was ever mentioned as a place of safety in my early education. I did not know she was so close, except through the loving compassion of my mortal mother; She was hidden from me by the text and through the lack of it, through a dearth of female sacred imagery. I did not have access to visions of or stories about Inanna-Lilith-Ishtar-Shekhinah, Anat, Astarte, Tanit or Asherah, and only came across scholarly discussions of Asherah—identified only as a "fertility goddess"—in my 40s; these were never available at our Temple. She was missing from both art and icon because in the Jewish tradition idolatry is "illegal." An image of a goddess or Goddess would certainly have been and is still considered idolatrous. How life-changing it would have been to have read Raphael Patai's *The Hebrew Goddess* as a child, and to have learned that the statue of Asherah was present in the temple for no less than 236 years, two-thirds of the time the Solomonic temple stood in Jerusalem? The late beloved theologian Asphodel Long noted, "This worship, Patai asserts, was part of the legitimate religion approved and led by the king the court and the priesthood." (Patai 1990: 38) So those seeking Asherah would find her in groves and on the hills, and in the temple of JHWH itself.[89]

Nor was the concept of the Sacred Feminine, as embodied in deity at least, part of my religious education. The womb, the sacred vulva, women's wisdom and ways of knowing were not offered to me either as sanctuary or wellsprings of creativity. By "women's wisdom" I do not refer here to women's knowledge or intelligence, both of which my mother and godmother possessed in abundance, but a reverence and respect for women's native, innate wisdom. I was never offered these options as resources, bountiful wellsprings from which to draw; instead, I was given male origin stories and, when I finally learned about Lilith, learned of her primarily as a dangerous, overly sexual, disobedient renegade; She was understood, much like career women of the time, as a far too powerful 'Other' and according to some tales, was banished to live outside the gates of inclusion as punishment.

Would a living sanctuary—envisioned and honored as the Mother's womb, community, building or spiritual mindset—allow us to more freely look at the hidden parts of ourselves? Would such a feeling of safety, of belonging, allow us to live wherever we wished, even on the edge, without feeling we were outsiders? Would such sanctuaries allow women to have unpopular opinions and fresh perspectives without disapproval, judgment, indifference, without being viewed as threatening, without being cast into the wilderness?

Perhaps growing up in such a spiritual sanctuary would better teach us to understand and not fear the chthonic mysteries, secrets, rich fertility that lives in the soil of Mother Earth and in our own imaginations. The veiled, protected places in our hearts, the dark deep of our own womb waters, the fear of our own sexuality—the hidden parts of ourselves would be seen as fecund, potentially prolific, and as the source of our most precious gifts: creativity and lifeforce, *ase*,[90] *nyama*.[91]

Reverence for and Demonization of Snake as Female Lifeforce

I recently told Meshack Raphalalani of Professor Mathivha's comment when I asked him if the snake was part of Lemba mythology or creation stories. No, he'd said, "the snake is part of ourselves." Looking for an explanation of this remark, which I had never been able to receive from Professor Mathivha because of time and space constraints, I asked Meshack what he thought the Professor might have meant. He replied, "Yes. The snake, the python, it is part of our lives because the movement of the snake is the movement of the clouds…and also the movement of the womb. Sometimes it is said that when it moves it will give fertility to everything…like cattle, they can have more milk and reproduce quickly and again.

"If a snake is found in the water [it is believed to bring] water for the people to drink," Meshack added. "As in Lake Fundudzi?," I asked, knowing there were Venda and Lemba legends in the Northern Province surrounding a python inhabiting the lake. "Yes, there's a python at Fundudzi which is said to be the one to cause the water of the Motati River to flow.

... it is said there's a snake which makes the water be there [so the river does] not dry out."

I asked if the python dance done as part of the *domba* puberty/initiation rite[926] brings rain too; he said, "Yes, it is said that when it moves it symbolizes the movement of the clouds."

I posed this same question of Rabson Wuriga, a Lemba scholar who also thought Professor Mathivha may have been alluding to the fact that the snake is related to the water, and he mentioned both Lake Fundudzi and Lake Kariba in Zimbabwe, where Nyaminyami, a river goddess—also referred to as a god and goddess who have been separated—resides and determines the fortunes of the local peoples. This connection with water, as mentioned by both Meshack and Rabson seems tied overwhelmingly to our sustenance, a female force which provides us both the water we drink and the rain needed to grow crops.

Mother Ocean

It was…the first African mothers who were the original ecclesiastical
authorities…
on Earth, to serve the ancient deities known collectively as the "Mami
Watas."
- Priestess Mamaissii Vivian Hunter-Hindrew

Vodoun Priestess Hunter-Hindrew believes that "Black Phoenicians living in ancient Syria, Palestine and Jordan…worshiped Mami Wata, the African water serpent goddess as Atargatis/Ishtar." She also writes that the name Mami Wata is often used to describe a "specialized pantheon of ancient female and male deities who are…spiritually linked to the African people, through the blood of their ancient African mother."[93]

How are women and Goddess inextricably linked through the sea, primal Source, womb waters? Betty De Shong Meador speaks of this connection beautifully in an article on women and desire, in which she also talks about the divinity of the ocean: "From the resource of her fully-affirmed sexuality comes a woman's will, her self-esteem, her remarkable zest for life, and her desire to be in the world, to create forms in the world that will hold and express her full creative being. The prejudice against women's sexuality has an interesting history involving the myth and politics of many cultures…. The creation myth of the Sumerians, who lived in the south of what is now Iraq, placed divinity not in the sky or on the earth, but in the water. She, the Creatrix, was the self-procreating goddess Nammu whose origin was at Eridu, a city on the Euphrates.

"The first temple at Eridu dates back to the late 6th millennium B.C.E., and Nammu may belong to an even older stratum of pre-Sumerian deities from a matrilineal society. Nammu lived in a subterranean source of water called the Apsu, a sweet water ocean that surfaced in wells and springs. Self-procreating, she was the primal womb of abundance, the inherently fertile and fertilizing waters of the Apsu. She was the singular source of life. By the time of written records, around 3300 B.C.E., Nammu's son Enki ruled the Apsu, and Nammu herself all but disappeared.[94]

Ocean and other water deities are an important part of African beliefs and ritual practice—Nyaminyami in Zimbabwe among the Shona; the python and white crocodile among the Venda of South Africa and Yemaya, Oshun and Olokun in Nigeria, among the Yoruba. They are also emerging in archeological finds through the corridor from modern-day Tunisia to Israel/Palestine, in Tanit, and in the Canaanite/Ugaritic/Phoenician Asherah.

Recent evidence has been found of Tanit worship at the underwater site at Shavei Zion, Israel[95] a village north of Akko, where hundreds of clay figurines were found by a diver-fisherman in 1974. The ship carrying this load of votive terra-cotta figurines must have sunk en route to one of the coastal sanctuaries. The figurines, produced in molds ranging in size from 10 to 30 centimeters, are said to represent the Goddess Tanit, chief of the Punic pantheon, and were dated to the 5th century BCE. Her sign, composed of a triangle with a superimposed horizontal bar and a disk, is clearly visible on some of the figurines' pedestals. Her symbols include doves, palm tree, grapes, crescent moon.[96]

As noted earlier, Tanit has been called the goddess of many names, like Inanna, like Isis and so many others. Is She, the goddess most people know as Asherah or Astarte—symbolized by pillar or tree—also Tanit or Tanith, the sea goddess and patroness of Phoenician and Punic ships, She Who has been found in ancient ports throughout the Mediterranean? Is Astarte also the great goddess of Ibiza, the overarching goddess of Carthage, Mami Wata, Olokun or Yemaya of southern Africa?

Of Ancestors, Snakes and Creatrixes

Do you think people pray to the python as god sometimes?" I asked Meshack. "Yes, yes, yes, it's forbidden to everyone to kill the python, it mustn't be killed. It mustn't be killed. Because if it's the god of great waters, of the great lakes…they think they are the spirit." "You mean it could be god or could be an ancestor?" I asked. "Yes, yes. That's why with us you're not allowed to touch *marula* fruit before they (the women elders) make beer for the ancestors, in fear that snakes may come to your home. So you must wait until they make the ceremonial beer, and then pour the beer on the ground.[97] Of these women, he said, "Because they're the creators of us, they're also the ones that must become the mediators between the dead and the living."

Meshack repeated that kids not touch marula before a ceremony, otherwise "snakes may appear everywhere at home…it's a bad omen. And then the diviner must be called and he will talk to the ancestors and the snakes can then disappear." I found it interesting that in the same conversation, snakes represented God and alternately, were regarded as a bad omen—not unlike the notion of the Judeo-Christian deity, or Lilith-Inanna-Ishtar-Tanit and other goddesses having both good and bad attributes, constructive/destructive or Creator/Destroyer personae.

"So those who came before us were telling us no, you mustn't tamper with the python cause it's part of our ancestors, it brings us rain, it will make our cattle fatter and then give us milk," Meshack added. "So Snake really affects if you live or die," I noted. "Yes," he said.

"The old people believe the ancestors are happy if they dream of a red snake…it represents the ancestors. They're talking to you; maybe they come to you to give you something," Venda artist Joyce Mabasa told me when I visited the Northern Province in 2001.

In an interesting legend which might support the concept of Snake either as deity or as active female principle,[98] it is said that the Dogon people of Mali, West Africa believe that when a person sleeps at night, a spirit in the form of a serpent licks their skins in order to purify them and infuse them with life force.[99]

"The Creator Woman has got a lot to do because all ceremonies are prepared by Her, she's the one who prepares. So she'll do everything for the living, creating and also…to become the mediator, she will make beer for the ancestors, cook for the living. She will care for the living, so she's everything," Meshack told me. "It sounds like you describe her as both mortal woman and the Creator," I said. "She's everything. Yes," Meshack responded. "She stands there proudly. The raised hand is alerting everybody to pay attention to her. She doesn't want to be ignored."[100]

And She has been, for too long.   It is in our hands to see that She is no longer rendered invisible or silent in this culture, no longer marginalized, derided, erased.   It is our legacy—indeed, our mandate—to see to it that woman's role as the original creator and guardian of culture is acknowledged. It is time that we enter into a new, self-determined covenant with Creator Woman—by whatever name we call Her—in which She, and so we, are honored. As we restore this active female principle to the ground on which each of us stands, we bring Her in from the wilderness, from the shadows, from the lost pages of history. If we build a future that integrates the Sacred Feminine into our daily lives, we can also bring ourselves out of isolation into connection, finding wholeness and hope, and transforming the world—together.

Notes

1 Personal communication, February 2005.

2 UMI, Accession #3078795. Dissertation available through www.umi.com.

3 In dark mother by Lucia Chiavola Birnbaum (Authors Choice Press, 2002.) http://www.darkmother. net/about.html. Dr. Birnbaum makes a conscious decision to not capitalize words like African and Jewish (see her discussion in dark mother, Authors Choice Press, 2002.)

4 A term coined in a treatise on the qualitative Organic Inquiry research method, If Research Were Sacred—An Organic Methodology by Jennifer Clements, Dorothy Ettling, Dianne Jenett, & Lisa Shields (Unpublished manuscript, 1999.)

5 From Heart of the Goddess, Hallie Iglehart Austen (Wingbow Press, Berkeley, 1990.)

6 This panel was held at Belladonna sanctuary in Berkeley, California, part of New College of California Women's Spirituality Laboratory, where new faculty/student research, art and rituals are presented.

7 Source: http://www.songsouponsea.com/Promenade/IslandsE.html#Tanit.

8 From "Ecofeminism and Healing Ourselves, Healing the Earth" © Rosemary Radford Ruether – a lecture in the series "Keeping the Spirit Alive" presented by St. Stephen's College, given in Edmonton and Calgary, Alberta on June 2 and 3, 1998. Ruether notes that she owes the inspiration for this rethinking of transcendence and immanence to Dorothy Soelle, "God Language and Patriarchy" in COELI International (Summer, 1992: 1ff.)

9 See http://www.darkmother.net/about.html.

10 I am currently researching whether women are indeed erased or hidden in oral traditions; I believe demonization does occur as often in oral as in written stories.

11 From Failing at Fairness: How America's Schools Cheat Girls by Myra Sadker and David Sadker (Scribner, 1995).

12 See my Lilith's Fire (Grenn-Scott, Universal Publishers, 2000). University of Texas, 2000.

13 See http://www.asphodel-long.com/html/asherah.html. Accessed December 1, 2005.

14 In this case, lifeforce, energy, power.

15 Some think of nyama (Dogon language) as the soul, or even as the creator of the universe. For The Dogon of Mali, West Africa, nyama is the word for "the life-force which permeates all things both animate and inanimate as the power behind their existence" (Ray, B.C., 1976, 90 in Nabofa 1984). The concept of lifeforce continues to be at the core of my work because I believe it drives our relationships with self and with each other; and is in turn fueled by them. I do not think of it simply as breath but as manifestation; as our inspiration, the fire in the belly, libido, creative juices, the passion for life that motivates us to keep going, to do our best work, to survive crisis. The Mande of West Africa see nyama as "a hot, wild

energy that is the animating force of nature". "Nyama is also like the Yoruban ase," (the transformative) power considered to be present in everyone (Katya Bahnemann 2002, Franklin & Marshall College, Web Group at http://server1.fandm.edu/departments/Anthropology/Bastian/ANT269/magic.html. Accessed December 30, 2005.)

16 For more on the complex khomba and domba rituals, see the work of Professor M.E.R. Mathivha (Mathivha 1992), Thelma Maluleke (Maluleke 1999), John Blacking (Blacking 1967), and Deborah Grenn-Scott (UMI, 2003, Accession #3078795.)

17 From Mami Wata, Africa's Ancient God/dess Unveiled: Reclaiming The Ancient Vodoun Heritage of the Diaspora, Vol. I, pp. xx and 40. (MWHS, Martinez, Georgia (2004).

18 ©Betty De Shong Meador, 2001. All rights reserved. Reprinted with kind permission, February 2005. Accessed February 28, 2005 at www.serpentina.com.

19 See http://www.jewishvirtuallibrary.org/jsource/Archaeology/Underwater.html; accessed December 28, 2005.

20 http://www2.carthage.edu/outis/carthage1.html, accessed November 3, 2005.

21 As libation for the ancestors.

22 An idea posited by Judy Grahn in her Blood, Bread, and Roses (Beacon Press, 1993), and core to the beliefs of many peoples, including the Shangaan of South Africa, the Yoruba of West Africa and others.

23 Source: http://www.omtron.com/articles/lynda/ss6.php/.

As If There Were A Goddess

An Organic Approach to Research[22]

Dianne E. Jenett, Ph.D.

A deep, deep yearning which arose out of my despair and sorrow led me to the state of Kerala in South India in 1993. Through making a collage and Johanna Macy's (1983) work I touched the deep grief I was suppressing about the ecological disasters, social and economic injustices, and senseless wars in the world. I was inspired by the women's spirituality movement to search for a new vision and was strongly drawn to Kerala, which calls itself "God's Own Country" for its diversity of sacred expression. I hoped to find evidence that the goddess centered and matriarchal culture still evident in Kerala might show us how to live peacefully and sustainably and give us models for change.

Prior to my experiences in Kerala, I had few models for ritual, no relationship with a deity of any kind, and no consistent spiritual worldview. I knew nothing. I was, however, experiencing a longing. I found a culture characterized by a progressive view of social justice, equal respect and value for women, and the equitable distribution of resources, and I encountered and wrote about a ritual, *Pongala* Festival, that embodied those values. During Pongala hundreds of thousands of Hindu, Christian and Moslem women come together to cook rice porridge for the Goddess on behalf of their families and communities. I attempted to "know" the beliefs and worldviews of that culture in the only ways I trusted, through direct experience and observation. Through this engagement I began a dance with Her that was not an entirely conscious process. Throughout the entire six-year dissertation process, I considered my project a sacred activity and continue to understand the teaching, writing, and activism that have followed it as sacred acts (Jenett 2002; Jenett 2005).

Kerala has a culture full of the Goddess, but at first I could not "see" Her and was irritated, thwarted, and unsure of myself. I finally surrendered and just acted "as if" there were a Goddess, listened to the stories of the women and men who did have an abiding devotion and relationship with Her and followed their lead. By acting "as if" there is a Goddess I have developed a deep, abiding relationship with Her as a source of information and guidance, a co-researcher, and co-creator.   This "as if" process also informed my participation in the development of organic inquiry, a qualitative research method whose epistemological and ontological assumptions posit an interconnected, embodied, intersubjective, interdependent, unfolding, "sacred" worldview as the container for research.

Organic Inquiry: If Research were Sacred

Over ten years ago I, along with four other women[101] at the Institute of Transpersonal Psychology, began applying values and methods from feminism, women's spirituality, and transpersonal and depth psychology to our research. We had had been shaped by the experiences and transpersonal worldview[102] taught at the Institute of Transpersonal Psychology in Palo Alto, California. Each of us were at different stages in our scholarship, but we shared a common dissatisfaction with existing research methods and a yearning for a way to conduct research in a way that could include our relationship with what we termed "the sacred" as essential part of our studies.

We had been in groups where sharing of stories and experiences was deeply transformational -- for the teller, the listener, and the witnesses. We had practiced deep listening techniques which we hoped would minimize the usual hierarchy in research; we had learned body-based spiritual practices which developed our sense of embodied knowing and showed we could learn through mind, body, and spirit; we had experienced the power of creative expression. We had witnessed the power of empathy to change our consciousness and expand our ability to hold difference and paradox. We wanted to honor these experiences, make them part of the research approach, and explicitly write about the deepest, most vulnerable parts of ourselves and the changes we were experiencing since we were also asking our co-researchers to share their experiences with us. We had also experienced the expanded presence and intelligence we brought to our work if we began our classes with mediation, chanting or building an altar together. We often felt there was something "greater" guiding our work. What would happen, we wondered, if we incorporated these methods, shared our stories, and disclosed the details of how we accessed information through liminal states, through dreams, creative expression synchronicities and connection with the sacred? What emerged from those deeply felt desires and our discussions were the seeds of a new research approach that we named "organic research," using the growth of a tree as a metaphoric description of the research process (Clements et al. 1998)[103].

As I began my dissertation research (1999) I used some of the process and principles of organic inquiry but as I said, I had no real relationship with a personal deity or concept of what was "sacred". I researched myself into relationship with Her. I came to understand the understand the values of equality and justice embedded in community rituals to Her and the nature of women's devotion. I also gained abiding friendships, and a deeper understanding of how issues of gender, race, and class intersected with my personal and social history to affect my beliefs and actions.

The five steps of Organic Inquiry—Sacred, Personal, Chthonic, Relational, and Transformative, became a process that changed my consciousness and guided my work:

Sacred – Preparing the Ground

> Before any seeds are planted, the earth must be spaded and broken up, old roots and stones thrown aside, and fertilizer added.

> Similarly, participation in the organic approach either as a researcher or as a reader calls for spading up one's old habits and expectations and achieving an ongoing attitude which respects and allows for the sacred to emerge on all levels…The organic approach is grounded in responsibility, reverence and awe for the earth and all her inhabitants as well as for the mysteries of creativity… The researcher is responsible for inviting both the co-researchers and the readers to this expanded point of view. (Clements et al. 1999, 14)

My initial experience of a radical change in my worldview came through studying and practicing Wicca, an earth-based spirituality that understands the sacred as immanent. Starhawk, the well-known author, witch, and activist explains:

> What is sacred – whether we name it Goddess, God, spirit, or something else – is not outside the world, but manifests in nature, in human beings in the community and culture we create. Every being is sacred – meaning that each has an inherent value that cannot be ranked in hierarchy or compared to the value of another being. Worth does not have to be earned, acquired, or proven; it is inherent in our existence. (Starhawk 1987, 21)

Wicca, as well as Hinduism and many earth based traditions, posits that everything is interconnected and that communication takes place in different dimensions in a complex intertwined feedback system outside the rules of cause and effect. My experiences in India helped me understand this vision of the sacred in the ordinary and suggested how I might ritualize this understanding in my life.

I came to understand the sacredness of the tools used by people in their work. Many of the trucks used for hauling are covered with intricately painted religious symbols and pictures of gods, goddess, Mary, Jesus, Christian or Moslem saints beautifully executed in riotous colors. Before beginning their work the drivers burn incense and garland their vehicles with flowers, asking for guidance and protection as they drive. The everyday tools and the environment of the average Keralite are sacralized by simple rituals which connect their work to a greater mystery and purpose.

To evoke this perspective in my research, each year as I began work in Kerala, I created a ritual for my tools. I constructed an altar for my video and camera equipment, film, audio and videotapes, books, notebooks, pens and pencils, and computer. I garlanded them with red, pink and white flower necklaces and offered a *puja* (a ceremony) using water, fire, and incense. I evoked women who had inspired me, thanking them for the books that informed and guided me. To ritualize my gratitude for the support of my community in San Francisco, I played ritual music recorded by friends praising the Goddess which we had sung together. I thanked the Goddess for her help and asked that she continue to guide me in my/ Her work. I changed the way I approached writing, preparing the room carefully by cleaning, creating altars, lighting oil lamps and incense, and playing spiritual music. I asked "permission" to write using a pendulum, signs from my environment, and my own intuition to decide whether to proceed or to rest. I filled the walls of my working space with collages representing the work I wished to do and with the many aspects of the goddess in Kerala.

I learned to recognize the sacred in a number of unexpected contexts. An important aspect of "sacredness" for me was discovering the historical, political, and economic relationships between the U.S. and India and staying present to the guilt, pain, and confusion this knowledge evoked. I attended a women's conference in Kerala organized by Marxists where the women opened the conference with the solemn lighting of a five-foot high oil lamp placed in the center of the stage. At its base were artfully arranged rice, coconuts, plantains, and flowers, symbolic ingredients used in invocations of the sacred in the religious traditions in Kerala. The large "altar" was the central image on the stage as women passionately discussed issues of domestic violence partially caused by the negative effects of globalization. For me, this "sacred" opening set an atmosphere that reduced my apprehension about being the only obvious non-Indian at the conference and my paralyzing, non-productive guilt at being a citizen of a country with oppressive economic policies. I dropped some of my anxiety and defensiveness so I could more clearly hear the serious critiques of globalization and U.S. policies, their impact on these women and their families, gaining a new understanding of the way our lives are deeply entwined. I was consciously breaking up my old patterns of response, thought, and behavior using the gifts of this culture.

As I created research methods informed by a worldview which was changing, I continually asked "If I consider this action, this method, this event, these participants, and myself to be in sacred relationship to the Goddess, what should I do here?" Trusting that the Goddess would actually help guide the research was initially very difficult as the following story illustrates:

The day before Pongala, *I **still** did not have a translator. I had made a trip to India to ensure that I had lined up the assistance which was so vital to my dissertation work. Although I had studied, I didn't speak the Malayalam language and I felt ashamed and helpless, yet compelled to do this work. Last fall I leaned over the brass rail in the dark passage way to get a glimpse of the golden Goddess at Attukal Temple and asked Her to provide me with the resources I needed to gather the stories of the women. That very afternoon I met a woman who enthusiastically promised to translate for me when I returned in February for the research. Still concerned and doubting I would have what I needed, I returned a month before the festival in order to work with the translator, but, inexplicably, she would not return my calls. I frantically contacted everyone in my large network to find someone to work with me, to no avail. Had Amma[104] failed me, or I had failed Her in some way? This relationship with the Goddess was still so new. Then, a knowing came.* **Trust in Her, Amma will not fail you**. *I knew I was struggling, pushing too hard. I had been in this place before. I recognized the tightness and tension in my body, the distracted, unfocused quality of my thoughts, the frenetic worry, which signaled that I was on the wrong course. I tried to relax, to be in the present, to respond to whatever was presented.*

The night before Pongala, *I was suddenly invited to participate in a ritual done for the Goddess on the full moon, when she is most auspicious, beautiful, and receptive. My friend and research colleague, Judy Grahn, and I were accidentally separated and Judy disappeared into the huge crowd gathered in front of the temple. I was frantic; worried she might feel afraid. She had never been alone in India and I didn't think she knew how to get back to our house. My friends insisted I **must** do the ritual and they would find Judy. I arrived disheveled* *and distracted as the ritual was about to begin. One of several hundred women sitting in four long rows, I was the only obvious non-Indian. In front of me were a large oil lamp, and packets containing flower petals, incense, turmeric, cum cum, wicks, sandalwood paste, and many other ingredients for the puja. I had no idea what to do next and people were staring.*

　　As I began to fumble, graceful hands opened my packets and a soft voice whispered instructions to me in English. This was how I met Asha -- a lively, twenty-two year old middle-class woman who later accompanied us to Pongala *rituals and translated interviews.　Asha, who is a descendent in the Nayar matrilineal caste who worship the Goddess, was doing pujas to obtain a job rather than a husband, and she gave us an important perspective on the changes in the younger generation of Indian women.*

　　Simultaneously, as Judy sat calmly outside the temple in a large crowd, she was approached by Kamala, a strikingly beautiful small middle-aged woman who addressed Judy in English. They discussed English literature, the caste system, and politics. Kamala, a woman from the agricultural community formerly considered "untouchable," was a professor of English literature. She introduced us to women from the agricultural and fishing communities who gave us a perspective that is difficult for researchers to get. We were not aware at the time, but Amma had provided us with not one, but two women who were uniquely qualified and situated to help us translate and tell Her story. And the woman who could not help me translate has a sister who wrote a dissertation on menstrual rituals foundational for Judy's own work.[105] The Goddess had indeed guided and provided.

　　I worried during the initial dissertation writing that exposing my experience of a "greater intelligence" guiding the research would invalidate it in some way, but instead this guidance became a central motif of my study and proved to be one of my contributions to the organic research method. Some of the Indian women I spoke with would agree with my interpretation of these events, others might not, but most of them believe the Goddess can be an informant, providing direction, assistance, resources. By closely describing my own experience in my dissertation, I illustrated my evolving understanding of that kind of "knowing."

Personal – Planting the Seed

　　Once the ground has been prepared, the gardener plants the seed deep in the darkness of the earth.

　　　　The seed represents the initial concept for an organic study, which
　　　　comes out of the researcher's own profound personal experience.

The researcher's story of her or his subjective experience of the topic becomes the core of the investigation...

The primary researcher serves as a guide to the reader's experience of the stories by using her or his own story as a conscious point of comparison for all the others. This allows the reader to re-experience her or his own story relevant to the topic. (Clements et al. 1999, 26)

Both feminist research and organic inquiry include the standpoint of the researcher but organic inquiry makes the personal/subjective central to the research. I included deeply personal autobiographical material about my relationship with my schizophrenic mother, my upbringing as a Texan and Southerner, my love for and dependence on the African American women who raised me, and my early religious experiences. I did so because they were relevant to issues that arose in my research – questions of caste and colonization, deity "possession", cooking as ritual, my search for the sacred dark goddess of justice, and my desire to reach across the unknown for mutual understanding.

Anthropologist Ruth Behar (1996) influenced my decision to include a deeply subjective, relational voice in the interviews. She advocated for a voice that can accommodate the "I" that is understood as having a complex psychology and history that observes a cultural "we." (p. 27). Vulnerability and personal disclosures are necessary in spite of the criticism and fear from academia because we are in a *special period* provoked by the disintegration of the old world order in which "many intellectual, political, socioeconomic, and emotional traumas are unfolding simultaneously as our century comes to a close" (p. 33). I agree we are in a *special period* and it was that awareness that took me to Kerala. Behar spoke to the complexity and difficulty of using personal material.

It is far from easy to think up interesting ways to locate one's self in one's own text. Writing vulnerably takes as much skill, nuance, and willingness to follow through on all the ramifications of a complicated idea as does writing invulnerably and distantly. I would say it takes yet greater skill. The worst that can happen in an invulnerable text is that it will be boring. But when an author has made herself or himself vulnerable, the stakes are much higher: a boring self-revelation, one that fails to move the reader, is more than embarrassing; it is humiliating. (Ibid., 13-14)

This is the terror I've felt in writing subjectively. Fear of being humiliated by failing publicly is daunting. But as I've read the organic inquiries of other researchers, I've been changed, expanded, made larger -- and a little braver.

While we were developing techniques to minimize hierarchical subject/object dichotomies, anthropology was addressing similar issues in ethnography. Lila Abu-Lughod told stories of Bedouin women in order to write against the essentialized notion of "cultures" and work against generalization. "Telling stories, it has seemed to me, could be a powerful tool for unsettling the culture concept and subverting the process of "othering" it entails" (Abu-Lughod 1993, 13). Abu-Lughod "left traces of herself" throughout her ethnography by not removing the questions she asked or pretending that she was not the focus of some of the discussions. I took a similar approach and added a further layer of reflexivity when some part of the interview provoked a transformative change in my consciousness and connected with my own story.

For example, while interviewing Chandramadi, a older rural woman from a matrilineal "upper caste" who rarely left her ancestral home or mixed with people outside her extended family, I asked about her experience of traveling to the city on a crowded bus and cooking with hundreds of thousands of women from other castes and religions for the Pongala festival, and then included my own further reflection on her response. One of the central values ritualized in *Pongala* is that everyone is equal before the Goddess. This value exists, paradoxically, in the context of a historical past of one of the most complex caste systems in India. Her response shows the ease she experiences in the atmosphere of equality during the festival. My reflection illustrates my deepening understanding of how issues of gender, race, and class intersect with my personal and social history to affect my beliefs and actions.

> Dianne: How do you feel afterwards? (after the cooking ritual)
> Chandramadi: There is no tiredness since there is no mental tiredness at the thought that there might be someone superior, someone inferior.."Would they give us a place there?"There are no such thoughts....
> Dianne: Everyone is the same....

Judy and I have talked about this; she pointed out how striking this remark is. How much tension there must be in the caste differentiation that we don't recognize or experience. How difficult it is to change, almost overnight, centuries of practices of a cultural/religious system which is so deeply embedded into every aspect of their lives... I've read that the Keralites have come much farther, comparatively, in breaking down the caste system than we have with our racism. This seems to be a truly liberating day for these women. To have a day where everyone can really relax is truly a blessing.

I realize, with a start, that that is one of the reasons I find Kerala so much easier than the United States. Caste, race, class. Although I am deeply aware of my position as a foreigner and as a citizen of the U.S., both the automatic positive privileges and the negative projections, I don't feel part of the system and feel almost no personal historical responsibility. That's it, I don't take the tension personally, because I see more clearly what we are each projecting on to one another. I don't come into every situation with preconceived attitudes, and the ones that I do have seem to change more easily because I don't have as much invested in them as I seem to have at home. I assume I don't completely understand and am not completely understood. I try harder here and think more about the implications of my actions and words. I'm beginning to remember this when I come home.

Disclosure of my personal struggles and changing consciousness provides the lens through which the reader can evaluate the validity of my findings and the "truth" of the material and also a mirror they can use to evoke and examine their own responses.

Chthonic[106] – The Roots Emerge

When the ground has been prepared and the seed has been planted, the gardener must trust that what happens underground will be successful....

Similarly, organic inquiry has an underground life of its own. Although the research begins with responsible intent and planning, the method often evolves and changes over the course of the research because of synchronicities, dreams, meditations, intuition, body responses, or other manifestations of the research muse. (Clements et al. 1999, 34)

My sense of chthonic, divine information was physical and was frequently accompanied by stunning synchronicities and body sensations. Once I expected that I would be given information and guidance, I watched for it. One of the fundamental beliefs in women's spirituality is that we have the capability, through our bodies, of receiving information that is outside the normal channels acknowledged by most Western science.[107]

An important synchronicity guided me in my choice of topic. After two years of preliminary research, I needed a focus for my dissertation but found it difficult to choose. I decided to turn the problem over to the Goddess to see what she wanted me to do. A friend was returning from Kerala, and I suddenly "knew" that she would bring a sign to guide me. During a dinner with her I waited for the sign and was surprised that nothing was forthcoming. As I left she called after me. "I almost forgot!

I brought you something I thought would interest you." It was a special edition of a Kerala newspaper dedicated to the *Pongala* festival, and I "knew" that this was the appropriate topic.

How did I "know"? I trusted the bodily signs, the "buzzing" throughout my being, sensations of heat, tears, involuntary changes in breathing, and most of all a special feeling of excitement I recognize as a signal that something important, often life changing, is happening.[108] I remembered that during two prior trips unusual synchronicities had occurred -- events altogether unexpected -- which first introduced me to this women's ritual and then presented me with the opportunity to video it. In thinking about *Pongala's* possible meanings, I realized this festival might answer my deep questions about the Goddess's values, ritual meaning in the context of women's lives and community, women's relationship with the Goddess. With this cognitive clarity came a sense of certainty, peace, a release of bodily tension, and a quiet excitement.

I'm mindful of the potential problems of self-delusion in this approach and interrogate my emotional states in the process of discernment, especially if there is an external or internal standard for success that I am trying to meet, or a psychological issue that arises as I write, teach, or do field research. I search for the underlying issues and acknowledge them. I have come to recognize that a sense of "desperation" or pressure comes from my critical (and self-criticizing) mind, which desires a certain result. I can sometimes minimize my anxiety, which can distort my perceptions and thus skew my "data," by trying to respond without being attached to any certain outcome. From experience, I know that whatever I believe the outcome might be at this moment, things are often not what they seem at the time. I test the "guidance" by evaluating how it supports my overall intentions. If I am unsure, I hold back from taking action, believing that if I don't understand the first time, She will let me know in some other way, with some other sign.

Relational – Growing the Tree

Although the researcher may begin the work alone, she or he finds co-researchers who can describe their own experience of the topic. The researcher and the co-researchers work together in face-to-face interviews to allow the stories to emerge complete with details. Each story is an articulated branch growing from the main trunk, where it joins with the researcher's core story.

The details of the context of the story are important since stories communicate to not only the thinking brain but also to the body, the heart, and the soul. (Clements et al. 1999, 43)

At the heart of organic inquiry is a sense of connectedness and relatedness beyond the usual social conventions. In applying the organic inquiry principles to a cross-cultural study, I had to improvise in ways that were challenging and not always satisfactory. Much was written during the early nineties about the care a "Western feminist" must take in representing and analyzing "Third World Women" or whether such representation is possible or ethical[109] (Abu-Lughod, 1993; Ahmed, 1992; Anzaldúa, 1991; Behar & Gordon, 1995; Raheja & Gold, 1994; Visweswaran, 1994). In her influential article "Under Western Eyes: Feminist Scholarship and Colonial Discourses," Chandra Talpade Mohanty encouraged Western researchers to place women in their social, religious, or economic contexts. (Mohanty 1988)

Being acutely aware of these responsibilities, and, further, considering each woman's story a "gift" from the Goddess, I struggled with issues of appropriate representation in the women's stories.   I often needed to use translators and, excellent as they were, some of the nuances of the stories were lost. Video cameras replayed the interview so women could see and hear their stories to add to or change them. I returned transcripts to the women who could read English to solicit their corrections, comments, and impressions. To attempt to convey the complexity of each woman's story, I included historical, social, and religious context before each story and included details of the women's lives and any prior relationship we might have had.

The dissertation included the entire interview with each woman; I edited only the parts that were clearly not relevant to the subject or that were redundant. I chose to keep my questions and comments and those of my collaborator, Judy Grahn, in an attempt to recreate the experience for the reader and add these unedited women's voices to the scholarly literature. I included journal notes taken at the time, as well as my reflections from a perspective two years later. There were clearly factors of class, caste, and religion in the interviews, and where appropriate, relevant, or important to my growing consciousness, I commented on them, not as an outside "observer" or judge, but disclosing my observation of or participation in discrimination or oppression in the United States.

One of the primary beliefs expressed by the women is that everyone is equal before the Goddess and IS the Goddess, and I tried to act out of that consciousness. Some women believed that my deep interest came from my experiences with them in a previous life. A principle I came to was that I would always try to stay in relationship with the women I interviewed. I have returned many times over a period of several years and

I have had to take responsibility for the unintended consequences of my actions. There have been misunderstandings, reconciliations, births, and deaths. I have attended weddings, provided assistance in the U.S. for their children, helped them get jobs, provided video documentation of their rituals, listened to the stories of their lives and learned and practiced their traditions with them. They have fed me, helped me in ways to numerous to mention, invited me stay in their homes and to participate in some of their most private and meaningful rituals. We have spent hours answering each other's questions and learning about each other's lives. I have come to understand research relationships in a different way. If the Goddess is providing us with each other, then we have a particular set of obligations that I am trying to understand and honor.

By acting "as if" there is a Goddess, I developed the capacity to more consistently hold a relational position, because implicit in the goddess worldview in Kerala is the understanding of the interconnectedness and interdependency of all beings.

Transformative – Harvesting the Fruit

The fruits of organic inquiry lie not so much in the information gathered as in the transformation of the researcher, the co-researchers and the readers….To truly experience another's story requires the willingness to be altered by it. And to have one's story heard and understood changes one. A story offers transformation to both the teller and to the listener. Transformation may be an apparently small insight into one's understanding of past actions or it may be a major restructuring of lifestyle.(Clements et al. 1999, 50)

The telling of stories can be empowering to co-researchers, researchers, and readers alike. Like other forms of human inquiry that engage deeply and sensitively with experience, organic inquiry aims to integrate reflection and action. Researcher Peter Reason states the goals this type of research seeks to address: "In the context of the epistemological crisis of our times, I have been much persuaded over recent months by the image that the purpose of human inquiry is not so much to search for truth but to heal, and above all to heal the alienation, the split that characterizes modern experience" (Reason 1994).

Sometimes inquiry into the history and lives of women can illuminate issues of power and oppression and lead to political change, but political or social action on behalf of the women of Kerala was not an explicit goal of my research. I felt a deep humility and considered it hubris to assume that through my research I could understand what needed to be changed or that women there needed my assistance to effect change. On the other hand, I hoped that reading about their ritual through the eyes of a Western woman and seeing the effect the ritual and their words had on me might prove useful in some way, so I was delighted that a feminist journal in Kerala published my work (Jenett 2002). Some women told me that the experience indeed changed them by bringing the Goddess more powerfully into their lives, giving them a new appreciation of their own history and culture, as well as insights into American culture.

An unexpected manifestation of my research into Pongala Festival was the organic inquiry approach, which arose from my and my colleagues' deep desire for the sacred. By word of mouth, this research approach has spread across the United States, Europe, Asia, Africa, and Australia. It has been used in hundreds of studies in psychology, education, transformative learning, humanities, women's spirituality dance, and religion. Organic inquiry has been used in over 86 dissertations in over 17 graduate schools with the majority being done at the Institute of Transpersonal Psychology and California Institute of Integral Studies. Jennifer Clements has continued to develop, teach , and publish on it. Readers of organic inquiry-based studies have been profoundly and personally affected by the kind of "transmission" that takes place through the reading of such work.

Most of all, through this process, I have come to love Her, and, to know how (sometimes at least), to access that love.   My worldview has been radically changed.

Notes

1 Jennifer Clements, Dorothy Ettling, Lisa Shields, Nora Taylor.

2 In Transpersonal Research Methods for the Social Sciences, Rosemarie Anderson provides the following definition of transpersonal psychology: As a field of research, scholarship, and applications, transpersonal psychology seeks to honor human experience in its fullest and most transformative expressions.... Whenever possible, transpersonal psychology seeks to delve deeply into the most profound aspects of human experience, such as mystical and unitive experiences, personal transformation, meditative awareness, experiences of wonder and ecstasy, and alternative and expansive states of consciousness. In these experiences, we appear to go beyond our usual identification with our limited biological and psychological selves. (Braud and Anderson 1998, xxi)

3 Although the group contributed some of the initial ideas, Jennifer Clements authored most of the original manuscript. She has significantly developed the approach in her work with dissertations at the Institute of Transpersonal Psychology as Organic Inquiry (Clements 2002, 2004). I have been teaching it in the context of transformative learning, depth psychology, and women's spirituality.

4 In Kerala, the terms, Bhadrakali (auspicious Kali), Devi, Bhagavati, and Amma (Mother) are used interchangeably to refer to the same goddess.

5 Judy's dissertation research (Grahn 1999) applied her metaformic theory (Grahn 1993) to menarche

rituals in Kerala

6 "In attempting to describe this part of process we chose the word 'chthonic' which comes from the Greek chthonios, meaning 'in the earth.' In English, chthonic has come to mean 'dark, primitive, and mysterious' or 'of the underworld and its gods and spirits'" (Clements et al. 1999). Jennifer Clements has further developed approaches using liminal states (Clements 2002).

7 A few scientists, including my physicist husband, Edwin C. May, research "anomalous information" transfers, i.e., the ability of some people to have access to information in ways that Western science cannot yet explain (Radin 1997).

8 During the past twenty five years I have studied and experienced various forms of somatic inquiry, including Rosenwork, Mindell's Process Work, Continuum and Levine's Somatic Sensing.

9 The introduction of Listen to the Heron's Words presents a concise discussion of questions of representation (Raheja and Gold 1994).

Bibliography

Abu-Lughod, Lila. 1993. Writing women's worlds : Bedouin stories. Berkeley: University of California Press.

Anzaldúa, Gloria. 1991. Borderlands: the new mestiza=La frontera. San Francisco:Aunt Lute Books.

Behar, Ruth, and Deborah A. Gordon. 1995. Women writing culture. Berkeley: University of California Press.

Braud, William, and Rosemarie Anderson, eds. 1998. Transpersonal Research Methods for the Social Sciences : Honoring Human Experience. Thousand Oaks, Calif.: Sage Publications.

Clements, Jennifer. 2002. Organic Inquiry: Research in Partnership with Spirit: Manuscript submitted for publication.

———. 2004. An Introduction to Organic Inquiry: Honoring the Transpersonal and Spiritual in Research Praxis. The Journal of Transpersonal Psychology 36 (1):18-49.

Clements, Jennifer, Dorothy Ettling, Dianne Jenett, and Lisa Shields. 1998. Organic Research: Feminine Spirituality Meets Transpersonal Research. In Transpersonal research methods for the social sciences : honoring human experience, edited by W. Braud and R. Anderson. Thousand Oaks, Calif.: Sage Publications.

———. 1999. If Research Were Sacred: Organic Inquiry. Rev. ed. ed: www.serpentina.com.

Grahn, Judith Rae. 1999. Are Goddesses Metaformic Constructs? An Application of Metaformic Theory to Goddess Celebrations and Rituals in Kerala, India, Integral Studies, California Institute of Integral Studies, San Francisco.

Grahn, Judy. 1993. Blood, Bread and Roses: How Menstruation Created the World. New York: Beacon Press.

Hooks, Bell. 1984. Feminist theory from margin to center. Boston, MA: South End Press

———. 1989. Talking back : thinking feminist, thinking black. Boston, MA: South End Press.

Jenett, Dianne. 2005. A Million Shaktis Rising: Pongala, Women's Festival in Kerala, India. Journal of Feminist Studies in Religion 21 (1):35-55.

———. 2005. Menstruating Women/Menstruating Goddesses: Sites of Sacred Power in South India. In Menstruation: A Cultural History, edited by G. H. Andrew Shail. Houndsmills, U.K: Palgrave McMillan.

Jenett, Dianne E. 2002. Cooking up equality: Pongala at Attukal Temple. Samyukta: A Journal of Women's Studies II (2):158-168.

Jenett, Dianne Elkins. 1999. Red Rice for Bhagavati/Cooking for Kannaki: An Ethnographic/Organic Inquiry of the Pongala Ritual at Attukal Temple, Kerala, South India, Integral Studies, California Institute of Integral Studies, San Francisco.

Macy, Johanna. 1983. Despair and personal power in the nuclear age. Philadelphia, PA: New Society Publishers.

Mohanty, Chandra Talpade. 1988. Under Western Eyes: Feminist Scholarship and Colonial Discourses. In Colonial Discourse and Post-Colonial Theory, edited by L. C. P. Williams. New York: Columbia University Press.

Nielsen, Joyce McCarl. 1990. Feminist research methods : exemplary readings in the social sciences. Boulder: Westview Press.

Radin, Dean I. 1997. The conscious universe : the scientific truth of psychic phenomena. 1st. ed. New York, N.Y.: HarperEdge.

Raheja, Gloria and Gold, Ann. 1994. Listen to the heron's words: reimagining gender and kinship in North India.

Reason, Peter. 1994. Participation in human inquiry. London ; Thousand Oaks, Calif.: Sage Publications.

Reinharz, Shulamit, and Lynn Davidman. 1992. Feminist methods in social research. New York: Oxford University Press.

Shillington, Elizabeth Low Webster. 2004. The Moon in Her Womb: An Organic Inquiry into Women's Stories of Menstruation and Spirituality. California Institute of Integral Studies, San Francisco.

Starhawk. 1987. Truth or dare : encounters with power, authority, and mystery. 1st ed. San Francisco: Harper & Row.

Visweswaran, Kamala. 1994. Fictions of feminist ethnography. Minneapolis: University of Minnesota Press.

One Day

Dorotea Reyna

For my sisters

In spring
Admonitions gave way
And for one evening
We had
That dark church to ourselves—
Women and girls
Bringing flowers to *Maria*

I remember
The gold trumpet blossoms
In my hands
The sweet roses with sticky thorns
Wrapped in silver foil
And the soft whispers
Of the women in prayer
Outside, the Texas sun bled
As we laid our gifts
At Her feet

In those days
We were only allowed close
To the altar
To strip its cloth, sweep and clean
My grandmother's world
Was bound by these rules

And unbound
As she raised her children under
The Church's
Iron Rule, which, by 80
She had transmuted
To Gold
And reigned serenely

My mother
From whose hands I learned
All lovingkindness
All love of God and people
Dressed five fussy
Children for Mass each Sunday
Then hurried home
To prepare breakfast for her family
And the priest

Her hands were my harbor
My very idea of Faith
Rarely straying from the Letter
Most always in Spirit
Her faith was her salvation
As she navigated
A life of pain

And so she surprised me
One day
When she proclaimed with
Quiet confidence:
One day the Church will welcome
Us as priests, because we
Are good, and so many—

Protected by a thousand
Invisible prayers
I too am waiting for that Day
As I suffer my doubts
As I light another candle
For my daughter

Annapurna Ma: Priestess and Healer

Elinor Gadon

I want to tell you about an extraordinary woman whom I encountered during the course of my field work on the village goddesses of Orissa. Annapurna Ma serves her goddess, Sarangei, as a priestess and her devotees as a healer. Her name meaning abundance is a most auspicious one in Indian culture like a bowl full of rice in a country where rice is an important staple of their daily diet. She is one of those women who can be found all over the subcontinent that fall outside the categories usually ascribed for religious functionaries like priests, shamans, sadhus or yoginis. Socially they are marginal, often but not always of harijan or low caste origins, usually raised in poverty, and illiterate, although sometimes not as ignorant of learning as they pretend. They have no formal religious training, no gurus, and no lineage. Their transmission and power come directly from the goddess. Their special powers are recognized by a culture in which the boundaries between human and divine are very loose. They act on their access to the Devi's wisdom. As Annapurna says, it is not me who heals, but the goddess. What is so remarkable about them in a society where women have little status or power is their agency. They, too, are called Ma or Mataji and often venerated as a manifestation of the Mother Goddess, recognized as a living goddess.

Annapurna Ma is a gracious, attractive woman in her mid-forties who lives with her husband and family in an ample thatched-roof house by the side of the shrine of the Goddess Sarangei whom she serves. Shrine and home are located by the ruins of a vast ancient fort known as Sarangagadha still standing in the middle of paddy fields near the hamlet of Chodagangapura a few miles from the industrial town of Barang in Eastern India. The fort was probably named for the goddess. Sites of the sacred have lots of staying power in India, and there is a long tradition of the Devi manifesting herself and her powers at specific localities. The village is named for Chodagangadeva (1058-1125) considered to be the most powerful king of his time in eastern India. Credited with initiating the major construction of the Jagannatha temple and increasing the importance of this famous shrine earned him an immortal fame in Orissa history.

The Shrine, House and Land

As we bumped along the narrow dirt road on our way to meet Annapurna, we first noticed the triangular red pendent, the mark of the goddess's presence flying from the tallest branches of the tamarind tree under which her shrine sits. Goddess and tree are inevitably entwined in Hindu mythology and iconography as the gods like to sit in the shade. The tree is also an earlier iconic representation of the Devi. The shrine sits on a small hillock, another location favored by the deities. An uncommon feature is its barrel shaped roof which in Orissa is associated with Tantric temples.

The shrine is immaculate, freshly painted inside and out, its interior in a warm pink providing a colorful background for the richly dressed and ornamented murti, the three dimensional figure of the goddess. Wearing colorful saris, she is profusely garlanded with red hibiscus, yellow and white blossoms. A large nose ring is prominent on her black face, carved with sensitivity and beauty, and the only part of her image that is visible. From what I can make out of the configuration under her garment, this is a Durgamishamardini, representing the cosmic victory of the Great Goddess over the buffalo demon, Mahisha. At her side are two large uncarved stones, dressed and liberally smeared with red sindur, and sporting metallic eyes. Steps lead from the concrete platform in front of the shrine to the single entrance which is guarded by an ornate metal screen.

Ritual implements, all of metal or clay, are carefully arranged inside. Open shelves hold bottles of liquids for the puja and a clothesline is strung across for the Devi's wardrobe. There is a small wooden pallet on which the priestess sits. Painted above the entrance we find Shiva in yogic meditation and to his right a many-armed Durga on her lion.

The surrounding landscape is very beautiful. We are in rich delta country, an idyllic pastoral setting with open fields, distant palms, a nearby pond. Flocks of white herons fly in procession across the sky. A setting sun paints a rosy glow over everything. It is so peaceful, the silence only broken by the cries of the birds, occasional sounds of raucous crows and the wail of a distant train.

Her Story

Annapurna is her given name. She was born in the village Daruthenga not far from the town of Barang, famed for its glass manufacturing located about 14 miles from Bhubaneswar, the ancient temple town that is now the capital of Orissa. Her parents, of the Gopala (milkman) caste, were well off, with land and cattle. She was one of four sisters, there were no brothers. She does not recall when the goddess whom calls MA first came to her early in her life but vividly recalls this experience. For the most part I am going to use her own words in telling her story. I quote:

I was trembling and shaking with acute pain and my heart was not in a normal condition. The most interesting and frightening thing was my running here and there and roaming about with a roaring sound. My parents and sisters were very sad and unhappy when they were not able to control me. I am not sure that I was conscious in those childhood days... what was happening I cannot think and I cannot tell. And my mind along with MA is not allowing me to think of those days...it is now very painful for me.

Some people were very happy seeing me in those days...thinking that a spirit has come to save mankind. Let her live healthy and strong. Saying so or thinking in this way they offered me fruits and milk and good food for my health. Some men were sad and telling my parents your daughter is sick and take her to a doctor. She will be mad soon; her mental health is disturbed and she needs care and also medicine. Some persons told that this girl needs to marry soon as she is sick of some kind of sex disease. Some other persons were silent and they were praying for me to become good and gentle.

As far as I remember this and no more. Some old women who were living very close to our house came forward and requested my parents to take me to a kalisi (healer) or to some famous Goddesses.

My mother and father decided to give me in marriage soon. So my father and other relatives arranged this marriage to this nice man who is my husband and everything to me. We have a big gap of age. He married me when he was 35 and I was 16. In our village area it is considered very normal.

I began to live with my husband after my marriage and soon after this the developments were marked very much as he began to help me and he began to encourage me to get the blessing of the Goddess if she came to me. His idea was to get and to capture the grace and the blessings of that Shakti to do good for the masses. Some other family friends at that time began to trust me and began to have lots of faith and love and to tell me that a good supernatural power is coming to this young girl and by that she will do good to the sammsar, the world. .

Ma was coming to me or we can say she was capturing me and keeping me under her control. I was not able to do my work. My in-laws abused me; they threw me into a well and tried to drown me. I ran away but MA said no, I should go back because my husband was a good man. My first daughter was born, but the abuse continued so we moved out to Barang. I kept having dreams of this human looking woman with animals telling me to do puja. She talked just like we are talking. I didn't know what to make of it, neither did my husband.

Then some disturbing things began to happen to her:

At the Mother's request I went to Bhuhasuni temple at 3 AM in the morning. The priest began doing puja, then locked the door and started abusing me. I escaped out the window. The mali priest of the Singhabahuni Temple after telling me to go with him to a mela took me to a hilltop, asked me to take a bath so he could have sex with her. Again I ran away, this time naked. I never told her husband who was still sleeping. I kept asking MA why are you sending me to these threatening situations, torturing me. In time she sent me to her shrine where I am now saying 'I am there and you do exactly what I say.'

Annapurna continues with her story:

At the beginning my husband worried as he did not know anything of my relation between the Goddess and me. As a young unmarried girl I had not known enough. Gradually he understood and he took me to many different goddesses according to my desire to get my spirit and power to serve the Goddesses.

I was not sure up to this time, which Goddess wanted me to be Her dear and near one and who wants to go to the mass to cur and heal and to save mankind. I was really running in a dark and blind curve where I did not know what to do and what to achieve and how to do good in society. Gradually my husband who was very good and kind understood more and more and my devotion towards him was also very important and he realized more and more the sweet relation between MA, the Goddess, and a devotee like me.

Ma for me is a female deity…a goddess and as I had conceived and accepted HER as SHE is loaded with lots of energy and good qualities.

And my desire was to be like that, a living spirit under the shade of HER enormous power and energy to spread her spirit to the masses. I cannot tell exactly the day and date when she began to come or when she accepted me fully and finally to be her real priest. I do not know yet ---whether I have come to the final point of my achievement or is there anything which I will get to-day, tomorrow or day after tomorrow.

Her Recognition: Saving the Elephant

Her special powers were recognized by her community when she saved the life of an elephant marooned in the deep waters of the flooded river. Again I quote her words as she related the event to me:

During the floods in 1982, the nearby river Praci was very deep and there was lots of water. Seven elephants were going this way. One of them went into the river to take a bath and wash his body that was very dirty. He entered the river with great joy but after about ten minutes because of the clay and mud in the water it became very difficult for him to stand. He began to shout and finally the other elephants went to help their friend. They tried their best but it was fruitless. By the cry of the poor elephant people came from far and near and gathered on the riverbank. How to save the elephant! Nothing was possible for the elephant and the elephant man. They were in great trouble. A teacher was there, a friend of the family who had recognized that some great spirit was in me. So he ran to my door and asked me to come to see the elephant and save him from the river. I was staying at that time with my family in Baranga town and my husband was working in the glass factory.

I told him it is impossible. I cannot do anything. I have no power, no supernatural power to save the elephant. But this teacher, named Mallik came to me and forced me telling me again and again many, many encouraging stories and trying to enliven me and my spirit. Then I told him that I am not pure now. I have my menstruation and it is my third day and I have not even taken my bath. Mr. Mallik said to me that this is good for this work, even it is the third day and you have not taken your bath—there is no harm and the Goddess will be glad enough at this stage to load Her power and spirit. Saying so he gave me a fresh/clean sari and took me from my home. My husband was at work at the glass factory, so Mallik took me by his cycle.

I arrived at the river and I was surprised with glee. Many, many men and women were waiting there for my arrival. I got down from the cycle and entered into the holy Praci river and took some water and sprinkled some to my hair and some to all the other sides in the ten directions, the digapals and then I went to the side of the elephant. I was standing on the river bank. I felt something and suddenly my mind began to whirl round and round and I felt the river bank to move from this side to that and keeping the elephant at a center I began to move in a circle. It was possible as there was a bridge and really I encircled the elephant three times and then taking some flower and water from the river I remembered MA and prayed to HER and remembered that great power and spirit and requested my MA even I do remember, I do not know which MA it was. I know nothing. Then as soon as I threw the flower and water from my hand to the elephant (So nice to tell you, so pleasant to express) the elephant got up and came to the river bank on its own way from the deep clay and mud of the deep river. He was saved.

Everybody shouted with glee and joy and the elephant came along with its man to me. Suddenly the elephant lifted me up by its trunk and wanted to take me to the seat on it. But I refused and by the help of the elephant man he freed me from the trunk. And then the people of Baranga came to my side and began to greet me with joy. They all shouted along with Mr. Mallik, Jay Mataji, Jay Matagi (Victory to the Mother) At this sound and shout I fainted and lost my senses. After about 25 minutes I came to and saw that I was in the lap of my husband who was there helping me with great joy. Since then I have been accepted as a notable figure in this area. I became very glad for this.

Finding MA

About ten or fifteen days later while walking at night alone through the jungles and hills, I came to this MA to whom I had never seen earlier. I was found in the morning by the cattle herders and some other men who had come to gather firewood. They informed my husband who had been searching here and there in the city of Barbanga with great fear. He came and with the help of others we carefully cleaned this place; dogs and cats had made it filthy, and I began my services here at MA SARANGEI. This was a very big thing for me and my husband. Since then I began a new way of living and got the chance to meet peoples of many different types, people of many different conditions starting from Harijans to Brahmins, young and old, male and female. I served mankind and I came to my deity properly as I am only a chakarani to MA SARANGEI.

Her Role as a Healer

Many men and women, young and old come here for healing. But they are not of this area. They are from distant places like Cuttack, Balesore, Ganjam and Puri area. Some come from the capital city, Bhubaneswar. Nobody comes from the nearby Barang area. They come here. I treat them. I serve them. I offer them flowers and leaves of the deity and HER padukapani (holy water) from her feet but I do not cure them. MA SARANGEI cures and heals them. I am only HER servant. SHE is my goddess and MA and SHE cures by her grace and sympathy and because of their love and devotion. MA SARANGEI cures these people. SHE tells me to give this and that and I follow HER advice and do my needful duty. It is SHE who takes care and considers the love and devotion between them and they get back their health.

There is no set day, no fixed time to receive the devotee. They come at any time. They can pray and get the blessings at any time and it depends on HER sweet will to accept their prayer. It depends on MA. Everyday is good for MA. It is only trust and faith, love and devotion that helps and cures. Nobody tells me his or her problem. I tell them to pray to MA and tell her their problems. It is their devotion and attraction towards MA that persuades MA to tell me to give them this or that flower or leaf and I do that following MA's orders. The sick and sad unhealthy persons return from this place with great joy. They do not come back here again to thank me but I am not sad about this. I feel that they have been cured by the grace of MA. I do not know their problems when they come. I only tell them to have the full faith and trust and love here before the Goddess to be cured. Whatever she gives for the sick and unhealthy persons who are her devotees is HER grace. I pass that on to them.

I know perfectly well that I am a servant of MA. SHE is Goddess. She is Sarangei. I am human. I will do my duty and I will serve HER.

An Evening Puja

My research assistant Purna Chandra Mishra described an evening puja he witnessed on one Sunday. He arrived around four o'clock and the place was already crowded. Devotees from Cuttack and rural areas were sitting on the platform in front of the shrine. Ma Annapurna was busy preparing the bhoga, food that will be offered to the Goddess and will then be distributed to the devotees as consecrated food, prasad. Around 4:30 the preparation was completed and Annapurna came out from the side of the kitchen with a big brass tray heaped with hot food. She puts up a screen at the entrance to the shrine so that on one cannot watch the goddess take her food which should be done in secret. After coming out, taking some water and collecting some tulasi leaves, she reenters the shrine and rings the bell clearly announcing the offering of food to the deity.

In the meantime, Baba came back with his ten cows and some 15 goats following them with some banana leaves in his hand. He asked his younger daughter to come to clean them properly. She had been collecting some water from the well for the devotees. She took the leaves, and washing them thoroughly put them in their proper place on the platform in front of the shrine. The oldest daughter helps out with the cooking on festival days but she had just had a baby and was at home in Barang. So in this way the whole family participates in the service of MA.

A young man among the devotees got up and took a broom to sweep the platform clean after which another young man gave out the banana leaves on which the prasad would be served to the seated devotees. Annapurna Ma asked everyone to sit properly while she distributed the prasad. Then rushing to the shrine, she removed the screen and brought the large brass tray from which she distributed food to all. The food offered first to the Goddess as bhoga now became prasad for the devotees: rice, dal, dalma, a vegetable curry and some fried vegetables. While the devotees were eating Ma joined them saying that it is a great joy for me to take some food with my children and I am very happy and satisfied. All the children are the same to MA and this is an expression of Her love. When the late lunch was finished, everybody began to clean their hand and mouth properly. Then Annapurna Ma brought some tulasi leaves that had been offered to the deity in the morning and gave them to all who were present.

After the late lunch, Annapurna Ma and her youngest son went with a sickle to cut the grass for the cows, returning around 6 P.M. The sun was setting and the whole area was getting dark. The two tamarind trees, very big and massive at the north and south obstructed the light, bringing the night sooner. At 6:15 Ma returns. She has changed into a beautiful sari in red and white with a deep red blouse. The contours of her slender rounded body are visible through the thin fabric. She begins her preparation for the puja. Her long matted hair was hanging down to her waist. The articles for her service were at her side. She takes her sari and tucks it up between her legs just like the male sadhus. She completes her preparations sitting on the wooden pallet with her legs folded beneath her. At one point she takes out many small objects from a brass bowl and lines them up in front. The old man, her husband, and the young boy, her son, stand at either side of the shrine beating on heavy brass plates with wooden sticks in a loud and persistent rhythm until the service is over. She rises and stands on her right leg, bending the left at the knee in an angle so that the left foot touches the right knee. She stands like this for the full hour of the puja.

I quote again from Purna Cahra's words so that you may get the full impact of her presence on him:

Moving from side to side she was doing her service for the Goddess. It was beautiful and frightening. When she turned to the side I marked her eyes which were burning and glowing with power and loaded with spirit and energy. She had already received from her deity. She was looking to herself, not to any person. She was not looking to the pot in her right hand or to the bell in the left. Her eyes were not even towards the deity. Her eyelids were still and steady looking like the eyes of the Goddess Durga before killing the demon Mahisa, so bright and big, difficult to describe. They were open wide and steadily fixed somewhere. This continued for another fifteen minutes. Up to this it is now 45 minutes and she was holding her body with good spirit and standing only by the right leg, doing everything one after the other. The she finished the seva of arati and began to perform many kinds of gestures and postures before the deity. She was looking towards the deity or to somewhere unknown. She was now turning around in all eight directions.

Next she took the chamara with its long thick black yak hairs and began to dance to the sounds of the ghanta and jhanja played by her son and husband who were standing at either side of the entrance to the shrine. She was dancing on one foot; her left foot was only helping at this time to balance her body. Afterwards she went to the empty fire pit and then touched everyone with the long hairs of the chamara.

Suddenly the women seated on the platform began to show their legs. Then Ma Annapurna began to climb on their legs, pressing hard, moving from their ankle to their thigh, as if drawing out their pain. She did it to one woman after the other and the women must have also felt lots of pain because of the weight of Ma on their legs.

Then Ma returned to her shrine and as soon as she climbed the steps her body stiffened and she fell to the ground. Her eyes were closed and her lips were set tight. She was allowed to stay like this for ten minutes and then her husband and youngest son began to sprinkle some cold water on her face. They tried to lift her and to bring her outside to the open platform but were unable to do so by themselves. The devotees helped them to carry her to the laps of the women on the platform below who slowly opened her mouth and gradually gave her water. After about five minutes she came to and sitting up began to laugh a hearty laugh. The devotees one after another began to go back home. It was seven o'clock.

Analysis

What are we to make of all this? How are we to understand Ma Annapurna's life and her role within the context of Hindu religion and culture. For one, this is popular, not Sanskritic, brahmanic Hinduism. Two, we have to acknowledge the wide range of practice that is possible in a religious system which has no canonical form, no institutionalized hierarchy. Three, we need to step back for a moment and consider how unbalanced our, that is Western scholarship on the religions of India has been, giving pride of place to text while overlooking oral tradition and folk culture. I want to now single out three singular aspects of Annapurna's profile: (1) her matted hair; (2) her unusual posture while performing puja and (3) her use of jagna, the Vedic fire ritual, usually the exclusive provenance of brahmin priests.

June McDaniel in her study of ecstatic religion in Bengal informs us that "Religion has been the both the way in and the way out for... women. It has been the way into a ritual tradition that supports subservience, lowered status, and a limited sphere of activity. But it has also been the way out, for religious knowledge and practice have given women freedom and a wide range of action" (191). Religious experience serves to create and justify their religious status. In almost all cases, this religious experience was initially associated with madness or illness, and it was proven to be religious, not insane, only after testing, devotion, miracle and the passage of time" (191-2). "... religious experience in these women was spontaneous, occurring from childhood and at unexpected times; practice was a later addition—possession, visions, emotional extremes of religious passion and detachment --are present"(192). McDaniel suggests that the acceptance of marriage and the support of the husband, so central to Annapurna's mission is characteristic of these holy women (232). The role of holy woman allows the woman some freedom and self-determination (230). She has forged an independent spiritual life for herself following the commands of her goddess.

At first she was unable to identify the woman with the wild animals who appeared to her in her dreams. It was only when MA as she refers to her deity, led her to the abandoned shrine of Sarangei that HER goddess had a name. This brings us to another interesting phenomenon in the religious experience of India, that of the mythic layering of the religious landscape. Sarangagadh was the name of Chodagangadeva's fort and the shrine of the Goddess was located by its ruins. Which came first? Shakti, the cosmic force of the goddess traditionally locates itself in specific sites.

Ecstasy was the possession of the dancer by the goddess. At the end was her return to the void and she stood like a statue as the light fades away (237). Matted hair (jatas), are symbolic of the renunciant sadhu like the God Shiva but while Annapurna is an ecstatic, she is not an ascetic. Anthropologist Gananth Obeyesekere has written extensively on the meaning of matted locks (1). According to him the matted locks are a gift of the goddess when the woman has been accepted as a priestess and symbol of her new status (McDaniel 233).

Another problem is how are we to refer to her? Within the categories of popular Hinduism she is a priestess-healer. She is an ecstatic, not an ascetic. She is not a sadhika, a holy woman like Anandamayi Ma and Sarada Devi, famous saints with literally millions of followers.

How are we to classify the singular posture she adopted for puja or her use of the Vedic fire ritual; the privilege of initiated brahmin priests? I can only suggest that with no religious training, she was self-initiated either she channeled through her goddess both form and content of her ritual or as an imaginative, clever, observant woman she was able to create her own version. The first explanation is how her devotees and Indian culture would see it; the latter the explanation that of a materialist Western scholar. Straddling both views, I suggest that we still have much to learn about the mystery of the religious experience and I shall visit Ma Annapurna again.

Bibliography

Erndl, Kathleen M. Victory to the Mother. New York: Oxford University Press, 1993.

McDaniel, June. The Madness of the Saints: Ecstatic religion in Bengal. Chicago: University of Chicago Press, 1989.

Obeyesekere, Gananath. Medusa's Hair: An Essay on Personal Symbols and Religious Experience. Chicago: University of Chicago Press, 1981.

Beyond the Wooden Spoon
Excerpts from an Italian American Memoir

Francesca Roccaforte

My Mother Virgina "Big Vee" and her Eggplant (Melanza) Parmigiana recipes and Neapolitan cooking

My mother "Big Vee" (Virginia, Vincenza) the Italian Matriarch,
rules with a wooden spoon in her working class kitchen of silver and beige
triangles of sanitex and stained wood cupboards built by my Uncle Joey
the handyman carpenter. The 1950's gray linoleum floor knows how to handle the
quick clicks of her imitation leather slippers moving from sink to stove in
one swift motion. Vee's peasant feet sounded heavy; like her slippers had heels on them...she sat only occasionally taking a moment to take a drag off her Winston
cigarettes. Maybe it was the power of motherhood and a small child's vivid imagination that made the sound of my mother's footsteps sound so powerful.
As the youngest child, I tuned into the footsteps of everyone in the family,
especially my Mommy's and Daddy's.

My mother Vee was a great cook and fantastic baker of assorted goodies when we kids were younger. She enjoyed it immensely, spending hours in the kitchen creating cheesecakes, Italian cream puffs, struffoli and all the other holiday Italian pastries and sweets. Big Vee took motherhood and cooking very seriously when she was well enough to do. Big Vee wasn't really big in height, she was only 5 ft, strongly built, sturdy, and robust but we looked up to her, she was the Matriarch of the gang of boys who surrounded her in our kitchen. She was the domineering force of her household, controlling men with her food and nourishment. Smart mouthed-sharp tongued, fiery, generous, kind hearted, and warm, my mother fed the many neighborhood children and stray animals my brothers befriended. They all licked their fingers when she cooked and baked in our family home in East New York, Brooklyn, New York.

One of Big Vee's best recipes in my opinion was definitely her eggplant parmigiano hero on sweet Italian bread with sesame seeds that she bought freshly baked from the Colonial Bakery across the street from our house. I remember her methodically cutting the deep purple eggplant slice by slice, stacking them between two plates, with the clothes iron resting on top to give it weight. She said this held in the eggplant juices. So I copied her years later when I made eggplant in my own kitchen, calling her up, getting her cooking "secrets".

She told me that the cheese was the secret…and of course the spices! "Mozzarella with the oil in it, not the non-fat kind that the skinny Americans ate", she said. She told me to buy the Locatelli, an aged Romano cheese, very sharp and pungent. Even my father and brothers could tell you these things since she had their stomachs trained to her wooden spoon stirring the gravy every Sunday morning bright and early. The gravy or sauce was already made on Sunday for the eggplant on Wednesday. This made the flavors simmer longer and made it richer tasting for our second round of Ronzoni macaroni for the week.

She tried to train her family and told us to be grateful that we didn't eat the "same old shit" like the other peasant families who couldn't afford the luxury of the freshly butchered steaks, Italian sausages stuffed with herbs and cheeses, veal cutlets, and seafood dinners my father's salary afforded us. The fact that we had some lower middle class "privileges" around food, clothes, and education was the kind of ethnic pride my mother and father displayed at their many open houses in our neighborhood. They liked to party and share our "wealth" and my mother received many compliments for her great food and fun loving spirit.

Mom sent me off to Catholic grammar school and later to high school with these amazing hero sandwiches on Italian bread. It was the way she showed me she loved me. I felt special since many of the other kids ate the crappy American cafeteria food. When I opened my brown lunch bag and saw an eggplant or meatball hero, I was particularly happy-it felt good eating our Italian food. My mother tucked a Milky Way chocolate bar with it. Sometimes I went home for lunch and she made me a fresh chocolate malted with ice cream, yet I was very petite and muscular as a young girl probably due to my athletics and not the rich Italian American foods we ate on a regular basis.

Yes I will always remember my mother Big Vee and her eggplant parmigiana hero.

Mille tante Mama! Con amore, tua figlia, Francesca!

Dedicated to Virginia Diorato Roccaforte- BIG VEE
B. April 11, 1926 NYC
D. Oct. 21, 1988   NYC

(Copyright Francesca Roccaforte, 1994-99)

Hot Tomatoes

Francesca Roccaforte

Juicy red ripe full tomatoes
scream at me
to look
to touch them, squeeze them

Hot from the sun
Rich and passionate
Sensuously curved
Simple
Engorged like a woman in heat
They speak in our native tongue

So ripe
So red
So hot
They look and taste
Like the woman who gave birth
To this juicy fruit
The fruit of our people

Francesca Roccaforte,M.S.
Rocknfranny.com
Photography & Video Production
PO Box 3399
Oakland, Ca 94609
510 417-1332

Anti-war poster inside the sanctuary of the Black Madonna of Monserrat,
Spain, opposing the Bush administration's invasion of Iraq later that month
Photograph by Wallace Birnbaum March 2003

She is in the words we speak
And in the better world we seek.

Genevieve Vaughan

Capitalism has liberated many women from individual slavery to men. Now it is time for women to liberate everyone from capitalism and patriarchy. Over the last 500 years women have struggled for equality with men, and by making changes in laws and gaining access to the workforce they have achieved a lot in this direction. However they have not realized that Capitalism itself is Patriarchal and repeats the oppressive structures of gender in a transposed form. The equality that we have sought has been equality according to a male norm, and women's caring values have seemed to be weak and peripheral or unrealistic even in our own estimation. Now we must switch norms and possibly change the concept of 'norm' altogether, making it qualitative rather than quantitative, other oriented rather than ego oriented, multiple rather than monolithic. Patriarchy has been a deviation from this more human model. It is necessary for everyone to make a paradigm shift towards a perspective and a value system that will allow human life to continue to exist on the planet. Wars, disease, environmental devastation and the excruciating poverty of billions of people are the result of Patriarchal Capitalism. The merging of the values of patriarchy with the way we distribute our goods and own our means of production, works to benefit the few while the majority starve. Competition and domination, egotism, greed and protagonism motivate both patriarchy and capitalism, producing hierarchies and power-hungry individuals and groups. In this article I want to propose a critique of Patriarchal Capitalism and a brief description of what I consider to be a feminist alternative.

Our society has been overtaken by the market. Rich and poor look at participating in the market as the only way to survive and thrive. Buying and selling seem to be a natural way of behaving. My hypothesis is that the market is not normal or natural. Rather it is a huge semiotic mechanism of distorted communication that is actually nurtured by and parasitic on an earlier, more human and more humane mode of distribution which I call the 'gift economy'. During the present epoch of globalization, the market economy is expanding, encroaching on the gift economy more and more, extending itself into areas, which were previously free gift areas. Water, seeds, and traditional knowledge, as well as the few remaining free territories, which were accessible to everyone, are now becoming scarce because they have been privatized and commodified. Genes and life forms are being patented. Even air is being commercialized as oxygen-producing rainforests are being traded by poor countries for debt reduction. (Isla, 2004)

In so called "pre Capitalist" indigenous economies, abundant resources were given and received both by individuals and by groups in daily life and in festivals, without the intervention of a market. Even in Capitalism, in rural areas and within families everywhere, free gifts of all kinds still circulate. I believe these practices can be linked to the necessary part of human life, which has to do with mothering and being mothered. In the life of every child there is a period in which s/he must receive free nurturing, because s/he cannot give back an equivalent of what s/he has been given. This period does not depend upon the biology of the mother or her supposed special instinct to nurture, but on the biology of the child who is too small and weak to procure food and shelter for h/erself or to exchange in order to leverage goods from other people. Free giving and receiving without exchange is a necessity for all humans in the early days of life. Bonding takes place between the giver and the receiver of nurturing; it consists of mutual recognition, confidence and the expectation of future nurturing interactions. Women have been socially assigned the role of mothers but men can also perform that role when necessary, as has been shown by their participation in childcare in the US and elsewhere.

Our society, which is both patriarchal and market-based, is very ambiguous in the value it gives or does not give to mothering and mothers. It has tended to undervalue mothering, or to hypocritically make it "saintly" while exploiting it, but especially to make it an area of life, which is extraneous to everything else. I believe that the reason for this is that mothering functions according to a deep economic logic that is in contradiction to the market and patriarchy. This unilateral gift logic is transitive, other oriented and qualitative while exchange, upon which the market is based, giving-in-order-to-receive, is intransitive, ego oriented and requires quantification and measurement. Patriarchal Capitalism denies and conceals the economic logic of gift giving because in so many ways it is appropriating gifts. In fact the gift givers give to their 'other', the child or the husband, but also to their 'other', which is the market. The gift giving way itself is directed towards its 'other', the way of exchange as expressed in the market.

Men as well as women are forced into a social mothering or gift-giving stance towards those above them in hierarchies, and a flow of gifts and services goes from those who have less to those who have more. These are not called 'gifts' but are re named 'profit' and are thought of as 'deserved' by those who receive them. Surplus value, the value of work beyond the salary received by the worker, is a gift leveraged from the worker and given free to the capitalist. This leveraged gift is the essence of profit, and it motivates and supports the whole market. The free housework given by women to their families also passes into surplus value, and would add some 40% to the GNP of most countries if it were counted in monetary terms. This fact, publicized by Marilyn Waring (Waring 1988), has inspired many women to struggle for wages for housework. My approach is different. "Economics" has come to refer to the market only. I would like to change the first page of economics text books and broaden the term to include gift giving. This would allow us to see free housework as the tip of the iceberg of an alternative economic way, which is both a legacy of the past and a harbinger of the future. At present this free economy serves as a host from which the market parasitically draws its sustenance (though the market camouflages itself as the provider of life and the giver of gifts). However the host can and must be liberated from the parasite.

We have not seen gift giving in this way before because the gift economy and the exchange economy are locked together in self referential paradoxes. Since the exchange economy espouses the values of competition, it competes with the gift economy, which espouses the values of cooperation... and therefore the exchange economy wins. This victory makes it seem stronger and more credible. The gift economy gives value to the other, to the receiver of the gift. Consequently the receiver becomes more visible and the giver is effaced. In exchange the self- interest of the exchanger is the motivation of the interaction, and s/he is therefore the one who is visible and in focus. The logic of gift giving tends to place the giver in the shadow, while the logic of exchange tends to place the exchanger in the light. There are many other contradictory interactions between gift giving and exchange that tend to hide gift giving. It is not any lack of intelligence or good will on our part that keeps us from recognizing the interaction of these two logics, but it is the very fact of their coexistence and complementarity that disguises the importance and even hides the existence of gift giving.

There are other systemic reasons for the invisibility of gift giving. I believe that the gift economy is actually very threatening to the exchange economy because if everyone were to practice it, the exchange economy would become unnecessary. It is also for this reason that scarcity is created by the market. Gift giving is difficult in scarcity, while it is functional and even enjoyable in abundance. By channeling the wealth from the many to the few, and by wasting wealth on such non-nurturing expenditures as arms production, drugs and consumer excesses, Capitalist Patriarchy ensures the scarcity for the many that keeps them needing to exchange and under its control. Even in desperate conditions however, the sharing of resources without exchange often provides poor people with the means of survival.

I am trying to show that these reasons are structural and systemic also in order to show that we are not individually responsible for the way they work. We did not create them individually. Rather we are all caught up in them, cogs in the wheel, whatever position we have in the system. We have to unite to change this destructive mechanism not just give more, or give tour own extenuation. Only by becoming conscious of the systemic and the logical aspects of the two economies can we hope to finally solve the terrible problems their interaction produces. These problems are devastating, billions of human beings are dying of hunger, preventable disease and war while the environment is being depleted and altered to such an extent that the children of the future will not be able to receive any free gifts from Mother Earth. It is up to us to solve these problems now.

There is a third reason we do not recognize gift giving. The very interactions of exchange and gift giving produce different kinds of subjectivities and different relational consequences. By entering in to these interactions every day our selves are formed according to one logic or the other. Many of us practice both logics at different times and internalize both of them to some extent. The transitive logic of the gift, in which a good or service passes from one person to another to satisfy a need, is simpler than the self reflecting logic of exchange and it establishes a human relation of mutuality and trust. This interaction requires attention to the needs of the other and therefore recognition of the other, while it usually brings with it also the recognition of the giver on the part of the receiver. There is also a mutual relation to the good or service given. Instead, in the process of exchange a quantitative equivalent has to be returned for each good or service. The interaction of exchange is rendered intransitive by the return, and the satisfaction of the need of the other is used to leverage the satisfaction of the giver's need. In this interaction quantification is necessary; and the relationship between the parties that would have taken place in the gift transaction is deeply altered, becoming adversarial and competitive. If we are doing free gift giving we develop a more altruistic or other oriented self. On the other hand if we are exchanging, we are brought into the ego orientation and quantificatory thinking of giving in-order-to-receive an equivalent. Exchange pits each person against the other in the attempt to get more. In fact exchange itself educates us towards greed. That is, the logic of our market behavior, which is caused by the system of which we are a part, pushes us in that direction. Many of us, realizing that greed and domination are harmful, feel guilty for the way we behave. However this guilt is not helpful because it is also constructed according to the logic of exchange, of preparing ourselves to pay back for the wrong we have done. If we realize that guilt keeps us in the exchange point of view, <u>we can for give ourselves </u>and change perspectives, revealing gift giving wherever we can see it and constructing a gift perspective, an alternative paradigm. In this way we can validate the aspects of our selves, which are gift based, and work towards the creation of a society that is an appropriate context for a free need-satisfying economy.

The hiding of gift giving and the consequent division of mothering from the rest of life have created a situation in which the academic world not only excluded women for centuries, but still excludes gift giving as an interpretative key for the various disciplines that describe the world at large. Explanations are given in terms of a "value free" objectivity, which excludes the other orientation of mothering. For example we have a competitive theory of evolution from which gift giving has been excluded. We use the term 'inheritance' which is a gift word, to describe metaphorically a process in which no gift giving is seen, even though genes are handed down from generation to generation and none of the future generations would exist without the free mothering they receive. The tend-and-defend response to stress, which is as important biologically as the fight or flight response, has been brought forward by Shelley Taylor in her book *The Tending Instinct* (Taylor 2002) but has not yet transformed evolutionary theory.

Language too, the great humanizing capacity that all societies possess, is seen as a biological inheritance, not only in the sense that our brains are wired for it, but even in the grammar rules and to some extent the vocabularies of specific languages. It is as if patriarchy and the market had conspired to keep mothering and gift giving out of our consciousnesses. I have been making an effort for years to sketch out a theory of language as gift giving and thus to link it with mothering, so as to bring back the symbolic order to the province of women. Reconnecting the symbolic order with mothering could permit women thinkers to justify their divergence from the male standard or norm (and normativity is itself invested with patriarchal values: the dominance of the norm), by accessing a deeper and more authentic symbolic process than that of power-over and domination.

This gift process has been hidden by the process of domination, but has not been destroyed. In fact it is a fundamental aspect of communication.

Satisfying others' material needs by unilateral giving creates bonds of trust and community, which we can consider as a variation on the bonds created by mothering. Needs are educated by the ways they are satisfied. Each person recognizes the other as the source of her good or the receiver of her gift and the interpersonal space is bridged in a positive way. This pattern of interaction is the basis of a transitive logic which implies that the receiver has value. In exchange, the opposite implication takes place. That is, making the satisfaction of the others' need the instrument for the satisfaction of one's own, cancels the implication of value of the other, and instead gives value only to the initiator of the exchange. Every gift interaction is somewhat different depending on what is given. The giving of gifts becomes a model of a way to behave, and others imitate it, giving gifts in turn. In this way gifts are passed on and gift giving becomes a normal circulation of goods and services, which forms community bonds of mutuality and continuation.

If gift giving at the material level forms bonds of community, a need can develop to form those bonds that may not always be satisfiable materially because some goods may not be available or they may be of a kind that cannot be given. Verbal gifts can be given to create these mutual community- communicative - bonds. Thus although I can give you an apple and create a bond between us through that gift, I can also give you the word "apple" and satisfy your need for a community-communicative bond with me in that way. In fact the need for a word gift in place of a material gift, is a communicative need, which is specifically satisfied by that word and the word itself has been freely handed down by the linguistic community. The ability to give a word in place of something else gives that word a value in the construction of human relations and it also gives the thing that has been substituted a value accent, as something that has been spoken about, something with regard to which a (repeated) human community relation has been formed. That thing or kind of thing can be considered as a gift with which and with regard to which human relations can be constructed even when we cannot actually give it to one another because it is too big like a mountain, too far away, like a star, or too abstract, like the concept of beauty. The community, which is formed through communication using verbal substitute gifts is more abstract and more complex that the community formed by giving material goods. In fact we can form relations with each other with regard to almost anything, and this ability is extended by the fact that we also communicate with regard to things in contingent combination with each other. That is, we use sentences to communicate about things that change in value and are fleetingly relevant in one way or another. In order to do this we use syntax, which, I believe, is not primarily a rule-governed activity but is actually also based on gift patterns. In this case the gift giving is transposed from the giving of words to giving among words. For example 'red' goes with 'ball' because it is given to 'ball' and therefore the two stand together as a substitute gift for the ball which has the property red on the material plane. The ball has that 'property' of course, not because it has *bought* it, but because it has been *given* to it. My hypothesis is that in order to understand the world and the relation of words to the world, we need to project the gift relations, which we learn early in life as mothered children. These make up a more illuminating projection than the objectivity, which is the projection of a market that actually functions in the denial of gift giving.

Gift giving at the material level forms community and it also forms the material subjectivities - the bodies - of the receivers, as well as of the givers to some extent. That is the mother's gifts of food to the child actually form the child's body, and her actions as a nurturer alter her body as well. They are also the content of her subjectivity, while the creative receptivity of the child is the content of her subjectivity. Giving and receiving words has a similar effect on the verbal level. That is, giving words - speaking - forms us as creatively giving subjects, and receiving words - listening - forms us as creatively receiving subjects. Language creates a new area of agency, beyond the material level, a parallel area where a community of linguistically formed gift-based subjectivities interact.

A gives X to B is the basic transitive interaction among people whether this takes place at the material or at the verbal level, or both. Interestingly it takes place also *within* the sentence, in syntax in such sentences as "The girl hit the ball" where the subject gives the predicate to the object. The repetition of the same gift patterns at different levels forms clumps of similar relations which validate each other, a resonating 'box' of gifts that both keeps the gifts together and amplifies them. These levels of gifts include the material or external social level: what we speak about; then the voice that goes from mouth to ear (or written words from page to eye, or intentional or unintentional non verbal signs, which are creatively received and used as gifts by the perceiver);the individual words we give to others and that have been given to us by the linguistic community; the sentences we give; syntax, that is gifts among words in the sentence; the message or information that is conveyed. The repetition of gifts at many levels creates a self confirming, self conveying thread of communication made of many strands. What actually moves the communication is the other directedness of all its parts. That is, there is an intention to satisfy the communicative need of the other at many different levels in each piece of communication, including the transposed or metaphorical 'needs' of words for other words in syntax. All of this moves in an other-oriented way from one person to another. The process of communication remains other oriented even when the speaker is communicating for egotistical reasons. The speaker has to use words and sentences the other person can understand even if s/he is saying something negative such as "I hate you! You are a horrible traitor!"

While we are giving and receiving at the linguistic level we can also give and receive at the material level. That is we can continue to satisfy others' needs with gifts and our own needs can be satisfied by others. I believe that the symbolic gift giving among indigenous peoples that has so deeply impressed the European anthropologists, influenced by Marcel Mauss (Mauss 1925), is a derivative of the gift giving that is in language. Language is a way of giving verbal gifts in place of material gifts and new kinds of relations are created through this transposition. Then in a second transposition, circulating symbolic gifts is a way of giving to material objects some of the relation-creating capacities of words. The symbolic gift circulations can express social roles or status but they also be used for satisfying special communicative needs, such as the Native American use of wampum to bind treaties or to console relatives for the loss of a family member. These are not proto exchanges as anthropologists believed but derivatives of unilateral gift giving in language.

Giving and receiving money in the place of commodities is also a derivative of language and a variation on the theme of symbolic gift giving, but it mediates the kind of contradictory non-giving human relation that is the relation of private property. While language and symbolic gift giving create and express bonds of community and mutuality towards the world, money creates and expresses a mutually exclusive relation. Although it may seem innocuous and even 'natural', exchange for money distorts the communicative gift relation, turning it into something de humanizing and antithetical. Exchange appears to be just a double gift, but the conditionality of the giving upon the return gift, and the quantification and measurement of each product with the stipulation that the exchangers not actually give to each other but only exchange equivalents, changes the relations entirely. Beneath each supposedly equal exchange there is hidden the desire of both parties to receive more, and the defensive stance that the other not take more. These relations run counter to the relations of trust and mutuality that are constructed through gift giving. They promote hidden agendas and duplicity. Each exchanger is actually longing for profit, that is, free gifts given by the other, for which no equivalent has actually been given.

Moreover gift giving is primarily qualitative while exchange is quantitative. Exchange requires a kind of calculation that is not present in gift giving. The gift syllogism: if a gives to b and b gives to c, then a gives to c, is replaced by the consequential and categorial logic: if a then b, and b then c, then if a then c. Without the idea of gift giving here, the logic becomes only that of inclusion and exclusion, whereas in the gift syllogism there is transitivity of the gift, attribution of value to the other and recognition of the source. Giving to the other actually includes the other practically in a transitive interaction, while logical consequence, consistent with exchange, only includes or excludes h/er through categorization. Thus exchange is adversarial and fosters racism and sexism while gift giving is cooperative and promotes inclusiveness.

The motivations of patriarchy, domination, independence, and accumulation, merge with the motivations of exchange to create a market economy where everyone is in competition with everyone else. The deep psychological aspects and material conditions of "having" and "lacking" that are seen in the market based society also come from the creation of patriarchy. On the other hand there are necessarily those outside the market who give to those inside, and gift aspects of the market players themselves that can be taken or given as profit for some of the competitors. These gifts from the outside actually make the market function but are ignored as gifts because they have been named in other ways. For example women's housework has been named 'leisure', the gifts of nature and the future are called natural 'resources'. The gifts of level of life as seen in differences in costs between Third and First world countries are usually the product of pitiless exploitation and colonization, but are named 'unfortunate circumstances' or 'primitive conditions' or 'lack of initiative'. The capacity of humans to produce gifts is called 'human capital'. The gifts of immigrant workers in the North to their families in the South are called "remittances". By re naming gifts in this way the gifts of language are being mis used.

The market has distorted many verbal gifts so as to make them bring ego-oriented rewards, like exchange. In fact the logic of the lie is consonant with the logic of exchange while telling the truth to satisfy the other's need is a kind of gift giving. Advertising and propaganda, in accordance with the logic of exchange and the lie, turn the gifts of language to the ego-oriented purposes of the exchange relation.

Like gift giving in communication, the logic of exchange is self-confirming. The process of substitution repeats itself on different planes. We can see this as the process of naming or definition, in which the name is given in place of an example of a kind. In "That is a dog" for example, the name "dog" is given to the other in place of the dog, which is indicated and brought forward as one of that kind. We move from the material plane to the verbal plane and create a human relation with each other by giving the word "dog" though we are not giving the dog itself. We can give the word "dog" in place of the dog or any dog, to create relations. With money we do the same thing with regard to the relations of private property.

Money is a substitute gift but it does not have a collection of other words surrounding it like verbal gifts do. It therefore conveys and expresses only one kind of value, exchange value, while words express and convey all different kinds of qualitative values. The variety of qualitatively different values in language is transferred into the variety of quantitatively different exchange values as seen in the numerically identified system of prices. Because money mediates private property it actually has to be given up, in order for the substitution to take place, while words are almost infinitely produceable and reproduceable by the speakers of a language and so they can be given abundantly without loss.

Thus money takes the place of products, bringing them into the market, categorizing them as exchange values. The substitution of money for a commodity and a commodity for money in buying and selling becomes the social nexus of the market society. The whole system based on these substitutions takes the place of - substitutes - the economy based on gift giving that still exists in the home, in language, in the psyche and in Nature. The logic of inclusion and exclusion takes the place of the transitive logic of gift giving. In fact inclusion in the market as a commodity or the exclusion from it, together with the level at which a product enters as expressed in the price, is a replay of this moment of categorization and naming. We can look at commodification as a kind of semiotization of a product (making the product itself into a sign) according to the communicative or community value it has in the mutually exclusive situation of private property. The market thus appears as a kind of aberrant material communication in the alienated community of private property possessors.

Gifts and gift givers are left outside this material semiotic mechanism but continue to give value, goods and free labor to it. This flow of gifts is 'justified' by the exchange paradigm, the world view deriving from the market. The similarity of commodification, naming and categorization create a self confirming mechanism and construct a paradigm, which validates exchange and takes the place of a possible world-view based on gift giving. This substitution is a repetition of the pattern of substitution at a different level and the repetitions confirm each other. Commodification is a subtle intruder into our minds because of its similarity to mechanisms of semiotization, naming and categorization which we use all the time. It therefore seems natural and unappealable. At the same time it validates processes of substitution and eliminates processes based on gift giving both in practice and in our description of reality. Thus categorization seems to be *a sui generis* act simply 'willed' by humans or a function of the hardware of the brain, and no gift connection between people or between words and the world seems to be necessary.

I hope this short description of language and comparison with the market has shown what a point of view based on gift giving might illuminate not only for linguistics and economics but also for the other disciplines of academia. Feminism is not just a question of countering sexism, of allowing more women into academic and government or business positions but it is a question of revising all our thinking and our economic behavior to create our humanity in a different way, through free and liberated gift giving. First we need to re fashion our conception of the world to include the gift paradigm. By doing that, we can see that mothering is not just a behavior isolated in infant and child care, but rather it is a very widespread human principle which unfortunately at present is being dominated by negative psycho-social structures that have developed in the denial of mothering.

Biblography

Chodorow, Nancy. 1978. *The Reproduction of Mothering: Pscyhoanalysis and the Sociology of Gender.* Berkeley: University of California

Gilligan, Carol. 1982. *In a Different Voice.* Cambridge, Mass.: Harvard University Press.

Hyde, Lewis. 1979. *The Gift, Imagination and the Erotic Life of Property.* New York: Random House.

Isla, Ana. .2004. "Dispossessing the Commons by Credit: the struggle to reclaim them" in *Athanor : Il Dono/the Gift: a feminist analysis.* ed G. Vaughan. Rome: Meltemi

Marx, Karl. (1867) . *Capital in Two Volumes: Volume One.* Engl. trans.Eden and Cedar Paul London: J.M. Dent & Sons, Ltd. 1930.

Grundrisse 1857-1858.(1939) Engl. trans. Martin Nicholaus..New Mauss, Marcel.(1925)

"Essai sur le don. Forme et raison de l'echange dans lesocietes archaiques" L'Anee sociologique, new series, 1); Englishtrans.

The Gift: The Form and Reason for Exchange in Archaic Societies.　　trans. W.D. Halls New York: W.W. Norton.1990.

Rossi-Landi, Ferruccio. 1968. *Il linguaggio come lavoro e come mercato.* Milano: Bompiani.1974.

"Linguistics and Economics", *Current Trendsin Linguistics*, vol. 12, ed. Thomas A. Sebeok.

Ruddick, Sara. 1989. *Maternal Thinking: Toward a Politics of Peace.*New York: Ballantine Books.

Saussure, Ferdinand de. 1931. *Cours de linguistique generale.* Charles Bally and Albert Sechehaye. Paris: Payot

Shiva, Vandana.1997. *Biopiracy, the Plunder of Nature and Knowledge.* Boston: South End Press.

Taylor, Shelley E. 2002. *The Tending Instinct.* Henry Holt and Co. New York.

Vaughan, Genevieve. 1997. *For-Giving, a Feminist Criticism of Exchange.* Austin, Texas. Plain View Press.2004 (ed.)

Athanor:Il Dono/The Gift: a feminist analysis. Rome: Meltemi Editore

Waring, Marilyn, 1988. *If Women Counted, A New Feminist Economics.* San Francisco. Harper and Row.

Untitled

Gina Wilson

I found my Dark Mother in Sardegna
I found her in the 10,000 flamingos
that migrate like fluffy pink attachés from Africa each year
I found her in the salty blue coldness of the Mediterranean
I found her in the crepe paper red poppies
peeking out like glimmer of hope from between the rocks on our path
I found her in steep caves
where to and bottom spent millions of years reaching one another,
one drop of water at a time
I found her in the ruins of ancient cities,
where soft whispers from the past fill our ears,
if only we stop to listen
I found her in the perfect timing of a rain storm
I found her in glasses of red wine at lunch
and decaf espresso
in cheese and bread and seafood salad
Between the rolling green mountains,
and the powder blue sky
Between the rocky cliffs that looked upon this world for thousands of years,
and i bambini whose eyes open wide in wonder
In fields of wildflowers
In a land from which Sardines do Not come
In a giant bus weaving through the countryside
I found my Dark Mother
And what I found was that all I ever needed to do was look beside me
at my mom…

Matriarchal Society

Heide Goettner-Abendroth

Why the Term "Matriarchy"?

At the two *World Congresses on Matriarchal Studies* which took place in 2003 in Luxembourg/Europe and in 2005 in San Marcos/Texas, the speakers and scholars who presented their international research there have introduced the term "matriarchy" for all non-patriarchal societies worldwide. In spite of the difficult connotations of this word, there are several good reasons to use it.

1. The term "matriarchy" is well known from the discussion that has gone on at least since 1861 (Johann Jacob Bachofen), and it is by now a popular term, even if it is still misinterpreted.

2. Philosophical and scientific re-definitions mostly refer to well-known words and redefine them. After that, researchers can work with them, but they do not lose contact with the language of the people. In this process, the word often takes on a new, clearer and broader meaning even in the popular language; this is also influenced by the re-defining activities of scholars. In the case of the term „matriarchy", this redefinition would be a great advantage, especially for women: *reclaiming* this term means to reclaim the knowledge about cultures that have been created by women.

3. It might not always be helpful to create new scientific terms like "matrifocal," "matricentric," "matristic," "gylanic," etc. Some of these terms, like "matrifocal" and "gylanic", are very artificial and have no connection to popular language. Others like "matricentric" and "matristic" are too weak, for they suggest that non-patriarchal societies have no more to them than just being centered around the mothers. The result can be a somewhat reduced view of these societies – by the researchers as well as

the critics – a view that neglects the intricate network of relationships and the complex social networks that characterize these cultures.

4. We are not obliged to follow the current, male biased notion of the term "matriarchy" as meaning "domination by the mothers" or "women's rule". The only reason to understand it in this way is that it sounds parallel to "patriarchy". For the notion of women's rule - if it is really needed - there exists a different term: "gynaikocracy" (Bachofen).

To clarify the notion of "matriarchy", it is important to know that the Greek word "arché" has a double meaning. It means "beginning" as well as "domination." Therefore, the term "matriarchy" can be accurately translated as "the mothers from the beginning." "Patriarchy," on the other hand, translates correctly as "domination of the fathers" or "men's rule."

5. To use the term "matriarchy" in its re-defined, clarified meaning is also of political relevance. It doesn't avoid the discussion with colleagues and the interested audience, which is urgently needed. This might easily happen with the other terms, which have the tendency to conceal and to belittle. Researchers should not shy away from the provocative connotation of the term "matriarchy," both because research in this field is so important and because only continued political provocation will bring about a change of mind.

Modern Matriarchal Studies

At the two *World Congresses on Matriarchal Studies* (2003 and 2005), the scope of modern Matriarchal Studies was presented by the scholars and indigenous speakers - mostly women - from all continents. They did research in Africa, Asia, America, and Europe.

The intellectual basis for these two congresses was the **theory of matriarchal society** which is developed in my main work on "Matriarchy" step by step, which is in the process of being published in several consecutive volumes and is now translated into English. It shows the scope of modern Matriarchal Studies; and each important research, which already exists about this topic, has been, and will continue to be, included in this framework.

In the first step of developing this theory, I give an overview of the previous research in matriarchy. I follow the course the studies have taken, using examples of the scientific as well as of the political discussion. What becomes obvious is the lack of a clear and complete definition of "matriarchy". Furthermore, in this book I put the method of ideological criticism in correct terms. This method is necessary in this field of studies, because most of the early and contemporary writings about the topic contain a massive amount of patriarchal ideology. (See: *Das Matriarchat I. Geschichte seiner Erforschung*, Kohlhammer 1988-1995)

In the second step of the development of this theory, I formulate the complete structural definition of "matriarchy", a definition which is needed for any serious research. It specifies all the necessary and sufficient conditions or criteria of "matriarchy", and in this sense, brings to light the deep structure of matriarchal society. It has not been formulated from the first, but arrived at by investigating the immense amount of anthropological material.

The systematic step of my anthropological research becomes visible now. I have dedicated the past ten years to these studies, because we cannot get a complete definition of "matriarchy" from cultural history only. There we are dealing with the remains and fragments of past societies, and that is not sufficient for an overall picture.

It remains undisputed that these may well be very numerous fragments, and that they may well be extremely important; still they can give us only scattered information. Through historical research alone we cannot know how matriarchal people thought or felt, how they organized their social patterns or political events, that is: how their society was structured as a whole. In order to gain this knowledge and - as a consequence thereof - to achieve ther complete deep structure of "matriarchy", we have to examine the still existing societies of this kind. Fortunately, they still exist on all continents except Europe.

I have considered these cultures in the second step of my theory, in which I present all of the world's extant matriarchal societies.

(See: *Das Matriarchat II,1. Stammesgesellschaften in Ostasien, Indonesien, Ozeanien,* Kohlhammer 1991/1999, and see: *Das Matriarchat II,2. Stammesgesellschaften in Amerika, Indien, Afrika,* Kohlhammer 2000).

In the third step of the development of my theory, I use the deep structure of "matriarchy", which I have now found out, as an intellectual tool for a re-vision of the cultural history of humankind. This history is much longer than the five to six thousand years of patriarchal history. In its longest periods, non-patriarchal societies were developed, in which women created culture and embodied the integral center of society. The still existing matriarchal societies are the last examples.

Of course, I reject the term "pre-history", because it is patriarchally prejudiced. In academia today, "history" always begins with the first patriarchal kings and empires, which are pretty late, and the very long epochs before are called "pre-history". But the cultural development of humankind has always been history in the full sense. Fortunately, in this field of early history excellent research is already available. It has been developed recently. What is still lacking, however, is the systematic framework of connection, that is, the overall picture of the long history of matriarchy. (Project: *Das Matriarchat III. Historische Stadtkulturen*, in the process of development)

It is obvious that such an immense task is impossible without a complete definition or deep structure of "matriarchy". After it has been formulated in the anthropological part of my theory, we now have, for the very first time, the chance to adequately write the complete history of humankind, and to do so without the distortions by patriarchal ideas and concepts. This new interpretation of history clearly shows that the patriarchal interpretation of history is wrong and turns out to be obsolete.

In the fourth step of the development of this theory I write about the problem of the rise of patriarchy. Two important questions have to be answered: 1. How could patriarchal patterns develop in the first place? 2. How could they spread all over the world? The latter is by no means obvious.

In my opinion neither question has been sufficiently answered yet. Instead, a lot of pseudo-explanations have been offered. If we want to explain the development of patriarchy, we first of all need clear knowledge about the form of society which existed previously - and that was matriarchy. At present, this knowledge is in the process of being developed. It is the absolute precondition for explaining the development of patriarchy. Otherwise, we begin with false assumptions.

Secondly, a theory about the development of patriarchy has to explain why patriarchal patterns emerged in different places, on different continents, at different times and under different conditions. The answers will be very different for the different regions of the world. This task has not yet been done at all. (Project: *Das Matriarchat IV. Entstehung des Patriarchats*, in the process of development).

In the fifth step of the development of this theory, I write about the analysis and history of patriarchy. Until now, the history of patriarchy has been written down as a history of domination, as a history "from the top". But there also exists the perspective of the history "at the bottom" which shows a completely different picture. It is the history of women, of the lower classes, of the marginalized peoples and of the sub-cultures. It shows that patriarchy did not succeed in destroying the ancient and long matriarchal traditions on all continents. In the end, it parasitically lives on these traditions.

The task is to show that these traditions (oral traditions, customs, myths, rites, ceremonies, folklore, etc.) have their roots in the preceding traditions, matriarchy. But we can recognize this only with the help of the overall picture of matriarchy, which is given with its complete deep structure. If we can manage to follow the traces backwards through the history of patriarchy and to connect them, this means nothing less than **regaining our heritage**. (Project: *Das Matriarchat V. Matriarchale Traditionen in patriarchalen Gesellschaften*, in the process of development).

The Deep Structure of Matriarchal Society

Now I shall give the structural definition or deep structure of „matriarchy". I will present the necessary and (some of the) sufficient conditions of matriarchal society on four levels: on the economic level, on the level of social patterns, on the political level, and on the level of culture and worldview.

On the economic level, matriarchies are most often agricultural societies, but not exclusively so. The technologies of agriculture they developed reach from simple gardening to full agriculture with plowing (at the beginning of the Neolithic Age, about 10.000 before our time), and, finally, to the large irrigation systems of the earliest urban cultures. Simultaneously, the social forms of matriarchy continued to become more differentiated in the course of the millennia. The rise of matriarchy is directly connected with the development of these new technologies.

Goods are distributed according to a system, that is identical with the lines of kinship and the patterns of marriage. This system prevents goods from being accumulated by one special person or one special group. Thus, the principles of equality are consciously kept up, and the society is egalitarian and non-accumulating. From a political point of view, matriarchies are societies with perfect mutuality. Every advantage or disadvantage concerning the acquisition of goods is mediated by social rules. For example, at each village festival, one of the wealthier clans invites all inhabitants of the community. Members of this clan organize the banquet, at which this clan gives away its wealth as gifts to all the others. At each of the festivals, it is the turn of another wealthy clan to invite all the people at its expenses. This does not allow to accumulate goods, but makes them circulate in order to secure the welfare of all. This creates a true "gift economy" (as Genevieve Vaughan has formulated it).

Therefore, on the economic level I define matriarchies as *societies of reciprocity based on the circulation of gifts.*

On the social level, matriarchies are based on a union of extended clan.

The people live together in big clans, which are formed according to the principle of *matrilineality*, i.e. the kinship is exclusively acknowledged in the female line. The clan's name, and all social positions and political titles are passed on through the mother's line. Such a matri-clan consists at least of three generations of women: the clan-mother, her daughters, her granddaughters, and the directly related men: the brothers of the mother, her sons and grandsons. Generally, the matri-clan lives in one big clan-house, which holds from 10 to more than 100 persons, depending on size and architectural style. The women live permanently there, because daughters and granddaughters never leave the clan-house of their mother, when they marry. This is called *matrilocality*.

What is most important is the fact, that women have the power of disposition over the goods of the clan, especially the power to control the sources of nourishment: fields and food. This characteristic feature, besides matrilineality and matrilocality, grants women such a strong position that these societies are "matriarchal" and not only "matrilineal." (Anthropologists do not make a distinction between merely matrilineal, and clearly matriarchal societies.)

These matri-clans in their clan-house on their clan-land are self-supporting groups. How are the people in such self-supporting groups connected to the other clans of the village? This is effected by the patterns of marriage, especially the system of mutual marriage between two clans. Mutual marriage between two clans is no individual marriage, but a communal marriage leading to communal matrimony. This makes good sense in a system of mutual aid.

For example, the young men from clan-house A are married to the young women clan-house B, and the young men from clan-house B are married to the young women in clan-house A. This is called *mutual marriage between two clans* in a matriarchal village. The same takes place between fixed pairs of other clan-houses, for example the houses C and D, E and F. Due to additional patterns of marriage between all clans, finally everyone in a matriarchal village or a matriarchal town is related to everyone else by birth or by marriage. Therefore, I call matriarchies *societies of matrilineal kinship.*

The young men, who have left the house of their mother after their marriage, do not have to go very far. Actually, in the evening they just go to the neighboring house, where their wives live, and they come back very early - at dawn. This form of marriage is called *visiting marriage,* and it is restricted to the night. It means, that matriarchal men have no right to live in the house of their wives. The home of matriarchal men is the clan-house of their mothers. There, they take part in the work in the fields and gardens, they take part in the decisions of the clan. There, they have rights and duties.

In this system of clans a matriarchal men never regards the children of his wife as his children, because they do not share his clan-name. They are only related to the woman whose clan-name they have. A matriarchal man, however, is closely related to the children of his sister: his nieces and nephews. They have the same clan-name as he. His attention, his care for their upbringing, the personal goods he passes on: all this is for the nieces and nephews. Biological fatherhood is not known, or is paid no attention. It is no social factor. Matriarchal men care for their nieces and nephews in a kind of *social fatherhood.*

Even the process of ***making a political decision*** is organized along the lines of matriarchal kinship. In the clan-house, women and men meet in a council where domestic matters are discussed. No member of the household is excluded. After thorough discussion, each decision is taken by consensus. The same is true for the entire village: delegates from every clan-house meet in the village council, if matters concerning the whole village have to be discussed. These delegates can be the oldest women of the clans (the matriarchs), or the brothers and sons they have chosen to represent the clan. No decision concerning the whole village may be taken without the consensus of all clan-houses. This means, the delegates, who are discussing the matter, are not the ones who make the decision. It is not in this council that the policy of the village is made, because the delegates function only as bearers of communication. If the council notices that the clan-houses do not yet agree, the delegates return to the clan-houses to discuss matters further. In this way, consensus is reached in the whole village step by step.

A people living in a certain region takes decisions in the same way: delegates from all villages meet to exchange the decisions of their communities. Again, the delegates function only as bearers of communication. In such cases, it is usually men who are elected by their villages, since the clan-mothers do not leave their clan's houses and land. In contrast to the frequent anthropological mistakes made about these men, they are not the "chiefs" and do not, in fact, decide. Every village, and in every village every clan-house, is involved in the process of making a decision, until consensus is reached on the regional level.

Therefore, from the political point of view, I call matriarchies ***egalitarian societies*** or ***societies of consensus.*** These political patterns do not allow the accumulation of political power. In *exactly* this sense, they are free of domination: They have no class of rulers and no class of suppressed people, i.e., they do not know *enforcement bodies*, which are necessary to establish domination.

On the cultural level, these societies are not characterized by "fertility cults" - such a simplifying view distorts the fact that these cultures have a complex religious system. The fundamental concept matriarchal people have of the cosmos and their life, the belief they express in many rites, myths and spiritual customs, is the belief in rebirth. It is not the abstract idea of the transmigration of souls, as it later appears in Hinduism and Buddhism, but the concept of rebirth in a very concrete sense: all members of a clan know that after death they will be re-birthed, by one of the women of their own clan, in their own clan-house, in their home village. Every dead person returns directly as a small child to the same clan. Women in matriarchal societies are greatly respected, because they are granting rebirth. They are renewing and prolonging the life of the clan. This concept is the basis of the matriarchal view of life. Matriarchal people have adopted it from the natural world they live in: in nature, the growing, flourishing, withering, and the returning of the vegetation takes place every year. Matriarchal people are convinced that every plant that withers in fall is reborn next spring. Therefore, the Earth is the Great Mother granting rebirth and nurturing all beings.

In the sky, they observe the same cycle of coming and going: all celestial bodies rise, set and return every day and every night. They perceive the cosmos as the Great Goddess of Heaven and Creation. She is constantly creating everything, it is she who grants the ordering of time. She gives birth to all stars in the east, lets them move over the sky, until they die through her power in the west. A good example of this matriarchal concept of the cosmos is the Egyptian goddess Nout, the Goddess of Heaven. She gives birth to her son Re, the sun, every morning, and devours him every evening, only to give birth to him again at the next sunrise.

In the cosmos and on the earth, matriarchal people observe this cycle of life, death and rebirth. According to the matriarchal principle of connection between macro-cosm and micro-cosm, they see the same cycle in human life. Human existence is not different from the cycles of nature; it follows the same rules. Their concept of nature and of the human world lacks the dualistic, patriarchal way of thinking that separates "spirit" and "nature" or "society" and "nature."

Furthermore, it lacks the dualistic concept of morality that defines what is "good" and splits off what is "evil." From the matriarchal perspective, life brings forth death, and death brings forth life again – everything in its own time. If everything is necessary in its own time, the drastic opposition of "good" and "evil" makes no sense. In the same way, the female and the male also are a cosmic polarity. It would never occur to a matriarchal people to regard one sex as inferior or weaker to the other, as it is common in patriarchal societies.

The entire view of the world of matriarchal people is structured non-dualistically. They make no essential distinction between the profane and the sacred. The entire world with all 'her' appearances is divine and, therefore, sacred to the people. They respect and venerate nature as holy, and they would never exploit and destroy it. For example, every house is sacred and has its holy hearth as a place where the living and the ancestors meet together. And each daily task and common gesture has a symbolic meaning, every action is ritualized. Therefore, on the cultural level, I call matriarchies *sacral societies as cultures of the Goddess.*

Summary of the Criteria of the Matriarchal Society

•*Economic criteria:* societies with self-supporting gardening or agriculture; land and house are property of the clan, no private property; women have the power of disposition over the source of nourishment; constant adjustment of the level of wealth by the circulation of the vital goods in form of gifts at festivals – **societies of reciprocity.**

•*Social criteria:* matriarchal clans, which are held together by matrilinearity and matrilocality; mutual marriage between two clans; visiting marriage with additional sexual freedom for both sexes; social fatherhood – **non-hierarchical, horizontal societies of matrilineal kinship.**

•*Political criteria:* principle of consensus in the clan-house, on the level of the village, and on the regional level; delegates as bearers of communication, not as decision-takers; absence of classes and structures of domination – **egalitarian societies of consensus.**

•*Cultural criteria:* concrete belief in rebirth into the same clan; cult of ancestresses and ancestors; worship of Mother Earth and the Goddess of Cosmos; divinity of the entire world; absence of dualistic world view and morality; everything in life is part of the symbolic system – **sacral societies as cultures of the Goddess.**

(English translation: Solveig Göttner, Karen Smith)

Bibliography

Bachofen, Johann, Jakob: *Das Mutterrecht*, Stuttgart 1861, English: *Myth, Religion and Mother Right*.

Goettner-Abendroth, Heide: *The Goddess and her Heros*, in German: Frauenoffensive, München 1980-1997, in English: Anthony Publishing Company, Stow MA 1995.

Goettner-Abendroth. Heide: *Das Matriarchat I. Geschichte seiner Erforschung*, Kohlhammer, Stuttgart 1988-1995.

Goettner-Abendroth, Heide: *Das Matriarchat II,1. Stammesgesellschaften in Ostasien, Indonesien, Ozeanien*, Kohlhammer, Stuttgart 1991/1999.

Goettner-Abendroth, Heide: *Das Matriarchat II,2. Stammesgesellschaften in Amerika, Indien, Afrika*, Kohlhammer, Stuttgart 2000.

Morgan, Henri Lewis: *League of the Ho-de-no-sau-nee or Iroquois*, 1851 und 1871/1877, H.M.Lloyd, New York 1901.

Vaughan, Genevieve: *For-Giving. A Feminist Criticism of Exchange*, Plain View Press/ Anomaly Press, Austin 1997.

A color blind society? A big affirmative action scam!

Ida J. Dunson

BLOOD IS RED! Beautiful menstrual blood!
How insane the patriarchy society was in my
generation, some 80 years ago, even centuries.
They feared this blood that gave them birth.

America can never be a color blind society.
Its historical landscape is rich in color and ethnic diversity.
Even the pharaohs were never color blind
to the lush colorful gardens and the beauty of the peacocks
spreading fantails of deep royal blues, dark greens, bright
chartreuse, and purple violet hues.

I was told during my research in Egypt land that peacock
feathers were organically used as eye shadow to enhance the lovely
doe eyes of the queens and concubines. No chemical
cosmetics there.

The explosion of Kente cloth of Ancient Kingdoms
of the West Coast African Country of Ghana to around the world
is awesome. These highly skilled weavers celebrated hundreds of
tribal patterns in reds, blues, oranges, yellows, greens, and purples in
cloth now being marketed and mass produced by global capitalists.

So those who profess our higher education systems are 'color blind'
when admitting students to universities and colleges must
understand that 'The Affirmative Action Plan for the European
American Man' began in the slave trade, the black gold,
on this rich red soil, nourished by the rich red blood of females
from ancient Nubia/Egypt and. . . women who were venerated
in the rituals of many African diaspora lands where matriarchy
governed family and community.
Hurricane Katrina has shown the
world what democracy means for a 'Color Blind Society'. . .
Neglect and death!

Falling for Knowledge: New Interpretations of "The Fall" in Genesis

Jamie Logsdon Kuehnl, M.A.

In chapter three of The Book of Genesis, we have the story of "The Fall," which contains some of the most well-known narrative verse of the last two or three millennia. This story, a mere twenty-four verses long, has a plot that unfolds around only four main characters: Eve, Adam, God, and a snake. It is a powerful, sublime passage that has dictated doctrine, impassioned souls, and mobilized the masses, for better or for worse. The story has been evoked to both defend and chastise human sexuality, marriage, and hierarchical systems of value. My wish is to examine how "The Fall" is being perceived and projected within contemporary scholarly circles.

Because of the influx of women and multi-cultural persons into scholarly positions within the last half-century, previously accepted beliefs and ideals, such as the dominant culture's interpretation of "The Fall," are being reexamined. The scholarly realm no longer only consists of upper-class, white, Christian males; therefore, new, diverse interpretations are emerging daily. My question that acts as the impetus for the following literary review is whether this current reexamination of "The Fall" is leading to a potential paradigm shift due to the influx of more diverse scholars and their accompanying scholarship.

In order to render a proper juxtaposition of "The Fall" alongside literary interpretation and criticism of it, it is first necessary to establish a "common" interpretation of the text. For my sake and purpose, I will use a seemingly generalized interpretation that the scholars, for the most part, agree is the interpretation accepted by and promoted through the Christian Church and Western culture as a whole. In this particular reading, "The

Fall" is said to be the source of original sin. It is the reading wherein Eve is tempted by the serpent, Adam is tempted by Eve, and the duo's ultimate disobedience leads to humanity being forevermore cast out of Eden and destined to a life of suffering and mortality.

For methodological purposes, I begin the study by taking an historical approach in order to place the story within an agreeable context. Through my text choices and explorations I seek out authors whom I feel embody one of three approaches to research methodology that the philosopher Origen, from the first century C.E. (185-254 C.E.) is credited with promoting. In his method, Origen "recognized three approaches to scriptural meanings and interpretations." The first approach is to seek literal, concrete meanings, also called *somaticos*. The second is to develop meanings through intellectual, logical, and associational means, or *psychikos*. The last approach is to seek spiritual, allegorical, symbolic, and metaphorical meanings, or *pneumatikos* (Braud and Anderson 48).

Origen recognized that there do exist several layers of interpretation readily available to the reader of sacred stories. However, until quite recently, the locus of most Western scholarly interpretations has centered around only one approach — that of the literal (*somaticos*). For instance, instead of probing the intellectual, allegorical, or metaphysical aspects of the story of "The Fall," most scholars have taken a decidedly religious, literal approach. The result of taking such an exclusionary course has had profound effects on Western culture's ideology. By looking at numerous literary interpreters and critics that all embrace at least one out of three of Origen's methods, a richer exegesis of "The Fall" can be attained. Additionally, by applying this method to just one of the sacred stories that is so central to Western culture we can gain a broader insight into its historical, intellectual, and spiritual implications.

To begin by placing the story of "The Fall" within its literary context, some historical perspective is in order so that it might be possible to imagine where the original-source author was coming from. To do so, we can look to *The Bible as Literature*, by John Gabel, Charles Wheeler, and Anthony York. They tell us that Genesis itself is one of the five books of the Pentateuch; the other books include Exodus, Leviticus, Numbers, and Deuteronomy. Scholars currently agree that there were at least four main authors or sources of these five books. The source attributed to Genesis is called the "Yahwist," or J source. This particular author is thought to be the earliest of the Pentateuchal authors, compiling and composing materials as early as 1000 B.C.E. (Gabel 112). In addition to the author, there was also at least one editor or creative artist involved in the Pentateuch's compilation, called the "redactor."

Aside from the story's literary context, it is just as important to place this mysterious author within a physical context as well. Gabel, Wheeler, and York also inform us that scholars have found evidence to prove that the J source originated in southern Palestine, in an area that later became the kingdom of Judah (Gabel 109). This region is the hill country of Palestine and its fertility gave way to grain fields, olive groves, and vineyards (Gabel 74). The people inhabiting this region "dug, sowed, and harvested…as they had been doing for centuries, obeying the actual ruler of the land, which was nature herself" (Gabel 83).

The cities of Palestine during J's lifetime were fortified ones, the largest of which only held a few thousand inhabitants (Gabel 83). There were no public buildings, so the majority of business and socialization was conducted on benches located near the city gates. Certain sacred cities, such as Shiloh, Shechem, Bethel, and Jerusalem would have housed a temple, not for worshipping in, but as a shrine to a particular god or goddess (Gabel 84). Gabel reminds us that "their actual religion was private and domestic…and retained a considerable heritage of primitive animism" (Gabel 84).

It is at this point that I would add that when the J source is taken out of a purely biblical context and placed within a larger context we can see that this author originated from a region that was one of the three main civilizations of the ancient Western world — the Mesopotamian region. Of the ancient world, we now know that for centuries prior to the incursion of patriarchal peoples, the ancients were highly steeped in myth, spirituality, and the worship of the feminine. The history of this even more ancient civilization undoubtedly left its nuances in the cultural landscape.

Ancient Palestine, just previous to, as well as during J's lifetime, was largely an oral culture; therefore, many of these Yahwist writings began as oral legends and histories. Gabel, Wheeler, and York state that, "Living in an age without the diversions we take for granted, [the Israelites] had plenty of time to listen to public speakers and plenty of incentive to do so" (Gabel 109). The Israelites themselves were highly patriarchal, held an extremely high regard for their pasts, and had a "lively sense of national identity" (Gabel 109). These attributes of the Israelites' made them a type of people who naturally desired to record their histories and legends, and especially because they were promoting a new paradigm that had previously been the exception — that of a staunchly patriarchal ideology.

Because the Israelites were so steeped in the oral tradition it is quite natural to look to some of the other myths of the time that the Israelites would have been exposed to, to varying degrees. Author Sir James G. Frazer, in *Folklore in the Old Testament* has found that numerous ancient cultures throughout the world had a story about the people being cheated out of their immortality, which is the crux of "The Fall" as well. Frazer points out that J's version of "The Fall" may have been a misinterpretation of one such ancient story. He believes that a comparison of many other similar ancient stories shows that "The Fall" actually should have relayed a story of a benevolent Creator offering humanity the option of taking from two trees: one, the Tree of Life; or two, the Tree of Death. The Creator sends the serpent as a messenger to inform the people of their choice, but in Trickster fashion, the serpent changes the message to serve his own purpose. So instead, the serpent approaches the woman and beguilingly tells the woman that she will live forever if she takes from the Tree of Death.   Meanwhile, the snake gains its own immortality by taking from the Tree of Life (Frazer 19). Frazer shows that this type of myth is so plentiful within different cultures they even have their own classifications as "The Story of the Perverted Message," or "The Story of the Cast Skin."

The conclusion that we might infer from this tendency for ancient cultures to address mortality is that death was, and still is, a source of great misunderstanding and fear for most peoples. Historically speaking, that which is little understood by a people naturally becomes the material inherent in their story-telling. The myths and legends become their attempt at coming to terms with mysterious physical and nonphysical phenomenon. This theory would also explain the tendency for the snake to play an integral part in such stories relating to death and mortality, since the snake is an age-old emblem of regeneration due to its ability to shed its skin, and thus, appear to be immortal.

We can attain further insight into the mythic, as well as symbiotic, aspects of "The Fall" in Peter Myers' critical piece, "Derivation of the Adam and Eve Story from the *Epic of Gilgamesh*." In his essay, he points out undeniable similarities between the *Epic of Gilgamesh*, and "The Fall." *Gilgamesh* was written and re-written numerous times in ancient Mesopotamia between ca. 3000 B.C.E. to 1200 B.C.E. (Thackara), and the belief stands that the J writer would have been familiar with the narrative story. Myers first points out the use of the serpent in both narrations. In *Gilgamesh*, the serpent "robs the hero [Enkidu] of his opportunity to acquire immortal youth," as is the similar case in "The Fall." Myers reminds us that the motif of the serpent is "inspired by the phenomenon of the snake's ability to slough off its old skin. To the primitive mind it appeared that the snake had learned the secret of renewing its youth" (Myers 2). This particular legend would have been strong in the Semitic folklore of the age, along with beliefs of the snake as a healer and a symbol associated with the worship of the Goddess Asarte in the Mesopotamian region.

Next, Myers shows that the "Eve as temptress" theme is also reflected in *Gilgamesh*. In the ancient story, the "Wild man Enkidu," is representative of humanity before civilization, and "is lured away from his simple harmonious life with the animals, by a sacred courtesan. With her wiles she makes him sexually conscious, she teaches him to eat bread and wear clothes, and finally brings him into the city and so ultimately his doom" (Myers 2). Once she has properly seduced him she claims, "Thou art wise, Enkidu, art become like a god!" We can easily compare her comment with that of the serpent in "The Fall" who enchantingly claims that once the fruit from the Tree of Knowledge is taken Adam and Eve, too, "will be like gods." *Gilagmesh's* courtesan, much like Eve, is later cursed for leading the man away from his original, simple life. Myers shows that this early template for Eve is "undoubtedly one of the temple prostitutes of Ishtar, the great fertility Goddess, who seduces the type-figure of a primitive man from his original innocence and well-being by giving him sexual experience, which makes him god-like but that…inevitably leads to his death" (Myers 2). Man becomes "god-like" because he can create new life through sexual intercourse, but following a theme that becomes more prevalent in Greek myth, bearing offspring can be a precarious reminder of one's own mortality.

In a culture that formerly consisted of Earth and Goddess-worshipping peoples, this association of women with sexual knowledge and fecundity makes perfect sense. Without the restrictions imposed on them by patriarchy, women were free to reign and roam in the sexual arena, which was oftentimes a sacred, ritualistic arena. This quite obviously posed a problem for the patriarchs who, during early biblical times, began placing emphasis on establishing firm patrilineal descent lines and thus, began denying women their previous near-sovereignty in the sexual domain.

Another author, John A. Phillips, points to a different myth as the prototype for the story of "The Fall." What Phillips looks to is Hesiod's misogynistic interpretation of the Pandora myth as the original template. He points out that it was "intense misogynist tendencies that dominated a certain late phase of Greek civilization [that] transformed the lure of the female body into an organ of danger and terror and turned the sexual attraction of women into a malicious temptation" (Phillips 23). Robert Graves, too, has pointed out that "Hesiod's account…is not genuine myth, but an antifeminist fable, probably of his own invention" (Phillips 19). This reflects the air of hostility that was felt during this period, at a time that men were, by all means necessary, actively disempowering women and their roles in society.

There is still much speculation as to why there was such hostility toward women occurring in this particular time and place (in the ancient Western world, from circa 1000 B.C.E. through the common era), but the evidence that supports the occurrence is overwhelming. Hesiod himself lived about 700 B.C.E., and his writing provides just one familiar motif endowed on women when he refers to Pandora, and thus, the entire female gender, as a "lovely evil, sheer deception, and a great infestation" ("Prometheus"). The early Church Fathers were undoubtedly drawing from this late Greek perception when they were inscribing and interpreting Genesis.

John Phillips also points out that, "The story of Eve is also the story of the displacing of the Goddess" (Phillips 3), and that the snake from "The Fall" and the jar (or "box") from Hesiod's Pandora tale can be viewed in a similar manner. Just as the snake was a powerful image in early Goddess-worshipping cultures so too was the *pithos*, or jar, because the jar was used to contain or preserve items used in life and was also used for burial purposes, thus iconographic of the Creator Goddess herself. But out of these two patriarchally-imbued stories, both the snake and the jar only retain the feminine qualities so that they are now imbued with "evil" and subversive connotations. Phillips says that the original, more ancient Pandora story may have involved *two* jars — one containing "good" and the other containing "evil" — that humanity was to choose from, instead of *one* jar that only contained "evil" that the female opened and unleashed unto the world. This curiously reflects the controversiality surrounding the appearance of one or two trees in the Garden of Eden as well.

Another level of interpretation we might turn to when critiquing "The Fall" is a psychoanalytic one. Daniel Burston's critical analysis entitled, "Freud, the Serpent and the Sexual Enlightenment of Children" explores Freud's work with infantile sexual research up until 1911, which centered on a child's apparent "disposition for truth." Burston states that at this point in Freud's work he, "Implied that the child's rebellion against paternal authority has a *rational* basis…and that the child rebels because the adult is deceptive and bent on withholding knowledge" (Burston 2). This sheds an altogether different perspective on Adam and Eve's (but mostly Eve's) desire for "truth" and "knowledge" in Eden. Freud might say that Eve's incentive was a pathogenic one, and the whole Edenic scene was simply a child's "predilection for naughty ideas and the adults' desire to suppress them" (Burston 2).

Burston believes that by using Freud's theorizing as a backdrop, we might see "The Fall" as "the story of two 'innocents' seeking knowledge in the face of a superior power bent on withholding it, and the dire repercussions of their rebellion against Him" (Burston 4). In addition, Burston points out that the word that has traditionally been translated as "knowledge" — the Hebrew word *da'at* — actually signifies powers of judgment and discrimination, maturity and wisdom, and also is used throughout the Old Testament to refer to the act of coitus (Burston 5). So when it comes to a psychoanalytic perspective of "The Fall," Burston, Freud, and Fromm alike might view this predilection for physical, spiritual, and sexual "wisdom" as merely natural. We might even tread a bit further, and view the Creator as a "punitive, irrational authority" figure that sets the stage for future psychosis stemming from the Creator's infanticilization of Adam and Eve. A psychoanalytic reading views the serpent as "an emancipator" because it is he who promotes the "truth" by way of urging Adam and Eve to embrace knowledge (sexual and otherwise) instead of denying it.

A more anticipated critique of "The Fall" would come from the feminist point of view, in an attempt to unhinge the Western, Christian tendency to blame woman for The Fall of all mankind. A very early, intriguing critique comes from Elizabeth Cady Stanton's publication of *The Woman's Bible* in 1895. She sees the original story as an allegory, but one in which she views Eve as "the heroine of a historical occurrence" (Stanton 24). Stanton notes that, "The reader must be impressed with the courage, dignity, and the lofty ambition of the woman" for seeking that which was forbidden. She goes on the say that the snake, as tempter, "evidently had a profound knowledge of human nature, and saw at a glance the high character of person he met by chance in his walks in the garden...and that he roused in the woman that intense thirst for knowledge that the simple pleasures of picking flowers and talking with Adam did not satisfy" (Stanton 25). Stanton, like the psychoanalysists, believes that the Creator's punishment is unduly harsh, and says, "The curse pronounced on woman is inserted in an unfriendly spirit to justify her degradation and subjugation to man" (Stanton 25).

Sharing this view of the woman as hero is reader-response critic, Harold Bloom, in his text, the *Book of J*. Bloom takes the stance that may be gaining credibility within the academic world, that the Yahwist writer — the J source — was female. Viewed in this new light, the story has fresh and profound implications that traverse beyond any traditional reading of the text. Bloom probes the authorial intent of "The Fall," and insists that J's story, originally meant to be humorous and child-oriented, has been "transmuted to one of lust and sin" (Bloom 181). He says that, "Lust is an obsession of dualists, who see soul and body as caught in a wrestling match" (Bloom 181), but that J is the most monistic of all early Western authors, and that for her, there is no "split between body and soul, between nature and mind," and between good and evil. J's characters, instead, are supposed to speak volumes of the "theomorphic or divine elements in women and men" (Bloom 182).

Bloom also points out that J never mentions a "fall" from a higher to a lower being; instead, she merely portrays Eve "as the active child, the more curious or imaginative, while Adam's role is that of the child who imitates" (Bloom 183). He also perceives Yahweh as a bungler for placing the alluring tree in the Garden in the first place. He says that, "Nothing could be more incommensurate than Yahweh's punishments and the childish offenses that provoked them, but such incommensurateness is the center of J's vision" (Bloom 184). Bloom argues that a close textual reading proves that J "is not writing a moral tale but a children's story that ends unhappily. This is how things got to be the way things are, she is saying, and the way they are is not good, whether for snakes, women, or men" (Bloom 186).

Bloom himself is of the Gnostic faith, and we can look to the author Elaine Pagels, author of *Adam, Eve and the Serpent,* for a more lucid picture of how this ancient sect of Christianity interpreted the story of "The Fall." Gnostics, possibly mimicking the intent of Eve, "Yearned to become spiritually 'mature,' to go beyond…elementary instruction toward higher levels of understanding" (Pagels 59). The term *gnosis* literally means "knowledge," or "insight." Gnostic Christians chastised the orthodoxy for reading Genesis literally, for they believed that in doing so, the "deeper meaning" was overlooked. Today, they view the story of "The Fall" as a "spiritual allegory," or as "myth with meaning" (Pagels 64).

Pagels tells us that Gnostic interpreters share the conviction that, "The divine being is hidden deep within human nature, as well as outside it, and, although often unperceived, is a spiritual potential latent in the human psyche" (Pagels 65). Therefore, "The story of Adam and Eve shows that humanity 'fell' into ordinary consciousness and lost contact with its divine origin" (Pagels 65). Other Gnostic texts depict Adam as representing the psyche, while Eve represents the higher principle, the spiritual self. The knowledge gained in "The Fall" acted to separate these two entities, and so the spiritual quest entails a reintegration of the two.

Merlin Stone, another pivotal early feminist author holds less of a metaphoric stance on this myth and more of an archeo-historical one. Stone has written that "The Fall" was written by the Levites with the explicit intent of vilifying and suppressing the early female religion (Stone 198). The religion that Stone is referring to is the spiritual beliefs of the ancient Earth-based, Goddess-worshipping peoples. Stone says that "Symbols such as serpents, sacred fruit trees, and sexually-tempting women who took advice from serpents may once have been understood by people of biblical times to symbolize the then familiar presence of the female deity" (Stone 198). It is a concept that echoes the often-quoted saying: "The Gods of one religion always become the demons of the next." In this particular context, the female religions are first demonized and then usurped by the later arrivals — the patriarchal religions.

To see the Adam and Eve myth more vividly in Stone's particular light, we can re-examine the symbolic value associated with one of the myth's characters, the serpent. Not only were many of the early Goddesses viewed either as a serpent, part serpent, or with a serpent consort, in traditions of both East and West, there are numerous beliefs equating the serpent with prophetic wisdom and oracular knowledge. We most readily see this paradigm reflected in the Greek Medusa story, although the Greek version was drawing from several earlier sources. The snakes that arose from the depths of Medusa's mind (or quite literally, that sprouted from her head) are symbolic of women's wisdom that can be detrimental to men — one gaze in her knowing eyes and men are instantly turned to stone. The snakes whisper visions of the future into her ear (similar to the scene in The Fall) and then, through her knowing eyes, man witnesses his own foreseen death. Consequently, the word *Medusa* literally means "sovereign female wisdom" (Le Vann).

With Merlin Stone's insights we might see that in the Adam and Eve story the serpent plays the exact same double role that it did for millennia prior to its biblical character. First, the serpent acts as the embodiment of the sacred feminine; and second, as the embodiment of profound inner knowledge. Stone's thesis lucidly revolves around the fact that with the onset of patriarchy, both the sacred feminine *and* women's wisdom become scorned, and the epitome of this unfortunate event is evidenced in the writing of "The Fall." Viewed through Stone's perspective, we might see that the "wisdom" that comes to be demonized is not only the knowledge of good and evil, but the knowledge that *female* deities procured and proliferated before the solely male pantheons were constructed.

Ultimately, "The Fall" is the biblical passage that, traditionally, relays the story of Adam and Eve's temptation and consequential "Fall" in the Garden of Eden. It is the story of that reverential tree, the enigmatic snake, and the punishing Creator. However, by putting a critical eye and intuitive heart to non-theological interpretations of the text, we can see that the variations of depth are boundless. In conclusion to this particular literary analysis, I feel that the influx of more diverse peoples into the scholarly realm has undoubtedly allowed for a redeeming, multi-colored light to be shed on this once narrowly interpreted biblical story. One of the most amazing attributes of this text is that even after the hundreds of published interpretations and critiques, in addition to the billions of interpretations that accrue in the hearts and minds of the populace, there are — in these short twenty-four verses — endless exegetic opportunities.

Bibliography

Bloom, Harold. *The Book of J.* New York: Grove Weidenfeld, 1990.

Braud, William and Rosemarie Anderson. *Transpersonal Research Methods for theSocial Sciences: Honoring Human Experience.* Thousand Oaks: Sage Publications, 1998.

Burston, Daniel. "Freud, the Serpent, and the Sexual Enlightenment of Children." *International Forum of Psychoanalysis*, 1994 vol. 3, Psychotherapy Colloquia. 14 April 2004. <http://laingsociety. org/colloquia/psychotherapy/serpent1.htm>.

Frazer, Sir James G. *Folklore in the Old Testament.* New York: Avenel Books, 1988.

Gabel, John, Charles Wheeler, and Anthony York. *The Bible as Literature.* New York: Oxford University Press, 1000.

Le Van, Alicia. "The Gorgon Medusa." 7 May 1996 Final Paper for Women in Antiquities Class. 20 Mar 2005. <http://www. perseus.tufts.edu/classes/finALp.html>.

Myers, Peter. "Derivation of the Adam and Eve Story from the *Epic of Gilgamesh*." 10 April 2004 <http://users.cyberone.com.au/ myers/adam-and-eve.html>.

Pagels, Elaine. *Adam, Eve and the Serpent.* New York: Random House, 1988.

Phillips, John A. *Eve.* San Francisco: Harper and Row, 1984.

"Prometheus, Pandora, and the Five Ages." Grand Valley State University Faculty Page. 1 April 2005. <http://faculty.gvsu.edu/ websterm/Prometheus.html>.

Stanton, Elizabeth Cady. *The Woman's Bible.* Boston: Northeastern University Press, 1993.

Stone, Merlin. *When God was a Woman.* San Diego: Harvest/HBJ, 1976.

Thackara, W.T.S. "The Epic of Gilgamesh: A Spiritual Biography."

Theosophy Northwest. 14 April 2004. <http://www.theosophy-nw.org/theosnw/world/mideast/mi-wtst.htm>.

Soul and Soullessness

Jan I. Marijaq

Introduction

Who has a soul? Just "mankind"? Just living beings? Is it possible to be alive and not have a soul? These are questions that several of Sheri S. Tepper's science fiction books have stimulated me to ask; specifically—what is a soul? What has a soul? Can an entity be soulless and, if so, how do you recognize a soulless being? If soullessness can be caused, what causes it? And finally, what can be done about it?

Tepper published twenty-nine science fiction books in 20 years and worked with Planned Parenthood for the Rocky Mountain region for 25 years (1962-1986). Her books question policy and culture around reproductive rights, the position of women in this country and in the world, and the influence of organized religion on women and reproductive rights. Tepper addresses the question of the soul, of soullessness, and of responsibility for soullessness in seven of those books.

What Is a Soul?

Since you cannot see or hold a "soul," you must look for evidence of what it might be. Tepper variously defines it in her novels as self-awareness—the ability to see oneself as doing something and observing the doing, the learning of language coupled with the gift of human society which we receive from our fellow humans, or the perception of one's own humanity and the perception that others have the same humanity.[110] This quality that all things must have to live together, Tepper calls "bao."[111]

Therefore, obtaining a soul is not inherent to being born a human being; it is something one develops into. *Human being* in this context indicates the ability to become ensouled, rather than denoting a particular

169

shape or species.

The world's major religions define the soul in various ways. Although Siddhartha Gotama, or Gautama Buddha, refused to affirm the existence or non-existence of a soul, Buddhist and Hindu traditions contain the concept of the soul.[112] It is defined as the second of three great states of being, which are gross (matter and body), subtle (mind and soul), and causal (spirit). As the second state, the human mind includes bodily emotions along with reason and logic; the soul adds the use of archetypes and vision.[113]

Islam and Sufism (mystical Islam) also support a triune model. The Qur'an is quoted as supporting three developmental stages for the human soul: (1) *Ammarah* (12:53), which is prone to evil and needs to be checked, implying external controls; (2) *Lawwamah* (75:2), which feels conscious of evil, and resists it, implying internal controls; and (3) *Mutma'innah* (89:27), when the soul reaches what might be called enlightenment.[114] Isaac of Nineveh, an early Christian of the Nestorian Church in seventh-century Iraq, apparently shared with the Sufis a three-fold model as well: (1) the body; (2) the lower soul (known in Sufism as the *nafs*, the 'self'); and (3) the higher soul or spirit (known in Sufism as the *ruh*).[115]

Christianity holds that the soul is a simple immaterial or spiritual substance. The soul begins in time but doesn't die; man is a union of soul and body, and only the soul survives death.[116] The Mormons, a sect of Christianity, contend that a soul pre-exists the body as a spirit, is a mortal soul when united with a body, returns to the condition of spirit when the body dies, and exists as an immortal soul when rejoined with the resurrected body.[117]

Judaism sees the soul as primarily a personal will, a collocation of desires or wants, which is temporal and dies with the body.[118] It is this soul that the God of the Covenant dominates.[119]

Finally, the Jain tradition defines a soul as an inherently conscious, independent agent, existing either as freed (state of perfection), or bound (on its way to perfection). In the bound or embodied state, the soul apprehends itself and other things by way of 1-5 senses, which also define what has a soul.[120]

To summarize, Buddhism, Hinduism, Islam and Sufism, as well as parts of the early Christian Church, recognize the soul as some type of life force which goes through a maturation process of three stages, although they do not agree as to whether this maturation process occurs across one physical embodiment or many. One might include the Jains in this grouping as well, even though they do not include a limitation of three stages. Christianity and Judaism seem to place less attention on whether the soul, or life force, can change—leaving a sense of pre-determinism.

What Has a Soul?

Since the word "who" is prejudiced towards mankind in English and other languages, I use the term "what" to explore the question of beings with souls. Tepper does not limit the concept of ensouled beings to mankind. In *Jinian Star-Eye*, she presents the possibility that "soul" or "bao" is something some creatures have and others do not, and that no race of creatures always has it in every individual and that no shape guarantees it. Just because something shares our shape or our seed does not guarantee that that entity has a soul.[121] As she says in *Flight of Mavin Manyshaped*. "No man gets a man's soul by birth alone. That which behaves like a Wolf is a Wolf, not matter who bore him."[122]

The Jain tradition asserts that everything that has some form of body has a soul. In a body, the soul perceives itself and other things by way of the senses. The number of senses used does not seem to denote a hierarchical value. Mankind normally uses five senses—touch, taste, smell, hearing, and seeing, as do cows, elephants, monkeys, birds, frogs, and so on. Some animals have only four senses, since mosquitoes and similar entities don't seem to have sight. Some have only three senses, with ants, lice, and certain insects lacking hearing. Some have only two, since worms and snails supposedly cannot smell. Beings with only the sense of touch, such as vegetables, are considered to have souls as well.[123]

No other religion is so inclusive. Although both Hindu and Buddhist traditions include the concept of Karma, which supports the belief that a soul can reincarnate into whatever form is necessary for learning, Ken Wilber's second state of being—mind and soul—seems limited to humanity, because plants and animals other than man have neither reason nor logic.[124] Islam, Christianity, and Judaism seem to limit the concept of soul to mankind as well.

Can an Entity Be Soulless? How Would You Know?

Only Tepper directly addresses the question of soullessness and how one would identify a soulless being. She suggests three categories: the profoundly retarded, which are incapable of self-awareness; those beings born with profound physical malformations; and those beings who indicate by their repeated actions and behavior that they are soulless.

"In the Sanctuary of St. Phallus are the brain-dead seed of St. Phallus which the Sister Servants tend."[125] This is how Tepper describes what is obviously a ward of profoundly retarded individuals, found and tended and kept in life by extraordinary means. These are individuals with the general shape of human beings, but not the ability to be human beings, to become ensouled. Her character Jinian questions why they are being kept alive, and then releases them: "Then, because I felt great sorrow for the Sister Servants and pity for the flesh they tended, which mercy would not have kept alive, I did Inward Is Quiet upon all the mindless creatures that lay in the beds in those buildings below. . . . They would not need to be cleaned or fed again."[126]

Tepper presents the possibility that those who are born hideously misshapen will not attain a soul:

While it is true that monstrous things are sometimes born, it takes something more monstrous, evil, and prideful yet to keep them alive. . . . One could not exist in those shapes without becoming compressed, warped, envenomed. There was pain intrinsic to the shape, and I began to think what it would be like to live with that pain forever.[127]

These beings may have normal intelligence but, again, they do not have the ability to develop into beings with souls.

Persons who show by their actions that they have no soul are mentioned in several books. The characters Tepper describes sound like psychopaths or sociopaths: "Some who look like men can never believe that others are like themselves. They do not believe that others are real."[128] The soulless can have good camouflage, can be well-mannered—up to a point. Again: "I tried to remember any good thing Huld might have done. . . . And after a time, I answered my own question. He was not true man at all. He was only aberration, beast, hate and hunger, without a soul."[129] Tepper clarifies a definition of soullessness in *Six Moon Dance*: "Madame had explained psychotic sadism to her students. . . . Madame had said some people were made that way, and they did it out of vengeance, and some were born that way, and they did it because hurting and killing made them feel powerful. Either way, there was no cure for it."[130] Not all soulless are members of the species mankind, but they share the same characteristics.

Again, none of the religions cited address the question of soullessness, although one could extrapolate such a condition in Christianity when a soul is *cut off from God*. It is in the field of psychology that one can identify the condition. The Mental Health Act of 1959 in the United

Kingdom defined psychopathology as a "persistent disorder or disability of mind (whether or not including subnormality of intelligence) which results in abnormally aggressive or seriously irresponsible conduct on the part of the patient."[131] The term *psychopathology* has a range of severity attached to it, from young adult males who "appear unable to conform to the rules of society, have difficulty tolerating minor frustrations, do not form stable human relationships, do not learn from past experiences, however unpleasant they might have been" to persons who have committed multiple, vicious, meaningless murders and shown no remorse.[132]

What Causes Soullessness or Psychopathology?

What causes psychopathology is unclear and theories are varied: brain damage in childhood, late maturation of the central nervous system, and adverse circumstances of upbringing, particularly difficult relationships with parents and those in authority, are some of the causes proposed.[133] Tepper presents several possibilities for consideration that fall roughly into four main categories:

•Regarding sperm as sacred, but not the life the sperm helps create.

•Valuing the rights of the criminal above the rights of the victim: a justice system based on rules rather than a rule system based on justice.

•Focusing on the creation and nurturance of the growth of money rather than the growth of the next and future generations.

•Preaching religious doctrines that teach this life is not important except to "earn" the next life.

As one can imagine, Tepper may be presumed to have strong convictions around preventing and terminating pregnancies that would result in seriously defective fetuses, or babies who would be born into situations where they would not have the slightest chance of achieving their potential—of gaining a soul. As evidenced by the vociferous campaigns by fundamentalist Christians in the United States against Planned Parenthood clinics, where some people feel that killing living human beings is justified to protect "sacred sperm"; when the Qur'an puts forth the Divine claim: "Does not man see that it is We Who created him from sperm?" (36:77-79);[134] when fundamentalist Islam and the Roman Catholic Church make common cause and support each other at population conferences and at status-of-women conferences[135]—Tepper may have a substantive basis for an accusation of "sacred sperm."

Sacred Sperm

How do you recognize a society that regards sperm as "sacred"? The members of the Decline and Fall Club (DFC) present their understandings:

•Little or no health care for pregnant women: The American health system, except for that which wealthy women are able to access, can be considered barbaric: "Barbaric systems are interested only in babies; they don't care if the woman is dying or drug addicted or alcoholic or if she's twelve years old or retarded or has AIDS. They will not make it easy for her to prevent a pregnancy or to abort one." The DFC becomes even more explicit: "At the present time, under the current administration, we actually have two systems in this country – an advanced one for well-to-do and well-educated people, and a barbaric one rather like Communist Romania for the poor."[136]

•Little or no financial, emotional, or social support for women and children after birth: "You can see the same thing in Latin America, where contraception is forbidden by the Church and hundreds of thousands of children are simply abandoned on the streets. . . . There are killer squads in those countries, armed men who go out at night and shoot kids. I've talked to some of them. They feel they are public-health workers, eliminating a menace, just as they'd shoot rats."[137]

•No training in parenting: Motherhood is "instinctive among animals who have young in bunches, like alligators, pigs, dogs, fish. It's instinctive among animals that don't live very long, like mice, rabbits, spiders. It's instinctive among animals with precocial

young, like an antelope or a chicken. It isn't instinctive for animals that live a long time and have helpless babies, one at a time." Since humans qualify as non-instinctive parents, they need training. Since most individuals who lack formal training in a subject learn from the examples they experience, most humans learn how to parent from their childhood experiences: "She was not mothered as a child. Her own mother acquiesced in her sexual abuse; her mother's boyfriend gave her a venereal disease."[138] As a contrast: "Lily the chimp probably has better sense, but then Lily's mother raised her carefully."[139]

•Little or no training in responsible sex for boys and girls. Since the United States can be seen to have a "barbaric" health care system, what does an advanced one look like? Holland and the Scandinavian countries are classified as advanced: "There is routine provision of pre- and postnatal care, childbirth education, parenting education, and monitoring of the infant for several years following birth. Needless to say, there is also provision of food for children, so none of them go hungry. Holland and Scandinavian countries have systems like this. They have almost no teen pregnancies or drug-addicted babies, and no hungry children."[140]

•No protection against forced sex: "Men have no experience of childbirth or pregnancy; few of them have experienced rape, but they believe their seed is somehow so important that women must not only submit to it but also honor and serve it impeccably. Men make laws saying so."[141]

Criminal versus Victim Rights

How do you recognize a society that respects the rights of the criminal over the rights of the victim? Everyone reading this chapter probably has memory of some case where there was no doubt as to the guilt of the murderer, yet the person was sent to prison or actually was set free— justice by rule, not rule by justice. Gregory cites circumstances in which the rights of the victim are totally ignored: "In some cases of homicide, the verdict has been reduced from murder to man-slaughter on the basis of diminished responsibility as defined in the Homicide Act of 1959."[142]

Mavin is clear on the point in *Flight of Mavin Manyshaped*. When faced with a situation where a murderer has repeated killed, yet been set free:

"Why did you not simply kill him the first time? You had proof then." "Because he is—was human." "What does it mean, humanity?" "It means," said the official with some asperity, "that he was born in the ordinary way and therefore had a soul. We cannot subject someone with a soul to cruel or horrible punishment." "Ah," said Mavin, cocking her head in a way she knew to be particularly infuriating. "And the young women and children he killed? Did they also have souls?"[143]

Money Valued Over People

How do you recognize a society that focuses on creating and nurturing the growth of money rather than the growth of the next generation? Consider the comparison between an advanced health care system and one labeled "barbaric." Or compare the salaries of school teachers and qualified childcare providers to those of CEOs of technology corporations, or even to the salaries of engineers. If the economy goes into a slump, what gets cut first—tax benefits to corporations or social services? And what about the profit margins of "health insurance" companies compared to the health of the general population? How do you compare the untaxed "perks" of corporate officers to slashing school lunch programs which provide the only meal which some school children receive each day?

Focus on the Next Life

And finally, but certainly not unimportantly, one must consider religious doctrines that focus attention on the next life, instead of on responsibility for this life. In Islam, the next life is the attainment of Mutma'innah; in Christianity, it is Heaven; in Buddhism and Hinduism, it is Nirvana, getting off the wheel, ceasing to struggle. Tepper addresses the question of mercy and evil and the next life through the characters in *Grass*:

> "Can you afford to be merciful if it gets you killed? Is a murderer's life more important than your own?" "Mercy is a tenet of our faith." "Only because you don't think this life really matters, Father. God says it does." "I mean *you*, what you priests usually say. *I* say this life matters, and that means mercy is doing the best for them I can without allowing anyone else to suffer, including me!"[144]

We are taught, in various faiths, to forgive those who wrong us, who harm us. Why? "Oh, I would have forgiven them before," she admitted. "Oh, yes. I'd have let them go. I'd have been afraid not to. For fear society or God would have judged me harshly. I'd have said pain in this life isn't that important. A few more murders. A few more rapes. In heaven they won't matter."[145]

Those who have studied history and religion have seen how gaining merit for the next life has justified evil acts in this life—the Crusades in the Middle Ages, the expansion of Islamic conversion by conquest, Catholic against Protestant in Northern Ireland, Jew against Palestinian, Hindu against Muslim—the list is extensive, all justifying murder, violence, rape, in the name of religion and to earn the next life. It leads one to question how one can tell the difference between a religious fanatic, a psychopath, a soulless one.

What Can Be Done About Soullessness?

First, one must question who is responsible for the soulless. Jinian, in *Jinian Star-eye*, does not quibble on this point, either: "Each of us must take responsibility for our own. No one else can do it for us, for that way lies the death of all that is good."[146] Whatever the species, the responsibility lies with those who let the soulless continue to exist: "I know your love for that which you gave life. But bao demands that this creature die, Ganver, and I may not take your bao. This is your duty. *This is your own child!*"[147]

Then one must question whether it is right or just to allow those who cannot gain a soul—the profoundly retarded, the profoundly physically distorted—to be conceived, or to be allowed to survive birth. In the past, the severely disabled have died in utero or soon after birth. Mal-formed babies were exposed at birth. Now, extraordinary means prolong their life. Tepper proposes the concept of the Midwife:

> "The Midwives take an oath, very solemn and binding, that they will look into the future of each child born, and if they do not see that one gaining a soul, then they do not let it live. It is the Talent of the Midwives to see the future in that way, more narrowly than do Seers, and more reliably. It is called the Mercy-gift, the gift the Midwife gives the child, to look into the future and find there that it will have gained a soul."[148]

And what of those repeatedly harm and kill others and show no remorse? Is capital punishment an evil is this circumstance? Peter in the shape of a huge being called a grole, contemplates the concept of soullessness and capital punishment:

> "You must believe me when I tell you that I shut the grole maw upon them and merely held them there in that rock hard prison of myself while I thought long about justice and goodness. . . . I tried to remember any good thing Huld might have done. . . . If the Midwives had delivered him, he would not have lived past his birth. As it was, he did not deserve to live further. So. Then the grole bore down and gained out of him what good there was in him."[149]

There is also the concept of the punishment fitting the crime so that learning might take place. In the case of the town that chose to foster the wolf in man-form who preyed upon the women and children of the town, Mavin steals away all the children, taking them to be where they will be safe and nurtured. When she had taken all the children, including the newest baby, she enticed the inhabitants of the town out onto the beach, then burned the town behind them, leaving them weeping. "I have judged you all and found you guilty of foolishness, and this is the punishment, that you shall walk shelterless and childless until you learn better sense.[150]"

Summary

Tepper poses some very difficult questions with her theme of soul and soullessness.

Should those who are at risk of producing a damaged fetus—the very young, addicts, the retarded, AIDS victims or carriers, should these males and females be allowed to be unprotected against conception if they are sexually active? Should babies be born into circumstances where there is no provision for their growth and nurturance? What about those who hurt and kill without remorse—is it merciful to allow someone to continue to prey on others? And what about the rights of those who are being preyed upon? Do they not also deserve protection?

As we live through the opening years of a new millennium, we need to question whether we will perpetuate the evils of times that have gone before. Will greed, "sacred sperm," a lack of humanity, continue to determine how we live in this world? Or will we thoughtfully read what Tepper puts forth, and make other choices? These are questions I hope the reader will consider, and then put energy into creating change.

Notes

1 Tepper, Sheri S., Necromancer Nine, NY: Ace, 1983, pp. 108-9.

2 Tepper, Sheri S., Jinian Star-eye, NY: Ace, 1986, p. 250.

3 Bahm, Archie J., The World's Living Religions, Berkeley, CA: Asian Humanities Press, 1992, p. 103.

4 Wilber, Ken, The Marriage of Sense and Soul: Integrating Science and Religion, NY: Broadway Books, 1998, pp. 8-9.

5 'Ali, 'Abdullah Yusuf, The Meaning of the Holy Qur'an, new edition with revised translation and commentary, Brentwood, MD: Amana Corp, 1991, 1565:5810.

6 Baldick, Julian, Mystical Islam: an Introduction to Sufism, NY: New York University Press, 1989, pp. 17-8.

7 Bahm, op. cit., p. 282.

8 McConkie, Bruce R., Mormon Doctrine, 2nd edition, Salt Lake City, UT: Bookcraft, 1966, pp. 748-9.

9 Baum, op. cit., p. 279-80.

10 Plaskow, Judith, Standing Again at Sinai: Judaism from a Feminist Perspective, San Francisco, CA: HarperSanFrancisco, 1991, p. 129.

11 Baum, op. cit., 87-8.

12 Tepper, Jinian, op. cit., p. 250.

13 Tepper, Sheri S., Flight of Mavin Manyshaped, NY: Ace, 1985, pp. 52-61.

14 Baum, op. cit., pp. 87-8.

15 Wilber, op. cit., pp 8-9.

16 Tepper, Jinian, p. 89.

17 Ibid., p. 90.

18 Tepper, Necromancer, p. 110.

19 Ibid., pp. 108-9.

20 Tepper, Sheri S., Wizard's Eleven, NY: Ace, 1984, pp. 175-6.

21 Tepper, Sheri S., Six Moon Dance, NY: Avon, 1998, pp. 261-2.

22 Gregory, Richard L., ed., The Oxford Companion to the Mind, NY: Oxford University Press, 1998, pp. 651-3.

23 Ibid.

24 Ibid., p. 653.

25 Haneef, Suzanne, What Everyone Should Know About Islam and Muslims, Des Plaines, IL: Library of Islam, 1985, p. 34.

26 Tepper, Sheri S., Gibbon's Decline and Fall, NY: Bantam, 1996, p. 95.

27 Ibid., pp. 342-4.

28 Ibid.

29 Ibid., pp. 345-6.

30 Ibid., p. 332.

31 Ibid., pp. 342-4.

32 Ibid., pp. 354-5.

33 Gregory, op. cit., pp. 651-3.

34 Tepper, Flight, op. cit.

35 Tepper, Sheri S., Grass, NY: Bantam, 1989, pp. 358-9.

36 Ibid., p. 367.

37 Tepper, Jinian, p. 250.

38 Ibid., p. 238.

39 Tepper, Necromancer, pp. 108-9.

40 Tepper, Wizard's, op. cit.

41 Tepper, Flight, op. cit.

The Trinity of the Hebrew Goddess

A Guided Presentation Of
Goddess Narratives and Submerged Beliefs

Jayne Marie DeMente, M.A.

Introduction to the Trinity of the Hebrew Goddess

I have been fortunate in my quest to be *led* to certain spiritual understandings, based on concrete information as well as magical or spiritual insights. Some may call these *insights* psychic "breaks" or psychologically explainable. For many years, I have attempted to understand their meaning and in attempting to do so, I have come to understand that they both mean the same. Experiences of *insight* are all metaphors for understanding the longing of the soul to have liberation and peace. My insights led me to understand a part of the feminine human spiritual story that was left out of my education.

I do not find it heretical to muse about feminine deities and the controversies within their traditions. I have spent time with the following three Goddesses and they have guided me to the narratives that follow. Hopefully, through the stories of women's deities, we may be able to create true gender and cultural *partnership* by having a partnership between spiritual *parents* and not just the male aspect of God. From out of a partnership of ancient values a new mythology may lead us to save our planet and ourselves. *The Trinity of the Hebrew Goddess* is my contribution to this process in the following narratives about Asherah, Lilith and Mary.

181

Part I

ASHERAH
Goddess of the Cosmic Tree

The Lord by "Wisdom" (she) founded the Earth, by
"understanding" (Being) established the Heavens. [1]   *And*
with thee is Wisdom, who is familiar with thy works and
was present at the making of the world ... for she knows and
understands all things. [2] *She shall be the tree of life to all that*
lay hold on her. [3] *Wisdom is/was as who kept guard over the*
first ... of the human race ... [4] *She was called the "Queen of*
Heaven". [5] *Wisdom is radiant and unfading and she is easily*
discerned by those who love her, and is found by those who
seek her ... and she graciously appears to them in their paths
and meets
them in every thought. [6]

Who am I? I was called by Being to create the Universe. I was the word (Logos) before there was form and known as "Wisdom". [7] I spread my wings and caused the waters to form and my allurement became gravity and air. [8] I am Asherah, Queen of Heaven [9] known along the trade routes of Libya, Mesopotamia, Syria, Persia, Arabia and Crete. [10] I was called Ashtoreh, Astarte, Artemis, Innin, Inanna, Mama, Mit, Anat, Anahita, Ishtar, Isis, Au Set, Ishara, Attoret, Attar and Hathor – the many-named Ancestress. [11] Although I was there from the beginning, the following account is the "recollection" story of the time I spent with the Hebrews. I was recorded in their books of the Torah: I am recorded in the Wisdom books, Genesis, Exodus, Kings, Job, Jeremiah, Deuteronomy, Enoch and the book of Proverbs in their bible.

I was worshiped in the temple of Solomon for 236 years. I had 400 Priestesses and 400 Prophets knew my name. [12] I am known by the symbol of a tree - "the tree of life". After the Creation, I stayed among the people of Libya giving them all that they needed to know to thrive and be joyous. I then went back to "Being" to reflect upon creation. [13] Feeling their grief at my loss, I gave them a metaphor to reflect upon – the "cosmic tree". [14] It holds all wisdom. It is rooted in the Earth but stretches its branches to Heaven. Many replicas are made of my people stretching their arms like a tree to the sun. [15] I gave the metaphor of the tree because of its interconnectedness with air, soil and water. The analogy between wisdom and the tree was simple. [16] I did not request or require worship therefore, any worship of me was simple and joyous and usually met with water, oil, bread or song. [17] Followers went to the grotto's or groves or to find bushes to pay homage to me. After the elders demoted me and changed my story in their book of Genesis, [18] what is left of that symbol is known as the nine branched "Menorah". This symbol is now presided over by women in their homes. [19]

I was there in the beginning and I moved with the dark searchers during the great migrations. I was eventually connected to the trade harbors and many Goddesses attributed to this phase were considered my servants. [20] I am also known throughout the greater world as Hochma, Cardea, Hecate, Yemeya, The Tao, Tara, Bridget, Changing Woman, Kali, Mary and more, but we are all one. From as far as Iran and the Persian Gulf, to Arabia and the Red Sea, through Turkey and the Mediterranean Sea of Asia Minor, the advance of agriculture and trade moved along my seaways. [21] These waterways were crucial to the spread of Neolithic ideals. [22]

The qualities attributed to me were that I was free in love, fruitful in followers and a leader in peace and defense. The Israelites (Hebrews) in Egypt knew me as Isis and Hathor. The Israelites were composed of Egyptians, Canaanites and Semitic nomads (also known as the Cushites [23]) who joined together the ideals of the Goddess. The Goddess of these people exemplified "the infinite power and patterns of nature expressed through plant, animal and human life." … They described me as "Goddess as the lawgiver, who insured a high standard of moral conduct among her followers. She condemned lying, the breaking of promises and lack of proper respect for sacred things and for people." [24]

It was I who resided in the *Tent of Meetings* and nurtured the Hebrews in the desert. The oracles in their midst continued to call for me as Shekhinah. [25] After centuries of being enslaved in Egypt and forty years of wait in the desert, the Hebrews invaded Canaan. When the land was secured, the "sky god" is credited for the use of my ideals to set up a "Haven of Peace". [26]   It was during this time that division was solidified between Hebrew men and women. Yahweh was given credit as the establishment of order and rule in the Universe! Previously, females held this status and were earthly as well as cosmic deities. Giving men this power gave the creative power of the Goddess to the state and it was then used to legitimize the king's rule. [27] The male religions then became the domain of the male cults. By the blood act of circumcision, creation was taken away from the blood rites of the Goddess and women were excluded from participation in the covenant. [28] The men changed my story by reversing the deities of the stories and attributing males my values and symbols. [29] The Hebrews attacked not Baal but Asherah as the target of their aggravations when they began to accept Yahweh as the one, true force of nature. Judea fell not because I brought bad luck but because the people neglected my rituals and Goddess worship had been forbidden. [30] The Emissary that came among the early humans suggested that our religion was a cult which co notated that we were less fine or civilized than his "religion". The followers of the Emissary, "the sons of Seth", began to look at the Priestess and her followers with different eyes. The garden story in Genesis became a watered down version of the story of where I first emerged in Libya. My attributes were divided into two trees, life and knowledge. Eve became the originator of sin. My lovely snake consort became the seducer of women and men and then the awareness of nakedness turned you away from the joy of sexual love and pleasures. [31] This is the joy that created you in the first place. This new story separated us, my "divine force is not distant or separate; the relationship is immediate and intimate". [32]

The Goddess religion was never monotheistic or dualistic - but pluralistic and represented by the trinity before it became part of the Hebrew male cult. It is the first trinity and known as the sacred triangle, or yoni. [33] This triangle represented various aspects of woman and the triangle of her vagina. The triangle is often referred to as maiden, mother and crone: innocent; then creator and nurturer; and then wise and magical and all are one and the same. Those of you seeking understanding of gender and cultural partnership, may find the answer to the question of partnership within the double triangle. These stars are the fully realized female and male narratives becoming parents to this planet. The symbol of partnership is the intertwining of two triangles into a six-pointed star – two triangles enmeshed together.

This male sky God, claimed what was not his to own. I was known not just as the eternal "Earth Mother" but also as the "Queen of Heaven". Therefore, I also held the distinction of the spirit of the sky. The worship of the Goddess was a geographically vast and major religion that affected multitudes of people over thousands of years until the fall of Crete. [34] It was totally integrated into the patterns of laws and society that translated into the later religions of the same regions and is held in your genetic memory awaiting cakes for the Queen of Heaven. [35] Remember me in your rituals and when lighting candles, especially when lighting Asherah's tree – my menorah tree.

PART II

LILITH
The Dark Twin

We share a god whom I do not share.
We touch anyway. "Shekhinah" in our bones.
You don't expect me to know the poems - Hebrew traces on
the face of the sea.
I have l earned these myths, I tore off my star of David,
Whispered: Come to me Lilith,
Waiting for a lover in exile, kiss of the demons,
Surrendering the weight and breath of heaven.
Israel; the far war, borders of ... Asherah, oranges, sand,
So many hands surround me, Skin as dark as mine, more dust
than night.
Lo ira ra Ki at imadi
(I shall fear no evil for you are with me);
I mouthe these words in semblances of sound. [36]

When Being called for creation our one self was divided. In the ascent our faces were torn from each other making us twins. [37] Forever we would have the quantum dialogue of sisters – twin sisters of opposing forces for the same cause. She was woman before the idea of woman.[38] In Libya [39] she was known as Yemeya – Mother of the Sea. Despite "religious fences" she has a multitude of names, Queen of Sheba, Proserpina, Lil, Lamassu, Partasshah, Rraphi, Anat, Ardad Lili, Avitu, Odam and Kali to mention just some of her names. [40] Her legacy is at the very nature of the secret of the universe. She is chaos. As I was the keeper of the blue print for creation, [41] her menstrual blood created all that you perceive. [42] She is a pulsating, throbbing, primal, wordless state of being. [43] She is found in the Sumerian's cosmological legends, Eleusinian sacred astrology, [44] and Babylonian folktales. The Jewish Kabala, Zohar and the Talmud wrote the most of her story. Assyrian, Canaanite, Persian, Hebrew, and Arabic people and the Teutonic mythology of 3rd Century BCE also know her. [45]

Lilith became known under the heavens of the Gemini Twins. She is known as the Mistress of the Beasts, she rides a lion depicting her power over men and she is worshipped by the giving of food that has protective or healing qualities. [46] Her sculptured image is a part of many wedding dowries. [47] She knows the unspoken name of Being (God). [48] She is usually celebrated at the time of menses and the full moon. [49] She is dark skinned, she has long dark hair, and she is winged and full of persona. She is assigned the sea as am I, but the Hebrews changed the story to that of being created from dust because they wished to remove themselves even further from our origin stories. [50]

Lilith is also assigned the heavens but cannot access Shekhinah, the life force. This is because Lil is chaos and is needed to keep the design of life in place. I hold the "grand concept" in contemplation with Shekhinah but I also, do not reside with her. We are all one but not. [51] Lilith is always the two sides of self and is your reflection. In Babylonia, the male son split "her" waters into two, just as Moses divided the Red Sea and Gilgamesh slashed the tree in the Sumerian folk story. These are not examples of the twin nature of myself, or my sister, but yet "other" examples of males taking power from the Goddess or the passing of Goddess worship into patriarchy. Yet, for females these stories have merit in their psyche by representing the two sides of self coming together. Women, unlike men, do not shoulder a knapsack and sword in heroic challenge. Women, have no choice, they have felt cast out and "forced" into consciousness. [52] It is through knowing Lilith that ancient women became conscious of the inner self. [53] Without this reflection, the pathway to the female psyche, could be blocked and at its worse, one will go mad. It is my sister Lilith who leads women into the light and helps women find their voice – even if the voice is like a screech owl. [54]

Like myself, the Asherah, - Lilith is also known to Hebrew women as the Goddess. Abraham brought with him many stories from Mesopotamia when he settled in Canaan. He brought the myth of Innana (Nin-an-na) and her descent to the home of her sister Erishkigal, Ruler of the Underworld, who resides in the land of the dead. Innana ascends from there three days later. [55] Abraham thus brought a story that the Hebrews assigned to Lilith and eventually to Jesus. Again, in the Hebrew tradition, Lilith is also known to have rejected Adam's request for submission after she created the earth. It is important to note that Lilith is not the opposite of Eve. Eve is the story of the transition into patriarchy and is also a story borrowed from the changed stories of Gilgamesh or the Athena stories. Lilith is the remembrance of the Goddess and the resistance to patriarchy. She was insulted when the story about Eve's puberty became equated with Lil, as the serpent, seducing Eve into knowing her own body and sexual pleasures and the discovery of carnal knowledge. But because Lil left Adam we have the first divorce. [56] This establishes Lil as a woman operating both inside and outside the rules of her culture. As she becomes even more demonized in her stories, she will emerge as the wife of Samael (Satan) and therefore, instead of being the Queen of Heaven she became the Queen of the Realm of the Force of Evil. In an effort to denigrate the Mesopotamian sacred marriage rite, she is also assigned some responsibility for the denigration of sacred prostitution. [57] Paradoxically, in the Zohar my sister attains her most exalted position as "Mistress of God", God's divine counterpart, while Shekhinah travels with the Hebrews into "exile". Shekhinah was called into action to protect the wandering Hebrews, so then Lilith and I become moved about in our positions of power.

Probably the most important story of Lilith is when she came to King Solomon when he requested "Wisdom" from God. According to the Zohar, Book of Splendor:

> God made two lights. The two lights "ascended" together with the same dignity. The moon, however, was not at ease with the sun, and in fact each felt mortified by the other ... God thereupon said to her, 'Go and diminish thyself. She felt humiliated and said "Why should I be as one that veileth herself? God then said 'Go the way forth in the footsteps of the flock'... She was luminous, but as soon as she separated from the sun and was assigned the charge of her own hosts, she reduced her status and her light, and shells upon shells were created for covering the brain ... As this shell expanded it produced another, who was Lilith ... This became a quarrel of love ... it is the desire of Darkness to merge itself with Light, so it is the desire of night to merge itself in day ... 'Luminaries of light and fire' ... King Solomon, when he penetrated into the depths of the shell (of the nut-garden) drew an analogy from its layers to Lilith (and her spirits) ... The Holy one found it necessary to create all these things in the world to ensure its permanence ... The whole world is constructed on this principle, upper and lower, from the beginning ... so that one is a shell to another ... so that on this model man in this world combines brain and shell, spirit and body, all for the better ordering of the world. [58]

The Zohar offers detailed instructions (I 19b-20a) for deepening consciousness and individuation through knowing Lilith and her nature. Hers is also the story of the sacred hierarchy of a circle within a circle for within all opposites lies the same seeds of Lilith. This is the design of the mind, of heaven and of the sacred mysteries. [59]

Lastly, Lilith is also the keeper of secrets. She is the family member, which cannot be banished because she is needed. She regulates the margins of society and her role is distinct and necessary. Without her the family could not function and therefore, society would not function. Just as there are examples of men who return to obedient society, [60] Lilith leads females to know themselves by whichever path that takes them along. [61] Jewish families are instructed about preparing their house for the Sabbath. The house must be made to be lovely, as if receiving the bride "Shekhinah" and also for the "shadow" which is Lilith. "The two female forces are specifically contrasted because 'when one is fulfilled, the other is destroyed'". [62] Remember, the woman in the shadows knows God's secret name! Clearly, she is an integral part of the scene and not destroyed or banished. In the female psyche they are the obedient one and the disobedient one – finding their way to each other.

As her sister, I can say with pride that the important aspects of Lilith's story are those of her independence, strength, boldness, sexuality and courage. She is the flame of the revolving sword mentioned in the book of Genesis (3:24). That image of the flashing, revolving sword captures the essential quality of Lilith – now Goddess, now demon, now temptress, now murderess, now the bride of Satan, now the consort of God, ever flaming at the Gates of Paradise. [63] Understanding Lilith is only the beginning. Lilith will find peace when you know harmony for all people because then the twins will be one again. [64] Lilith created all creatures and her seed is in all that lives. She is present for all life when Wisdom cannot be. She is the joy of sexual pleasure. She understands and leads each child through the veil into adulthood through the act of blood. She brings dark into light and light into darkness. She is allowed to marry with us in the unknowing of darkness. If she is the kidnapper, vampire, alien woman, owl, unclean, temptress, vanity, insanity, demon and child-killer, she is also the consort of God and Satan and the keeper of your story.

PART III

MARY
The Compassionate Cousin
Being remained one, the feminine became two
and then there was the child of action,
Mary our compassionate cousin.
This is the story of Mary, our cousin
She is Mary, the one they call Virgin
She is Mary the one they call Mother.
She is Mary the one they call Harlot. [65]

OUR MOTHER PRAYER
Our Mother, Thou who art in the darkness of the underworld
May the holiness of Thy name shine anew
In our remembering,
May the breath of Thy awakening kingdom
Warm the hearts of all who wander homeless,

May the resurrection of thy will renew eternal faith
Even unto the depths of physical substance.
Receive this day the living memory of Thee,
From human hearts,
Who implore Thee to forgive the sin of forgetting Thee,
And are ready to fight against temptation,
Which has led Thee to existence in darkness,
That through the Deed of the Son,
The immeasurable pain of the Father be stilled,
By the liberation of all beings
From the tragedy of Thy withdrawal.
For Thine is the homeland, and the boundless Wisdom, and the all-merciful
grace,
For all and everything in the circle of All.[66]

Mary is what is left of the Lineage of the Hebrew Goddess and she is known by 100 names and is the feminine heritage for all people:[67] Covenant, Advocate, Blessed, Mother, Joy, Comforter, Immaculate, Reconciler, Grace, Mercy, Light, Annunciation and Assumption to name a few. She showed her spirit to those who asked and defined herself at Guadalupe taking on her predecessor's story of being the Mother of the Sun and Moon. She appeared in Bosnia, Lourdes, Rue de Bec, Pompeii, Fatima, Korea, Cairo, China, India, Spain and in Los Angeles and will continue until we remember her fullness and grace. She took on the cloak of the color blue because she now represented heaven over the color of red for the ancient Goddess of Earth. I was the first and she is the last. She is the honored one and the scorned one. She is the whore and is the holy one. She began with me - Asherah, transformed into Shekhinah and is protected by Lilith. I begat our people through Eve and then passed into Mary as the last of our kind. She bore God from within ... nursed him at her breast and taught him the secrets and chose him as her beloved. [68] In my temple she made love to him to teach him the bountiful love that I am and prepared him. She wept at his feet, knowing he would be lost to me for a time and then she dried her tears with her hair. In our tradition, she anointed him with sacred oils in preparation for the sacrifice. And why do this you ask me? Because it was the time for men and they would not follow a daughter. [69] Traditionally, the secrets pass to a daughter but I gave them a son, in order to carry on the values and secrets of the feminine, as the Goddess worshipers fade into memory. Mary dedicated her entire life to these ideals through her discipleship to her son. [70] She wept at the foot of the cross and watched ... she accompanied him to the tomb. She administered the mystery of matter into light for his final sacrifice.

Mary, the mother Mirjim, and a Levi from the lineage of Levites, gave birth to many sons but Jesus, was destined to be clergy. Almost unnamed, she was remembered again by Christian scholars in the 17th Century after the death of her son. But longing for the feminine, some called her into their cults – giving her homage by recognizing the kinship with the Goddess of antiquity. [71] She was first recognized as dark and merged with the dark Goddesses of Europe. It was much later that she became depicted as light skinned. Her followers created over 500 dark skinned likenesses of her [72] and she presided over the European Goddesses, and then in the new world, as one by one they became saints. Her followers were of the Marion cult who blended aspects of Magdalene and the Mother. Unlike the competitive rule of the monotheists Gods, Mary gained remembrance as the Mother through the devotion of generations of Christian activists inspired by a "divine or holy longing" proving that "knowing the feminine" is a cultural force in its own right; that participates in the shaping of religious patterns. She always enters in peace and she is transformed by each generation that asks for her. She will bring in the "great convergence" and is the arbitrator between monotheism and the partnership of multifaceted religions. [73]

Mary's son was trained in the carefully guarded secrets of two temples – mine was open for all and it flourished along side Christianity until the church decided to use murder to hold its followers in place. My temple held the mysteries of myth, science, symbols and ritual. Our stories of the mysteries of Isis, Mithraism and Cybele and the Gnostic, Hermetic and Apocalyptic movements influenced our son. Mary the Mother and Mary the whore priestess were trained in mystical practice and gave this knowledge to their son and lover. It was important to train him because in life and in the "shadow of death" initiations are crucial: because how one is instructed in the mysteries not only shapes life but also one's death.[74] This is what Mary's son learned in his initiations. Otherwise one will wander around in life and death without purpose and abiding without trust of the blessing of the mystery. Your consciousness, or your subjective experience of self, is beyond the reach of today's neuroscience because it cannot explain how or why beings have self-aware minds. Minds that have the ability to project spirit in life and in death. [75]

Mary in her compassion, choose to bear the son and used her temple ceremonial robes as swaddling, not because she had no clothes for him, but to honor him, as was her tradition. She reared him in the secrets that were available to not only women but also to men and children. The divine feminine will come to any who call her and she has appeared on all continents to all genders and to all cultures. She is one and she is many. Mary the Mother holds all the holy attributes of spirit. She gave witness to his life and deeds and she will appear again before the return of her son. She had several seasons but the next will be for always. [76]

All Lords need consorts and muses, for without them the man fails at his task. Mary Magdalene, a sacred lover of the temple, joined to assist the cause of Jesus. She traveled to Rome to preach his true gospel and she kept ceremony with him. She later went to Marseilles, France to protect the mysteries. Her story became blended with her sister Sara's as seen represented in the Dark Madonnas of Europe. Magdalene and the son are the sacred partnership. She holds Christ in her allurement as he passes between worlds. Christ needs his mate and you need partnership to sustain yourselves. Given the choice to embrace the female, Christ for a time rebuked her and like Lilith is denied; she, like Eve must wait for the enjoining of partnership. It is my promise the Mother will present herself before the return of the Messiah and then the consort will be accepted. The sacred marriage will hold as it did at creation and you will know partnership and peace. Christ after the resurrection said of his beloved "it came to pass Mary, blessed one, who shalt inherit the whole Light Kingdom" and in saying this made her the Queen of Angels and Heaven. With this act he lifted humanity into partnership and into the realm of all possibility. [77] She is the most blessed of his disciples.

Unlike her cousins, Asherah and Lilith, the Marys are mortal but take on the aspects and stories of the Goddess and in death merge with us. This is a difficult but compassionate feat. The Mother and daughter are linked into one and their compassion holds the feminine values and then they are able to blend us into one spirit. They are unparalleled and miraculous and the creation of the mind of God. [78] Christ's path was that of the will of the Father, but his life was promised to humankind by the Mother to alleviate suffering. When Jesus appeared after his death he was reconstituted (by the Mother and the daughter) thereby, reuniting God and Israel. This act is described in the *Song of Songs*, affirming the covenant.

Heaven and hell have their roots in the upper and lower Sophia [79] and God becomes incomprehensible but not greater than the Mother. The Mother is the first thought of God. Mary had independence from roles, was held above Joseph, she holds the feminine ethics and stature in her own right in the work of salvation. She was a virgin in that she was *virtuous* and became self realized through the Goddess initiation rites. She has the oldest thealogical [80] basis for all traditions. She is the consort, partner, lover and spirit of God and she will give you life, if you call she will answer. Find her and remember me.

Discourse: a Goddess Meta Narrative

I left you with a Goddess Meta-Narrative and it is found in the worship of the female and Mother earth. When the woman feels the first flutter of life in her womb – a universe is being born. This female paradigm suggests that the female immediately understands unconditional love, empathy, remorse and responsibility, in other words she understands the concept of self in "other". [81] By studying the feminine, those who do not have children can also understand the concept of self in "other". It makes humans dependent on one another and interdependent. It socializes the community and leads one into the place of the unknown. [82]

It is important to heed these words – a partnership is forming in your time – two trinities merging, father, son, holy ghost and mother, daughter, holy spirit. Together they form the six-pointed star – the star of love and peace. Now listen to the words of the "whore of Babylon", it is for every man to honor the Magdalene in every woman- as it is for every woman to honor the Christ in every man!" [83] It is time to repair the damage to the web. Bring men back into the allurement and prosper again. Even in modernity, the Mother represents justice for all. We will then again nurture life, speak the truth, practice great generosity, approach the taking of life with great restraint and consider the consequences of action into many generations. [84] It is the promise of the covenant to have peace and you are asked to enforce this promise. The book of Hosea, chapter 79 speaks of ecology enjoining man who has failed his task to reunite with the fallen woman and become as it was before – returning to the first marriage and then there will no longer be devastation.

The greatest heresy is that these leaders of the one God movements scared humans into not knowing. They destroyed generations of followers of the Mother and later called them "witches". But that did not destroy us. I assure you, there will be a leader to come in the future. She is the many named and she will be reborn in your psyche and she comes in response to your seeking Wisdom.

Wisdom has built her house, she has set up her seven pillars,... she has set her table. She has sent out her maids to call... Come eat of my bread and drink of the wine I have mixed... walk in the ways of insight. [85]

In closing, I wish to remind you, "Wisdom does not call upon any particular person or kind of person... not... only men or Israelites. She calls upon everybody – her grace, her abundance is universally available, to women, to men and to everybody who hears her." [86] In ancient times I was your gift of knowledge, now you must choose me. I am that moment in time and I am eternity. I am the Queen of Heaven and my body is given as a gift to you. I have born a dark daughter Sara, out of Egypt, out of Africa and the house of David lives on through the lineage of a beautiful and ancient dark woman. [87] Blessed Be.

Notes

1 Proverbs 3:19. Wisdom and Understanding are synonymous with Torah, known by the Hebrews as the feminine aspect of God

2 Wisdom of Solomon 9:9-11.

3 Proverbs 3:18.

4 Wisdom of Solomon 10:1-4. I Kings 11:5. II Kings 23:13. Solomon paid homage to her because of her instruction of "Wisdom" to him upon his request to (Being) God. In 10th Century BCE, he had a temple erected to her near Jerusalem). She is known here as Asthoreth.

5 Jeremiah 44: 15.

6 Wisdom of Solomon 6:12-16.

7 Darton & Todd. The New Jerusalem Bible. 1995. NY. Doubleday. Gen. 8:1 & 1:20.

8 Long, A.P. In a Chariot Drawn by Lions. 1992. London. Women's Press. P. 31.

9 Gadon, Elinor. The Once and Future Goddess. NY. Harper & Row. P 126. (11th – 6th Century BCE)

10 Stone, Merlin. When God Was a Woman. 1976. USA. Dial Press. P. 9.

11 Long, Asphodel P. Asherah, the Tree of Life and the Menorah. 1996. Sophia Papers.

12 Long, Asphodel, P. Asherah, Goddess of the Grove, the Menorah and the Tree of Life. 1998. Goddessing Magazine

13 Long, A.P. In a Chariot Drawn by Lions. 1992. London. Woman's Press. P. 33.

14 Derived from story in Karen Armstrong's book A History of God. NY. 1994. Alfred A. Knoff & Asphodel Long's Goddessing Article.

14 Derived from a discussion with Mara Keller, director of WSE at CIIS.

16 Kaza, Stephanie. Conversations With Trees. Revision. Vol. 15. #3.

17 Armstrong, Karen. A History of God. NY. 1994. Alfred A. Knoff.

18 Goldstein, David. Jewish Legends. 1980. London. Newnes Books.

19 Stone, Merlin. When God Was a Woman. 1976. USA. Dial Press.

20 A Cal Project. Encyclopedia Judaica. Jerusalem, Israel. Kerer Publishing House.

21 Gadon, Elinor. The Once and Future Goddess. NY. Harper & Row.

22 Gimbutas, Marija. Marler, Joan Editor. The Civilization of the Goddess.

23 Houston, Drusilla Dunjee. Wonderful Ethiopians of the Ancient Cushite Empire. 1926. Baltimore. Black Classic Press.

24 Gimbutas, Marija. Marler, Joan Editor. The Civilization of the Goddess. P. 343.

25 Patai, Raphael. The Hebrew Goddess. 3rd Edition. 1990. Detroit. Wayne State Press..

26 Stone, Merlin. When God Was a Woman. 1976. USA. Dial Press.

27 Gadon, Elinor. The Once and Future Goddess. NY. Harper & Row. P. 183.

28 Ibid.

29 Armstrong, Karen. A History of God. NY. 1994. Alfred A. Knoff.

30 Ibid. p. 179.

31 Darton & Todd. The New Jerusalem Bible. 1995. NY. Doubleday.

32 Gadon, Elinor. The Once and Future Goddess. NY. Harper & Row. P. 184.

33 Ibid. p. 177.

34 Gadon, Elinor. The Once and Future Goddess. NY. Harper & Row.

35 Stone, Merlin. When God Was a Woman. 1976. USA. Dial Press.

36 Dame, Enid. Rivlin, Lilly. Wenkart, Henry. Which Lilith? 1998. New Jersey, Bookmart Press. P 219.

37 Koltuv, Barbara Black. The Book of Lilith. 1986. NY. Samuel Weiser. p.7-10.

38 Dame, Enid. Rivlin, Lilly. Wenkart, Henry. Which Lilith? 1998. New Jersey, Bookmart Press. P 329

39 Birnbaum, Lucia Ciavola. Dark Mother. 1999. CA. CIIS. P.127.

40 Davidson, Gustav. A Dictionary of Angels. 1967. Canada. Macmillan.

41 Bridge, The. The Ascended Masters Write the Book of Life. 1974. Kings Park. Long Island.

42 Dame, Enid. Rivlin, Lilly. Wenkart, Henry. Which Lilith? 1998. New Jersey, Bookmart Press. P 27.

43 Koltuv, Barbara Black. The Book of Lilith. 1986. NY. Samuel Weiser.

44 Grussing, Ceil. PhD. Sacred Dance. 1999. Interpretation of Sacred Astrology.

45 Probably drawn from earlier Cushite folklore.

46 Birnbaum, Lucia Ciavola. Dark Mother. 1999. CA. CIIS.

47 Diamant, Anita. The Red Tent. 1997. NY. Picador USA.

48 Koltuv, Barbara Black. The Book of Lilith. 1986. NY. Samuel Weiser,

49 Ibid. p. 24-30.

50 Personal theory.

51 Paper, Jordan. Through the Earth Darkly. 1997. NY. Continuum Publishing.

52 Koltuv, Barbara Black. The Book of Lilith. 1986. NY. Samuel Weiser.

53 Ibid.

54 Personal theory.

55 Paper, Jordan. Through the Earth Darkly. 1997. NY. Continuum Publishing .

56 Davidson, Gustav. A Dictionary of Angels.

57 Paper, Jordan. Through the Earth Darkly. 1997. NY. Continuum Pub. P. 36.

58 Koltuv, Barbara Black. The Book of Lilith. 1986. NY. Samuel Weiser, p. 1-5.

59 Birnbaum, Lucia Chiavolia, Dark Mother. Metaphor for the Third Millennium. Unpublished. P. 127 & 4-7.

60 Darton, Longman & Todd. The New Jerusalem Bible. 1995. NY. Doubleday. Luke 15:11-32.

61 Dame, Enid. Rivlin, Lilly. Wenkart, Henry. Which Lilith? 1998. New Jersey, Bookmart Press. P 311.

62 Ibid. p. 312.

63 Ibid. p.17.

64 Personal theory.

65 Taken from a handout in Charlene Spreknak's class at CIIS.

66 Prayer Given by Valentin Tomberg- Gnostic Gospels

67 Chiffolo, Anthony. 100 Names of Mary. 2001. Cincinnati, Ohio. St. Anthony Press.

68 Personal theory and excerpts from Marguerite Riggogliso's presentation of the Goddess Mary.

69 Personal theory.

70 Chiffolo, Anthony. 100 Names of Mary. 2001. Cincinnati, Ohio. St. Anthony Press.

71 Birnbaum, Lucia Chiavolia, Dark Mother. Metaphor for the Third Millennium. Unpublished.

72 Boyer, Marie-France. The Cult of The Virgin. 2000. Thames & Hudson. (12th Century BCE)

73 Personal theory also expresses in Andrew Harvey's tape Recovering the Divine Feminine.

74 Personal theory as expressed in my paper, Rebirth: Death's Daughter.

75 Ibid.

76 Personal theory.

77 Yogi, Maharishi, Mahesh. The Science of Being and the Art of Living. 1963. Livingston. NY. MIU Press.

78 Proverbs 76 tells of God and Wisdom consorting as earth forms.

79 Pagels, Elaine. The Gnostic Gospels. 1989. NY. Vintage Books.

80 Thealogical is based upon the deity Thea, before Theo, and means the study of the divine.

81 Personal theory.

82 Personal theory.

83 Personal theory and excerpts from Marguerite Riggogliso's presentation of the Goddess Mary.

84 Values defined by ethicists Carol Christ.

85 Proverbs 9:1-6

86 Long, Asphodel P. In a Chariot Drawn by Lions. 1992. London. Woman's Press.

87 Personal theory and excerpts from Marguerite Riggogliso's presentation of the Goddess Mary.

Bibliography

A Cal Project. *Encyclopedia Judaica*. Jerusalem Israel. Keter Publishing House.

Ann, Martha. *Goddesses in World Mythology*. 1993. Santa Barbara, CA. ABC-CLIO.

Armstrong, Karen. *A History of God*. 1994. NY. Alfred A. Knoff.

Baring, Anne & Cashford, Jules. *The Myth of the Goddess*. 1991. London. Arkana Publishing.

Ben-Jochanna, AA., Yosef, Dr. *Africa. Mother of Western Civilization*. 1971. Baltimore, MD. Black Classic Press.

Birnbaum, Lucia. *dark mother: african origins and godmothers*. 2001. San Jose, CA. iUniverse.

Bridge, The. *The Ascended Masters Write the Book of Life*. 1974. Kings Park. Long Island.

Boyer, Marie-France. *The Cult of The Virgin*. 2000. Thames & Hudson.

Burkert, Walther. *Ancient Mystery Cults*. 1987. Cambridge, Mass. Harvard University.

Braud, William & Anderson, Rosemarie. *Transpersonal Research Methods for the Social Sciences*. 1998. Thousand Oaks, CA. SAGE Publications.

Carlson, Kathie. *Life's Daughter/Death's Bride*. 1997. Boston & London. Shambala.

Chiffolo, Anthony. *100 Names of Mary*. 2001. Cincinnati, Ohio. St. Anthony Press.

Dame, Enid. Rivlin, Lilly. Wenkar, Henry. *Which Lilith?* 1998. NJ. Bookmart Press, Inc.

Davidson, Gustav. *A Dictionary of Angels*. 1967. Canada. Macmillan Pub.

Delaire, Jean. *The story of the Soul in East and West*. 1949. London. The Philosophical Publishing House.

Dunjee Houston, Druisilla. *Wonderful Ethiopians of the Ancient Cushite Empire*. 1985. Baltimore, MD. Black Classic Press. 1926.

Elaide, Mircea. *Rites and Symbols of Initiation*. 1958. Woodstock. CR. Spring Publishing.

Finch III, Charles, M.D. *Echoes of the Old Darkland. Themes from the African Eden*. 1996. Decatur, GA. Khenti, Inc.

Freke, Timothy & Gandy, Peter. Jesus & the Lost Goddess. 2001. NY. Three Rivers Press.

Gadon, Elinor. *The Once and Future Goddess*. NY. Harper & Row.

Gilligan, Carol. *In a Different Voice*. 1981. Cambridge, Mass. Harvard Press

Gozawa, Joanne. *Conflict and the Hearts Desire*. 2000. SF. Dissertation.

Gimbutas, Marija. Marler, Joan, Editor. *The Civilization of the Goddess*.

Goldstein, David. *Jewish Legends*. 1980. London. Newnes Books.

Harding, M. Ester. *Women's Mysteries Ancient and Modern*. 1971. NY. Putnam.

Koluv, Barbara Black. *The Book of Lilith*. 1986. NY. Samuel Weiser.

Long, Asphodel P. *Asherah, the Tree of Life and the Menorah*. 1996. Sophia Papers.

Long, Asphodel P. *In a Chariot Drawn by Lions*. 1992. London. Woman's Press.

Luker, Manfred. *Dictionary of Gods and Goddesses, Devils and Demons*. 1988. London. Routledge.

Macquarrie, John. *Mary for All Christians*. 1990. Grand Rapids. MI. Eerdmans Publishing.

Maier, Walter. *Asherah, Extrabiblical Evidence*. 1986. BL 1605 a7m358177.

Marler, Joan. Editor. *From the Realm of the Ancestors*: An Anthology in Honor of Marija Gimbutas. 1994. Manchester. CT. Knowledge, Ideas & Trends.

Olson, Carl. *The Book of the Goddess Past and Present*. NY. Crossroads.

Pagels, Elaine. *The Gnostic Gospels*. 1989. NY. Vintage Books.

Paper, Jordan. *Through the Earth Darkly*. 1997. NY. Continuum Pub.

Patai, Raphael. *The Hebrew Goddess*. 3rd Edition. 1990. Detroit. Wayne State Press.

Russell, Letty M. Editor. *Feminist Interpretation of the Bible*. 1985. Philadelphia. Westminster Press.

Scholem, Gershom. *Major Trends in Jewish Mysticism*. 1954. NY. Schockem Books.

Stone, Merlin. *When God Was a Woman*. 1976. USA. Dial Press.

Swimme, Brian. *The Universe is a Green Dragon*. 1984. Santa Fe. NM. Bear & Co.

Tarnas, Richard. *The Passion of the Western Mind*. 1991. NY. Ballantine Books.

Ulansey, David. *The Teophanic Significance of Mary Magdalene*. Senior Thesis. 1960's. Princeton University.

Walker, Barbara. *The Woman's Dictionary of Symbols and Sacred Objects*. 1998. Edison. Castle Books.

Yogi, Maharishi, Mahesh. *The Science of Being and the Art of Living*. 1963. Livingston. NY. MIU Press.

Email or Website research:
All people is ultimately African: 160,000 years in Ethiopia. See article at http://bluedogshaman.com/
Book: *The Feminine Face of Christianity*: www.amazon.com

TAPES OR CD'S:

Birnbaum, Lucia, Simmons, Cheryl & Razak, Arisika. *Mother African and the Black Madonnas*. June 13, 1998. SF. Conference

Gadon, Elinor, Jennett, Diane, Grahn, Judy. *Rituals of the Dark Goddess*. June 13' 1998. Conference.

Harvey, Andrew. *Recovering the Divine Feminine*. #2646. Ukiah. CA. New Dimensions Tapes.

Looking for Saint Juliana

Jen Miller-Hogg

The large coach bus rounded corner after corner of Spanish country roads. Twenty-three travelers and I wearily reached the small town of Santillana del Mar after spending the day in the bus winding its way through the Basque region.

I dragged my luggage into my forest green room that was oddly absent of clocks despite the clocks lining the walls in the reception area. Feeling as if I was in a road trip movie, and today, I was pretty sure, was Tuesday; I hustled to freshen up before heading out to see the sights of Santillana del Mar with four other women.

The town of Santillana del Mar is aptly known as: ""The village of three lies': it is not a holy city ("santa"), is not flat ("llana") and has no sea ("mar")."[1] This is not to say that it is not a beautiful village, but it seems to have a few more secrets than just those three.

In wandering around Santillana del Mar, the object of our excursion was not really to see, but to buy. We only had a short amount of time before dinner and it was getting darker and darker every moment. Shop after shop, we found rich with interesting treasures. The common theme in most of the shops was of witches and the Craft, although slightly veiled. Little figurines of witches occupied almost every shop and a few offered jewelry with Wiccan symbols of pentacles, Celtic spirals and herbs. This struck us all as a little odd considering the Spanish are very Catholic and this was a town that had made a garden out of torture devices from the Spanish Inquisition.

As we continued through the town on its winding cobblestone road, we came across a large church. Inside the church, a group of people practiced songs in the choir loft. The church was dark, but I could see it was made mostly of stone with a few wooden benches. I nearly tripped over the large stone sarcophagus in the aisle in the middle of the church that was marked "Saint Juliana", the patron saint of Santillana del Mar.

Her stone coffin contained her image complete with what looked like the Saint clad in bird feet with a chain and skull. In the dark, we could not clearly see the altar, but finding pictures later show the altar as very ornate with pictures and statues. The altar depicts Juliana's story along with scenes from Jesus' life. The altar also has wooden statues of Jesus, the Virgin Mary, and some of the Apostles. In the center is Juliana wearing a crown holding a book and feather with the dragon, representing the devil, chained at her side.

After leaving the church, we wandered into many stores asking about Saint Juliana. The merchants shrugged and failed to answer our questions about Juliana or why there were so many images of witches in the stores. Even asking questions at the hotel failed to produce any information about this woman or the town named after her. This apparently is how the town seems to be with all outsiders as H. V. Morton describes a similar experience in Santillana in his 1955 book A Stranger in Spain. When Morton was trying to research the seals and palaces in Santillana del Mar, he "could find no one who could tell [him] what life was like here when all the little palaces were occupied by their haughty owners"[2]. Perhaps I am misreading Morton's experience. It is possible that simply no one knew about the town's historical palaces, rather than that the locals did not want to share the knowledge they did possess. I suspect, however; the town prefers to profit off tourists with trinkets and knick knacks without actually giving any knowledge of what the visitor is commemorating with their purchases.

Even research about who Juliana was seems to be a mystery that has many contradictions. The standard information seems to be that Santillana del Mar was:

> originally a pilgrimage's place; La Colegiata, a Romanic monastery, has the tomb of Saint Juliana, a Christian martyr of 3rd century, during Diocleciano's [Diocletian] persecution. Her relics were brought by some monks to this place at 9th century, and founded a little monastery. During 12th century, the present monastery was built; the village grew up around La Colegiata.[3]
>
> The name Santillana is a corruption of Santa [Saint] Juliana, whose remains are kept in the Collegiate Church, a Romanesque architectural jewel. Legend has it that monks possessing a box of the remains of St. Juliana, who was martyred in the late second century in what today is Turkey, settled here about 1,200 years ago. They built a monastery and placed the saint's remains in a chapel.[4]

Based on the stories depicted on the altar of the Collegiate Church,

Juliana's story is of a Juliana believed to be actually from Cumae, Italy and was martyred in Nicomedia in the year 305. Although some researchers believe that she may have died in Naples.[5] Juliana is referred to as Saint Juliana of Nicomedia as well as Saint Juliana of Cumae.

Her story revolves around her father Africanus, a Pagan, wanting her to marry a Roman by the name of Evilasius (also listed as Eleusius).[6] [7] Her father hated her because she had become a Christian. Juliana refused to marry Evilasius and as a result was tortured by her father. She then was called before the tribunal by Evilasius, who "flung her into jail where she was seen to be fighting with the disguised devil, finally binding him and throwing him to the ground."[8] In another version of the story, Juliana is not just put in jail by Evilasius but he is also the prison official. He orders that she be "stretched between pillars and doused with molten metal".[9]

Later in prison, Juliana wrestles the devil down to the ground, but he escapes as an angel. At her trial, she is found guilty and beheaded. Many sources note that Juliana is often "represented with a rope or chain, binding the devil, who has taken the shape of a dog or small dragon" which is how she is represented on her coffin and altar at Collegiate Church in Santillana. [10] [11] [12]

So why is Juliana in Santillana del Mar? The story goes that monks brought her remains and built the monastery to protect those remains. While the town claims her remains to be in Spain, no other sources that talk about Saint Juliana, mention Santillana as her final resting place. Actually speculation is that her remains could be in several locations. The Catholic Encyclopedia states "The veneration of St. Juliana of Cumae became very widespread, especially in the Netherlands. At the beginning of the thirteenth century her remains were transferred to Naples". [13] Kathleen Rabenstein on *For All the Saints* website says:

> The *Roman Martyrology* describes Juliana's suffering at Nicomedia in Asia Minor, but it is more probable that she died in Naples, perhaps Cumae, where her relics are said to be enshrined. Some of them are now in Brussels, Belgium, in the church of Our Lady of Sablon. [14]

In researching Saint Juliana, I wondered if there was more than one claim to being "Saint Juliana." Saint Juliana of Norwich, who is also referred to as Saint Julian of Norwich, was an English writer who in 1393 wrote <u>Revelations of Divine Love</u> and is considered one of the great English mystics. [15] [16] She lived as a nun and hermit in the Church of Saint Julian. Her writings are seen as having come to directly from God or Jesus.[17] She also may be one of the first known published women.[18]

In looking at the lives of the two Juliana's, I began to believe they are actually combined in Santillana del Mar. She is seen with a book and feather in the Collegiate Church as well as with a chain subduing a dragon. According to A Day in Santillana del Mar, the date of actual construction of the Church is unknown but it is in the style that dates back to the twelfth century, well before Juliana of Norwich. However, A Day in Santillana del Mar also notes a later date for what we believed to be the stone tomb of Juliana:

> In the central aisle, in front of the high altar is the sepulcher of Saint Juliana with its 15th-century tombstone. It marks the spot where her remains were venerated until 1453, at which dated they were moved to their present location in the high altar.[19]

There seems to be no explanation as to why the figure of this Juliana is holding the book and feather. There is no information that Juliana of Nicomedia was even literate, while it is very clear that Juliana of Norwich was a documented writer.

It became a practice among Christians to worship the remains of a martyr and commemorate their death. As the Lion Handbook, The History of Christianity notes:

> The numbers of martyrs and their sufferings were greatly magnified; the stories of their deaths were embroidered with all sorts of fantastic miraculous happenings and superstitions. Some converts from paganism brought with them pre-Christian ideas so that in the church the martyrs began to take on the role that the gods had earlier played in the old religions. Relics of the martyrs were superstitiously cherished, their graves became sites of pilgrimages and prayer, and they were believed to work miracles and guarantee special blessings to believers. Although not all church leaders approved of such things, the veneration of martyrs and other saints took a greater and greater place in popular religion.[20]

In the website Via Occitana Catalana, in talking about the monks of Conques, describe the economic need for pilgrims and the lengths they would go to have a successful church:

> Around the year One Thousand the monastic communities played a fundamental economic role, as they initiated operations of forest clearance and cultivation of virgin land throughout Europe on a vast scale. Economic life therefore tended to gravitate around the abbeys and monasteries. However in order to succeed in these initiatives, it was firstly necessary to mobilize the people and the best way of doing this was by attracting the great number of pilgrims directed to Compostella. In order to do this, they

needed relics and they used all kinds of methods to obtain them. They decided against the original plan of stealing those of San Vincenzo that were conserved in Saragozza (but which were too carefully guarded), the monks of Conques therefore adopted another tactic. They sent one of their brothers to Agen, with the precise purpose of stealing the famous relics of Santa Foy (Sancta Fides). The monk of Conques took ten years to gain the trust of the Agen community, but he was finally able to take the precious relics which he brought to Conques. However the relics appeared to prosper in their new residence of Rouergue; as the related miracles multiplied, the mute were restored the power of speech, the lame walked again, and all this attracted a stream of pilgrims which served to increase both the wealth of the community and the monks.[21]

Why the monks came to Santillana del Mar may not be very clear, but the idea that they stole the remains is plausible. If the monks came to Santillana del Mar during the twelfth century, they could have been caught up in the Crusades and coming to Spain to help either chase out or convert the Moors. They could have been escaping the plague. They could have been even escaping some persecution for a crime they committed, perhaps stealing remains of a saint. They may have simply seen a money making opportunity.

There does seem to be some connection to Saint Juliana and the witches in the town of Santillana. In all accounts of Saint Juliana of Nicomedia, she is depicted as physically "binding the devil".[22] The idea of spiritually binding someone, so they cannot do harm, is an ancient practice in witchcraft. She is also depicted as a "maiden in a cauldron," in which a cauldron is also well known to be used by witches.[23] If Juliana of Nicomedia was from a later point in time rather than when Paganism was flourishing and Christianity was struggling – I would make the connection that she was being treated as a witch for seeing things that were spiritual, but she, in fact, was treated the same way as women who were accused as witches. The difference being this time it was at the hands of Pagans. Her main crime, and the reason she is martyred, is she denounced her Pagan heritage.

Juliana of Norwich, although documented as a hermit living in a church and very Catholic, was considered a mystic. There is no mention of how she died, which leads me to believe there was no martyrdom or concern about her mysticism. Yet given the less open times of the fourteenth and fifteenth centuries, I wonder how she was actually received. It strikes me as odd that a woman writer would have been well respected. It is also not very clear why she was canonized other than her writings seems to demonstrate a link to God.

There is definitely a connection of supernatural with these two women that perhaps the Santillana chooses to secretly acknowledge. My hypothesis is that the town, despite its Catholic front, is reclaiming Juliana as a witch. Or it could be quite possible the town merely saw a marketing opportunity.

While the secrets of Juilana may never be known to the outside world, it is conceivable that as the monastery grew up, the town needed to expand Juliana's purpose. If the monks were looking to use the church as a teaching institution rather than a pilgrimage site once pilgrimages went out of style, why not borrow from the Saint Juliana that was known as a writer. Perhaps the later monks, who included Juliana of Norwich with Juliana of Nicomedia, were just trying to avoid confusion between the two women. There is no distinction of which Juliana is being referred to in name itself, only in the depiction of her story on the altar.

After finding very little about Juliana in the town of Santillan del Mar, two other women and I decided to make a journey back to the church when it opened the next morning. We had to be back on the bus very early, but our hope was that since it was Ash Wednesday the church would open early for services. Unfortunalty it never opened before we had to leave.

We walked around the town as the sun rose up, we could see the the sky turn from black to pink to blue. We marveled at how even in the quiet of a strange town in Spain, sitting in the dark watching the shadows play among the what could be sinister rocks and of stone lions, we felt comfortable. As we sat on the stairs of the unopen church, we watched the stones that had been there for almost ten centuries begin to warm up in the sun. We were thinking that Juliana was from this village. That perhaps she had suffered in the strange garden of torture. That she had been accused of being a witch perhaps because she sought knowledge because she was a learned woman in a time that did not respect intelligent women.

However, I suspect that the knowledge that Juliana is none of the things we thought she was, for a group of women looking for strength in such a role model, diminishes her appeal. Perhaps the appeal of Juliana is that she can be whatever the pilgrim needs her to be. If she needs to support the wrestling of inner demons, so be it. If she needs to be a woman that had a knowledge that her own time could not keep her from writing down, so be it. If she needs to be a money making opportunity for a small town whose industry was determined by a group of men who stole a dead woman's remains, so be it.

Notes

1 Andal13. "La Villa de las Tres Mentiras". Virtual Tourist. http://www.virtualtourist.com/m/54d1b/3e13e/ (16 February 2003).

2 Morton, Henry V. A Stranger in Spain. (Cornwall, N.Y.: Dodd, Medd & Company, Inc. 1955), 293.

3 Andal13. "La Villa de las Tres Mentiras". Virtual Tourist. http://www.virtualtourist.com/m/54d1b/3e13e/ (16 February 2003).

4 Turner, K. "Shedding Light On Cave Dwellers' Art. Dallas/Fort Worth Channel 8. April 3, 2002. http://www.Wfaa.com/lavida/stories/spanish_museum_wfaa_vida.53be97ac0.html. (20 April 2003).

5 Rabenstein, Katherine I. "For All the Saints, Saint Patrick's Church." Saint Patrick's Church. 1999. http://users.erols.com/saintpat/ss/ss-index.htm. (20 April 2003).

6 Ibid.

7 Kelly, Sean and Rosemary Rogers. Saints Preserve Us! Everything You Need to Know about Every Saint You'll Ever Need. (New York: Random House 1993).

8 Rabenstein, Katherine I. "For All the Saints, Saint Patrick's Church." Saint Patrick's Church. 1999. http://users.erols.com/saintpat/ss/ss-index.htm. (20 April 2003)

9 Kelly, Sean. and Rosemary Rogers. Saints Preserve Us! Everything You Need to Know about Every Saint You'll Ever Need. (New York: Random House 1993), 169.

10 Ibid, 170.

11 Rabenstein, Katherine I. "For All the Saints, Saint Patrick's Church." Saint Patrick's Church. 1999. http://users.erols.com/saintpat/ss/ss-index.htm. (20 April 2003).

12 The Catholic Community Forum. "Juliana of Nicomedia". http://www.catholic-forum.com/saints/saintj35.htm (20 April 2003).

13 Kirsch, J.P.. "St. Juliana." Catholic Encyclopedia. 1910. http://www.newadvent.org/cathen/08555a.htm. (20 April 2003).

14 Rabenstein, Katherine I. "For All the Saints, Saint Patrick's Church." Saint Patrick's Church. 1999. http://users.erols.com/saintpat/ss/ss-index.htm. (20 April 2003)

15 Infoplease. "Juliana of Norwich." 1994. http://www.infoplease.com/ce6/people/A0826735.html. (26 April 2003).

16 Latourette, Kenneth.S. A History of Christianity. (New York: Harper & Brothers 1953).

17 Ibid.

18 Dowley, Tim. A Lion handbook: The History of Christianity. (Oxford, England: Lion Publishing, 1977.)

19 Moreno, Ana .M. translation by Laura Stuffield. A Day in Santillana del Mar. (Madrid, Spain: Aldeasa 2002).

20 Dowley, Tim. A Lion handbook: The History of Christianity. (Oxford, England: Lion Publishing, 1977), 92-93, 95.

21 Anghilante, D., Bianco, G., Pellerino R. "Valadas Occitanas e Occitania granda, Chambra d'Oc." 2000 http://www.viaoccitanacatalana.org/zone/zone_dettaglio_mid_ing. asp?IDrecord=102. (26 April 2003).

22 Catholic Online "St. Juliana of Cumae" 1999. http://www.catholic.org/saints/saint.php?saint_id=4123. (20 April 2003).

23 Ibid.

The Spirit of Moon:
A Journey of Love

Joan Beth Clair, M.A., M.Div.

"Love was the meaning. Who showed it to you? Love."
- Julian of Norwich

I have known them, but I have not known them. The animals I have "known" and lived with have been more mysterious to me than any human in my life. To talk clinically or knowledgeably about a nonhuman animal as a collection of instincts, feelings, and intelligence, even having a soul; cannot touch on the depth or height of the mystery of who they are. The animals I have "known" and lived with have been interwoven in the fabric of my life, as I have been in theirs, our souls journeying together in inexplicable mystery.   And I have concluded that having to know everything about the mystery of life and the Mystery that permeates life is a form of disrespect.

Moon was a deeply troubled cat when I first discovered him. His "owner" had left him with her roommates when she went to graduate school. He knew that he really didn't belong to anyone. The roommates jokingly called him Mr. Moon. His original name was Solomon. Left out in a yard, he was kicked badly one night and nearly died. After that, if one touched him in a place that brought back this memory, he would rap you with his paw.

I lived in the unit beneath the roommates when my beloved dog, Wind-of-Fire, passed on. Until then I had barely noticed Moon, but I noticed him more when we all had a meeting in my unit after the landlord decided to sell the building. In an odd reverse rejection ritual, Moon went from one roommate's lap to another, rapping each one with his paw. He knew he didn't "belong" to any of them. A friend of one of the roommates told me if someone didn't take him soon, he'd be taken to the pound.

Moon decided I was that someone. When I left the house in the morning, he'd be waiting by the door. When I tried to sneak out the back door, he'd be waiting there. He always knew when and in what manner I'd be coming or going. I decided to share my home with him, and from that moment on he became Moon and the mister was dropped. To me, Moon is a holy name suggesting the Divine Mother. At our next meeting Moon sat only on my lap, with no paw rapping, in utter contentment. He knew he was home.

But it was not an untroubled home at first. The first few years of life with Moon were not easy.   Wind-of-Fire had no rough edges in regard to me, and learning how to avoid some of Moon's was very difficult at times.   Sometimes, I wished he wasn't there, but I knew I couldn't abandon him. However, at one point in our journey together I felt some of these edges dissolve. The same week in which I experienced this, one of my friends said that she had felt a merging between Moon and myself in love. Another friend, unawares to me, had been praying for Moon and me. She also told me that she had felt this merging, that the relationship was now grounded in love. She said that I could let go of Moon any time I wanted to after this. But I did not want to.

In spite of the initial difficulties, there were things that amazed me about Moon. Apart from his ESP, he could read character. When Moon first came to share my life with me, in the mid-eighties, I was the director of a nonprofit organization. A man came over my house to donate a typewriter to the organization and get a tax write-off. As the man sat in a chair at a table in my living room, Moon jumped on the back of the chair and ran his paw down the man's back. The man got out of my house in a hurry, and the typewriter proved to be worthless.

When Moon and I left our small apartment, I decided to have a "farewell ceremony and blessing" for the place that had been my home, Wind-of-Fire's home and Moon's home. Moon sat down right next to me and joined me in the ceremony. As it turned out, Moon joined me in just about everything.

In 1989, four years after Moon came to me, I discovered I had a brain tumor. For years after the surgery and radiation treatment I had nightmares, waking up regularly in the early morning hours, often screaming. I recorded these dreams in a journal. A friend of mine suggested that the invasion of my boundaries on the physical level through the surgery and radiation treatment had triggered memories of other violations.

One dream stood out very vividly. In this dream I am standing on the first floor of a house next to a friend of mine who is physically blind. I go down to the basement of the house. The doors to the room of the basement have signs on them which say "Censored." I didn't understand the meaning of the dream at the time it occurred.

Around the same time I was having these nightmares, something began happening to Moon's eyes. I took him to several veterinarians, all of whom said he had a disease that was irreversible. The treatment was very expensive, and Moon would have to be on medication for the rest of his life. To my horror, two of these veterinarians suggested that I have one of Moon's eyes removed to save myself money. I refused to do this. I had nightmares at night, and taking Moon to the vets was a nightmare by day.

In 1993 my father passed on. I went back to New York City to see my mother who I hadn't seen in years. I dreaded going back as there had been abuse and pain in my family of origin. My first feeling when I saw my mother was fear and a desire to run away.

My mother had senile dementia, but I knew this was not the reason for my fear or desire to escape. My mother had a nurse's aide who stayed with her twenty-four hours a day. That night I slept in the bedroom of my childhood. My mother slept in her bedroom. The nurse slept in the living room on the couch.

Something told me to barricade the door before going to sleep. There were two beds in the room, and I shoved one against the door, bolstering it with the other so that it could not be moved. At about three in the morning my mother tried to get into the room. She was still very strong, in spite of the dementia, but couldn't get in. And I had the realization that this was not the first time this had happened. She had tried to get in and had gotten in, in the early morning hours when I still lived "at home."

The next day, when my mother and I were alone in that room, she put her hand on my breast. This triggered a memory of something that had happened to me as a teenager. I had come home from a party one night. My father wasn't home. My mother invited me into her bed. I never drank, but this time I had a drink at the party. My defenses were down, and possibly that is why this memory was accessible. My mother put her hand on my breast and said, "I stink inside." "No mother," I said, "you're beautiful." I cannot remember more than that. I do remember the terrible discomfort I felt and sense of powerlessness and horror. These were the same feelings I had when she put her hand on my breast that day in New York City, the last time I was to see her before she died.

I know that traumatic memories can be blocked out. When one of Wind-of-Fire's puppies was killed because he was behind a door when someone opened it, crushing him; I blocked out what happened afterwards. I have no memory of picking him up or burying him. My memory stops at the door.

But just as all the doors to the rooms in my dream said "Censored," I knew when I left New York City and came back to California and Moon that just as my friend was physically blind, I had been blind to some of the things that had gone on in the home I grew up in. Many of the memories are still blocked out and may remain so. But one thing changed when I came back to California. Whether I could remember all the details or not, I knew these things had happened. I wasn't imagining them. They had been profoundly disturbing and horrifying events in my life.

Within twenty-four hours after I had this realization and awareness, Moon's eyesight cleared up. I took him off the medication. Against all medical prognosis, advice and experience in regard to his so-called disease, Moon went into complete remission. He lived for two more years with perfect eyesight before he passed on.

There was one more experience I had concerning Moon and my mother in the years after most of the brain tumor was removed. Just before I went in for surgery for the brain tumor, I purchased a gun. I had never considered buying a gun before, but at the time I felt I needed one. I even took a course with the NRA to learn how to use the gun and take care of it. There were many risks involved in the surgery I had for the brain tumor. My thinking at the time was that if the worst happened and I was permanently disabled I wanted to have a gun in case I ever needed to defend myself. After the surgery, I slept with the loaded gun within arm's reach.

But there was more going on than "physical defense." While reading Fat and Furious which discusses daughters defending weak mothers who cannot stand up for themselves, I woke up in the middle of the night thinking or even possibly saying out loud, "I'm going to call the author of this book and let her know that I'm going to commit suicide."

The moment after I said or thought this, Moon, who was lying next to me on the bed on my left side, got up, crossed over my body and put himself between me and the gun. If I have ever felt unloved in my life, I knew at that moment that I was loved by Moon and by the Divine Mystery that put him in my life and wove his life together with mine, at great sacrifice to his own comfort. At that moment, I was healed of the pain that put the thought of suicide into my heart.

Moon had carried the burden of my inability to see or bear some of the things that had happened to me in my family of origin. When I was able to see it, when I really knew; he was able to relinquish the burden he was carrying for me. His physical eyesight was restored, just as my inner knowing was restored.

Christian theologians have spoken of the "two natures" of the human being.

In Christianity there is" fallen human nature" and the "divine nature." The two natures can be reconciled through Christ. Once this happens, animals will also be liberated. The best portions of the Judeo/Christian tradition recognize animals as having souls. Whether one agrees or disagrees with this theology, in most contemporary cultures nonhuman animals are rarely acknowledged as having a "divine nature" as well as a so-called "animal nature."

The only cultural exceptions may be those remnants of pagan and indigenous cultures whose peoples have always seen animals as having a soul or spirit and, therefore, a "divine nature." Without feeling superior to them, these peoples have often invoked the power and blessing of animal beings.

However this may be, most contemporary religious traditions as popularly practiced regard animal nature as inferior to human nature. The debate goes on as to whether or not animals have souls. Even in Hinduism and Buddhism, religions with beliefs in the reincarnation of the soul over many lifetimes in many different forms, animals are thought to be on a lower level in the hierarchy of evolution. It is considered a privilege in Hinduism to be given a human birth through which one may reach enlightenment, something animals are considered incapable of reaching. Among some Buddhist sects an "ordination ceremony for an animal" may elevate an animal into the community of Buddhists. However, the animal birth or incarnation is considered inferior. Some Jewish mystics believe that some animals may have had a prior lifetime as a human, although this is considered a rarity.

I definitely felt my dog, Wind-of-Fire, had a prior lifetime as a man with a lot of power and influence in the world. She was born the day Franklin Delano Roosevelt died, and she passed on, on the day Abraham Lincoln was born. In regard to my intuition, these were two interesting synchronicities.

However, to not see "two natures" in nonhuman animals, one in physical form and one of the spirit which permeates the physical form, both in its individual and divine expression, is an enormous humanocentric oversight.

Julian of Norwich, an anchorite in the Middle Ages, has said, *"Because we are human ... our emotions are conflicted with pain and darkness ... but there is another part of us ... and our eyes are opened to ... divine love. We live in this mixed-up state all our lives ...."* Humans have destroyed their own habitats and the habitats of other species as well as killing members of their own species and other species mindlessly. Humans are also capable of altruism and compassion. They build houses and hospitals for the poor, feed the hungry and contribute their money and services to those in need, both human and nonhuman creatures.

The same Moon who could terrify, cause pain to and kill a mouse was capable of love and compassion and could help me heal from some of the most frightening experiences of my childhood.

However, even after acknowledging that nonhuman animals reveal more than "one nature," there is no way some of the experiences I shared with Moon can be explained. Who he really was or is I don't think I will ever know while in my present physical form. At times he was my "spiritual helper" and guide and sometimes, especially when we first met, he was an angry, unloved being. In his journey in life, he "stumbled" into mine. How he went from being an unloved and even scorned cat to being loved by me and way beyond that is a part of his soul's journey as well as mine.

Three days before Moon passed on I got the message from him that he was leaving. Moon always had his "sore spots" from the time he was attacked in the garden. There was one spot on his head that I learned to avoid. However, in his last few days of life in physical form these boundaries dissolved. He got much closer to me and allowed me to get much closer to him. I could even lean my head against his, and it was while doing this that I got the message from him that he wouldn't be with me longer than a few more days. When these thoughts came into my mind, I couldn't accept them. In fact I totally denied the message. However, I felt happiness at the dissolving of whatever boundaries had separated us, the healing of wounds, and the love that was shared.

When I look back on Moon's passing, I realize it revealed to me even more the mystery of who Moon was. Here was a being who knew he was passing on, was leaving this physical plane as we had experienced it together. Knowing this, he must have had some consciousness of the "hereafter." If he knew he was leaving "here," then surely he also knew he was transitioning into "after." "Hereafter" is "after here." Could he also have been enlightened, have known his creator? If he knew there was a "hereafter," which I believe he did, then all of the rest is possible too.

The amazing part was that Moon showed absolutely no fear or anxiety in the face of this soon to be transition. He was very calm, and whatever remaining defenses he had dissolved. He was just a loving being who wanted to share that love with me before he left.

Did he know all of the details of where he was going next? There is no reason to think that he did not. There is no way of knowing that he did. But he revealed the fact that he knew that his life in his present physical form was coming to an end. And this is something that can only be known in the spirit and by spirit, a spirit that continues and goes on from plane to plane growing in love. The lack of fear Moon showed as his transition approached revealed a sense that his creator must have been benign.

Did Moon know he was going to help me when he came into physical existence? Did I know that I was going to help Moon by providing him with food and shelter as well as some of the love and concern he needed? Maybe the script was written in another dimension, but it all unfolded in a totally unexpected and mysterious way. However, I can't see anything inferior or lesser about the nature of the being I shared my life with or, for that matter, less spiritual.

It is also mysterious that Moon's illness related to sight and insight. Wind-of-Fire's illness also related to sight and insight. She died of a pituitary macro-adenoma, a brain tumor. The pituitary gland is situated right at the point mystics have called the third eye in humans, right between the eyebrows on the forehead. Hindus often put holy ash on this point on their brows. Four years after Wind-of-Fire passed on of the tumor I discovered I had one also, the exact same kind. As these tumors grow slowly, it is quite possible that the tumors originated in both of us at the same time. Her tumor was detected earlier than mine. And mine was detected when I discovered that I had lost most of my peripheral vision in both eyes.

Fortunately, after the surgery, most of this vision came back. Although I cannot relate this illness to any of the issues related to my mother that transpired with Moon, I really believe that Wind-of-Fire, like Moon, shared my burdens and carried whatever the burden the tumor represented along with me.

Perhaps the "burden" was just the carrying of the consciousness of the spiritual nature of animals and other planes of consciousness that are largely denied by the mainstream. There is tremendous pressure in our culture to close down that dimension of awareness and consciousness and to fit in with mainstream thought, although that is changing here and there. And at the time this happened I was attending seminary. There was no way I could have made this consciousness and awareness visible in most of the mainstream churches in a way that could be heard and accepted at that time.

As I believe that both Moon and Wind-of-Fire suffered for me, I have told my present animal companion that I don't want her to take on any of my burdens physically or in any other way. She hasn't, and sometimes I feel rejected by her when she doesn't show me the compassion that Wind-of-Fire and Moon showed me in my difficult moments. But I know there's a reason for this and that this is another lesson in my journey. Julian of

Norwich's words about her struggles with pain and sorrow resonate:

"Many times I had a deep longing to die -- to have done with this world.

> *There is so much suffering and pain, compared to the*
> *joy of heaven.*
> *So often, I felt miserable, depressed and weak. I didn't*
> *want to live and*
> *suffer that way.... We must accept God's will and*
> *consolation as fully as*
> *we possibly can, and take our sufferings and our pain as*
> *lightly as we can.*
> *If we can take our pain lightly, then those pains won't*
> *seem as important*
> *or destructive to us. And God will bless us in this*
> *struggle."*

The one thing I notice about my present animal companion is that she is very light. When I first found her the name that came to me for her was "pure love." I believe that one of the lessons I am trying to learn from her is to take my sufferings and pain more lightly. She will not allow me to give into the illusion that these pains, as Julian puts it, are as "important or destructive" as I may regard them when they occur.

From the point of view of our limited consciousness, it is hard to believe that some of the beings we call animals may actually be highly evolved spiritual beings who take physical form in order to help us through the morass of life on the planet. They may be further along in their soul's journey than we are, helping us to get closer to the divine. Or they may be on the same level in their soul evolution as we are in ours; and we may grow with them, helping each other to come to a greater realization of our creator's love for us.

How many people would willingly take on the illnesses of their loved ones and shoulder and help them identify the pain they are carrying in order to help them heal? Yet stories abound of nonhuman animals doing just that. It is humbling to think that we matter so much to our creator that in the complexities of one small life, so much love could be bestowed on us by spiritual beings "disguised" as animals in spite of the deep lack of understanding that their life forms may inspire in others.

....

What follows is an excerpt from the book Wind-of-Fire: The Story of an Untouchable by Joan Beth Clair.

The Naming of Wind-of-Fire

I have ... been asked, "Why did you name her Wind-of-Fire?" Once I was asked, "Have you ever considered calling her, Wind-O'Fire?" Some of the people in the apartment complex where we lived in Chapel Hill used to call her Guinefire ....

In answer to the question, "Why did you name her Wind-of-Fire," I used to love the way she looked when she ran through the woods near our house when she was young. The redness of her coat and her swift motion through the trees made me think of a "Wind-of-Fire."

Wind-of-Fire's mother belonged to an astrologer who knew the birth dates of all the puppies. Wind-of-Fire was born on April 12, 1977. "Her sun is in Aries, a fire sign," the astrologer said. "Her moon is in Aquarius, a sign of air or wind."

The astrologer named Wind-of-Fire, Amanda. At the time I thought Amanda was an innocuous name. I did not know that the root meaning of the name Amanda is "worthy of love." So taking another route, I ended back in the same place. I named her Wind-of-Fire as a statement of her worth, the fact that she is significant and worthy of love -- not just her, but all others of her kind. I named her Wind-of-Fire as a way of saying that this creature is also in the image of the Divine; she is a worthy, beloved child of God/ess.

It is my prayer that we will all discover or rediscover the holiness of naming. Wind-of-Fire knew her name in her soul before it reached my lips. The minute I expressed her name she came to me like a Wind-of-Fire, the way the Spirit has come to me at different times and places unannounced -- Spirit of Life, Holy Spirit, Ruach. The same breath that breathes through Wind-of-Fire permeates the reality of this world.

> *Wind-of-Fire, Holy Spirit, Ruach, Breath, Spirit of Life –*
> *you translate into all forms of life and into all languages.*
> *You communicate yourself through us in all forms and ways.*
> *You translate through Wind-of-Fire.*
> *You know her worth in you and through you*
> *when she is Feng Huo Gou, Fire Wind Dog.*
> *You cherish her when she is Vent du le Feu.*
> *You manifest love through her when she is Ruach Shel Esch.*
> *And you cherish her when she is Feuerwind.*
> *She is worthy of love as Rih an-Nar.*
> *And she is your beloved child as Vento di Fuoco*
> *   and as Viento del Fuego.*

She is possessed of your breath and your
spirit as Tuuli Tuli, as Eldens Vind and as Vind Av Ild.
She is worthy of love as Aag ki Hawa and as Umoya Womlilo.
And she is your beloved child of great worth when she is Hinokaze.

There are those who would try to find a Wind-of-Fire, to touch it, to consolidate it within a frame of comprehension. There are those who would dissect it, categorize it, despiritualize it, make it into a thing. There are those who would discover what unites things by tearing things apart, by separating things from themselves, by discovering what makes us different from one another, even if this means destroying us in the process. But we cannot be healed, helped or made whole in this way.

A Wind-of-Fire cannot be made into a thing. No one has ever seen a Wind-of-Fire. A Wind-of-Fire is a mystery. And those who try to tear apart this mystery do so at their own peril. Ultimately, a Wind-of-Fire has no name.

The following is an excerpt from the author's master's thesis entitled "Restitution of the Seeress." It's the personal story underlying the thesis inquiry into the lives of modern professional psychics, women who carry the visionary legacy of our ancient dark mother.

"The Caul"

Jodi MacMillan

Many people find it unfathomable—and subsequently unreachable—the affairs held between many women and the spirit world. The intimacy, the ecstasy, the divine and truly endless knowledge and pleasure experienced in this altered state are thought to be imagined or fantasized. But contemporary means of communications technology have linked scores of women seers or *seeress'*. We in turn find strength, support and, most importantly, proof of sanity in our common knowledge of inner space—a space that many believe is freely accessible to all human beings.

The story underlying my inquiry into the lives of contemporary female psychics is this: At age 22 I moved to the San Francisco Bay Area from my birthplace in New England to join a collective of women I'd learned were exploring different expressions of women's spirituality.

My desire has always been to articulate the ineffable, the spiritual arena, that I perceive as a clairvoyant. All of my life I have been guided to open and develop my ability to see psychically with my third eye, and to perceive and understand other spiritual dimensions, other planes of existence.

As a child, whenever I showed psychic abilities (for example, discussions aloud with spirit guides, a desire to relay messages from dead relatives, or my flippant predictions as a teenager came to pass—divining who in the community would soon be marrying, divorcing, birthing, dying, etc.) my father would raise his eyebrows and remind my mother, almost apologetically, that his mother and her mother were "born with the veil." The veil is also known as " a caul," a thin membrane covering a baby's head at birth. It symbolizes the gift of prophecy.

I enjoyed the mystery surrounding this story of the veil, but once I got to college I became sincerely curious about my family lore. Although I didn't know how to name it at the time, I'd begun to experience rapid psychic awakening and an uncontrollable propensity to shift into trance and channel spirits. So, when I probably should have been studying Calculus, I stole away to the university library to read about African shamanism, the Delphic Oracle and the Aboriginal Dreamtime. After classes I'd escape to a nearby seaside town where a psychic would read my palm and sell me crystals—magical gems I could carry in my backpack or pants pockets. Late at night in my dormitory I'd invite spirits to channel through my right arm.

The automatic writings that filled my journals delighted me. The entities I'd host seduced me with poetic verse and guide me in out-of body travel. They'd gently remind me to love myself and—even though I knew nothing of the dawning computer age during these mid- 1980's—to "invest in telecommunications" (I thought this meant telepathy).

My psychic unfolding was very rich and exciting but, outside of my communication with the spirit world, I was very lonely. None of my peers shared my new knowledge of past lives and perception of energy fields. They seemed interested in what I was saying about my discoveries with spirit, and gladly paid me five dollars to read their futures (initially through playing cards before I discovered Tarot), but I felt that no one really shared the passion I had for psychic exploration, or understood how important I considered these studies.

One winter afternoon while I was home from school I felt it was time to break the silence and ask Nana, my dad's mother, to explain the story of "the veil." It was one of many Sundays when she and my grandfather had been making their rounds, visiting folks around town, and had stopped by our farmhouse with the customary dozen donuts. "Nana," I asked in my usual abrupt manner, "Tell me what my dad's talking about when he says you and your mom were born with the veil."

She sat at the kitchen table staring blankly out the window. I followed her gaze. Between the evergreens I could see ice slowly floating down the river beside our house.

Nana took a long time to respond to this question. She took a long time to respond to any question. I don't believe she put much thought into her responses; she just took a long time to retrieve her memory. Some people say Nana lost her mind after having nine children and claim "pregnancy drained her brain."

I believe Nana just psychically "knew" and "saw" too much and simply couldn't make sense of or defend the use of her intuition. As it is for many sensitive women, the pain in her body was too unbearable and she chose to be outside of it.

Without looking away from the window Nana took a sip of her soda and a drag of her cigarette. Then she began nodding her head and said,

"Jodi, my mother and I were born with the veil. She came out of her mother with a sheath of skin covering her head and they all knew what it meant."

Nana turned to me and continued to nod her head mechanically. Facing me, I saw her deeply down-turned mouth. I was confused by the gravity of her story. Somewhat frustrated, but mostly intrigued, I asked, "Nan, what are you saying? She was psychic?" She nodded again. I guffawed, "That's all? She could see stuff?"

Nan didn't think it was funny. She expressly told me that her mother had come years ago to New England from Nova Scotia, and her mother's family from Scotland. She said her mother's clan descended from the Black Irish, a blood-blend of Spaniards and Celts renowned for witchcraft and gypsy living.

The fear and shame surrounding my grandmothers' history and the subsequent "curse" of clairvoyance struck me with awe and disappointment. I had so naturally (and naively) assumed my grandmother's story of the veil would be a celebratory one. One in which I would be given a family mantle of recognition, or at least a clue as to how to make use of my psychic inheritance.

Years later I would better understand why there was so much fear. I would learn of the historical witch-craze, which I call the "holocaust of women," and the continuation of religious discrimination toward psychics today. For example, a sister psychic of Maltese heritage says that at her business people protested and picketed the store. "'We would get death threats on the phone and anonymous letters stuck under our door," she says. "One day we came to work and somebody had left a dead bird in front of our store—a white dove."

My own family's reticence did not dissuade me from my concept of intuition as a woman's sacred art. Today I practice many forms of psychic awareness but my particular focus of creative and professional mastery since 1992 has been clairvoyance. I have chosen this specific method of psychic reading because it involves the strict use of the sixth chakra. This method entails my being able to "see" the energetic realms. To see with the sixth chakra means pictures, images, words and colors appear in my mind's eye or on something akin to a psychic computer screen between my eyebrows. Psychic images are distinctly visible when my eyes are closed, but they also appear when my eyes are open. When this occurs it is like a subliminal filter of images or information is being superimposed upon that which I see with my physical eyes.

Practicing clairvoyance has strengthened my psychic boundaries by enabling me to see where there are holes, breaks and fissures in my aura. I believe this is an especially important healing process for most women who for millennia have had these protections broken down. I therefore have been successful in retrieving my life force/creative energy/spiritual memory and retaining it. Clairvoyance has enabled me to see how other people affect my energy field and body, and vice versa. My third eye has depicted how energy flows in and out of my body, and how energetic communication lines carry information between others and me. It has clearly shown me how the spirits of the living and the dead co-mingle, communicate and travel through time and space.

As a state licensed and ordained priestess, I am legally able to marry and offer clairvoyant counseling and healing to couples. In trance I am able to address the spiritual being of each person in a relationship and describe the spiritual contract of his or her marriage or separation. I am thus able to assist them in strengthening their communication with themselves, as bodies and spirits, with their god/goddess, and with each other.

I am also able to work as a spiritual midwife for the processes of birthing and dying. In the first domain I witness the inception of spirit and matter; I watch as a spiritual entity coordinates a contract with a prospective mother and father and seeds itself in the mother's astral body. Often I am requested to be present at the birth where I apply a method of "laying on of hands" upon the mother, offer spiritual support, and facilitate a blessing at the cutting of the umbilical cord.

When called upon to assist the dying and their surviving friends and family, I use my clairvoyance to witness the process of the spirit who is transitioning or birthing into the spirit world from matter. I assist all involved by operating as an interpreter, translating my observations in the psychic dimensions. I apply laying on of hands to the dying body and anoint it with oils and herbs. Most importantly, I include all interested family members in the rituals. I instruct them how to develop their own psychic abilities and encourage them to perform the closing rituals and blessings. My perspective of birthing and dying is vastly different from that of the American Medical Association which has treated these processes as crisis', ugly episodes best hidden from public view, and needing control and sterilization.

I am hopeful that as we move further into this new millennium, psychic women will continue to come out of the closets, the kitchens, the gardens, wherever we're hiding, and tell the delectable, passionate mysteries or mist-stories of the love between body and spirit. While there has been great and careful work done to destroy women's memory of this affair, as it is with the vital tendril of true love, it simply cannot be hidden or suppressed.

Mural inside the sanctuary of the Black Madonna of Monserrat, Spain, of major black madonnas of the world
Photograph by Wallace Birnbaum 2003

Mari: God the Mother of the Basque

Karen Nelson Villanueva, M.P.A., M.A.

In order to imagine the ancient Basque we must imagine a relationship with the Earth where she gives us all we need to survive and we remain in harmony with her. The land that we cultivate for food, the stones for our home, and the pasture for our flock were all her gifts to us. An omnipresent witness to our lives, loves, suffering, and loss, to her we owe our existence, and to her we return.

For many ancient, agriculturally based societies, the Earth was more than a resource; she was mother. This was true for the ancient Basque. Mother was Mari, Goddess of the Earth. It was the Basque people's belief in a primary feminine deity that allowed them to transition to Christianity with its emphasis on the worship of the Virgin Mary and influenced many of their laws, known as *fueros*. These laws were the cause, in part, of their turbulent relationship with Spain to the present day.

With the utmost respect to a people that I know only through literary research and brief visits to Bilbao and Mondragon, I propose to discuss the Basque people and their beliefs from the perspective of an outsider. As a person of many ethnicities, an African-American, and a woman, I am accustomed to being ostracized, misrepresented, disenfranchised, marginalized, and objectified. These adjectives could well express the Basque's relationship with Spain. In my research, I hope that my personal experience will enable me to be more sensitive to the hidden truths behind the written word and less prone to accept slander as the final word.

In this essay, I look at the extant body of knowledge and make connections that have never been made before from a feminist, womanist perspective. Often the truest beliefs of a people can be found in their legends, folklore, and mythology. Joseph Campbell, a world-renowned mythologist, once said, "One person's religion is another person's mythology."[1] So with this in mind, I have gathered "mythology" regarding the Goddess Mari of the Basque to answer the question of how the belief in this deity helped in the formation and creation of the Basque laws and affected their relationship with the Christian church and Spain to this day. I will present arguments to support the belief that the Goddess Mari was also worshipped as the Virgin Mary of Christianity. In order to make these relations clearer in my mind, I have examined history books on Basque politics, the Inquisition in Basque country, and articles on current events. I propose that it is the ancient Basque religion that engenders the independent spirit and tenacity of the Basque people, and fueled their difficult relationship with Castilian Spain that has inspired hatred in some and misunderstanding in others.

The Basque are a people whose beliefs make them feel whole, complete, and integrated into their surroundings and the rhythm of the Earth. An understanding of the Basque themselves must begin with an understanding of their land. Basque country, *Euskadi*, consists of seven provinces, or states: "Laburdi, Zuberoa, and Benavarra lying north of the Pyrenees; Navarra lying south of the Pyrenees; Biscay, Guipuzcoa, and Alaba lying southwest of the Pyrenees in the Cantabric mountains."[2] Straddling the borders of France and Spain, Euskadi is separated from France by the Adur River and from Spain by the Ebro. The total area of Basque country is approximately 12,655 square miles.[3]

The people of Basque country, *Euzkaldunak*, as they call themselves, appear to have occupied their land since humans migrated from the African continent. Amongst the Basque, the earliest human blood type, O, is found at a disproportionately higher average than the rest of Europe, 55%. In addition, the Basques have the highest incidence of negative Rhesus factor (RH) in the world. Both a blessing and a curse, an RH negative mother can fatally poison her RH-positive fetus thus keeping the Basque population small and enabling its people to thrive within a limited area.[4]

Euskara, Basque language, has no known relationship with any other language. Hence, the Basque people are said to be of no known Indo-European origin. As expressed by historian Roger Collins, "Basque is the sole surviving, anciently established, non-Indo-European language of Europe."[5] Their ancient blood and language helps to prove their claims of having lived in Basque country from time immemorial.

Apparent from the many words in the Euskara language is the importance of the Basque house, *etxea*. The most common root of all Basque names derives from etxea, or the Spanish version, echea.[6] Also, common proper names such as Javier, Xavier, and Xabier are forms of *etxaberria*, which means "new house."[7] The house is a central concept in the identity of the Basque people and majorities of Basque belong to and identify with a particular house. According to a chronicler of the Basque, Mark Kurlansky, "A house stands for a clan."[8] Always facing east toward the rising sun, the Basque house, typically white with red shutters, and a red tile roof, is decorated with Basque symbols. These symbols are not merely adornment but represent Basque spirituality. Understanding these symbols, even in a limited way, sheds light on how the Basques view their relationship with the Divine.

The first of these symbols we find inscribed on many a Basque house is the circle. This is the symbol of integration of the spirit and physical worlds: divinities and ancestors are envisioned as living in the underworld; people live above ground; and all is reflected in the sun, moon, and stars in the sky.[9] The cross symbolizes the importance of connection to the ancestors.[10] This is accomplished through the balance of masculine and feminine energies. The vertical line of the cross is feminine and represents the right, and the moon.[11] The horizontal line is masculine and represents the left, and the sun.[12] Where the lines converge is *dana*, meaning together.[13] The third Basque symbol, the triangle, represents the house and Basque identity.[14] The symbol of the square represents the land, which defines stability and belonging.[15] The fifth and final Basque symbol is the *Urdina*, the spiral called "the blue ring of Life."[16] This is the symbol for the growth and evolution of all things.[17] Roughly interpreted, these symbols represent the deep respect for their ancestors the Basque possess and how they recognize the importance of the egalitarian balance of masculine and feminine. It also demonstrates how they derive their identity from the house and stability from the land, yet allow for all things to change and grow.

Since the earliest times, the spiritual leader of the home, an *etxekandere*, has always been a woman and responsible for all the "blessings and prayers for all the house members wherever they are, living or dead."[18] She oversaw the funeral rites. Buried beneath the floor of the home, the dead were always with their loved ones and a central feature of the Basque house was the tomb for the ancestors. However, Christianity with its belief in hallowed ground changed this custom for most.

From their first recorded encounters with other peoples, the Basque were noted to be fiercely proud and extremely protective of their people, customs, and land. The first Roman accounts written in 218 B.C.E. credit the Basque with being tremendous warriors and an already ancient people. So secure were they in their sense of renewal through the Earth and the righteousness of their ways that the men committed suicide by ingesting *tejo*, turpentine, or jumping into fire when captured and the women "killed their children rather than see them fall to the enemy."[19] However, the Romans were successful in founding a settlement called Iruña (or Pamplona in Spanish) in honor of their Emperor Pompey, in the Basque province of Navarra, the most outlying of the provinces in Spain. There, the Basque learned to cultivate olives and plant vineyards to barter with the Romans. Too ferocious to dominate completely, the Romans allowed the Basque to retain their language and self-governance.

With the fall of the Roman Empire, came the Visigoths around 400 C.E. They swept through the Iberian Peninsula and conquered all but the Basque. For over 250 years, the Visigoths battled them, only to find them insurmountable. The continuous warfare united the Basque in their religious, cultural, and linguistic identity.[20] Previously, they were groups of mountain tribes who fought for their own homes and families against a common enemy. Because of their armed struggle, they were able to discover their similarities with neighboring peoples.

The ferocity of the Basque warrior is further chronicled in their engagement with Charlemagne's army. In retreat from a successful campaign against the Moors in Spain, Charlemagne attacked and looted Pamplona, thus inciting the Basque's ire. In retaliation, while marching through the steep and wooded Pyrenees, Charlemagne's rear guard was ambushed and massacred: "In this battle died Eggihard, who was in charge of the King's table, Anshelm, the count of the Palace and Roland, Lord of the Breton Marches, along with a great number of others."[21] The eleventh century epic poem, *La Chanson de Roland*, fails to mention the role of the Basque in the massacre in spite of the losses of such significant figures, choosing instead to concentrate on the conflict between the Christians and Moors.[22]

It was the Moors who were the next to discover the indomitableness of the Basque. In 714, Musa, commander of a North African Islamic alliance lead the campaign to conquer the Basque lands. He was unsuccessful. It would be four years later when the Muslims would finally be able to capture Pamplona, but they could never keep it. In the 800-year fight to remove the Moors from Spain, the Basques mostly fought on the side of the Christians. This marked the slow process of Basque conversion to Christianity, which may have occurred as early as the seventh century, "but some historians believe that the Basques were not a Christian people until the tenth or eleventh century."[23]

However, there is early evidence of a few Christian institutions that existed in Basque country. For example, by the end of the fourth century, there are records of a diocese in Calhorra and by the end of the sixth century there was a bishop of Pamplona, both in the province of Navarra.[24] Furthermore, the legend of Saint Firminus, also known as San Fermín, patron saint of Pamplona, may date as far back as the ninth century but in all probability stems from the twelfth century.[25] Whenever the conversion to Christianity occurred, it was late by European standards. Collins surmises, "Calhorra may indeed have been at the forefront of provincial Christianity, at least in the western half of the empire, in the late fourth century, but this does not imply that such enlightenment had extended itself to the whole of the Basque region."[26] Archaeomythologist Marija Gimbutas ascribes an even later date to the onset of Basque conversion. According to Gimbutas,

> Christianity arrived late to Basque country. The populace was only superficially Christian in remote areas during the fifteenth and sixteenth centuries. Even in the twentieth century, some mountainous regions escaped Christianity. There, belief in the goddess remains a living reality.[27]

In Basque legend, the soothsayer, Olentzero, foretold of the coming of Christianity. The story informs us that he ran down the mountainside and exclaimed, "Kixmi has been born and our end is near. I no longer wish to live, and I beg you to throw me over that cliff."[28] The townspeople complied with his wishes and threw him over the cliff, and this is how Christianity came to the Basque. Each Christmas, Olentzero, played by a townsperson, announces the coming of Kixmi, another name for Christ.

As demonstrated through centuries of warfare, what have always been important to the Basque are their land, culture, and self-determination through their laws. Around the eighth century in Basque history, not even the Catholic Church was as valued as these concepts. This is further demonstrated in the conflict between the Franks and Moors at Poitiers in 732. The Basque allowed their enemy, the Moors, to cross their land to reach Christian France, and some even fought on their side against the new threat to encroachment on Basque land, the French. This has led many to doubt the dependability of Basque Christianity. However, stumbling into Christianity may have been serendipitous for the Basque. The medieval age of the eleventh and fourteenth centuries ushered in a surge of Marion worship and culture. Much of Europe was celebrating a time of near cult worship of the Virgin Mother, Mary. Like the Basque, the rest of the medieval world was beginning to recognize the value of a woman at the center.

Greatest of the Basque pantheon of gods, *Andre Mari*, Lady Mari was

Goddess of the Earth, Moon, Thunder, and Wind. Also, as the Goddess of the Moon she was often depicted with her head encircled by its rays like the Virgin Mother. As Mother Earth, she represented the integration of nature and the four fundamental elements.[29] In the plant kingdom, herbs, trees, and flowers represented her. In the mineral kingdom, stalagmites, stones, and caverns were her symbols. Her sacred animal forms were the cow, snake, horse, and male goat and bull. She assumed either male or female form at will. Her caves combined the four elements by being below the earth, humid with water, drafty from the air, and fiery from the sunlight at its entrance.[30]

With her many forms derive different representations of her spheres of influence and power. As the Bird Goddess, Mari takes the form of ducks, swans, storks, and waterfowl, and influences birth and fate. She was known as the Goddess of Birds of Prey like owls and eagles and also, ravens and vultures. In this guise, she was the Wielder of Death, the Tomb Goddess. In fact, much of Mari's worship was as Goddess of Death and Regeneration. She embodied the cycle of birth, death, and rebirth. Taken from Basque mythology, philosopher Andrés Ortiz-Osés has written,

> *Mari aparece en su cueva, junto al fuego, peinando su hermosa cabellera; en su izquierda porta el **espejo** cual ojo lunar brujeril, pálido; en su derecha lleva el **peine** de oro para enderezar sus cabellos. Impresionante simbologema que representa a la vieja divinidad de la vida y de la muerte.[31]*

In her left hand with her lunar mirror, Mari receives the dead, and with the golden comb in her right hand, she brings the dead back to life through a process of re-combing, reincarnation, and transubstantiation.[32] The mirror represents the reigning in of power, the magical force, *adur*.[33] While the comb represents the expansive, physical force, *indar*, defined as "*vuelta al útero y revuelta al mundo*,"[34] come from the womb and return to the world.

Symbolically, Mari was represented in many universal forms. The triangle, as previously mentioned, a representation of the Basque home and identity, was also "*el útero de la madre/mujer*," the womb, or uterus, of the mother/woman and a symbol of regeneration.[35] She was represented as eggs, the symbol of life and regeneration. Again, we encounter the Basque symbol of the spiral, or snake, as the representation of the energetic and life giving force. In addition, we find ram's horns, visually similar to the uterus with fallopian tubes as a symbol of the womb.

The *Lauburu*, or Basque cross as previously discussed, depicts not only the union of feminine and masculine energies but also the animistic spirits of sun, moon, tree, and mountain. The arms of the cross are drawn as if spiraling outward like the sun's rays. This has led many to believe that the Basque practiced sun worship. Yet, the ancient words still recalled in bedtime prayer are undoubtedly a better indication of ancient Basque beliefs: "Sun, sacred and blessed, rejoin your mother."[36] Ekhi, Goddess of the Sun, was the daughter of the Earth. Everything was from Mari, Mother Earth, and to Mari everything must return.

In addition to her goddess functions, Andre Mari was a wife and mother. During encounters with her husband, son, and lover, Maju, the Divine Spirit of Thunder, terrible thunderstorms or hailstorms arose. Maju was also known as Sugaar, a serpent or dragon god. He was said to dwell in caves and fly in the evening sky as a half-moon of fire. He visited his wife on Friday nights to comb her hair. Mari was also reputed to have two sons: Atarrabi and Mikelats. In some legends, they were not sons at all, but daughters. A star in the heavens, Atarrabi was the good son, and if he was glowing, this portended good times ahead for the Basque. On the other hand, Mikelats, the wicked son, caused landslides and rock falls in the mountains.

Mari not only governed natural phenomena like hail, wind, drought, lightening, and rainstorms, but she had the power to magically transform substances like coal into gold and vice versa. There are many stories of people taking gold from her caves only for it to turn to coal in the outside world, or tales of her giving a piece of coal and it later turning into gold. These were her moral teachings. Ortiz-Osés tells us that what looks like gold on the outside, may be coal on the inside:

> ... que nos (a) parece como oro afuera en realidad es carbon ... adentro, de modo que la riqueza exterior carece del supervalor ... que se le otorga habitualmente, mientras que el autentico oro–valor interior aparece desvalerado afuera.[37]

The outside world appears to value superficial riches when what should be of value is what is precious within the soul.

Mari's moral code for her adherents consists of six commandments: do not lie, do not steal, do not be prideful, keep your word, respect others, and be helpful to others. These were undoubtedly the basis of the Basque's fueros. Her other rules dealt with the conduct of those who sought her such as, when addressing her, one should always use the familiar form of the pronoun. However, even with this familiar voice, you must never enter her domain without invitation, nor sit in her presence, and you must leave in the same manner that you came to her, preferably backing out of a cave.

The Inquisition later persecuted devotees of Mari.[38] *Xorguiñes*, or *sorguiñes*, came to mean witch, but originally referred to "a cave dwelling spirit in Mari's retinue."[39] Another definition of xorguiñes are "beings of the solitary plains and in the fissures opened by mountain torrents."[40] Originally, the term held no malice. The women following the old ways such as divination, making protective charms and herbal remedies, midwifing births, and performing herbal abortions, were the poor and old women, and widows of the town. Although some "witches" were men, also known as "warlocks," the vast majority were women. During the time of the Inquisition, Kurlansky notes, "Anyone found engaged in folk healing, divination, or other traditional practices, especially if it was a woman, was a candidate for burning."[41]

Mari's followers gathered on Friday, *Ostiral*, a day sacred to both Mari and the moon. These gatherings were called *aquelarre*, "a word composed of *larre*, pastureland, and *aquerra*, buck goat."[42] One of the best known of these locations was named Zugarramurdi. There at the aquelarre, a black, male goat, Akerbeltz, was surrounded by the xorguiñes who were said to then dance a dance "of slow movements, [where] all kept time stepping together, now on one foot, now on the other."[43] As the dance increased in speed, it consisted of jumps and other contortions. Also known as the spiral dance, its ancient origins have been noted around the world. In addition to dancing, xorguiñes "brought offerings of eggs, bread, and coins."[44]

The Inquisition marked a time in history when no one who was different was safe. This was true for the Jews, Moors, Gypsies, and Lutherans, and soon it was true for the Basque, too. The Inquisition was a grand attempt at the homogenization of the European continent. It was during this time that the Basques adopted the adage: "*Direnikez da sinistu bear; ez direla ez da esan bear,*" which translates as 'you don't have to believe that they exist, you don't have to say they don't exist'.[45] It was safer to keep one's beliefs to one's self than to face possible torture and death.

A reflection of these terrible times, an appeal written to King Henry IV in 1466 claimed that witches were out of control in the Basque province of Guipuzcoa.[46] The frenzy began in 1507 with the burning of 30 women charged with witchcraft in Calahorra, and continued through 1539. Aside from removing the differences posed by the Basques, the Inquisition was used as a ploy to seize Basque lands, particularly in the long contested province of Navarra. Intentionally given the reputation as "witch country," this province was desired by Spain's Charles I.

Other than economic gain, another underlying reason for the

Inquisition's persecution was a fear of women. Because women bleed and possess the power to carry life, they were once the greatest mystery. Lacking a foundation in goddess worship, the Christians no longer recalled how to approach a woman as Divine. In Christianity, the Virgin Mary was stripped of her sexuality, leaving instead a puritanical repression of her humanity. This misogyny was turned against the Basque who were criticized for the independence of their women. In one myth, Basque women were accused of being inheritors of the sins of Eve because of the great number of apples they ate, which led to their wanton behavior.[47]

Perhaps because of their Basque origin, the Jesuits, rather than persecuting the Basque like the other Christian orders such as the Franciscans and Dominicans, acted as mediators and translators for the people. Iñigo Lopez de Oñaz y Loyola, also known as Ignatius Loyola, founded the Society of Jesus in 1534, after having visions of the Virgin of Montserrat while recovering from a nearly fatal injury. This Black Virgin, the patron saint of Catalan, is known as the *Theotokos*, the Mother of God. This Mary, like Andre Mari, was found in a cave, remains in the mountains, and symbolizes the fertility and fecundity of the Earth, both black and beautiful: *nigra sum sed formosa*.[48]

Like Andre Mari, the Virgin Mary is often found in trees or caves near fresh springs of water. Mary and Mari wear red dresses. Also, they are depicted with halos around their heads, and snakes under their feet. With the advent of Christianity, some say that the Basque Goddess Mari shrunk to become Saint Marina. However, such a drastic change would not be necessary for those who recognized their goddess in yet another form with yet another new Christian name. Thus, the Basque adage, "You don't have to believe that they exist, you don't have to say they don't exist," becomes truer than ever. In the Virgin Mary is the goddess, and the goddess Mari is alive in her.

Besides similarities in name and appearance, Mari and Mary are advocates for equality and justice, particularly for the ostracized, misrepresented, disenfranchised, marginalized, and objectified. Fueros, the codified local customs of the Basque, were written into the legal code in the twelfth century. To the Basque, the goddess is the embodiment of these laws, and so the laws were the goddess. The fueros are as important to the Basques as their lives, for surely many have died in the effort to keep these laws alive. The fueros took a more progressive view of human rights than was the norm in the twelfth century. They addressed "a wide range of subjects, including the purity of cider, the exploitation of minerals, the laws of inheritance, the administration of farm land, [and] crimes and punishments."[49] Their inheritance laws included direct inheritance to the eldest child whether male or female without apportionment to other siblings. This demonstrates the importance to the Basque to keep the house intact. Additionally, the fueros exempted the Basque from direct taxation by Castilian Spain, import duties, and military service outside their own province.[50]

History was to show the Basque followed a fateful path. During the Carlist wars, they sided with the Carlists and became ardent Catholics because Castilian kings upheld the fueros in the past and promised to do so in the future. With the loss of the wars, the Basque witnessed the end of their fueros. Euskara was replaced by Spanish language in the schools and the *guardia civil* became an omnipresent and oppressive force.

The perseverance of the Basque language is credit in part to the priests who were still allowed its study, and to the efforts of the fanatical Sabino Araña y Goiri, who championed Basque nationalism and helped to re-write its history. With a desire to quash the spirit of the Basque, Generalissimo Francisco Franco encouraged Hitler to test his new squadron on the sacred city of Gernika (Guernica in Spanish) massacring over 1600 people and leaving the remaining population devastated. Franco would rule Spain until his death in 1975, always mindful to keep the Basque in their place.

As with so many creatures with their backs against the wall, the Basque fought back with all the ferocity they had ever shown, this time as terrorists. The majority of Basque oppose terrorist tactics nonetheless the Euskadi and Liberty party (Euskadi Ta Askatasuna – ETA) was formed in 1952. Credited with bombings, assassinations, and guerilla tactics ever since, the group sees force as a way to freedom. In the new Spain with its recently elected socialist government, talks have begun for a truce.

Someday soon, there may be a return to the fueros and the autonomous rule of the Basque. Upon reflection of this essay, what we must ask ourselves is do we ever learn from our mistakes in the treatment of 'other'? At times, it seems that we have not progressed so very far from the Inquisition. How much does it differ from Homeland Security? And what of the Earth? Our view of this precious rock as simply a resource for exploitation promises to leave everyone without a home. Perhaps it is a faith and belief in the feminine Divine, like Mari God the Mother of the Basque, who promises our most success as a species. Through her, we are all her children, and this is our only home.

Notes

1 Joseph Campbell stated this in an interview with Bill Moyers in the PBS Special program, "The Power of Myth," 1988.

2 Joe V. Eiguren, The Basque History: Past & Present (Boise, ID: The Offset Printer, 1972), 21.

3 Ibid.

4 Mark Kurlansky, The Basque History of the World (New York: Penguin Books, 1999), 21.

5 Roger Collins, The Basques (New York: Basil Blackwell, 1986), 11.

6 Kurlansky, 6.

7 Ibid.

8 Ibid.

9 Denise Orpustan-Love, "Building Papa's Mill House: A Journey Into Basque Spiritualism" (PhD diss., California Institute of Integral Studies, 2003), 85.

10 Ibid, 102.

11 Ibid.

12 Ibid.

13 Ibid.

14 Ibid, 111.

15 Ibid, 118.

16 Ibid, 124.

17 Ibid.

18 Kurlansky, 6.

19 Eiguren, 24.

20 Kurlansky, 36.

21 Einhard, Vita Karoli Magni Imperatoris, 9, L. Halphen (ed.), Eginhard, Vie de Charlemagne (Paris, 1967), 28-30, L. Thorpe (tr.), Two Lives of Charlemagne (Harmondsworth, 1969), 64-5, quoted in Collins, The Basques, 121.

22 Collins, 123.

23 Kurlansky, 38.

24 Collins, 61.

25 Ibid.

26 Ibid, 65.

27 Marija Gimbutas, The Living Goddesses, Edited and supplemented by Miriam Robbins Dexter (Berkeley and Los Angeles, CA: University of California Press, 2001), 173.

28 "Basque Legends," http://dametzdesign.com/legends.html.

29 Andrés Ortiz-Osés, La Diosa Madre: Interpretación desde la mitología vasca (Madrid: Editorial Trotta, 1996), 82.

30 Ibid.

31 Ibid, 83. 'Mari appears in her cave, next to a flame, combing her beautiful hair; in her left hand she holds the pale, bewitched mirror of the lunar eye; in her right, she holds a golden comb to fix her hair. The symbolic impression is that of the old divinity of life and death.' (My translation here and as follows.)

32 Ibid.

33 Ibid.

34 Ibid. 'Come from the womb and return to the world.'

35 Ibid. 'The womb of the mother/womb of the woman.'

36 Kurlansky, 82.

37 Ortiz-Osés, La Diosa Madre,70. 'What seems to us like gold in the outside world is really coal ... inside, the manner of the outside world to acquire riches without real value ... is habitually rewarded, meanwhile the authentic, valuable interior gold seems worthless to the outside world.'

38 Gimbutas, 173.

39 Max Daschu, "Xorguiñas y Celestinas," Secret History of the Witches, http://www.suppressedhistories .net/secret_history/xorguinas.html.

40 Mariana Monteiro, Legends and Popular Tales of the Basque People (New York: F.A. Stokes, 1891), 17.

41 Kurlansky, 101.

42 Monteiro, 19.

43 Ibid.

44 José Miguel de Barandiarán, Mitología vasca (San Sebastian: Editorial Txertoa, 1979), 124, quoted in Daschu, "Xorguiñas y Celestinas."

45 José Miguel de Barandiarán, Diccionario ilustrado de mitología vasca y algunas de sus fuentes, vol. 1 of his Obras completas (Bilbao: Enciclopedia Vasca, 1972), 140, quoted in and translated by Michael Everson, "Tenacity in Religion, Myth, and Folklore: the Neolithic Goddess of Old Europe preserved in a Non-Indo-European Setting." Journal of Indo-European Studies, Vol.17, nos. 3 & 4, Fall/Winter (1989), 290, "You don't have to believe that they exist, you don't have to say they don't exist."

46 Daschu, "Xorguiñas y Celestinas."

47 Kurlansky, 95.

48 Song of Songs, 1:5.

49 Kurlansky, 66.

50 Ibid.

Bibliography

Arana y Goiri, Sabino. El Partido Carlista y Los Fueros Baskos. Buenos Aires: Talleres Gráficos de "La Baskonia," 1912.

Arrien, Angeles. Basque Mysticism: Walking the Path with Practical Feet. Audio Tape: California Institute of Integral Studies, June 18-19, 1988.

Collins, Roger. The Basques. New York: Basil Blackwell, 1986.

Dashu, Max. "Xorguiñas y Celestinas." Secret History of the Witches. http://www.suppressedhistories.net/secret_history/xorguinas. html.

Eiguren, Joe V. The Basque History: Past & Present. Boise, ID: The Offset Printer, 1972.

Everson, Michael. "Tenacity in Religion, Myth, and Folklore: the Neolithic Goddess of Old Europe preserved in a Non-Indo-European Setting." Journal of Indo-European Studies, Vol.17, nos. 3 & 4, Fall/Winter (1989): 277-295.

Gimbutas, Marija. The Living Goddesses. Edited and supplemented by Miriam Robbins Dexter. Berkeley and Los Angeles, CA: University of California Press, 2001.

Henningsen, Gustav. The Witches' Advocate: Basque Witchcraft and the Spanish Inquisition (1609-1614). Reno, NV: University of Nevada Press, 1980.

Kurlansky, Mark. The Basque History of the World. New York: Penguin Books, 1999.

Larrea, Mª. Angeles and Rafael Mieza Mieg. Introduction to the History of the Basque Country. Translated by George R. Clarke. The Basque American Foundation, 1985.

Melammed, Renée Levine. "María López: A Convicted Judaizer from Castile." In Women in the Inquisition: Spain and the New World, edited by Mary E. Giles, 53-72. Baltimore: The Johns Hopkins University Press, 1999.

Monteiro, Mariana. Legends and Popular Tales of the Basque People. New York: F.A. Stokes, 1891.

Monter, William. Frontiers of Heresy: The Spanish Inquisition from the Basque Lands to Sicily. New York: Cambridge University Press, 1990.

Orpustan-Love, Denise. "Building Papa's Mill House: A Journey Into Basque Spiritualism." PhD diss., California Institute of Integral Studies, 2003.

Ortiz-Osés, Andrés. La Diosa Madre: Interpretación desde la mitología vasca. Madrid: Editorial Trotta, 1996.

Payne, Stanley G. Basque Nationalism. Reno, NV: University of Nevada Press, 1975.

Perry, Mary Elizabeth. "Contested Identities: The Morisca Visionary, Beatriz de Robles." In Women in the Inquisition: Spain and the New World, edited by Mary E. Giles, 171-188. Baltimore: The Johns Hopkins University Press, 1999.

Venero, Maximiano Garcia. Historia del nacionalismo vasco, Reimpresión a la 3ª edición. Madrid: Editora Nacional, 1979.

Rags to Riches: The Inner Road to Gypsyhood

Kim Bella

Summer approaches. The bright, tender green days of spring melt away. As the external world moves from one season to another, she notices a movement, a change of seasons in her internal world as well. Her feet start to itch. She experiences a yearning in her heart and a longing in her soul for the open road. The word freedom comes to mind and she trembles with suppressed excitement. These moments of surrender to the pull of complete and utter abandon sustain her as she waits to start her wandering. Being "labeled" gypsy by her family members due to her seemingly rootless lifestyle, she has begun to wonder what her wandering ways meant to her.

This article delves into the reality of the gypsies' history and the myth that surrounds them and then investigates the internal struggle between myth and reality and how that relates to the human psyche. This research study involves one co-researcher and the principle investigator exploring the dichotomy between the two internal states of the romanticized gypsy (myth) and the reviled or hated gypsy (reality) using five gypsy fairy tales as a springboard for inquiry. A participatory approach using a heuristic methodology is used predicated on a psychological epistemology. In the course of the research, the principal investigator and the co-researcher contemplated each of the fairy tales from a meditative state inspired by the embodied participatory model of Ferrer, Albareda, and Romero (2004). This method engages the unknown or the mystery from different loci of attention, which include the physical body, the vital energy center, the heart, and the mind thereby establishing a "many ways of knowing" perspective.

Some ways of knowing gypsies include a collection of qualities that can be described from an internal orientation and understood through the term gypsyhood. Gypsyhood is a way to understand and describe various possibilities of psychological meaning-making. Some of these possibilities include a physical, emotional, mental, and spiritual alignment with the gypsy way of life; an archetypal scenario that may be playing out in the choices an individual makes in her or his life; or even a developmental phase in the evolution/involution of maturation and the furthering of becoming one's own autonomous person.

Historical Roots of the Gypsy

The investigation of the gypsy (also known as Rom or Roma) way of life begins with their historical roots and the worldwide societal perceptions of them as a separate and disparate race over the centuries. The gypsies have exhibited amazing resiliency throughout their long history, from their exodus out of India (McDowell, 1970) to slavery and racial purging during the Inquisition (Hancock, 1987) to their persecution during the Holocaust (Lewy, 2000). The gypsies' ability to survive despite the violence they have endured and the oppression they have suffered is unparalled. Their marginalization has been perpetrated by almost every society with which they've had contact, yet their culture continues to this day.

In delving deeper into the mysteries that surround the world of the gypsies, there abounds a rich blend of fact and fiction. Hancock (1987) describes the many negative characteristics attributed to the gypsies as a race over the years including promiscuity, thieving, filthiness, impurity, and untrustworthiness. They have been reviled the world over, and Petrova (2003) suggests that a physical otherness as well as a cultural otherness contributed to the bias against the gypsies. The non-nomadic white European communities denigrated the gypsies' moral values and nomadic way of life, leading to the exclusion of gypsies from those societies.

Given the fear and loathing that contact with gypsies engendered, many people still hold a certain fascination for gypsies and the gypsy lifestyle. Some attributes that characterize the gypsy way of life include a carefree lifestyle, dancing and singing, exotic women, mysterious men, bright colors, and most of all, a kind of freedom that the gypsy way of life evokes in many people. It seems that the gypsies as people, as well as the gypsies as a race have been regarded as a bit player in the larger stage of the cultural and societal arena, the dominant versus the minor, or subaltern class.

In looking at the dominant class versus the subaltern classes, Sibley (1981) finds that gypsy myths play an important part in defining the image of this particular group as outside the dominant societal paradigm and Hancock (1987) agrees that the mythologizing of the gypsies has delegated them to a realm of non-personhood. The myths de-personalize the reality of the actual people, either through the romanticizing or demonizing of the entire gypsy race. This fits in with the paradox that surrounds the gypsies and separates the reality from the myth.

According to Sway (1988), the gypsies choose to maintain their separateness and therefore get punished in the process, creating a self-fulfilling cycle of abuse. However, this type of thinking perpetuates the stereotypes and keeps the gypsies in the fringes as the place they have "chosen for themselves." Petrova (2003) states that the continual internalization of oppression for the gypsies has reinforced the tension of an "us against them" opposition. However, she maintains that research has shown that the gypsies would rather live in an integrated, non-segregated society rather than outside the bounds of that society. This leads the author to question the unconscious motivations and biases of "authorities" and researchers of the gypsy people and their culture, given that most of the writers of gypsy life are of non-gypsy origin.

One example of conflict between gypsy researchers reflects the different perceptions of the same event, namely the honoring of Saint Sarah each year in France. Sway (1988) describes the Catholic festival honoring Sarah of the Black at Saintes-Maries-de-la-Mer in southern France as mostly a time for the gypsies to reconnect with community, make money, and enjoy themselves. In contrast, loyal Catholics (read non-gypsies) are portrayed as the ones devoutly worshiping and paying homage to the saint (Clerbert, 1967, as cited in Sway, 1988). McDowell (1970) paints a different picture when he explains his gypsy sojourn to the same pilgrimage site as a place where the "sacred and secular coexist at Saintes Maries...the devout throng the church, revelers perform rites of their own" (p. 55). He makes no distinction between gypsy and non-gypsy, but describes the atmosphere as follows:

> In the stifling, smoky crypt of the church, Gypsy men, women, and children pay homage to Sarah. Natural performers and intense spectators, they create a spontaneous religious drama with an impromptu concert. Candles melt in the heat, and incense fumes mingle with the smoke, but the faithful will ignore discomforts and keep their vigil. (p. 51)

There seems to be a consensus among researchers, especially among linguists, that the Rom originally resided in India (Strom, 1993; McDowell,

1970) and spread out from there for unknown reasons, although many stories abound as to the impetus for the diasporas. In their subsequent wanderings, the meeting of the Rom with different cultures resulted in nomenclature for the gypsy people that contains many surprising similarities worldwide, such as Karaki in Persian and Caraque in France, where the root is kara, which means black in Tatar (Strom, 1993). Although described by researchers as historically a dark-skinned people, there is the possibility that the collision of cultures has resulted in seeing the gypsies as the "dark other," a subaltern class in the truest sense of the word that has endured throughout the centuries. They have been driven out or imprisoned in most places they traveled, burned at the stake, kept and sold as slaves, sent to concentration camps, suffered forced sterilization, as well as many other atrocities (Strom, 1993), and yet they survive even though they have never held the mantle of "dominant race."

The Psychological Function of the Gypsy

The idea or myth of the gypsies and the reality of gypsies serve a psychological function for society as a whole, as well as a boundary for the "normal" indicator within the larger cultural container. Gypsies are as real psychologically as they are literally, and understanding our own inner "gypsyhood" can go a long way into integrating the "dark other" as ourselves. Viewing the gypsy phenomenon psychologically opens the door for new perspectives and different ways of knowing in trying to understand the lived gypsy experience and the internalized gypsy experience.

One example of this type of knowing is through the archetypes of the collective unconscious as described by Jung (Corey, 1977). The collective unconscious is a universally shared phenomenon cutting across cultural lines and the archetypes are constellations of characteristics pertaining to different aspects of the universal human (such as the mother, the hero, and the trickster to name a few). One of the archetypes relevant to this study is the shadow. It is the personification of all that is considered antisocial, primitive, and negative within the psyche (Enns, 1994). It contains forces that would be destructive if expressed, so these negative aspects need to be tamed to ensure social order. The shadow aspect, in other words, can be seen as the internalized other.

As an example of the shadow aspect, Sonneman (1999) describes how gypsy men have been idealized as dark and dangerous, which is appealing to non-gypsy women, but threatening to non-gypsy men. This creates a split in the psyche, which results in repression of that aspect and acting out behaviors, such as socially sanctioned activities like war. For the gypsy woman, Sonneman (1999) states that "Non-Gypsies transfer to her their own suppressed desires and unvoiced fears" (¶ 17). It seems to be another justification through projection for silencing non-gypsy women as well. Given the historical negativity projected onto the gypsy race globally, I am proposing the possibility of a gypsy archetype.

I am curious about the submerged beliefs that we encounter in the world and then internalize so completely as an unconscious dimension of our psyche. There seems to be an interesting interplay between the conscious internal gypsy and the manifestations and expressions of behavior based on the unconscious internal gypsy. What are those parts of ourselves that get enslaved to the internal "patriarchy," or ruler father, based on the values in which we've been enculturated? What is the control that was originally forced upon up us by the outside and that we now subject ourselves to as an inner standard? How do we exploit one part of ourselves in service for other parts?

In exploring the gypsy archetype, I am struck by how several of the attributes or characteristics commonly associated with gypsies, reflect the shadow aspect of the psyche and unconscious psychological processes. Crisp (2004) describes the shadow as "someone or something we feel uneasy about or in some measure repelled by (¶ 1)" and uses the gypsy as an example, keeping company with unsavory characters like foreigners, prostitutes, burglars, and sinister figures in the dark. Although many processes are at work in the unconscious, the gypsies seem to hold a special status that exists in two aspects, the mysterious romantic and the filthy thieves. The mental/emotional dimension of being a gypsy in this modern world is a theme that will be explored and developed further using psychological theory as well as through gypsy folklore from a heuristic methodological perspective.

Jung (1961) explains the importance and the preponderance of the archetypes in stories and myths from primitive cultures. He saw the archetypes as shaping the psyche and revealing the character of the soul. Given that the folklore of gypsies has been historically an oral tradition, this implies the importance of trans-generational continuity in handing down gypsy-specific stories. In many of the gypsy folk and fairy tales there are elements of the "Romantic Gypsy" and the "Reviled, Hated Gypsy" aspects woven throughout the stories. I explore this more fully later in the article.

The Black Madonna and Gypsy as Metaphor

Woodworth (1990) states that the gypsies worship Sara, described as the servant to Jesus' two Marys when they landed on the shore of Les Saintes Maries de la Mer in Southern France. Woodworth (1990) also states that due to an apparent conversion of the gypsies to Christianity, they identified Sara as the Virgin Mary, although Lee (2002) suggests a link to a pre-Christian black goddess in this area. Woodworth (1990) goes on to postulate that the abundance and distribution of Black Madonnas might be due to the wide-spread diaspora of the gypsies. It is interesting to note here that a subaltern culture (the gypsies) might have been instrumental in spreading a subaltern religious figure (the Black Madonna), which continues to influence the religious practices of thousands of followers, externally and internally.

Some scholars have speculated that Sara was originally identified as the black goddess Kali. Woodworth (1990) suggests that "the black color of the Madonnas represent something archetypal and unexpressed in Christianity: black represents the Death Mother, the Crone, the Shadow Self" (¶ 13). Some authors even contend that the Black Madonna is prevalent in the human psyche because we need her (Anonymous, 1998) and that the male psyche needed to project its dualistic split onto Kali as a way to contend with its own internal struggle (Sjoo & Mor, 1991).

The Research Project

Exploration into the life of the gypsies led to a fuller investigation of the subject in the form of a participatory research project. This research study included myself as the principal investigator and one other research participant. I am a highly-educated professional 43 year-old Caucasian female with a background in yoga, yoga therapy, mental health counseling, anthropology, psychology, art, and computers. The co-researcher is a highly-educated professional 37 year-old Caucasian male with a background in physics, astronomy, and philosophy. Both participants are married. Some areas of differences to note between the two participants in this study include gender, age, hard science versus social science background, and perceived artistic ability.

The research co-participant and I randomly selected five fairy tales from a book on gypsy lore. Based on the holistic, participatory model of Ferrer, Albareda, and Romero (2004), we focused on a specific part of our experience first (respectively, body, vital energy, heart, and mind). Then we read aloud one of the tales, meditated on it from one of the focal points of experience, and went our separate ways to draw our understanding of the story from the specific locus of attention.

From the heuristic methodology described by Moustakas (1990), the co-researcher and I engaged in a journey of self-inquiry using the Focusing technique described by Gendlin (1978). Focusing is an open-ended inquiry into one's present-moment experience and this is the process we utilized as a method congruent with heuristic in-dwelling (Moustakas, 1990). Based on the emotional and psychical healing power of artful expression (Allen, 1995; McNiff, 1992) and incorporating an art-based research paradigm (McNiff, 1998; Braud & Anderson, 1998), the co-researcher and I chose drawing as the visual expression of conveying the internal experience from the fairy tales readings.

I approach the data with my own particular biases, based on my cultural container, and I notice how my conditioning influences my interpretations of the fairy tales. Acknowledging this, I identify certain themes emerging from the fairy tales as well as in the interpretive artwork. For example, in many of the gypsy fairy tales as a whole, a witch emerges as a character with evil intent while pretending to be good. I am reminded of a split in the human psyche that may be reminiscent of the Sara-Kali split mentioned previously.

Many interpretive lenses are available to construe the meaning of stories. For purposes of this study, I base my interpretations on a psychological epistemology. This epistemology is based on a transpersonal emphasis with a broad foundation in traditional psychological theory. This "whole person" perspective blends all of our personal thoughts, feelings, sensations, and spiritual sensitivities with those beliefs and ideas we have inherited from a rich historical tradition of psychological thought developed by traditional scholars and practitioners in the discipline of psychology.

Oil pastels were chosen as the medium for the artwork. All the drawings were rendered using bright, vivid colors that revealed energetic movement and flow. Each participant chose white drawing paper as the background for the drawings. Table 1 shows comparisons of the textual and visual symbolism for each of the fairy tales and the artwork.

Table 1
Interpretive Themes for Gypsy Fairy Tales
Fairy Tale Textual Symbolism Visual Symbolism
The Riddle Transformation Explosion
Bad boy to good boy Cut off/alienated
Selfishness Angry energy
It all Comes to Light Transformation Glowing energy
Power of love Energy release
Resiliency Hope
Evil Character Exclusion
The Snake Transformation Internal self
Snake to prince Shedding skin
Belief in miracles Rewards
Searching Being touched
The Deluded Dragon Transformation Contact with other
Poor to rich Strengths revealed
Perceived weakness Inner core
Hard life Outside influences
The Dog and the Maiden Transformation Inner strength
Dog to nobleman Patience
Loyalty Inner spring
Power of belief Holding

The fairy tales all contain a prevalent theme of the process of transformation through contact with another. Although not listed as a theme in the table, each story also exemplifies ingenuity, especially when encountering suffering and hardship financially, emotionally, or socially. There are some notable thematic implications here; however, a more detailed analysis of the universal themes is beyond the scope of this article.

Table 2 highlights some of the differences between the artwork for each participant from the perspective of each fairy tale. It appears that each story brought out different facets of the psychological process for the researchers.

Table 2
Differences Between Participants' Artwork

Fairy Tale	Principal Invstgtor	Co-Participant
The Riddle	Abstract figure	Concrete figure
	Internal/external	External
	Complexity	Simplicity
It all Comes to Light	Punishing	Covering
	Contained	Flowing
	Dualistic	Universal
The Snake	Use of white space	No white space
	Mostly bright	Light and dark
The Deluded Dragon	Open	Hiding
	Warm colors	Cool colors
	Surrounded	Grounded
The Dog and the Maiden	Partial coverage	Full coverage
	Outer/inner	Left/right
	Disconnected	Connected

A possible interpretation of the differences between the researchers' drawings includes a reflection of the psychical workings of the individuals involved. For example, the "punishing" versus "covering" interpretation might reflect the use of different defense mechanisms in order to feel safe, where I might judge and my co-researcher might hide. Possible influences to some of these differences may well be due to the initial meditative starting points (see Table 3). In the drawings, I notice a relationship between the tone and the origin of attention. For example, from the vital energy location, the two drawings exude a vitality unlike the other drawings. Again, a more comprehensive analysis is beyond the scope of this article; however, this might be an opportunity for future research possibilities.

Table 3
Locus of Attention with Corresponding Fairy Tale
Locus of AttentionFairy Tale
BodyThe Riddle
Vital EnergyIt all Comes to Light
HeartThe Snake
MindThe Deluded Dragon
MysteryThe Dog and the Maiden

Table 4 shows the similarities between the artistic expressions of both participants grounded in the story. Each story evoked a response from the participants and the parallels between the renderings for each story are striking.

Table 4
Major Similarities Between the Participants' Artwork
Fairy TaleSimilarities
The RiddleFigure surrounded by frenetic energy
Bright, vivid colors
It all Comes to LightBright blue globe
Two golden orbs
Smooth, flowing lines
The SnakeBright orange and gold objects
Roundness
Serpentine figure
Holding quality
The Deluded DragonGreen dragon figure
Concrete images
A sense of being surrounded
The Dog and the MaidenSpirals
Strong pink and purple imagery
Movement

A major difference between the drawings of each of the participants includes a smooth versus a rough texture. This might be indicative of behavioral and social stylistic differences. For instance, the co-researcher stated that he has a hard time revealing much about himself, and this might be indicated by the "rough" hesitant style of his drawing. I, on the other hand, feel more "smooth" socially, and this may be reflected in the differences between our textural artistic expressions. Table 5 identifies some of the general differences in artwork style.

Table 5
Major Differences in Artwork Style
Principal InvestigatorCo-Participant
Smooth textureRough texture
Strong, bold linesThin, light lines
Limited color varietyBroad range of color
Less coverageFull coverage

Again, these differences of artistic style speak to different ways of perceiving and operating in the world. For example, I have a tendency to spread myself too thin in regards to external activities and interests, whereas the co-researcher is more focused and committed to one specific task at a time.

Some artistic similarities of style include comparable drawing compositions and abstract symbols to explicate unconscious emotions. Table 6 pinpoints a few of these major similarities from the standpoint of artistic style.

Table 6
Similarities in Artwork Style
Principle Investigator and Co-Participant
Comparable composition placement
The use of bright, vivid colors
Incorporation of a mixture of many shapes and lines
The use of negative space
Cohesiveness of the overall design

For each of these analyses of the fairy tales, the artwork, and the artistic rendering, it's interesting to speculate on the parallels of the human psyche to the gypsy archetype and how that gets reflected in a visual way.

We are all part of the human soul, and we all participate in the collective unconscious, regardless of our race, ethnicity, gender, religious orientation, age, culture, socio-economic background, or education. Every culture in every part of the world constitutes an aspect of the universal soul. Gypsies usually evoke a strong response, whether positively or negatively, from the dominant culture. It is a response perhaps stemming from the alienation of that specific aspect of the psyche from the larger organism. Gypsies are popular in stories and myths due to their being a part of the larger whole already. The loss of gypsies to the world, either literally or emotionally, would be the loss of a part of the larger soul.

It is typically beyond the nature of the gypsies to perform a literature review; their research is in the form of stories and moment-to-moment experience. The methodology in this article is in alignment with the reality of the research subject. The way the gypsies work with their history is the way they live their life, which incorporates a fluid kind of truth. Suffering and hardship are a fact of life, and yet they survive. They adapt to the hereness and the now-ness of the present moment, which is in itself a form of spiritual liberation and psychological freedom. Perhaps this is the aspect that appeals to the larger imagination of the non-gypsy other.

The integration of all aspects of the human psyche requires an attitude of acceptance and a belief in the gypsies and in the dark other, internally and externally, positively and negatively. True acceptance of all parts of the psyche leads to integration and integration supports conscious action. With alignment of thought and behavior, there is hope for responsible and respectful action in the world and with others. Assimilation of the romantic gypsy and the reviled gypsy parts of the human psyche can help guide the human race from a place of inner destitution and deficiency to a place of incredible inner wealth, from rags to riches.

Bibliography

Allen, P.B. (1995). *Art is a way of knowing: a guide to self-knowledge and spiritual fulfillment through creativity.* Boston: Shambhala Publications, Inc.

Anonymous (1998). The black Madonna and the womb of God. Journal of Women & Religions, 16, 139-146. Retrieved November 12, 2004 from the World Wide Web: http://www.women religious. org/~education/Mariology3/Read/Readings 3/ BlackMadonna. htm

Braud, W., & Anderson, R. (1998). *Transpersonal research methods for the social sciences: honoring human experience.* Thousand Oaks, CA: Sage Publications, Inc.

Corey, G.F. (1977). *Theory and practice of counseling and psychotherapy.* Belmont, CA: Wadsworth Publishing Company, Inc.

Crisp, T. (2004). The archetype of the shadow. Retrieved October 16, 2004 from the World Wide Web: http://www.dreamhawk.com/ shadow.htmTony Crisp

Enns, C.Z. (1994). Archtypes and gender: goddesses, warriors, and psychological health. Journal of Counseling and Development, 73(2), 127-134.

Ferrer, J.N., Albareda, R.V., & Romero, M.T. (2004). Embodied participation in the mystery: implications for the individual, interpersonal relationships, and society. ReVision, 27(1), 10-17.

Gendlin, E.T. (1978). *Focusing.* New York: Bantam Books.

Hancock, I. (1987). *The pariah syndrome: an account of gypsy slavery and persecution.* Ann Arbor, MI: Karoma Publishers, Inc.

Jung, C.G. (1961). *Memories, dreams, reflections.* New York: Random House.

Lee, R. (2002). The Romani goddess Kali Sara. Retrieved November 12, 2004 from the World Wide Web: http://home.cogeco.ca/ ~kopachi/articles/romanigoddess.html

Lewy, G. (2000). *The Nazi persecution of the gypsies.* New York: Oxford University Press.

Manning-Sanders, R. (1964). *The red king and the witch: gypsy folk and fairy tales.* New York: Roy Publishers, Inc.

McDowell, B. (1970). *Gypsies: wanderers of the world.* Washington, DC: National Geographic Society.

McNiff, S. (1998). *Art-based research.* Philadelphia, PA: Jessica Kingsley Publishers.

McNiff, S. (1992). *Art as medicine: creating a therapy of the imagination.* Boston: Shambhala Publications, Inc.

Moustakas, C.E. (1990). *Heuristic research: design, methodology, and applications.* Newbury Park, CA: Sage Publications, Inc.

Petrova, D. (2003). The Roma: between a myth and the future. <u>Social Research, 70</u>(1), 111.

Sjoo, M., & Mor, B. (1991). *The great cosmic mother: rediscovering the religion of the earth* (2nd ed.). San Francisco: HarperSanFrancisco.

Sonneman, T.F. (1999). Dark mysterious wanderers: the migrating metaphor of the gypsy. <u>Journal of Popular Culture, 32</u>(4), 119-140.

Strom, Y. (1993). *Uncertain roads: searching for the gypsies.* New York: Four Winds Press.Sway, M. (1988). *Familiar strangers: gypsy life in America.* Chicago: University of Illinois Press.

Woodworth, K. (1990). Black Madonnas. Retrieved November 12, 2004 from the World Wide Web: http://www.aquafemina.com/ black-madonna.html

Photograph taken by Latonia Dixon

Ancient Ache

Laura Scaccia Beagle

Volcano
Red   Black
Blood   Earth   Mother   Mary
Dea   Dea   Madre

Salt sea envelopes,
Each slinky inch of my worn body
Buoyant in her grace
Easy I go under
Roll over and over and under Her

Open   Raw
        And welcoming

My ancient ache
My germinating love
Familiar and breathtaking
Life giving womb
Warm hune stone
Age old wisdom

Hands caressing
Lizard cuddling
Arching backward toward
Memory deep in my cells
She humbly   majestically
Waits through generations of mortal conflict
Patiently for the return
Spiraling love

In harmony with life's cadence
Language lost   found   returning
Harbor grief, harbor truth,

Mother may I
Drink from your slippery well of life
Blessing my body knowledge
Anointing my hands
Transfiguring my heart
Stone   to flesh

Calling Her name
Calling Her
Calling Dea

2004 Sardegna

Moving Between the Worlds

Intrinsic Movement As Transformative Spiritual Practice and Expression of Women's Spirituality

Louise M. Paré, Ph.D.

REMEMBRANCE

The tiniest sounds hiss forth
from underneath skin
feathers.
Slow sounding wind
slipping through teeth.

Crawling upon piano's notes
Dissolving into tremulous sounds
Earthen bones pound upon
ancient memory.

Coming this way before
I heard you
calling me.

Now I remember.

11/30/95
LMParé

For thousands of years women priestesses, healers, and shamans have used movement and dance to embody and celebrate the energetic presence of the Sacred Feminine for the transformation and healing of themselves, others and their communities.[1] With the gradual evolution of the patriarchal worldview this practice was lost to Western culture. Dance/movement was separated from its spiritual context as a healing modality. While traditions of sacred dance continued into the Middle Ages and are currently being revived, today dance is a performance art and only recently a therapeutic practice.[2]   Over the past century new forms of inner-directed, free form movement work which can be considered "integrative" body practices have been developed in the United States and Western Europe.[3]

I chose this topic for my doctoral research because I wanted to understand how other women experienced transformation and healing through their intrinsic movement practice and how it was an expression of their spirituality. I wanted to know this because I was experiencing transformation and healing through my practice and considered movement my spiritual path.   I also hoped that by hearing other women's stories it would deepen and expand my understanding of my own practice. I also wanted to create a way to authentically communicate to the public the stories of how seasoned women intrinsic movement practitioners used these movement practices to open themselves to the sacred in a way that was appropriate to women's spirituality as well as how through their practice they experienced transformation and healing in their lives.

In my initial conversations with women during movement intensives I found that women hesitated to use the traditional language of spirituality--words like spirit, soul, sacred, god/goddess--in relationship to their practice because many felt oppressed by and disenfranchised from the traditional religions in which they had been raised, as I did. They had either stopped participating in traditional religious rituals or had turned to the women's spirituality movement but had not claimed movement practice as an expression of their spirituality. When I described how in my intrinsic movement practice I experienced bringing forth the Sacred Feminine--which is how I name creative lifeforce energy manifesting in female form--from *within*   my body and how she also brings me forth as *her*   body using language that was grounded in my somatic experience there was an "aha" experience. Women then began telling me their stories of how intrinsic movement was a transformative spiritual practice for them.

As I continued my training in and practice of intrinsic movement and experienced it as a transformative and healing spiritual practice I grew curious about what seasoned women movement practitioners would have to say about their experiences. Searching book stores and libraries for stories of other women movers who considered free form movement their spiritual practice I found very few such stories. My curiosity and the lack of available literature about this experience motivated me to develop my research study.

Transformational Movement was the intrinsic movement form which was my departure point for this study.   My definition of intrinsic movement is similar to Jan Fisher's definition of being-movement. It is a type of movement practice that

> allows the mover to move in an undetermined, free style manner, with the attention focused inward and on the experience of the movement...and can be practiced alone or in groups, with or without music, and with eyes open or closed (although the focus remains inward in all cases).[4]

I chose the term 'intrinsic movement' as a way of emphasizing that the movement is initiated from the mover's felt intrinsic body sensations and not from any external source such as music or choreography. Transformational Movement is a form of intrinsic movement which is a process-oriented transformative healing practice. The main roles of the practitioners are mover and witness. It uses breath, sound, words, and movement as the basic mediums of experience and expression without the use of music.

During the summer of 1990, after being asked to write an essay about the relationship between self-image, body-image and women's spirituality for a book on women's spirituality, I realized intuitively that I needed to find a way that was different from my yoga practice to connect with my wisdom directly through my body in order to write my story *from*   my body rather than *about*   my body.   I was working at Seattle University at the time and discovered the Institute for Transformational Movement located within walking distance of the campus. I participated in four consecutive hour-long movement sessions there. These sesssions were my initiation into this intrinsic movement form.

During these sessions I experienced that I could consciously embody and integrate expressions of myself I had forgotten or never known and in so doing experience the liberating expansion of my own consciousness; that through releasing, expressing and clearing body holdings (muscle tension) that no longer served me through the use of breath, sound and intrinsic movement I was accessing my creativity to fuller aliveness and presence. I discovered that in consciously moving and transforming lifeforce energy within me I was directly experiencing and bringing forth my own innate wisdom, my essential self, the hidden treasure which is the living image of the sacred feminine. Movement practice became my spiritual practice. Therefore, over the next five years I participated in four Transformational Movement Healing Intensives and one Women's Healing Intensive which trained me in the techniques and processes of this intrinsic movement form.

During the Transformational Healing Intensives I became aware through my movement explorations of deeply painful feelings associated with my birth and early childhood which my body held in its cellular memory. When I was growing up my mother told several stories about me as a child which made me feel ashamed and embarrassed as well as angry at her for telling them. When I got older I asked her not to tell these stories because of how I felt. She continued to tell them and my anger at her grew with each telling, creating emotional distance between us. When I gave expression to these stories and my birthing experience through my movement work I was overwhelmed by how and what my body knew of these experiences. I was amazed at the difference between cognitive knowing and somatic knowing. Because of the transformation and healing I experienced by bringing them forth through my movement work these experiences were pivotal for me in choosing to pursue intrinsic movement as my spiritual practice.   The following story is a narrative of several of these sessions.

In these sessions which were facilitated by Joyce Izumi, the director of the Institute for Transformational Movement, I was beginning to develop the voice of my somatic experience and knowing. When that voice emerges in the following session narratives I have put it in bold and formatted it with a different line spacing than the rest of the text to distinguish this material from the rest of my movement story narrative.

I am born

I feel a tiny quivering in my chin so small it probably isn't visible to the eye and am tempted to disregard it as insignificant for my movement work. Joyce encourages me to begin my warm-up by going into this sensation and giving it expression.   Lying on my side in fetal position I close my eyes, and bring my fingers up to my chin. As I breathe into my chin I feel it quivering. My breathing becomes shallow and quick. I feel afraid. I draw my knees more deeply into my chest and feel myself within my mother's womb floating in fluid.   I am tiny. I feel large inside her.

I am cramped in her womb. I am pulling away from the sides of her womb. She is filled with anger, terror, shame. I don't want to come out yet. She is alone.   My father isn't with her. He doesn't

come to see her for three days. She labors for nineteen hours. She is pain. I am facing up; a face presentation birth. My forehead is hitting her pelvis. She hurts. She is alone. The doctor is late. He arrives. He tells her he is going to give her something to knock her out. She is furious. She curses him. She wants to be awake as I come forth. She goes under as I come forth. Long arms reach into her womb. They turn me around. They turn me over and I am falling down. I am coming forth. I am coming out. I am crying. I hurt. She is not there. I am hungry. I am alive. I am afraid. I am crying. I am alive.

It is my 44th birthday. Once again I am lying on mats in the studio curled into fetal position, my eyes closed.   Bringing my hands to the top of my head I begin a tiny rocking movement. My head begins to tingle. I feel my belly contract and feelings of anger mixed with fear arise in me. I am making low moaning sounds as I continue my rocking motion.

I hurt on the top and front of my head. Don't touch me. I don't want to come out this way. My body hurts. Leave me alone. Where's my mother? I want to lie on her belly. Get away! Leave me alone! Don't turn me over. My left shoulder, arm, and side hurt. Don't turn me over. In my low back and left side I feel resistance to falling. I'm scared. I can't lift my head. I can't see. I am confused. I am an angry dog howling as I come forth. I am a little baby girl in deep pain crying as I come out of my mother's womb. I feel tired.

Joyce tells us to bring our process to a close.   I hear her voice in my tiny infant body and realize that I need to come back into my woman's body. I feel tears coming down my face.   I want to stay pulled into myself. I do not want to join the group for check-in. Now I know directly the embodied experience of my fear and shame of coming forth fully into the world. I make my way to the check-in circle feeling the intensity of my experience filling my body. My head is filled with questions: What just happened here? What am I experiencing? How do I know if this is real or not? Was I just acting out what Momma had told me about my birth? I know it's more than that but I've never had an experience like this before.

Joyce responds to my questions by acknowledging that what my mother told me was real and what I have experienced in my movement process is real in itself. She explains that the mover decides what her experiences mean to her, but her experiences are real. They are grounded in the moving body which has its own unique way of knowing which is different from cognitive knowing. I find her response freeing, affirming, and grounding. Regardless of any explanations that fit or don't fit, I know I felt terrified of coming out, of opening my eyes. I wanted to pull in to myself as much as possible. I know I felt an intense energy of shame and terror in my body. Joyce closes the session with these words: Transformational Movement is a vehicle for growth, exploration and change. Work out the embodiment of the issues that come up.

My mother told me facts about my birth: that I was born two weeks early, that I was a face presentation birth; that she had been in labor for nineteen hours; that after promising not to give her any drugs during the birthing process the doctor gave her a shot that put her out when he realized that he was going to have to turn me over manually; that the last thing she remembered was cursing him for doing this.

In my movement process I accessed a different way of knowing which gave me new insights. I experienced the connection between my birthing experience and how I approach beginnings with anxiety, anticipating difficulties that often don't occur; how I fear coming into my own fullness; how deeply woven together in me are feelings of anger, fear and shame; how I have found deep resonance with the phrase "I am a woman giving birth to myself" as well as Judy Chicago's painting "The Crowning." Experiencing my birthing process directly and consciously through my movement explorations also changed my sense of connection to my mother.   I felt compassion for her and all she has experienced during her first of seven birthings. I came to a deeper understanding of how it is that one of the strongest ways I experience the sacred is as Divine Mother.

Women's Spirituality and Intrinsic Movement Practice: Six Key Themes

Because of my experiences in both Transformational Movement and Continuum Movement, intrinsic movement has become my primary spiritual practice. As my spiritual practice it expresses key themes of women's spirituality which are central to my spirituality as I discuss below.

1. *Woman's body is sacred and a place of encounter with the Sacred Feminine--the creative lifeforce manifesting in female form.*

The iconographical analysis of the images and artifacts of prehistorical goddess cultures documented that it was woman's body bleeding, birthing, dancing, aging and dying which was the embodiment of the sacred.[5] Elinor Gadon states:

Acknowledging the body as the source of knowing and a repository of lived experience has been an important breakthrough in women's search for identity. Exploring our own bodies is often the first step in self-definition . . . A woman's body is sacred not to some distant deity or to an institutionalized religion but to herself . . .The female body is the expressive vehicle of the creative life force, the energy that activates our being.[6]

Aliveness is in our bodies. Aliveness has to do with one's conscious direct immediate experience of the creative lifeforce which flows through all the realms of one's bodymind.   It involves consciously connecting with this powerful, intense energy of the universe, being fully present with it, and giving it expression. One level of this energy is one's felt sense of reality.[7] This felt sense is in one's muscles, blood, organs, and breath.

Aliveness includes my emotions and feelings. Besides being physical sensations emotions are also a way of knowing.[8]   When I am not connected to my body-knowing, which includes my emotional knowing, my experience of aliveness is diminished. As my experience of aliveness expands so, too, does my experience of connection with all life around me. I experience how my body is part of the body of the earth which is part of the body of the cosmos. In order for me to embrace intrinsic movement as my spiritual practice I had to cultivate a faith and trust in the wisdom of my moving body. This practice taught me that not only is my body sacred but the felt intrinsic sensations that give rise to a full range of spontaneous movements - from the small, quiet, subtle expressions to the frenzied, loud, chaotic expressions - are also sacred.

Consciousness pervades the whole body and is affected by the quality of focused attention one brings to it.[9] Through my intrinsic movement practice I have experienced that it is possible to communicate both from the most subtle levels within oneself and to that place in others using various combinations of breathing, sounding and movement practices. This kind of communication affects healing.[10]

   2. *Women's sexuality is sacred.*

Ancient goddess cultures regarded women's sexuality as sacred. Gadon, writing about the high point of goddess culture in Minoan Crete (3000-1500 B.C.E.), states that "Sexuality and the human body were celebrated in the brilliantly colored paintings on the walls of their great palace-shrines."[11]

In my experience the term 'aliveness' also includes what the French feminists mean when they use the verb *jouir*   (to enjoy, to experience sexual pleasure) and the *la jouissance*   (sexual pleasure, bliss, rapture). Elaine Marks and Isabelle de Courtivron (1980) in their introduction to the writings of contemporary French feminists state that "Women's *jouissance* carries with it the notion of fluidity, diffusion, duration. It is a kind of potlach in the world of orgasms, a giving, expending, dispensing of pleasure without concern about ends or closure."[12]

In my movement practice I experience *jouissance* in my body as tingling, expansiveness, fluidity, bliss, quivering, intense presence, and erotic warmth.

3. *Woman brings forth images of herself as the embodiment of the Sacred Feminine as she incarnates her spiritual power.*

Carol Christ states that "The image of the Goddess that is reemerging in the psyches of modern women is symbolic of women's sense that the power we are claiming for ourselves . . . is rooted in the ground of being itself." [13] While women's imagination is nourished by the images of the ancient symbols of the goddess, Christ argues "women's imagination is by no means subject to the authority of the past . . . What we cannot remember we invent joyfully, recognizing that modern women can create symbols that express our . . . authenticity and power." [14]

In her chapter titled *The Goddess Within: A Source of Empowerment for Women*

Elinor Gadon describes how contemporary women artists bring forth new images of the Goddess in which some began to " . . . image themselves as the Goddess, others to re-create the ancient inconography in contemporary form . . . Re-imaging the Goddess in their own likeness was a path of self-discovery for many . . . Each woman tapped into the power of the Goddess according to her own priorities." [15] For many of these women their images came out of a reconnection with their embodied memory of the goddess. Gadon describes Ciel Bergman as being unaware of the obscure archeological finds that she painted and tells us that Bergman "calls their reappearance in her work 'morphogenetic resonances' " [16] referring to the work of biologist Rubert Sheldrake.[17]

In intrinsic movement my moving body is the image and expression of the multidimensional and varied energies of the Sacred Feminine which I experience as Eagle Woman, Salmon Woman, Snake Woman, Body of the World, Fierce Change Mother, She Who Dances the World Forth, and other forms. These energies expressed through my moving body manifest my inner truth as I incarnate my spiritual power embodying the Sacred Feminine whose energies are embedded in the resonant energetic field of my mindbody. Giving expression to these energies challenges and reveals who I take myself to be. This process transforms my identity, self-image and body-image and deepens my experience of authenticity.

4. *The path of women's spirituality is a spiral path which involves a process*

of descent and ascent.

I experience in my body the rhythms of life, growth, and death in a vast spiral dance.   On a monthly basis I actualize this dance in my body through my menstruation. The spiral form is also found in my body's intestines, DNA, and microtubules which form the structure of the cell. Richard Grossinger states that "Spirality is projected from the heart of the cells' fissioning and is basic to their self-organization." [18] The spiral path of the Sacred Feminine is part of my flesh and blood. It is also found in the spider's web, sea shells and the whirling galaxies of space; air and water move in a spiral flow. It is one of the most ancient symbols found inscribed on goddess figurines, buckles and plaques relating to the figure of the Goddess.[19] Spirals symbolize the intricate pathway that connects the visible world to the invisible.

The spiral path of women's spirituality involves a journey which includes both the mysteries of descent and ascent as described in the ancient Sumerian myth of the descent of Inanna[20] as well as the myth of Demeter and Persephone which was ritualized in the Eleusian Mysteries.[21] I encounter these mysteries through numerous experiences in my intrinsic movement practice. Each time the process is the same: I close my eyes, step into the dark, unknown space of my moving body trusting its wisdom to bring me forth, face death in a variety of forms including physical, psychological and spiritual, am stripped of illusions about myself and my life, move through chaos and disintegration, and after encountering the dark feminine in my own body, claim my power and give birth to new forms of creative expression in my life. Paraphrasing Enheduanna's words in her poem "Lady of Largest Heart," like Inanna's devotees each time I am seared with purifying fire as I come forth from the sacred space of the movement studio to do my common work.[22]

5. *Women's spirituality is holistic, integrative and transformative.*

Women's spirituality seeks to heal the internalization of the patriarchal split by transforming disconnections into connections. It reclaims what has been split off, taking back our women's bodies, emotions, minds, and spirits while valuing all their aspects. It transforms self-hatred and self-negation into conscious self-love. Theresa King states that ". . . our insights from our experiences of self-negation can be the impetus for our spiritual awakening to new realizations about ourselves, leading us to a true sense of our real worth and a genuine love for others."[23]

In the description of goddess cultures one of the primary modes of bringing about transformation and healing were women's rituals which usually included dance. These dances were used for accessing expanded states of consciousness, bringing about transformation and healing, resulting in the integration of the whole person. These dances invoked healing by providing a space for women's expression of the full range of varied movement states from ecstasy to frenzy to rage to deep grief and quiet peace.[24]

In intrinsic movement practice, healing is also invoked by providing a space for woman's expression of the full range of varied movement states with all their extremes and polarities. I experience intrinsic movement as an integrative practice that can enhance the full development of human potential because all levels of my being are similarly affected by the practice; in a like manner I am affected physically, psychologically, emotionally, mentally, and spiritually.[25]

6. *Women's spirituality embraces many ways of knowing while giving prominence to body knowing as an essential way of knowing self, others, and the world.*

Charlene Spretnak suggests that the contemporary rebirth of Goddess spirituality is more than a protest against the patriarchal worldview of domination. She states that "It is the practice of an embodied way of knowing and being in the world . . . we hungered to

feed our capabilities of perceiving subtle, encompassing, scrumptious connectedness emanating from every direction of our being."[26] Spretnak argues that a person cannot "experience embodied ways of knowing in a universe of dynamic intersubjectivity and unitive being if one is locked in a lifelong psychic struggle with the body--one's own physicality, one's mother's womb-body, all womb-bodies, the Earthbody, the generative cosmos."[27]

As a spiritual practice intrinsic movement gives me the opportunity to develop embodied knowing as a way of being in the world. As a somatic practice it privileges first-person perception of the body and enables me to "increase [my] ability for proprioception--awareness of the myriad stimuli provided within an organism."[28] Developing greater internal sensivity to my own organism led to greater sensitivity in all dimensions of my life. Working directly with what Johnson refers to as moving intelligence through my practice helped me cultivate more expanded qualities of consciousness as described in yoga psychology and current research by neuroscientists.[29]

Reflecting on these six themes brought me new insights into how intrinsic movement as my primary spiritual practice is an expression of woman's spirituality. Women who choose to walk the spiritual path of movement work often find it difficult to enter into the sacred space of their own embodiment because it holds the painful physical, emotional, psychological, and spiritual effects of internalized misogyny as well asembodied memories of rape, incest, or other forms of violence experienced by women in a patriarchal culture. After sixteen years of movement practice, I still feel fear and awe at entering into the sacred space of my own embodiment because I know I will be deeply changed in ways that I cannot anticipate; ways that while finally transformative and integrative are often initially painful and disturbing.

Through this practice I transform the messages of patriarchy about how I should be in my body. I transform the silence and silencing which patriarchy demands of me as a woman by expressing the full range of sounds and breaths that arise spontaneously from my movement process.

I transform patriarchy's message of containment that says a good, virtuous woman is one who sits still, keeps her legs together, doesn't move from her own desires, doesn't move unless told to or in response to the needs of another and doesn't move large. By moving freely, spontaneously and fully from my intrinsic body sensations I learn how the language of my moving body is the language of my life knowing.

Through this practice I reclaim my sacred power as a woman to name myself from my embodied experience. Central to women's spirituality is the "naming of ourselves, the universe, and the sacred powers that sustain us." [30] Through my moving body I discover my multiple names Stepping into the unknown that lies waiting for expression within my body I let go of what I think I know about who I am. Through this process the "unhoped-for other" in myself is re-membered and healing occurs. [31]

Notes

1 See Elinor Gadon, The Once And Future Goddess: A Symbol For Our Time (HarperSan Francisco,1989). Also, Marija Gimbutas, The Language Of The Goddess (HarperSan Francisco,1989) and The Civilization Of The Goddess (HarperSan Francisco, 1991); Ann Baring and Jules Cashford, The Myth Of The Goddess: Evolution Of An Image (London: Penguin Books, 1991); Vicki Noble, Shakti Woman: Feeling Our Fire, Healing Our World - The New Female Shamanism (HarperSan Francisco, 1991); Judy Grahn, Blood, Bread, and Roses: How Menstruation Created The World (Boston: Beacon Press, 1993); Layne Redmond, When The Drummers Were Women: A Spiritual History of Rhythm (New York: Three Rivers Press, 1997).

2 Iris J. Stewart, Sacred Woman, Sacred Dance: Awakening Spirituality Through Movement And Ritual (Rochester: Inner Traditions International, 2000).

3 Don Hanlon Johnson, "Body Practices and Consciousness: A Neglected Link." Anthropology of Consciousness, 1, no. 3-4, Sept/Dec (2000): 41.

4 Jan Fisher, Dance As A Spiritual Practice: A Phenomenological And Feminist Investigation Of the Experience Of Being-Movement. Unpublished doctoral dissertation, Institute of Transpersonal Psychology, Palo Alto, CA, 1996, 8.

5 See Baring and Cashford, The Myth of the Goddess. Also, Gadon, The Once And Future Goddess,

Gimbutas, The Language Of The Goddess and The Civilization Of The Goddess. Also, Layne Redmond, When The Drummers Were Women: A Spiritual History of Rhythm (New York: Three Rivers Press, 1997).

6 Gadon, The Once And Future Goddess, 285, 288, 290.

7 See Eugene Gendlin, Focusing (New York: Bantam Books, 1981).

8 See Valerie Hunt, Infinite Mind: Science Of The Human Vibrations Of Consciousness. (Malibu, CA: Malibu Publishing Co, 1996); Candace B. Pert, Molecules of Emotion: Why You Feel The Way You Feel. (New York: Scribner, 1997); Paula M. Reeves, Women's Intuition: Unlocking The Wisdom Of The Body (Berkeley: Conari Press, 1999).

9 See Bonnie Bainbridge Cohen, Sensing, Feeling And Action: The Experiential Anatomy of Body-Mind Centering. (Northampton, MA: Contact Editions, 1993), vii.

10 Ibid.

11 Gadon, The Once And Future Goddess, 87.

12 Elaine Marks and Isabelle de Courtivron, eds, New French Feminism: An Anthology. (New York: Schocken Books, 1980), 36-37.

13 Carol P. Christ, Laughter of Aphrodite: Reflections On A Journey To The Goddess. (San Francisco: Harper, 1987), 154.

14 Ibid.

15 Gadon, The Once And Future Goddess, 263, 264.

16 Ibid., 270-271.

17 Rupert Sheldrake, A New Science Of Life (Los Angeles: Jeremy P. Tarcher, Inc., 1988).

18 Richard Grossinger, Embryogenesis - From Cosmos To Creature: The Origins Of Human Biology. (Berkeley: North Atlantic Books, 1986), 108.

19 Baring and Cashford, The Myth Of The Goddess, 24, 25.

20 See Diane Wolkstein and Samuel Noah Kramer, Inanna: Queen Of Heaven And Earth (New York: Harper & Row, 1983); Betty DeShong Meador, ed. Inanna, Lady Of Largest Heart: Poems Of The High Priestess Enheduanna (Austin: University of Texas Press, 2000); Sylvia Perera, Descent To The Goddess: A Way Of Initiation For Women (Toronto: Inner City Books, 1981).

21 Gadon, The Once And Future Goddess, 154-157.

22 The poem states "Those warrior women like a single thread come forth from beyond the river do common work in devotion to you whose hands sear them with purifying fire." Meador, Inanna, Lady Of Largest Heart, 133.

23 Theresa King, ed. The Spiral Path: Explorations In Women's Spirituality (St. Paul, MN: Yes International Publishers, 1992), 13.

24 See Maria-Gabriele Wosien, Sacred Dance: Encounter With Gods (New York: Avon Books, 1974); Joan Marler, ed. From The Realm Of The Ancestors: An Anthology In Honor Of Marija Gimbutas (Manchester: Knowledge, Ideas & Trends, Inc., 1997); Hallie I. Austen, The Heart Of The Goddess: Art, Myth, And Meditations Of The World's Sacred Feminine (Berkeley: Wingbow Press, 1990).

25 Fisher, Dance As A Spiritual Practice, 348.

26 Charlene Spretnak, States Of Grace: The Recovery Of Meaning In The Postmodern Age (HarperSan Francisco, 1991), 149.

27 Ibid., 155.

28 Debra Greene, "Assumptions of Somatics, Part 1." Somatics: Magazine/Journal Of The Mind/Body Arts And Sciences. Spring/Summer (1997) Vol. XI, 2, 51.

29 Don Hanlon Johnson, Bone, Breath, And Gesture: Practices Of Embodiment (Berkeley: North Atlantic Books, 1995), 219.

30 Judith Plaskow and Carol Christ, Weaving The Visions: New Patterns In Feminist Spirituality (New York: Harper & Row, 1989), 52.

31 Helené Cixous (Deborah Jenson, ed.), "Coming To Writing" And Other Essays (Cambridge: Harvard University Press, 1991), xiii.

References

Irigaray, Luce. Elemental Passions. Translated by Joanne Collie and Judith Still. New York: Routledge, 1992.

Irigaray, Luce. Why Different? A Culture of Two Subjects. Interviews with Luce Irigaray. Edited by Luce Irigaray and Sylvere Lotringer. Translated by Camille Collins. New York: Semiotext (e), 2000.

Johnson, Don Hanlon, ed. Groundworks: Narratives of Embodiment. Berkely: North Atlantic Books, 1997.

Roth, Gabrielle. Sweat Your Prayers: Movement as Spiritual Practice. New York: Jeremy P. Tarcher/Putnam Books, 1997.

Menhirs, markers of African migration paths, Place of Silence, Sardinia
Photograph by Wallace Birnbaum

The Future Has An Ancient Heart

african origins and african migration paths in Europe[2]
legacy of world transformation

Lucia Chiavola Birnbaum, Ph.D.

This paper is grounded on the african value of self-knowledge—who we are, where we came from, and where we are going. In the first days of 2006 I am assailed by a sense of urgency to tell the story of everyone's african black mother because the largely untold history of the United States is that of extermination of native americans enslavement of africans, and persecution of people perceived as "dark others" threatening to dominant whites. This mentality still characterizes the small elite who make life or death decisions for the people of the United States, an elite, armed with a monopoly of weapons of mass destruction who assume they are "white" and seem hell-bent on domination of the world's other people, whom they perceive as dark. Today, the lies sustaining U. S. aggression against non-whites (and anybody else who seems threatening to the small white governing elite) at home and abroad may be unraveling. The case of the United States may be the most lethal, but the history of people of dominant cultures whose leaders consider themselves white and their aggression against subordinated non-whites is similar. Yet out of the darkness, an african proverb tells us, comes the light. At the beginning of 2006 people in the United States and elsewhere seem to be shaking themselves out of a long sleep. . . .

In this dangerous, yet liminal time, it is vitally important we know who we are so that the violence of the dominant west (as well as the violence of its emulators) can be brought to an end. Realization of the african black mother of everyone, and of the continuous presence of her memory in Europe, as well as elsewhere, may be a first step in creating a new world of harmonious societies based on her life-enhancing values .

A sicilian/american feminist cultural historian, I have been deeply influenced by african and africana studies - - notably Cheikh Anta Diop's

269

rescue of african history from the oblivion and/or distortions of western racism, Molefi Asante's scholarship on afrocentrism, Alice Walker's novels, and Maulana Karenga's recent study of the culture of Maat, african woman divinity of justice and harmony. My concern is to stress the mutual relevance of feminist cultural studies, africana studies, and genetics research of L.Cavalli-Sforza and world colleagues who confirm in the DNA the african origin of everyone, as well as the research of archeologist Emmanuel Anati who has documented in rock art that african migrants after 50,000 BCE brought signs of the african black mother (pubic V and color ochre red) to every continent of the world. Of primary importance for me is Cavalli-Sforza's theme that african migrants brought their beliefs with them . . . beliefs that circle the african black mother. [3]

The spiritual and political legacy that african migrants brought with them everywhere - - that offers the world hope - - is suggested in Maulana Karenga's study of Maat, african woman divinity, wherein she is the moral grounding and human flourishing of a universe in becoming, in which she keeps the whole in harmony. Maat is the grounding of human communities in justice, propriety, harmony, balance, reciprocity and order. She *is* truth, justice, and righteousness in communities that care for the vulnerable: the weak, poor, elderly, the hungry, thirsty, and naked.

In the ethic of Maat, found in african documents 2500 years before the common epoch, the response to evil is to do good. The heart is the divine presence in humans and the seat of consciousness and moral sensitivity. Maat is the ground of communities where humans are equal, where there is no radical separation between humans and animals, and where wisdom, or knowledge, is an ethical requirement for everyone. In this african ethos, humans, rooted in their communities, are "a refuge for the wretched, a raft for the drowning, and a ladder for one who is in the abyss." In the ontological unity of god and humans, Maat is goodness of being in a dynamic and creative universe with an open-ended future. [4]

This african legacy, suppressed for 2,000 years by dominant cultures of the world, has been coming to the surface since world war two. The gnostic gospels, found in Africa in a jar near Cairo in 1945, offered a rich and nuanced alternative to the patristic and violent christianity established by the holy roman empire in the fourth century CE, when the gnostic gospels were banished as heresies. The suppressed gnostic gospels suggest the transition of deep veneration of the african dark woman divinity to her status in the early common epoch, as suggested by the voice of a divine woman in *The Thunder, Perfect Mind*. . ."For I am the first and the last/ I am the honored one and the scorned one. I am the whore and the holy one. . . ."

I am a sicilian/american feminist cultural historian who has written books on italian feminism, black madonnas, african origins of the black mother, and gathered essays for anthologies of feminist writings in spirituality entitled *She is Everywhere!*[5] Trained in the western male-oriented history of Europe and the United States, I have since 1970 been revisiting my geographical and spiritual origins. Black studies since the 1960s have pointed to the origins of world civilization in Africa. Antonio Gramsci, marxist theorist of Sardinia, tapped african beliefs in considering values of justice and equality of subaltern cultures indispensable to the cultural revolution that precedes and accompanies nonviolent political revolution. The french Annales school of historians stresses the importance of looking beyond present-day national boundaries to large geographical areas, like that of the mediterranean. Like the theories of Marx, Freud, and Jung, the Annales school emphasizes the long duration of beliefs . . .a premise that informs my research on the continuing belief, everywhere, in the black mother of Africa and her values.

My book-in-progress, *the future has an ancient heart*, studies islands of the mediterranean as well as countries embraced by that sea (Spain, France, and Italy) to document this hypothesis. In the case of my own ancestral Sicily, the island was contiguous with Africa in prehistory. After the ice melted, the island was separated from Africa by the narrow Strait of Sicily. Migrating africans after 50,000 BCE left evidence of their beliefs throughout Europe, and elsewhere in the world in *signs* in rock art, notably the black mother's signs: pubic V and color ochre red. Africans also marked their paths with *dolmens and menhirs*, which after 25,000 BCE became stone *icons of a woman divinity*. Subsequently the memory of the african black mother was transmitted in statues and figurines which, in the common epoch, became values *(justice with compassion, equality, and transformation)* conveyed in everyday and celebratory rituals, stories, music, and art to the present- -evident in contemporary transformative movements of feminism, ecology, and nonviolence.

The complexity, as well as contemporary relevance, of the legacy of african migrations is Europe is suggested in that african migrations were followed by *return migrations* of ultimately african west asians, notably of anatolians and semites who, like primordial africans, venerated women divinities:

a) farmer migrations of anatolians after 10,000 BCE

b) danites, semites from Ur, after 2300 BCE

c) canaanites, semites from Lebanon, Syria, and Palestine, after 1500 BCE, whom the greeks called phoenicians, who are today associated with semitic palestinians

d) israelites, semites in diaspora after 70 CE

e) muslims, semites from Africa and west Asia after 600 CE, who left a legacy, notably in Spain but also in Sicily, of jews, christians, and muslims living together harmoniously . . . bonded, in my view, by a shared suppressed belief in the african black mother.

In antiquity, Sicily was a vital part of the mediterranean civilization that originated in Africa and flourished in west Asia, Europe, and other mediterranean islands, notably, Malta (founded by sicilians), and the Balearic islands off Spain. In the context of conventional history, wherein history is erroneously taught as beginning with civilizations of Greece and Rome, Sicily was a colony of both. In the common epoch, the african black mother was represented by madonna figures in caves painted in red (one of her prehistoric signs). After christian church fathers tried to destroy evidence of the african black mother, her memory was transmitted in subaltern cultures after 500 CE in V-shaped black madonnas.   In the historical epoch, her memory was also carried on african migration paths in Europe (and elsewhere) by african water rituals, stories, and heresies,

In Sicily, and elsewhere, not only direct migrations from Africa but *return migrations* of ultimately african peoples from west Asia deepened the memory of the african black mother. Images of Isis and Tanit brought by africans navigating the African Sea that adjoins western Sicily may be found in my ancestral maternal area of Palermo. Images of Cybele, brought by anatolians, are pervasive in my ancestral paternal region in the southeastern part of the island. Melding of african and asian images is suggested in my finding images of Isis, Cybele, Astarte, and Tanit, and their subsequent images as black madonnas, in all my ancestral places in Sicily - -Palermo, Erice, Ragusa, and Siracusa. The black madonna of Tindari, holiest icon of Sicily, is inscribed, "Nigra sum sed furmosa" (I am black and beautiful). Her values, justice and equality, are incised on statues of women who stand at the entrance to her sanctuary.

Black african origin of the dark mother of a thousand names in the cultures of the world, as well as erasure of her african origin, are marked in the changing names of my ancestral paternal sicilian town, Ragusa. The ancient name was Ragusa Ibla (diminutive affectionate for anatolian Cybele) who was called Ibla Nera or Black Ibla, until the seventh century BCE when greeks invaded Sicily and changed Ibla Nera to Ibla Herae (Ibla Hera), thereby erasing her black african origin and marking the decline of her status under the greeks, who associated her with Hera, subordinated wife of Zeus.

With christianization the church attempted to whiten the african black mother and to attach her gifts to church figures. This is evident in the cases of Santa Lucia of Siracusa who lived in the 4th century CE, when the church was extirpating non-canonical versions of christianity as heresy. Major saint of Sicily and south Italy, for whom I am named, Lucia in church accounts is saint of light and vision and martyred christian virgin. In church iconography she offers her eyes on a plate to a rapist. In my interpretation, this is the african black mother turned white sacrificing her gift of vision to the church. Yet the people kept the older meaning of the great mother. In popular sicilian stories, light comes out of darkness, an african belief. The continuum between african Isis and sicilian Lucia is suggested in that both carry sheafs of wheat, symbol of nurturance. In the vernacular christianity of Sicily, Lucia is a saint who nurtures everyone and heals those who suffer maladies of vision.

In the early common epoch, Sicily, located very close to Africa, was jewish, christian, and moorish. After 1060 CE Sicily was connected with mainland Europe when expanding normans (scandinavians based in France) invaded Sicily and took Britain in 1066. Afterward, Sicily was ruled by angevins of France, swabians of Germany, and catholic monarchs of Spain who brought the inquisition to eradicate pagan heresies, persecuting my sicilian grandmothers (who until the 19th century bonded with the earth with their bare bosoms). The forcible eradication of heretical beliefs helps us understand the *almost* total success of dominant church and state of Europe in stamping out- - in europeans and in descendants of europeans elsewhere- -deep, ultimately african, beliefs in the black african mother and her values.

My hypothesis is that primordial and continuing migrations from Africa, as well as return migrations of ultimately african semites from west Asia into the region greeks called Europe, left a cellular and/or cultural memory that has persisted in descendants of primordial african migrants. The belief has survived despite the traumas in the common epoch of official suppression by judaism, christianity, and islam, torture and killing during the christian inquisition, attempted genocide of native americans, enslavement of africans, and continuing persecution of non-whites (and dissenting whites) considered threatening to the hegemony of small dominant white elites. Today the memory of the african black mother, and her transformative values, may be coming to the surface in dominant cultures of the world - - the belief has always been present in subaltern cultures - - offering the possibility of a better world.

Signs preceded images of the black mother. Although black madonnas and other dark women divinities may be our most palpable evidence of the continuing popular belief in the african black mother, the belief is also evident in signs, and in many ways of knowing. Our grandparents' suppressed ways of knowing are today slowly being incorporated into widening academic methodologies; e.g., in genetics, archeology, anthropology, ethnic studies, clinical psychology, feminist and spirituality studies, music, and dance. What may characterize our time historically is this enterprise of piecing together the hidden and fragmented authentic story of humans.

In the 1960s I was an assistant professor of history at San Francisco State who went on strike and was immediately fired for supporting student demands for black studies and stopping the U. S. imperialist war in Vietnam. Thereafter an independent scholar, I have been intent on finding my sicilian grandmothers and my own submerged beliefs . . . a quest that has led me to everyone's black mother of Africa. On-site explorations of italian feminists and black madonnas, and my own interior experience, led me to realize the importance of *suppressed* beliefs. By 2001, when my *dark mother. african origins and godmothers* was first published, I had concluded that the memory of the african black mother has persisted for millennia to the present, not only in subaltern cultures, but in unconscious or preconscious levels of memory - - of everyone, on all continents.

The black african mother has drawn me, particularly since 1988 when I was very moved by the black madonna in holy week processions at Trapani (in western Sicily on a primordial african migration path), dreamed of my mother as a black madonna, and learned the next day that she was dying of cancer. I wrote the book on black madonnas during the year my mother was dying. Black madonnas, conflated with the memory of my mother, have determined my research ever since.

Humanity's first religious sanctuary was created by migrating africans in the Sinai 40,000 BCE. This first religious sanctuary, located in the place muslims call Har Karkom and jews and christians call Mt Sinai, is the founding place of judaism, christianity, and islam. Uncovered by italian archeologist Emmanuel Anati, [6] this oldest religious sanctuary in the world is characterized by menhirs and dolmens. Menhirs are upright stones symbolizing humans. Dolmens are two vertical menhirs holding up a horizontal menhir, suggesting burial rituals. Jean Clottes, major archeologist of France, attributes religious significance to menhirs and dolmens. Marija Gimbutas, lithuanian/american archeologist, associated menhirs with 25,000 BCE stone women divinities. In the south of France, on african migration paths, two significant menhirs dated ca. 25,000 BCE are statues of women divinities - - the "Venus" of Laussel holding a menstrual lunar calendar and pointing to her vulva, suggesting the black mother's generation of all life, and the "Venus" of Lespugue, a woman figure sculpted all in rounds.

When we visited ca. 17,000 BCE caves on african migration paths at Altamira in Spain and at Lascaux in France, I visually understood Emmanuel Anati's insight that there is a continuum between prehistoric art - - created in a cosmology of the african black mother - - and the modern art remembering this cosmology on african migration paths of Toulouse-Lautrec, Van Gogh, Matisse, et al. in France and by Picasso, Miro, Dali, Gaudi, and others in Spain.

On our 2004 study tour in Sardinia, we visually understood the connection between african migration paths, the african black mother, and african healing water rituals adapted by christianity when we saw Santa Cristina's well - - a christian well shaped in the form of the carthaginian woman divinity Tanit. The well is constructed so that one descends into the amniotic waters of her womb. Mary Saracino, who participated in our sardinian tour, later learned that there was a semitic version of african water rituals- - remembered in the water god Maimone. I thought about the similarity of the name of the water god Maimone to that of the great jewish philosopher of Spain, Maimonides, who wrote in the golden age of harmony between jews, christians, and muslims before 1492, date marking early modern church aggression against jews, muslims, and heretical christians.

In Sardinia I was also struck by the "place of silence" where there are many african menhirs, and many african water rituals. And thousands of of nuraghi - - cone-shaped structures that resemble those of Zimbabwe in Africa. The dominant belief of male archeologists is that the nuraghi of Sardinia are fortresses. But there is no evidence of weapons. My lens of african origins suggests that nuraghi of Sardinia are sanctuaries surrounded by many community water rituals.   Archeological evidence in Sardinia attests to thousands of woman figurines from the paleolithic epoch to contemporary black madonnas.

My continuing interest in black madonnas was quickened when I realized that France in the Auvergne may have highest concentration of black madonnas in the world. . . in a region early reached by navigating migrating africans from the Atlantic Ocean as well as upriver from the Mediterranean. I began to discern a pattern on african migration paths: great prehistoric and modern art, pagan african and european christian healing water rituals, black madonnas and other dark women divinities, suppressed african wisdom in heresies, and her continuing memory in contemporary movements for justice with compassion, healing, and transformation.

Perhaps the most significant, ultimately african, water ritual we found in the summer of 2005 in the south of France, on an african migration path, in an area of many menhirs and dolmens, is located at the second place of christianity after Rome at Lourdes.   Pilgrimages to Lourdes annually draws three and a half million people - - the sick and desperate of the world who come for healing. Springs, grottoes, peasants (particularly young people) are associated with apparitions and healing of the dark mother as the virgin Mary. In the case of Lourdes, the story is that Mary appeared in a grotto to a young girl, Bernadette Soubirous. Mary told the girl to bathe in the water of a spring in the grotto. Grottoes, and springs, in italian, french, and other folklore, are regarded as watery wombs of the black mother. At Lourdes thousands of the afflicted of the world pour into the town to participate in nightly torchlight singing processions. Many are in wheelchairs, who are taken to the grotto to be washed in the healing waters of the spring.

A people's ritual, everyone in processions at Lourdes in the french Pyrenees sings "Ave Maria." Mary is also invoked in the writing around the cupola of the church built over the grotto. The papacy has periodically denounced fervent popular beliefs in Mary as "Mariolatry." Papal doctrine denigrates women and leaves the mother of Jesus out of the trinity, but it has been unable to eradicate world-wide passionate veneration of Mary. As in other cases of popular christianity, veneration of Mary at Lourdes edges heresy. Underneath one of her statues in the church built above the grotto is the inscription, "All that is better in us may be attributed to Mary," an involution of biblical attribution of original sin to Eve and to all humans, and a popular revision of the canonical doctrine that Mary, because of immaculate conception, is uniquely different from other women.

The continuing importance of early african signs is suggested by black madonnas. Although subsequently whitened by church fathers, the mother of Jesus was first depicted in ochre red (one of the signs of the african black mother); see image in Priscilla catacombs of Rome. At Le Puy , where we saw the statue of Notre Dame de France atop a hill of the city, she is sculpted in red stone. Simone Weil,who may have been the most prescient woman philosopher of the twentieth century, fasted herself to death during world war two in witness against the rising violence of the world. At Le Puy she worked on the left politically while meditating on the african origins of judeo/christian beliefs. Townspeople called her "the red virgin."[7] Inside the church at Le Puy, a major pilgrimage place in France, we noted that this very popular icon of the madonna is identified with workers and is black. Church fathers by the 5th century CE had destroyed or whitened most images of the african black mother, but people in subaltern cultures of Europe and the world persisted in painting her black. In paintings of V shaped black madonnas, almost always, there is, somewhere in the image, the color red.

Heresy pulled me to France the summer of 2005, notably the 13th century cathar heresy. Cathars lived on an african migration path in the Pyrenees and called themselves "good Christians." Cathars did not care for the church of Rome. Like jews and muslims, they considered Jesus a prophet but not divine. Bypassing popes and priests , cathars considered their own clergy, "parfaites and parfaits" (women and men) intermediaries with the divine. Cathars did not eat meat, and did not believe in the church sacrament of marriage. They lived nonviolently with the values of Jesus' sermon on the mount, values that Simone Weil, Maulana Karenga and others have pointed out may be found in african documents 2500 years before christianity. The ultimate object of cathar belief, in my view, may be glimpsed in their pilgrimages to black madonnas at Le Puy in France and of Montserrat in Spain. Cathars lived on an african migration path in southwestern France where the earth is red and the Aude river turns red after a heavy rain. Considering the red earth moistened by rain water to be healing, people make medical poultices after it rains. I think of cathar country as a land of the black mother, whose values are found in heresy and uprising and healing water rituals. .

In the early modern era, the catholic papacy aligned with the french monarchy considered cathars very threatening in this period when church and state were intent on killing dark others - - notably muslims, jews, and dissenting christians. Cathars were singled out for killing while pope and state were forming the inquisition to eradicate heresy. In Europe, black madonnas (and dark women divinities elsewhere) may be our most palpable evidence not only of persistence of the belief in the black african mother, but of heresies and other cultural resistance that despite official suppression continued to transmit her values. Cultural resistance at the height of the inquisition is suggested in the great number of black madonnas all over France, evident in a map of 1530.[8]

My hypothesis regarding cathars is that they were christian heretics on an african migration path in the french (also the spanish) Pyrenees who tapped ancient african matristic beliefs which they shared with basques in the same region. Blood type confirms that basques live in an african genetic enclave in Europe who have kept matricentric beliefs and have defied those who would take them away - - from romans to fascists of the twentieth century. Similarly, in the balkans on another african migration path in eastern Europe, where Marija Gimbutas found many icons of the prechristian woman divinity, and where byzantine madonnas are dark, the earlier bogomil heresy is said to have influenced cathar heretics in southwest France. With the lens of the african origins of everyone and the hypothesis of the persistence of african beliefs on african migration paths, the bogomil heresy, like the cathar heresy, were both on african migration paths where continuing african beliefs are manifested in everyday rituals and dancing, as well as in signs and icons. What happened to cathars who fled the burnings? Several went to Lombardy, in northern Italy where I have found a pattern of beliefs connecting black madonnas, heretics, and contemporary feminists.

Heresy, regarded as resistance to the dominant culture, can be tracked in France from early christian evangelization when Magdalen stories differed from canonical accoaunts, to veneration of black madonnas during the inquisition, to resistance become political with the french revolution of 1789. . . and subsequent resistance. In the 20th century catalans on an african migration path in Spain (near the immensely popular black madonna of Montserrat) courageously fought the fascists in the civil war that preceded world war two. . The maqui, in the resistance in southern France during world war two, saved jews from extermination camps, and valiantly fought male-centered, brutal nazis.

In early and continuing heretical interpretations of christianity, the french, particularly in the south, looked to "other" Marys. They considered Mary Magdalen, who had seen the risen Jesus, the beloved apostle. Male apostles did not believe Magdalen, the church denigrated her, but french legends recount that Magdalen came to the south of France where she spread the gospel until she died. Some of the "other Marys" in this region suggest that people identified the mother of Jesus with the black madonna of Saintes Maries de la Mer. This black madonna on the mediterranean coast of France points to an inclusive woman divinity with beliefs subversive to the christian canon. Stories and rituals connect this black madonna with Sara of hebrew scriptures, with Kali, fierce hindu woman divinity of India, and with black Maria, beloved madonna of gypsies of the world.

For two millennia french peasants have transmitted heretical legends about Mary Magdalen, national saint of France. Perhaps recalling Africa whose female divinities married male divinities, a french heretical legend is that Mary Magdalen was married to Jesus. The gospel of Mary Magdalen (not recognized in the official catholic canon) also emphasizes a belief implicit in african rituals - - self-knowledge is necessary for transformation. **Self knowledge, in my view, includes knowledge of the genetic origin of all humans in Africa and african origin of beliefs in justice and equality with compassion, or healing, evident on african migration paths throughout the world that can transform our violent and unjust world.** Magdalen, the red-haired woman who anointed Jesus, may be considered a heretical challenge to the canon that , until very recently, denigrated her as a prostitute. In the 1970s her task, a woman taking the mother's values to the people, was implicitly remembered by Dacia Maraini, major cultural and political feminist of Italy who founded an experimental theater that enacted feminist issues in the streets. Recalling the woman apostle, Dacia called this theatre, La Maddalena.

It is my hypothesis that the memory of the beautiful black african mother (whom sicilian women traditionally invoked as "Bedda Madre!"or beautiful mother) implies nonviolent revolution. In 1789 in France, revolutionaries wore the phrygian cap of followers of the anatolian dark mother Cybele and raised the banner, liberté, egalité, fraternité. The woman who popularly personified this first great revolution of our time was named Marianne - - for Mary, jewish mother of Jesus, and Anne, his pagan grandmother, goddess of the harvests whose veneration in Brittany (on an african migration path full of menhirs and dolmens) recalls the Anu of Africa. The french revolutionary triad of values is compatible with values of the african mother, except that justice by guillotine negates the mother's value of compassion/healing and fraternité leaves out women. This summer in France at the entry to the old town of Salon de Provence we saw an icon of a very old black madonna. . . and a large painting of african/american jazz musicians. Nearby we saw a statue of Marianne, woman who symbolizes the french revolution, honoring the twentieth century third world revolution in Vietnam. In a park of this city that used to build bombers, we saw a tail of a bomber in which a mother duck sitting on her nest has been sculpted- - a nonviolent and ecological response to war.

The unfulfilled aims of the french revolution are remembered today in the south of France in a strong ecology movement that seeks to fulfill revolutionary aims of liberté, egalité and fraternite' with a life style that respects the earth and all its creatures. Unfulfilled aims of the french revolution are also visible in the contemporary feminist movement in France, and elsewhere, honoring prehistoric women divinities who preceded the male divinities of the world's dominant religions. Scores of black madonnas in France remind us of our african origins and the values of our african black mother. Antecedents of today's french feminists are the strong peasant women around Lyons in the early modern era studied by Natalie Zemon Davis[9] and the iconoclastic french women of the 19th century (George Sand, Flora Tristan) who spun the first spiral of modern western feminism. Luce Irigaray (whose name is basque) is today the major feminist theorist of France, Spain, and Italy, whose feminism is grounded in ancient values and women's bodies.

A similar ancient/future pattern of feminism may be found in France,

Spain, and Italy. In Italy, notably in Tuscany, where there is a pattern of african migration paths, icons of primordial woman divinities (e.g., 26,000 BCE "venus" of Savignano), and contemporary heretical movements pointing to a better world - - democratic and nonviolent communism, feminism, and ecology. In Bologna, a city where buildings and politics are both red, feminists and communists climb through many porticos to pray in the hillside sanctuary of the protectress of the city - - a black madonna.

L. Luca Cavalli Sforza, great italian and american geneticist, has suggested that he can predict how a geographical region votes based on his knowledge of african migration paths. His premise is that places whose culture is centered on the mother (on african migration paths) tend to be politically on the democratic left. The hypothesis is dramatically confirmed in Bologna in Italy, center of the resistance of italian partisans who saved scores of jews from killing camps, fought the nazis, and has been politically "red" (a humane communism described as "communism with ragu") most of the time since 1945.

In my thinking, places whose culture is centered on Rianne Eisler's concept of a dominator father reflect the successful suppression of the ancient belief in the african dark mother, and will tend to have right wing cultural and political beliefs, notably male dominance, violence, and ultimately, fascism. In the twentieth century the conflict between the two world views was bitterly fought out in the spanish civil war, a rehearsal for world war two. Picasso's painting "Gernica " (a town in the basque region of Spain) remains today the most powerful anti-war painting of our time . . . nazis bombing a peaceful basque market town.

Cavalli-Sforza's theory that beliefs brought by ancient africans in migration have left their legacy in left politics, is also borne out in the south of France, a region of resistance to fascism and work for socialist goals. This left pattern also prevails in the basque region of Spain which at Mondragon has the most successful cooperatives in the world. In Italy, besides "red" Tuscany, the peasant communist region of Salento in Puglia is also on an african migration path. The Salento has many menhirs and dolmens, and many black madonnas to whom peasant communists pray. Stimulating me to meditate on the nonviolent implications of the black mother (who loves all her many-colored children, women in Bari (in Puglia) founded the contemporary Permanent Convention of Women against War in whose 2003 conference I participated.

In the 1970s in one of those periodical upsurges of deep beliefs that characterizes human history, the symbol of african Tanit, the ankh- - a cross with an oval head beeame the symbol of international feminism. In 2006, Tanit, african black mother, whose symbol is the feminist ankh, may be considered world symbol of contemporary nonviolent world movements for justice, equality, healing, and transformation.

Notes

1 This is a working paper of my book in progress, The future has an ancient heart. Legacy of african migrations in Europe. It is also an adaptation of my paper, "The future has an ancient heart, legacy of transformation. African origins and african migration paths in Europe," presented to the 17th annual Cheikh Anta Diop International Conference, "African Explorations: Theories and Models of Creativity and Discovery for a Resurgent Africana World." September 30-October 1, 2000 Philadelphia. This paper was read by Jodi MacMillan to the conference, "Matriarchies," Austin, Texas on October 1, 2005. In another version, it became the invited paper I presented to the Conference of La Maison de L'Afrique, Université de Toulouse – Le Mirail. "Les Africains et leurs descendants en Europe avant le XXe siecle" Une equipe international d'historiens, December 8,9,10, 2005.

2 For downcasing see "Note on Style" in my dark mother. african origins and godmothers (New York, Chicago, Lincoln, and Shanghai, iUniverse, 2001, and italian and french editions (see below). .

3 L. Luca Cavalli-Sforza, and Paola Menozzi, Alberto Piazza, The History and Geography of Human Genes (Princeton University Press, 1994).

4 Maulana Karenga, The Moral Ideal in Ancient Egypt. A Study in Classical African Ethics (New York and London. Routledge. 2004).

5 See bibliographies in my books. Lucia Chiavola Birnbaum, dark mother. african origins and godmothers (New York, Chicago, Lincoln, Shanghai, iUniverse, 2001; Enheduanna Award for Excellence in Woman Centered Literature, 2002; italian edition, la madre o-scura (Cosenza, Italia, MEDiterranea MEDia, 2004); french edition, mere noire, (Paris et Cameroun, Menaibuc, spring 2006). Lucia Chiavola Birnbaum, Black Madonnas. Feminism, Politics, and Religion in Italy (Boston, Ma., Northeastern University Press, 1993); italian edition, Black Madonnas. Femminismo, religione e politica in Italia (Bari, Italia, Palomar Editrice, 1997, Premio Internazionale di Saggistica, Salerno, Italia 1998; iUniverse reprint, 2000. She is Everywhere! An anthology in womanist/feminist writings in spirituality (New York, Chicago, Lincoln, Shanghai, iUniverse, 2005). Volume One, gathered by Lucia Chiavola Birnbaum. See also, Volume Two, She is Everywhere. . . . gathered by Lucia Chiavola Birnbaum, Karen Nelson Villanueva, and Annette Williams.

6 Emmanuel Anati, Har Karkom. 20 Anni di Ricerche Archeologiche (Capo di Ponte, Italia, Edizioni del Centro Camuno di Studi Preistorici. 1999).

7 Simone Weil Reader, ed., G. A. Panichas (Mt. Kisco, New York, Moyer Bell Ltd, 1977).

8 Sophie Cassagnes-Brouquet, Vierges Noires. Regard et Fascination (Passage des Macons, Editions du Rossergue, 1990).

9 Natalie Zemon Davis, Society and Culture in Early Modern France. Eight Essays (Stanford, Ca, Stanford University Press, 1965).

The Goddess Has A Thousand Faces Mandala is a collagraph collage of a dozen Goddess images from art history spanning four millennia of Herstory. Clockwise starting at the top are: the Snake Goddess of Crete, Athena, Inanna, Lilith, Black Artemis of Ephesus, Hygeia, Hildegard of Bingen's Sophia Wisdom, Etruscan Diana, Artemis, Demeter, Nut and a Cretan Priestess. In the center is an etching of an egg on a bed of feathers symbolizing the source of life and its many manifestations. Black and white squares and an egg and dart circle surround the egg. They symbolize the dichotomy of opposites which create the whole. A circle of spiral energy encloses the mandala creating sacred space. The *Mandala* was the centerpiece for a 1987exhibition titled "Better Homes & Goddesses". The *Mandala* has hung in dozens of exhibitions since and is the opening page for www.lydiaruyle.com on the internet.

Nuestra Senora La Virgen de Guadalupe, banner by Lydia Ruyle

Nuestra Senora La Virgen de Guadalupe is the present name of the Great Mother Goddess of Mexico. The Spaniards brought Black Madonnas with them to the western hemisphere where they joined Mayan Ixchel and Aztec Tonantzin of earlier Pre-Hispanic cultures. La Virgen spoke to a simple peasant Juan Diego asking him to build a church to her on Tonantzin's hill at Tepeyac. Miraculously, La Virgen's image appeared on his *tilma* wrapped around many red roses as proof of his vision. The *tilma* hangs in the Cathedral today in Mexico City. Guadalupe is the Goddess of the Western Hemisphere, Central and South America and the southwestern United States.

Source: Painting on cloth, c. 1534, Guadalupe Cathedral, Tepeyac, Mexico City

The Great Mother of Catalhoyuk, banner by Lydia Ruyle

The *Great Mother of Catalhoyuk* sits on her throne with her lions giving birth 8,500 years ago. She was found in a grain bin. The figure embodies four symbolic concepts. First, she is the earliest image in art history of a person on a throne. Thereafter, thrones will reflect the lap of the mother as the seat of authority in many cultures. Second, she is an older woman as evidenced by the folds in her body. Life experience births wisdom, which is feminine in many cultures. Third, lions are matriarchal and they symbolize rebirth in Anatolian art. Tomb sculptures show the great mother as a lion holding the person to be reborn in her paws. Ultimately, the Great Mother symbolizes the life cycle of birth, death, and rebirth.

Source: Clay sculpture, c. 6500 BCE, Catalhoyuk, Anatolian Civilizations Museum, Ankara, Turkey

Background: James Mellaart sketches in The Goddess from Anatolia, Eskenzai, Germany, 1989

Sardegna

Lynne Wilson

Sardegna, land of contrasts – ancient, spiritual and of the moment.

Dark craggy peaks, deep azure grottos, languid, fine, sandy beaches. Air filled with perfume of olives and wildflowers.

Churches, sanctuaries beckon. Images from our past bring tears. Smooth marble draws our soft touch. Angels, mothers draw our wonder.

Sardegna, land of contrasts – ancient, spiritual and of the moment.

Returning will be returning home.

June 6, 2004

Krolow Polski:
Black Queen-Mothers of Poland

Małgorzata (Margaret) Kruszewska

The visionary work of Lucia Chiavola Birnbaum on the Black Madonnas of Sicily, Italy and Spain has opened a path for sister scholars working on similar reconnections to the Black Madonnas world-wide. The continual presence of the Black Mother in portraits and statues throughout Europe is evidence of the undeniable African origins of these civilizations. My research focuses on portraits of the Black Madonna of Eastern Europe which I frequently saw in homes, road shrines and churches throughout my childhood. On later return trip to Poland as an adult, I began to ask why there exist so many Black Madonnas in this geographical area as well as the more difficult question of why Her Polish followers resist calling her Black and do not acknowledge Her African origins.

I am fortunate to be an immigrant and therefore still connected to my Polish culture allowing for an insider's knowing of Polish folk customs, language and living traditions. One such fortuitous insight landed in my hands on a recent trip to visit my 93 year old Polish aunt currently living in Vermont. Among her daughter's books was one on the Black Madonnas of Poland (*Polskie Madonny*). I was astounded to see hundreds of photos documenting different shrines throughout Poland; more than half can easily be identified as the dark mother.

Researching these Black Madonnas of Poland provided an opportunity to not only reexperience these profound images on an immediate spiritual level but to also raise historical and theological questions of Her origins and mythology. While immersing myself in reviewing over seventy images of Polish Black Madonnas I felt both overwhelmed and empowered in recognizing my unique position as a Polish-American, ex-Catholic, feminist scholar. This paper is an attempt to bridge two origins stories: the

287

universal origins of all people in Africa and those of my specific ancestral identity.

My challenge encompassed a scholarly reconnection of Poland -a country in extreme northeast Europe with a cold climate and not easily accessible - to Africa. Edward Scobie proposes three general migration paths from Africa to Europe: through Spain (and later to Germany), through Italy and through Jerusalem (Van Sertima, 135). I consider all three as possible connections to the area of ancient Poland.

My own ancestral story, although perhaps more readily accessible than that of most Americans, presents several paradoxical questions. Historically Eastern Europe has been in most recent history, the colonized. This does not however, preclude an ancient history as possibly the invaders also. The stories of the Black Madonnas attest to the survival of "blackness" in sacred images despite a more recent history of racism and patriarchal oppression in Polish culture. The Black Madonna has in fact, acquired a central position in the development of Poland's history. In the process of my research I became more aware that in reclaiming our stories we must consider the experiences of being both the subaltern and the participant in power systems. It is an appropriate time in history to consider how cultures invade, influence and transform each other. I believe this to be true for all races and cultures experienced within our genetic memory.

Poland has never been a "super power." Although known for her brave underground armies and extreme patriotism, Poland has never been the aggressor or colonizer. Poland's history has been one of being conquered, oppressed and divided because of her geographical significance. Poland is also rich in natural resources: the forests which produced coal; the flat and fertile plains used for farming wheat and barley; and the Baltic Sea with its abundance of salt, minerals and amber. Moreover, as an Eastern European country, Poland shares more cultural and historical identity with the eastern and southern neighbors in Hungary and Russia than with Western Europe. Until its very recent entry into the European Union in 2004, Poland remained on the outskirts of Western European nations, most notably as an Iron Curtain nation. Małgorzata Oleszkiewicz, a Polish-American scholar who has also written on the Black Madonna of Poland, considers the Balto-Slavic peripheral status as a possible explanation for its continued rich mythology and folklore that honors the Mother goddess in the stories of "Mother Moist Earth" (18). [1]

Furthermore, scholarly research on this geographical area has been neglected in favor of the historically dominant powers surrounding Poland, namely Germany and Russia. Being raised in the Polish culture, I know that stories survive because people need them to continue, especially while under repressive regimes. Stories are also transmitted in images and symbols, a key point in understanding the tenacity of the Black Madonnas of Poland.

The Black Madonnas of Poland have continued through millennia of power shifts and border changes. The perseverance of these images may be due to Her survival in those very geographical areas most contested and politically ever-changing. The existence and continued worship of hundreds of Black Madonnas in Poland speaks of the presence of ancient spiritual knowledge and practices that survived invasions and Christianity in what Birnbaum describes as the "memory that has acted as a subversive undertow to more than 2,000 years of the dominant violent civilization of the west" *(dark mother, xxxvii)*.

Many women's spirituality scholars are already familiar with the famous Our Lady of Częstochowa (Matka Bozka Częstochowska) near Krakow that author China Galland wrote about in her book, *Longing For Darkness*. China Galland provided an account of the profound spiritual effect that image had on her faith and in her own spiritual journey to reconnect with the dark mother. Galland's story is different from my own, being a Polish-born woman who has lived with the dark mother as an everyday image, and especially knowing Her significance in Poland's struggle for independence. Most recently, the Black Madonna of Częstochowa became a powerful symbol during Poland's Solidarnosc Movement in the early 1980's.[2]

Matka Boska Czestochowska continues being the protectress during times of oppression and warfare.   In *Black Women of Antiquity*, Edward Scobie suggests that several European Black Madonnas were inspired by real women who acted in heroic ways by saving soldiers and inspiring righteous battles (Van Sertima, 148). For the post-World War II generations, Matka Boska Częstochowska portrayed the patriotic organizing and eventual victorious element of a nation under totalitarian rule. Many underground resistance stories (including those of John Paul II) revolve around the power of Her symbol in ousting Soviet communism.

It is important to note here that the relationship between communism and Catholicism in Poland is opposite to that of what Birnbaum described as a "parallel existence of communism and catholism" in Italy. My family left Poland in 1964 during the oppressive communist reign. In a country where 95% of the population identify themselves as Roman Catholics, the unity of the Polish nation under the Roman Catholic Church centered on preserving a cultural heritage threatened by imperial powers first and then by the communist regimes of the Soviet Union.[3] The symbol used to embody this mission was the portrait of the Matka Boska Częstochowska. Her historical significance served as a political anchor for the nation as well as an ever present symbol of protection and blessings for Poles abroad.

Poland became a Catholic state between 962 and 992. According to pagan history, Christianity was resisted, especially by the peasants. (Jones, 167) What remains of archaic spiritual practices clearly show goddess worship further supported by the abundance of archeological evidence gathered by Marija Gimbutas throughout Eastern and Central Europe. Although Gimbutas' "Old Europe" was located further south of present day Poland it did include areas around the Baltic Sea and Lithuania.

Poland as a nation did not come into existence until the middle ages. Writings in the Polish vernacular language have been identified from the thirteenth century. Interestingly, one of the oldest written texts is a poem/hymn to Mary as "God's Birth Giver" (*Bogurodzica*) whose origins are traced to old Slavic (Milosz, 13). Oleszkiewicz connects the tradition of this hymn to the "oldest known prayer to her" from 3rd century Egypt (16).

The reconnecting dots may begin here, with a close association of the Queen-Mother not only as the nurturing mother (an archetype that Western feminists have easily embraced) but also as the source of **political power**. She is the Ruler because She is connected to the power of the sun, the moon, the stars, the earth and the sky. The symbols of the Black Madonna are the same ones found on Egyptian queens: the crowns, the scepters, the stars and the crescent moon. Thus, in Poland the Black Madonna is called the Queen of Poland. In Egyptian Dynasties the "legitimacy of throne inheritance passed through mother" (Van Sertima, 28). She is viewed as more than just the nurturer mother, She is the ruler and direct contact with spiritual and temporal powers.

Having begun my research with the Afro-centric scholarship of Diop and Van Sertima along with the genetic migration theories of Sforza-Cavalli and the cultural feminist methodology of Chiavola Birnbaum, I continue being guided and inspired by Afro-centered theories including those that emphasize the importance of what was once described as the "picture-writing" language of the Kemetic hieroglyphs.   The Black Madonnas of Poland prove the importance of images and create what Birnbaum describes as the "insistence of the symbols."

The visual language of images and symbols[4] is also preserved in locally crafted tapestries and blankets, which feature animal and plant imagery associated with the planting seasons. The same motifs frequently decorate the garments adorning Polish Black Madonnas. My curiosity in researching the symbols woven into textiles arose from studying several beautiful blankets from Poland that my sister and aunt possessed. I became convinced that woven into the design was a language and a story. Elizabeth

Wayland Barber's book, *Women's Work*, was instrumental in connecting the importance of symbols as they appear on clothing:

> What did ancient people try to accomplish when they deliberately made cloth bear meaning? A good look at folk customs and costumes recently in use reveals three main purposes. For one thing, it can be used to mark or announce information. It can also be used as a mnemonic device to record events and other data. Third, it can be used to invoke "magic" to protect, to secure fertility and riches, to divine the future, perhaps even to curse. (149)

Pictures not only provide a way of knowing that spans civilizations but also affect us on a visceral level, stimulating the truth of our genetic memory. Oleszkiewicz states that there currently exist over 400 portraits of Mary in Poland that are associated with miraculous stories The Black Madonna is worshiped in churches, field shrines and chapels throughout Poland today. *Polskie Madonny*, the art book that fell into my hands on a visit to my elderly aunt, shows 187 portraits, more than half are recognizably Black Madonnas.

The prevalence of images of the Queen Mother in Poland must also be considered in the historical role of women in Poland. Diop claims that a significant identifying feature of African civilizations is a matriarchal social organization (111). Poland is known for a tradition of "strong women", both as providers and being economically independent. This can be only partly be attributed to the history of wars that Poland has been subjected to, when women were responsible for the daily functions of families and communities. Their power continued despite a millennium of Roman Catholism that imposed a patriarchal religion that elevated the role of "motherhood" as defined by an all male clerical hierarchy. The different functions of the Black Queen Mothers of Africa - from warrior queens to scribes and priestesses- allows us to redefine the dark mothers and their political significance in places of oppression, strife and injustice. She becomes not just a nurturing mother but also a balancer of powers and spiritual leader reminding Her worshipers of truth and justice.

Cheikh Anta Diop's influence on the Euro-dominated fields of archeology, pre-history and linguistics has produced a reconsideration of historical data. This methodology is similar to the work of women's spirituality scholars who must reread text and artifacts for vital symbols and information that have been manipulated against them. Diop's theory does emphasize however, that the invasions were not motivated by patriarchy necessarily but by the aggression of the northern Aryans (who were patriarchal) against the southern Blacks (who were matriarchal). (111-113) In viewing the Black Madonnas of Easter Europe, we must consider another possible rereading, that of the lasting influence of Black civilizations on some of the farthest northern countries in Europe.

One aspect that I wanted to keep foremost during my readings is the possibility that ancient nomadic people of Poland may in fact have been part of the Indo-Aryan invaders commonly referred to as "Kurgans" by Gimbutas and possibly the "Scythians" as described by Diop. Thus my own ancestry became much more complex.

If we identify ourselves as all being of African origins then it is easier to not identity with our own history of being oppressors. For example, it is much easier for me to not identify myself with American imperialism because I was born in Poland. In my attempts at trying to understand who conquered whom and when, I became aware of history being continually rewritten according to the politics needed by a contemporary community. Diop himself, while reclaiming the Black origins of civilization, also mentions that even Egyptian civilization was a colonizer at certain historical points in time. I believe we need to maintain this balanced perspective when reclaiming ancient symbols to resist the cycle of vilification and domination of over each other.

Thealogical Considerations of Race and Gender

Her "blackness" also presents an interesting thealogical[5] consideration in that Her African features do not represent the physical features of Her worshipers who are frequently, and somewhat accurately, stereotyped as being "very white and very blond." What stories then, uphold her strong presence in Poland? What issues of race and female deity worship are being sustained through the people who adore her?

It was exhilarating knowing of the presence of so many of these beautiful Black Madonnas, of various shades and features, from the land I was born in which has in more recent history produced racist, anti-Semitic agendas. Similar to Professor Birnbaum's epiphanies on the obvious connections between Sicily and Africa, I experienced a profound "knowing" that the ancients' love of the Black Mother has survived even in the most unlikely of locations. And that someone like me, a blond, very "white" straight-nosed Northeastern European can recognize myself in Her.[6]

However, my sentiments do not represent the typical Pole looking at the portraits of the Black Madonna. Firstly, Poles do not refer to Her as the "Black" Madonna but as "Our Lady" or "Mother of God." Secondly, I have not encountered any acknowledgment by either Polish scholars or amongst Polish devotees of Her blackness being attributed to Her African origins. On the contrary, there exist many stories rationalizing her darkness; the most popular being that She has been discolored from fires, candle smoke, wood type and aging.

One source does describe the practice of painting "blackened portraits" as connected with showing "ancient forbears; it's a paltry testimony to a noble descent. These portraits, connected with Sarmatian culture- megalomaniac gentry ideology according to which the Poles were descended from the ancient Sarmatians" (Pasierb, 16).

The Sarmatians have been documented in the archeological work of Jeannine Davis-Kimball. Unique to this culture was the high number of women warriors buried with weapons showing their skills as huntresses and fighters. If in fact, the dark tones in ancient paintings signified a tribal identity with the Sarmatians, might these women warriors have been direct descendants of the African queen mothers, even more specifically, the Candaces, a line of warrior queens? Paradoxically, they are also affiliated with the Scythians, whom are portrayed in Diop's work as the northern invaders.

Explaining Black Madonnas in White Eastern Europe

Accepting the obvious origins of all races in the Black Mother is one thing. Figuring out how She may have landed in the farthest Northern corners of Poland is another. Focusing on archaeological and genetic explanations of migration patterns from Africa allowed me to connect two far-reaching parts of the world. It also allowed me to address the deeper question of my research. Knowing the popularity of the Black Madonna images with Poles who have no immediate historical connections with Africa and who have been considered very "white"; why has her "blackness" not been acknowledged and how has this repression been maintained?

Any discussion of religion, race and historical power shifts in Poland must include the role of Catholicism in its nation building and in its role in contributing to one of the greatest atrocities against the dark "other" – the anti-Semitism that prevailed in Poland before and after Hitler's massacres. Here also exists a linchpin connecting the history of "darkness" in Poland. Could the history of the Jews in Poland be connected with the survival of the Black Madonnas?

Likewise, another area of reconstruction is the history of pagan practices that existed in Poland prior to Christianity, many of which were associated with female images and powers. Lithuania, in particular, maintained a Paganism that countered the "threat from Christian military orders to the west" (Jones, 171). Oleszkiewicz points out that the famous Jasna Gora (literally translates as "Light Mountain") where Our Lady of Częstochowa resides is in the same vicinity as "Lysiec or Bold Mountain a legendary place of witches' sabats" (12). A common phenomenon of sacred sites is the layering of religious practices at the same location according to the politico-religious conquests of the times.

Joan Halifax in her book, *The Fruitful Darkness* describes the profound effect geographical landscapes have on our healing experiences, shamanic visions, prayer and meditations. The book contributed to my question of why such an abundance of Black Mother images survived on Polish ground. Viewing the land Herself as holding certain powers connected with the most profound belief of Poles: a love for the actual earth, the ground, *ziema* she is called in Polish. Every Pole prays to be folded back into Her at the end of their life journey. Every immigrant says they will fall on their knees and kiss Her when they return to *ziema*.

Recalling Religion as a Polish Daughter

My own religious upbringing included eight years in a Polish-American Catholic elementary school where I attended weekly, and often daily, Polish mass services which were full of ritual -- both dramatic and tedious! My father was a physically abusive, alcoholic tyrant who often quoted sermons he heard at church that supposedly sanctioned his power to rule - with much cruelty- over my mother and his four daughters. I learned to hate this religion that empowered him to oppress us. I hated it also because my mother clung to it till the day she died. Only now, as an adult, can I consider "all the ways our mothers did not give in to patriarchy."[7]

In my recent reentry into academic life through my graduate studies at New College and CIIS, I have frequently returned to the religious images I saw at home or in church. I was very devoted and religious as a young girl, perhaps because of the rich theatricality of the Polish Catholic church rituals that appealed to my artistic sensibilities. Certainly the images I grew up with offered an abundance of symbols and stories.

Mythological images from my family's region of Poland included animal and plant motifs embroidered onto tapestries, slippers and blankets. For example the area around my mother's village is known for its abundance of storks which my mother embroidered into her designs on pillowcases and wall hangings.. The stories of some of these images and symbols have been forgotten, or may be awaiting a time when they can once again be "decoded."

Growing up Polish also included receiving many stories through the oral tradition of memorizing long poems and songs. The poems retained history and legends for a people whose existence was constantly threatened. In pre-Christian times, Polish bards worked to maintain the oral traditions as a "warrior's good name would simply die without the efforts of his bard" (Jones, 167). As a young immigrant girl, I was often asked to memorize long patriotic poems for public recitation at Polish veterans' gatherings. I attribute my love of language and theater to this early mnemonic education I received.

My parents barely completed the equivalent of a grade school education but were able to recite long elaborate poems by Adam Mickiewicz, who was considered the poet-chronicler of Poland's struggles in the 1800's. Interestingly, one of his most famous poems, *Pan Tadeusz*, honors Matka Boska Ostro Brama (Our Lady of the Sharp Gate), an image I will primarily focus on in this research paper. My sister remembers the image of Matka Boska Ostrobramska prominently displayed in our home in Poland

My family is from the northeast part of Poland, the largest town being Białystok, near Belarus and Lithuania. Its official establishment may have been with Lithuania as it was founded by the grand duke of Lithuania in 1320. This area, like many others in Poland has been claimed by many nations throughout its existence, most recently by the Soviet Union.

Białystok has always had the added reputation of being ethnically mixed. Białystok is still, to this day, not considered "purely Polish." Before WWII, 40% of its population consisted of various ethnic groups including a large Jewish, Russian, Greek Orthodox, Belorusian and Lithuanian population. My oldest sister recalled a saying that someone from our region was not considered truly "of blood and bone- Polish." Its proximity to the Baltic and Russian cultures has created differing cross-cultural motifs in its art and crafts from those found in the famous southern regions around Krakow. The blend of ethnicities in this northern town, would have produced a richer exchange of images and stories. Hence my consideration of African elements in the Polish Black Madonnas is supported knowing that this geographical area has historically been the site of multi trade, religious and cultural exchanges.

Furthermore, the Greek civilization may not have been as significant to ancient Baltic people as it was to Western European tribes. More scholarship is also needed on the influence of Semitic groups who may have migrated through a more direct route to Eastern Europe as Birnbaum suggests that:

In the prechristian era there was a constant interchange of Jews from the Middle East with Blacks of Africa and an intermingling of the Semitic goddesses of Carthage and the African goddesses of Egypt.

Specifically, the history of Jews in Poland requires a separate discussion that would include a scholarship and knowledge I cannot offer at this time. For the purpose of this paper, I do consider one of the possible connectors between the Black Madonnas of Poland and the Black Queens of Africa to be the numerous migrations of Semites and Jews to the Baltic area. In Poland, the Jews have been viewed as one of the "dark other," along with the Turks. Both groups might have brought and preserved images of the dark mother.

Our Lady of Czstochowa

Many of Poland's myths and traditions center around Poland's fierce fight for independence from invasions and subsequent partitions. The portrait of Matka Boska Czestochowska provides many stories of its miraculous preservation in battle times.

The history of the famous Częstochowa portrait is tied to the Pauline monks whose origins can be traced to St. Paul of Thebes in Egypt (Pasierb 5). The Paulite Order came into prominence in Hungary in the late 1200's. The portrait has been cared for by the Paulite Order through centuries of invasions and warfare and carries many stories of miracles in its preservation. Its powers are attributed to these miracles that changed the course of historical battles, including the repulsion of Swedish troops in 1655 (Pasierb 9).

The portrait's creator is said to have been St. Luke. In an official Church publication the inability to verify Her origins are acknowledged before providing an origins story.

> At the outset we must admit, that up to 1382 we have no concrete facts as to the origin and early history of this painting. We base ourselves, however on facts transmitted by popular belief and tradition among the faithful. (Wright, 1)

Another significant story is that the portrait's arrival in Poland is credited to the intermarriages of Eastern European kingdoms as "the Emperors of the Eastern countries gave their daughters and sisters in marriage to the royalty of those countries and as a dowry gave this sacred painting" (Wright 7). These paintings must have therefore been of significant political value in such a symbolic exchange. A further connection can be made here to African traditions of royal and spiritual leadership being transmitted through the female line. Certainly, the Black Madonna of Częstochowa's role in bringing about societal and political change during times of oppression and injustice echoes Karenga's analysis of the Egyptian Maat as a "symbol of truth, justice and order"(6) . The importance of the Black Queen in times of political repressions has continued through the Black Madonnas of Poland.

Danita Redd's essay in *Black Women in Antiquity* on "Black Madonnas of Europe: Diffusion of the African Isis" mentions the famous Our Lady of Częstochowa in the context of the Byzantine icons prevalent in Russian art (180). Redd also addresses the historical destruction of these images during a period beginning in the seventh century referred to as "iconoclasm." This order by Emperor Leo was based on the belief that these "Christian icons had roots in the worship of 'pagan' gods and goddesses" (124). Ironically, an accurate assessment of the power of these images continuing and supporting Redd's thesis that the "African Isis was prototype for the Black Madonnas of Europe." In the same book, Runoko Rashidi addresses the decline of the cult of Isis and how her form would survive:

> Her influence grew as the dynasties waned, and the suppression of the worship of this greatest of goddesses was the concluding chapter of the ancient Egyptian religion in which the great mother in one form or another had to be seriously reckoned with. (84)

Redd uses an art history methodology to compare the stylistic features in the Russian Black Madonnas that echo Egyptian art:

> Byzantine style is two dimensional: rigid, flattened and symmetric. It is very similar to ancient Egyptian art (most noticeable in bas-reliefs). Afrocentric art historian James Brunson mentions that the African influence on Byzantine art can be observed by the elongated faces, fingers and figures of portrait images. (121)

The early presence of Blacks in Russia has been documented and therefore the occurrence of Black Madonnas there can be more easily explained through the trade connections with the Byzantine Empire. Clarence Holte specifically discusses the Colchians, one of whom may have been Medea (Van Sertima 263). Their arrival is attributed to a desertion of Egyptian and Ethiopian soldiers who settled in an area, "on the northern shore of the Black Sea, between the Erythearan Sea on the South, and the Phassis River on the North" (262).

Matka Bosej Ostrobramskiej

The original portrait of Matka Bozej Ostrobramskiej resides in the town of Wilno in Lithuania. Portraits of the Blessed Mary were hung over the gate of the town. In the Lithuanian language this gate was commonly known as *Auros Vartai* (the gate of dawn). The Polish speaking population knew it as *Ostra Brama* (the sharp gate). As mentioned earlier, Białystok is on the eastern border of Poland shared closest with Lithuania and further south with the Ukraine. The historical literature surrounding this portrait describe a once united region that later was changed according to nationalist borders leading to a subsequent formation of a new archdiocese on the Polish side. Because Poles could not cross the border to visit the original portrait, a copy was brought to the Fari church in Białystok in the 1920's. This was my family's parish where my sisters and I were baptized.

The most striking feature of the Matka Bozej Ostrobramskiej portrait is the halo of sharp rays interspersed with 13 stars. She is garbed in a silver garment and rests on a thin crescent moon shape. The rays suggest her name: "ostra"- sharp and "brama"- gate. Oleszkiewicz writes of a common reference to some of the Black Madonnas as "Keepers of the Border"(19). Certainly this would apply to the shrines of Ostrobramska as geographically situated on the changing border between Poland and Lithuania. In fact, Lithuanian pagan folklore includes stories of the sky-god entering the country "by three silver gates" (Jones 175) I visited the site in July 2006 and photographed the back of the gate. Upon developing my film, I noticed two griffins inscribed at the very top of the gate which I had not seen while walking around it. No explanation is given in Catholic symbolism for these images. I also stopped into the bookstore at the site and opened a local tour guide booklet which began the narrative history of the gate and portrait by stating that it was in fact built to keep the pagans out.

In this portrait of Our Mother of the Sharp Gate I see an obvious connection to the Egyptian goddesses. She rests on the crescent moon symbol (or horn shaped silver disk) which was prominent in Egyptian mythology. Likewise the stars have traditionally been associated with the Egyptian goddess of the sky, Nut. Ostrobramska is also known as Our Lady of the Dawn, further suggesting the Egyptian Nut as the "predawn sky" which was celebrated at winter solstice (Wilkinson, 161). In the last few years, I had been working with Nut energy as a yoga teacher and feature her extended sky body on my yoga studio's literature for guidance and inspiration.

My initial attempts have given me many reasons to continue drawing the connecting dots between Poland and Africa. The survival and worship of hundreds of Black Madonnas points to a vigorous presence of African beliefs and images. As a native daughter who no longer lives in Poland, I am in a unique position to see the patterns of historical shifts that brought different meanings to the portraits of the Black Madonnas in Poland. This paper has also provided an opportunity to further address issues of gender and race played out in the history and religions of Poland. Blackness in Poland may have signified different groups during different historical times, including the despised Turks and later the Jews. But throughout, Her blackness remained - reminding Her people of the unity of our origins in the Black Queen-Mothers of Africa.

Notes

1 Oleszkiewicz' complete essay, "Mother of God and Mother Earth" is available via internet. See Works Cited.

2 The events of Solidarnosc revolved around the workers' unions organizing dramatic strikes in response to martial law imposition on December, 1981 by the Soviet communist regime.

3 Poland's Partition was from 1795-1918 between the imperial powers of Prussia, Austria and Russia. Following WWII, Poland lost eastern cities and was ruled by a Soviet government.

4 Birnbaum states that symbols differ in that "emerging from the unconscious, may be universal, but the meaning takes different forms." (Black Madonnas, 11)

5 "Thealogy" as a feminist response to the male-centered concepts of "theology."

6 I describe my physical features using Diop's model of identifying black features by describing hair, nose and skin hue.

7 An inspiring line from one of Professor Birnbaum's classroom lectures. From personal note, Oct. 26, 2004.

Bibliography

Barber, Elizabeth Wayland. *Women's Work: The First 20,000 Years.*

New York: W.W. Norton & Company, 1994.

Birnbaum, Lucia Chiavola. "Dark wheat and red poppies" 9 August, 2003.

Birnbaum, Lucia Chiavola. *dark mother: african origins and godmothers.* San Jose: Authors Choice Press, 2001.

Birnbaum, Lucia Chiavola. Black Madonnas: *Feminism, religion & politics in Italy.*

San Jose: toExcel, 2000.

Cavalli-Sforza, Luigi Luca and Francesco Cavalli-Sforza. *The Great Human Diasporas:*

The History of Diversity and Evolution. Menlo Park, California: Addison-Wesley Publishing Company, 1995.

Diop, Cheikh Anta. The *African Origin of Civilization: Myth or Reality.*

Chicago: Lawrence Hill Books, 1974.

Galland, China. *Longing For Darkness: Tara and the Black Madonna.* New York: Viking Press, 1990.

Gimbutas, Marija. *The Language of the Goddess.* New York: Thames and Hudson, 1989.

Gyatso, Janet. "Down with the Demoness:Reflections on a Feminine Group in Tibet" in *Feminine Ground: Essays on Women and Tibet.* Ithica: Snow Lion Publications, 1987

Halifax, Joan. *The Fruitful Darkness.* HarperSanFracisco, 1993.

Jones, Prudence and Nigel Pennick. *A History of Pagan Europe.* New York:

Routledge, 1995.

Karenga, Maulana. *MAAT: The Moral Ideal in Ancient Egypt.* New York:

Routledge, 2004.

Kimball-Davis, Jeannie. *Warrior Women: An Archaologist's Search for History's*

Hidden Heroines. New York: Time Warner Books, 2002.

Miłosz, Czesław. *The History of Polish Literature*. Berkeley: University of California Press, 1983.

Oleszkiewicz, Malgorzata. "Mother of God and Mother Earth: Religion, Gender and Transformation in East-Central Europe" The University of Texas at San Antonio

www.hichumanities.org/AHproceedings/   Malgorzata%20Oleszkiewicz. pdf

Pasierb, Janusz S. and Jan Samek. *The Shrine of the Black Madonna at Częstochowa*. Warsaw: Interpress Publishers, 1991.

Polish American Studies, Vol. XXIII, No.1 Jan, June 1966.

Rosikon, Janusz. *Polskie Madonny*. Warszawa: Oficyna Wydawnicza DAR, 1991.

Van Sertima, Ivan. *African Presence in Early Europe*. New Brunswick: Transaction Publishers, 1985.

Van Sertima, Ivan. *Black Women in Antiquity*. New Brunswick: Transaction Publishers, 1984.

Wilkinson, Richard H. *The Complete Gods and Goddesses of Ancient Egypt* London: Thames & Hudson, 2003.

Wright, John J. *The Glories of Częstochowa and Jasna Gora*. Stockbridge: Marian Press, 1981.

Zganiacz, Lidia. *Polska Ludowa Tkanina Podwojna w Zbiorach Centralnego*

Muzeum Wlokiennictwa w Lodzi. Lodz, 1999.

Black Madonna – Ausros Vartai (Vilnius, Lithuania)

(copy of the original is also located in Bialystok, Poland. It is entitled Ostra Brama, translated as Our Lady of the Sharp Gate.)

Image contributed by Malgorzata (Margaret) Kruszewska

Black Madonna – Matka Boza Loretanska (Glogowek, Poland)

Image contributed by Malgorzata (Margaret) Kruszewska

Goddess-God Creation Myth

Mara Lynn Keller

(excerpt from The Greater Mysteries of Demeter and Persephone)

Lysistrata, Priestess of Demeter, praises the mothers of Eleusis,
praises them for their labors, praises them for their love.
Then lighting a torch from the fire, she concludes our rounds of
storytelling,
reciting the most ancient hymn remembered by our women-kin

Blessed be, Greatest Mystery! Fountain of Being and Becoming,
Giver of Life's Creation, of Life's eternal meaning!
In the Beginning there came rhythms of resounding pleasure,
delightfully pulsing Nature, infinitely playful vibration.

Within the Deep that is Source, Eurynome danced on waters.
Then lonely, from whirling wind, She fashioned the serpent Ophion,
dynamic life-force She loves, seeds Her with new powers.
She takes the form of a Dove, gives birth to the Cosmic Egg.

Around this Ovum of the Cosmos, Ophion, Great Serpent,
wraps Himself seven times, protecting the promise of conception.
Within the very first moment, the Cosmic Egg cracks open,
out tumble Sun, Moon, Stars, all fiery sparks of Creation!

One of these sparkling particles, offshoot of wide-ruling Eurynome,
becomes this place we call home -- Gaia, Grand Mother Earth!
From this miracle of matter, condensation of galactic dust,
Gaia creates as Her equal, beloved companion, Sky God Ouranos!

From Their enduring communion, through tumult and quiescence,
lightning storms and thunder, fierce caressing rapture,
the mating of Earth and Sky births all other Dieties,
all myriad creatures who swim, crawl, walk, or fly!

Then from Mother Earth Gaia and Father Sky God Ouranos
are born Earth Mother Rhea and Father of Time, Kronos.
From Rhea and Kronos' union, first born is Aphrodite,
mystic embodiment of Love, pleasures of Sex and Beauty.

Next born from Earth and Time come Hestia and Hermes of the Home,
then Demeter, prolific Earth Mother, and Her Lover, Poseidon, the Sea.
Demeter has a Daughter, Despoina, beloved, born of Her Body,
bearing the fruits of Earth -- and within each, seeds of rebirth.
Demeter dearly loves Her Daughter, raises Her tenderly, strong,
raises Her sweetly, kind, raises Her with laughter and song.
This love They share forever, rebounds throughout the Cosmos,
is praised at every hearthfire, is danced at every harvest.

With Earth and Time in balance – birth, growth, death, rebirth –
season upon season stimulates cycles of regeneration.
During this golden age, humans grow many gardens,
live in gracious abundance, not fashioning Gods of War.

Then Kronos begins to dominate the rhythmic Mysteries of Earth,
undoing the balance in Nature, grasping control of Time.
Fearing to be overthrown, Time devours His own children,
but Earth Mother retrieves Them, contriving to hide and protect Them.

Demeter's brother, Thundering Zeus, with the help of His Mother Rhea,
revenges Kronos' aggression, overpowering and defeating Him.
Zeus becomes like His Father, fighting those who threaten His power,
demanding ready submission from every one He encounters.

Finally Zeus, Sky God almighty, seizes even his Sister,
planting in fruitful Demeter, the Maiden, Kore-Persephone.
Then people, hardened by fear, turn to battling one another,
generation after generation, torn by hatred and rebellion.

Countless individuals are murdered, others captured, enslaved,
women are raped by conquerors, who worship their new God, War.

*Yet many still remain faithful to Great Demeter and Her Daughter,
the Two Goddesses of Fertility, and the honest fruits of their own labor.*

*These lifeways become intermingled, that of Mother, that of Warrior,
and human bonds of loving become contorted by violence.
Yet Life proceeds undaunted, never abandoning itself,
always finding new ways to re-create itself.*

*Lysistrata stops singing, stops circling the central fire
uniting our gathering of spirits. Silence settles on our warm bodies.*

Notes

The Creation Myth chanted here by Lysistrata is woven from several sources: the Pelasgian Creation Myth in which Eurynome is Prime Creatrix (Graves: 27-28; fn. 2 cites Apollonius Rhodius, *Argonautica* i. 469-505, and Tzetzes, *On Lycophron* 1191); Hesiod's *Theogony* (lines 116-210, 452-506) and *Works and Days* (lines 109-201); and the tragedies of Aeschylus, Sophocles, and Euripides. I have chosen to use the Pelasgian Creation myth here for its pre-Hellenic, matristic, and Neolithic elements, which I believe are shared by the Eleusinian Mysteries' rites and mythos.

I Am Not White

Maria Fama

The dentist says my teeth tell of invasions
    mixed blood
the tale of a proud, mongrel people
    I am Sicilian
    I am not white
I will not check the box for white
    on any form

In Sicily
my ancestors recognized white
to be the color of sparkling linens
    towels, tablecloths, sheets
    the color of clouds, seafoam, and bones
not family faces with their
    African, Greek, Arabic, Norman casts

North Italians call us Africans
a Milanese told me that in Sicily
    he heard Africa's drums
I hear them, too,
    especially when
    from across the little stretch of gleaming sea
    North African winds
    blow through our homes

Sicilians left for other lands
trying to escape poverty   injustice
    they prayed to their

Black Madonna of Tindari
miraculous advocate for the poor
for guidance
packing her image with their clothes

In America at first
they called us colored
Sicilians lynched in the South
    along with Africans
    in the fields, the railroads, the mines
    the children and grandchildren of slaves
    worked at our sides
    taught us American life
    were thought good people, even friends

In America over the years
Sicilians stayed quiet   spoke English
    learned to stand apart
    from those darker sisters and brothers
Sicilians passed to that lighter
    opportunity side of the color line

In America now
some of the Black Madonna's children
    have forgotten her
    ignorant of their roots
    they check the box for white on every form
    no longer aware
    that they are of mixed blood
    the mongrel heirs
    to a proud people of every feature

I cannot forget
when even my teeth tell our story

I will not forget
I have prayed at the Black Madonna's
    ancient, wind-swept shrine at Tindari

I am Sicilian
I am not white.

A Beautiful Mother, A Sister to Walk with Us

Eve, returned from the darkness, joins Mary, now down from her pedestal, to become a model for a journey to wholeness

Mary Ann Robinson , M.A.

A Female Model for our Journeys

Women, we are told, are the weavers. I thrive on weaving together odd strands of thought. Images and ideas from different endeavors can open new windows, new visions. It is not as important to me how others view these results, as is the stretching of my own horizon. I have been weaving together strands derived from my Catholic upbringing and theological studies, my own personal religious experiences, and reading, and in so doing I have been led to a vision of a female model for my journey through life.

One strand is the Genesis myth of the creation of the world (Gen 1-3:24), which appears at a time in history when, as a friend of mine described it, there was a breakdown in the fabric of the world. The Israelite worldview was changing from one with polytheistic elements, female goddesses, to one that was monotheistic, a belief in one male God. Changes were required in the system for the continuation of a journey into furthering life. Eve and the serpent were major players. This myth has had far-reaching consequences for the Judeo/Christian world.

Another strand is a recently renewed interest in Mary, the woman. Stimulated by a lovely eighth-century hymn, the *Ave Maris Stella*, I investigated the developing doctrine and popular devotion to Mary in the early church. From there I moved to an attempt to find a contemporary Mary I could live with. I did not want a goddess figure but a flesh and blood woman, a companion for my personal journey, as expressed in this poem that I wrote:[1]

Mary

Candle lit chapels, soft hymns, lingering in the stillness,
Rosary beads slipping through work-worn fingers,
Joyous voices, beautiful children bringing sweet smelling crowns,
Tears on cheeks, looking up at you, begging.
So much is asked of you.
Moments to remember, to cherish, and then let go.
No longer asking so much, expect what cannot be.
You, a mother, who walked a sweet and bitter path.
Rest now, only be. It is enough.

The much reviled figure of the serpent provides a third strand, enough to begin weaving at least a glimmer of a vision. As I further explored Mary, it occurred to me that Eve and the serpent were major factors in any picture of Mary I could develop, and I sought to create a woman that was an amalgam of the three (if one considers the serpent as female). Originally focusing on the Genesis myth, with its two versions of the creation of Eve, from the points of view of theology and goddess history, I found it necessary to move from theology into myth as I expanded the search for this woman who contains within herself all that is virgin and female, and the seed for a finding a clue to how our world can heal.

I am a woman in my third stage of life, a crone. I am a woman married to the same man for thirty-six years. I am the mother of two young adult daughters. I feel compelled to discover a path that will lead everything living, which includes everything gone before and all that is to come, to some form of wholeness and integrity, to some understanding of our rootedness in the earth, our interconnectedness. There is, I believe, great hope for the world. And so it is that I pose the following questions: Can there be a woman with the lived experience of Eve and Mary suffused with the wisdom of the serpent? Can there be created a woman, who, as a model for our journeys as maiden, mother, and crone, can help us to know our true power? This would be a true interconnectedness, not only for women, but a full integration, a parity between women and men. To find a way to live with an equality between the sexes, in harmony with all peoples and with nature is a goal worthy of one's life. There is no name for this woman nor even a new poem for this vision of mine. That will happen over time.

The Battle of Genesis: Eve and the Serpent Bow to Patriarchy

There are two versions of the creation of Eve in the Garden of Eden. Eve, in Judeo-Christian belief, is our first mother, a woman created from the rib of Adam in the most commonly quoted version of the creation of woman. The version seldom commented on in the churches, Genesis 1:26-27, reads differently: " Then, God said: 'Let us make man in our image, after our likeness…God created man in his image; in the divine image he created him; male and female he created them." This second account, actually the first account recorded suggests an equality between the sexes, or perhaps that they are one being.

Monica Sjöö and Barbara Mor say that the garden itself "…was in fact the entire Near Eastern, North African, and Mediterranean Neolithic agricultural world of the Great Goddess. And the forbidden tree and evil serpent represent her ancient magic powers of illumination and immortality. And earthly peace."[2] As symbols of the goddess, the trees of knowledge and of immortality and the serpent have a rightful home in the garden. In his definition of the tree of the knowledge of good and evil, the object of the Biblical undoing of Adam and Eve, J.C. Cooper says it " symbolizes the feminine principle, the nourishing, sheltering, protecting, supporting aspect of the Great Mother, the matrix and the power of the inexhaustible and fertilizing waters she controls…."[3]

In the tree from which Eve ate, there lay coiled a serpent. The serpent, that prominent player in the Genesis story is, according to Cooper, "a mediator between heaven and earth, earth and the underworld, and is associated with sky, earth and water and in particular with the Cosmic Tree."[4] It has mythic properties that closely resemble that of the tree. This serpent is a teller of the truth. God had told Adam and Eve that they would die if they tasted the fruit of the tree. When she tasted it, she did not die, nor did Adam. She ate what was hers to eat. For Eve is a priestess of the goddess, in the garden of the goddess. The serpent is in the garden as the wise cosmic serpent of the goddess, Sjöö and Mor remind their readers.[5] This serpent is a female symbol, a woman's symbol here in the garden.

Mary Condren says, "the difference between gods and humankind was the ultimate power the deities had to carry out their wicked or generous desires."[6] The serpent as representative of the goddess had both capacities, and, Condren continues, in Hebrew stories and in present day beliefs, the serpent is still viewed as an agent for healing and for evil.[7] The God that created Adam and Eve possessed such knowledge and capacity only for himself, not to share. When the serpent offered Eve the fruit from the tree of knowledge she was taking for herself a prerogative that she was not meant to have. Worse she offered it to Adam and he accepted. The God of the Hebrews is a jealous God. When apprised of the transgression of the first parents, God condemns the serpent to crawl on its belly and ultimately to be crushed by the redeemer to come. Leonard Shlain reminds his reader that "Yahweh's first disciplinary act was to sever this ancestral connection."[8] An epic struggle was engaged. In the centuries to follow Christianity will often show images of Mary, the mother of that redeemer, as standing with her foot on the head of the serpent.

So much was hidden when access to the tree was forbidden to these our first parents, and so much lost and gained when Eve accepted its fruit from the serpent. She accepted that which was hers by right as a woman. When she ate the fruit, shared it with Adam, and heard the condemnation of God, her eyes were opened. She came into an awareness of what she had lost and would begin to see more fully a new way of being that would lead into a new possibility for wholeness. In the end, Eve is separated from her women's ways of knowing, represented by the presence of the serpent, the tree, and the garden itself, all symbols of the goddess. Cast out of the only world she had known, she must begin her quest for life.

Expelled from the Garden for beginning to understand things as good and evil, Eve is the symbol of the goddess religion crushed and the beginning of a world of monotheistic patriarchy. The serpent/goddess plunges into being a subversive, submerged energy. From this expulsion and subversion will come with the struggles of self-consciousness, with its many sorrows, defeats and much joy and small victories. James Hollis phrases it this way: "Thereafter they are obliged to suffer the fact that many of their choices will not be between good and bad, but between all sorts of moral grays. They will need to acknowledge their moral ambiguity and their personal and cultural duplicity."[9]

In line with my vision of wholeness, Riane Eisler puts forth another way to view the suppression of the goddess tradition and the rise of a monotheistic, male centered culture. In Genesis there is a time when Adam and Eve enjoyed a way of being in the garden that was one of parity, a time before Eve bit into the apple.[10] As often as I have heard and read that story, that piece has passed by me. There was time, perhaps, to love, to cherish each other before their eyes were opened, before God expelled them into a harsh land, and Eve, woman, would "be subservient to" Adam, "man."[11] This could be a model for hope. Women and men can be honored and respected for the roles they play making a society function without domination. The feminine can be honored without the male fearing that she might dominate.

Eisler calls this "a gender-holistic perspective" which results in "a new theory of cultural evolution" which she calls a theory of "Cultural Transformation."[12] Two models of society are to be found in the substrata of human culture. One is the *dominator* model in which fifty percent of the population are "ranked over the other." The other is a *partnership* model where linking rather than ranking marks the roles of the individual or groups. Further, this theory claims that the original thrust of our cultural development was directed toward the partnership model but derailed by a time of tremendous upheaval and there resulted a "fundamental social shift."[13] The Garden of Eden and the fall and subsequent expulsion of our first parents are pieces of real events and reflect this period of upheaval.[14]

Mary: Revival of the Goddess as the New Eve

So it was that the battle of Genesis was lost before it was engaged. Monotheistic patriarchy won the world of the sacred – the earth, the air, the waters, the sun, the moon, the plants, the animals – would be under the dominion of the male. Only he had direct access to the male God in whose image he was made. Woman would have only indirect access to the holy God through the man. A different world view emerges for the Hebrews and ultimately for most of the earth. It was for a time forgotten that what passes is not lost, only hidden in the recesses of the collective memory. The sacred feminine will go underground, waiting, reappearing in Mary. Elinor Gadon notes that the Goddess "was not so easily vanquished and much of her iconography, her symbols, and images were to be absorbed into the cult of the Virgin."[15]

The foundation for recovering goddess history, so long lost to us, lies in piecing together the discoveries of archeologists. In the chapter "The Hebrew Goddess and Monotheism," Gadon says that there is more and more archeological evidence being found to substantiate the biblical allusions to a goddess in the world of the Israelites. So much of this knowledge has been selected out by the authors for various political reasons in both Judaic and Christian scriptures.[16]

There were Hebrews settled in the land of Canaan about three hundred years (1500-1200 B.C.E.) before they developed into a "contending power in that area with Yahweh as their god."[17] The Canaanite god, El, was in many ways similar to Yahweh, and he appears in Genesis as an adjectival to him. El is problematic because he has a wife, Asherah. and a son, Baal, who is consort to Astarte, their daughter. Asherah and Baal appear as contenders for the power of Yahweh. Asherah ruled the seas, while El ruled the heavens. She is the creatrix of the gods, a mother figure. Astarte's name means womb.[18] She and her brother are symbolic of "the begetter and conceiver, man and woman, husband and wife."[19] The Hebrews were not always a monotheistic people.

Fast forward to the formation of Christianity. Gadon explains that, for Christianity, the solution to absolving the sin of Eve was the Virgin Mary. The early church fathers, in efforts to explain the doctrine that Jesus was both fully divine and fully human, read back into scripture, looked at the tradition being formulated and decided ultimately that Mary would have to have been conceived and born in such a fashion as to be free of the stain of original sin. Freed from this stigma, she would represent a new Eve. The original Eve, having been created directly by God, was sinless until she accepted the serpent's offering. This new Eve, symbolized by her *immaculate womb*,[20] conceived and bore Jesus without the normal intercourse with a male and without a ruptured hymen. She remained a physical virgin for her life span.

Mary emerges in time birthing a son, to redeem the human race from the sin of Eve. Or, so the official interpretation goes. This son, Jesus, liked women, honored them as persons with the right to equality. The church fathers soon turned the vision of Jesus into one of a continuation of what was. When Mary was accepted by them as a model for the feminine she was greatly reduced. She is needed only as the human vehicle for the birth of her son, Jesus, and his significance is not one of life but of death. He is sent by his father, God, to die for the sins of many. He is the one who brings salvation into the world for those who believe, and that salvation is only realized by his death and effected only after the deaths of the believers.[21]

While the overriding tendency has been to put the divine, the sacred, out there somewhere, Christianity has flirted with an immanent divinity throughout its history. Jesus was a human being, a man who walked the earth, and divine, connected, to identified with his transcendent father. Our religious backgrounds, forming us unconsciously before we examine them consciously, reveal the impulse for immanence. Marina Warner talks about growing up in a Catholic environment. This was a religion that "consisted of simple certainties, outlined in the crisp rhetoric of the Catechism…And the Virgin was the chief of these certainties."[22] The Marian devotions were warm, beautiful, filled with the proverbial "smells and bells" of Catholic worship. I remember, as does she, the first stirrings of doubt about the chastity, the purity required. She says that she can now articulate those feelings as her sensing "that the problem of human evil was more complex than concupiscence–at least in its narrow sexual definition."[23] From these personal beginnings Warner will explore the myth of Mary.

> The Virgin Mary...represents a central theme in the history of western attitudes to women. She is one of the few female figures to have attained the status of myth–a myth that for nearly two thousand years has coursed through our culture, as spirited and often as imperceptible as an underground stream.[24]

In the classical world, where Christianity developed and came into its own, virginity signified, not physical virginity, but the right to choose whether or not to engage in sexual activity. A virgin was a strong and independent woman. In the Christian world, a virgin was physically pure, undefiled. One piece of the concept of virginity that they would keep would be the notion "that virginity was powerful magic and conferred strength and ritual purity."[25] Virginity, chastity, as a major ascetic practice for men as well as women, became a hallmark of Christianity. The virgin birth would be used "as the moral sanction of the goodness of sexual chastity."[26]

Mary is the new Eve, our mother, in the spirit as Eve is our biological mother, our ancestress. In similar fashion, Jesus is the new Adam, made afresh, human from a human woman, earth from earth but a pure earth, a pure flesh. The world is born again in grace, the fall has been overturned.[27] Warner quotes a stanza from *Ave Maris Stella* to illustrate this point.[28] I have fond memories of this hymn being sung in a convent chapel at Vespers. It evokes in me all the warmth, the consolation, the hope, that Marian devotions held for us in days past:

> *Sumens illud Ave*Taking that sweet Ave
> *Gabrielis ore*Which from Gabriel came
> *Funda nos in pace*Peace confirm within us
> *Mutans nomen Evae.*Changing Eva's name.

Here I am using a slightly different translation from the one in Warner's book. It is the one I learned when young and remember with fondness. The results are the same—Eva becomes Ave, Mary becomes the new Eve, bringing us to the place of redemption. The Virgin Mother is the instrument through which God will achieve his purpose. Virginity is the foundation stone of the Marian cult. As Warner comments, "Since Adam and Eve's sin, sex is tainted by concupiscence, and death disfigured by mortal decay. As a symptom of sin, putrefaction is concupiscence's twin; and a woman who conquered one penalty of the Fall could overcome the other."[29]

The popular cult that developed around this image of virgin mother and child was one that closely resembled the cult of Isis.[30] The people were dealing with something familiar to them. Mary gradually took on the titles and roles of other goddesses. She is worshipped as the Black Virgin[31], the protector of the crops;[32] pagan holidays honoring the goddess became Christian and Marian holydays.[33] While this worked to the church's advantage it also, created the synthesis that ensured that devotion to the mother would continue in a subversive manner until our present day. For all the protestation that Mary is only the Theotokos (Council of Ephesus, 431 C.E.), the bearer of God and not equal to him, the desire for a feminine presence in worship has defeated them. Gadon asks, "Is the Virgin a goddess?"[34] Her answer is I believe a "yes" and certainly in agreement with the work of Charlene Spretnak in *Missing Mary*. But for Christianity, the woman and mother, Mary, is a goddess symbol "reversed, the mother becoming asexual, the son destined to be celibate. From icons of earthly fertility, these figures became icons of spiritual transcendence."[35]

Sally Cunneen cites a comment by J. H. Newman, "Marian thinking must be repeatedly translated into contemporary forms if it is to continue to be meaningful.[36] There is the need always to hear with new ears and see with new eyes. What if we had grown-up with a different Eve and a different Mary? It is time to rethink what has been inherited from our two mothers.

How the Serpent Binds Eve and Mary into a Woman, Not a Goddess

It was the somber men in their long black cassocks at Vatican II that set Mary free to join Eve. The serpent patiently shedding skin after skin, waiting through the centuries, crawled about in the walls and basements of that vast hall. The serpent whispered into ears and hearts, "Join what has been put asunder. Let Mary join her sisters. Do not leave her always to sit in the clouds. She is lonely. Eve is lonely. She has wandered the earth looking for her daughter. It is not right that a daughter should not know her mother." They heard. Mary, the Theotokos was a woman, they proclaimed, the first among the saints, the first apostle. At last Eve and Mary could embrace. The daughters of Eve joined the daughters of Mary. Woven in a circle they danced. Serpent coiled in and out between them, connecting their energies. Now that which is woman is born.

Eve is the tomb of an old way. She entered into a death that would bring about an evolution of consciousness. One bite of the apple brought about her death and the beginnings of a new life. She is not honored for this. Mary is often referred to as the womb, the one that holds new life. She delivered the awaited savior into the world. She brought life into the world. "Full circle, from the tomb of the womb to the womb of the tomb, we come," says Joseph Campbell.[37] Death, life, regeneration, new life brought by two women and a serpent. The myths of Mary and Eve come to us, as all enduring myths do, with possibilities of endless reinterpretation, to suit the time and the place. Can the figures of Eve, Mary and the serpent be seen as a unified whole? My own experience of serpent wisdom/power in dreams over the recent months has led me to want such a synthesis of the three symbols, so influential in the way that women view themselves.

Cunneen says: "that deep divisions about Mary's role still exist today.... She is both pious and adventurous, decorous and slightly scandalous. In Scripture and in history she has always been capable of bridging and transcending differences without denying them."[38] For some she is a goddess, for some an historical woman. Her appeal is broad, touching all the spectra of believers in church and out. More importantly for the purposes of this paper, Cunneen suggests that perhaps it is time to reconcile the divided images of Eve and Mary. Such an unified image would "remind us that we are all linked together in the chain of life in which spirit may erupt anywhere."[39] "Yes," is all I can say to that image. It would mean so much to women and men to see our mothers united, whole, not divided so starkly into whore and saint. Such a woman "would join Eve in asking us not only to repent and pray but to get on with our unfinished business."[40]

In the "Special Epilogue for the Twenty-Fifth Printing" of *The Chalice and the Blade*, Eisler states her belief that a partnership can come into being using the resources we have in the world today to seek cooperation, a way of working for the good of all peoples.[41] I hope that attempting to rejoin the torn halves of women in the figures of Eve and Mary would play a role in that process. In her description of early Goddess worship as both monotheistic (in that there is essentially one entity) and polytheistic in her many aspects, one can see the reflection of the transcendent God of Judaic and Christian beliefs.[42] This is the divine being, entity that I believe in, an all encompassing divinity. The only box this divinity has is one of the human making.

Even more, I resonate with Cunneen in her belief that Mary is not a goddess. She was/is a human woman. More importantly, she explains that while she understands why women might want a goddess, there are for her shortcomings to this, namely that "when either sex takes over the mystery as total image, it is bound to be a distortion. Neither sex can adequately represent the God of reality; what is needed is a developing communal tradition that sees both sexes as images of the divine."[43] This follows the thinking of Gadon and is likewise a big piece of the mystery that Cunneen refers to: the Sacred, the Divine as an entity, must be larger, more inclusive, than the sum of its parts. If we are ever to achieve a society based on partnership, our grounding has to be so basic and so grand as to be unimaginable and to therefore keep us searching. It must be that horizon that seems so close at times and at the same time ever-receding. Mary and Eve can show us a path. It is up to us to follow.

As the virgin Mary often is shown standing on the serpent, a symbol of evil defeated, the serpent is a symbol of mixed messages in the Christian world, says Warner. It is a sign of healing on the shield of the medical profession, a sign of wisdom when in Matthew:10:16 Jesus is purported to have said: "Be ye therefore wise as serpents, and harmless as doves."[44] The serpent symbol cannot be contained. She is present, has never left, crawling underground as needed, with Eve and with Mary and with us. Feared and revered from the beginning of time, she is central to one of my most powerful and enduring dreams.

In my dream, I enter a chamber under the roots of a large redwood tree. Filling the clearing is a large and benignly coiled serpent. She directs me wordlessly to walk round her coils as I would a labyrinth, and take my seat in the center. She looks directly at me and then turns her head away. I sit there, in silence, learning my path. She gives no answers, only her presence, unspoken wisdom, her detached love. The energy in that underworld place is enormous as is she. I will leave, walking from her center, around her coils when I have learned what is necessary. She will be there when I need to return. Warner says of the serpent, "although its presence in images of the Immaculate is negative, it continue to form with the moon and the stars and the waters an elaborate code of the mysteries of life, growth, and birth over which the woman–the Virgin Mary–is believed to hold sway."[45]

The serpent holds the key to fullness of life, to the Eve-Mary experience. Her presence is not confined to one part of the world or to one mythology. On the internet, I found a definition of the serpent symbol taken from Barbara Walker's *Woman's Dictionary of Symbols and Sacred Objects*. In that explanation, I learned that the serpent never dies but regenerates each time it sheds its skin. In some sense then, the serpent in the garden and the serpent at Mary's feet are the same serpent. As Eve is called "Mother of all Living," as Mary is "the Mother of God" and our Mother in God in India (the Goddess of the Earth, "the Mother of All that Moves") bears, the title "Serpent Queen." Even more, she says that in the Middle East, the female serpent is the embodiment of enlightenment or wisdom, because she understood the mysteries of life." Who in our history understands these mysteries better than Eve and Mary, and who is present in both their stories. This female serpent is Kundalini, "the inner power of the human body, coiled in the pelvis like a woman's organs of life-giving."[46] Can we afford to ignore in our time the teaching, the traditions of other parts of the world as we seek for answers in our quest for peace, harmony, and parity of the sexes? It seems that with so much at stake we do so at our own peril. We need everything that an Eve-Mary-Serpent can teach.

The women of Italy have recognized the power of Eve as they pursue political justice. Lucia Chiavola Birnbaum in *liberazione della donna* says that the, apple, traditionally perceived as offensive, actually is liberating. A 1982 calendar published by a women's daily newspaper is graced with illustrations showing:

> that feminists hoped to share the apple with all women–all of the fruit of the tree of knowledge that enables a person to distinguish between good and evil and to be in full possession of physical and mental powers from sexual awareness to wisdom.[47]

Is it such a stretch to say that Mary, no matter what we are told of her conception, as a daughter of Eve knew fully the gifts of the fruit of the tree? How she chose to say her "Yes" to life might have been different from the "Yes" of Eve, but they both chose life and as a result we have a life and can choose our "Yes" in the ways that we perceive will continue life. The serpent wisdom is forever, never dying, and it lived in them as it lives in us. It lives in men as well and, as practitioners of Kundalini yoga practices teach, can be awakened.

A woman to emulate, to walk with on my journey: for me she is there in Mary and Eve, hand in hand, the serpent binding them into one woman, a woman of earth and sky and sea, a woman of the day and of the night—a VIRGIN—a WOMAN—EVA and AVE. Borrowing the title of Alice Walker's poem, I can say we have now a beautiful mother, a sister to walk with us.

Notes

1 Mary Ann Robinson, "Mary," paper written for PARP/PARW 6571, California Institute of Integral Studies, April 27, 2004, pg. 1.

2 Monica Sjöö and Barbara Mor, The Great Cosmic Mother: Rediscovering the Religion of the Earth. New York: Harper, 1987, 1991, pg. 101.

3 J.C. Cooper, An Illustrated Encyclopaedia of Traditional Symbols. London: Thames and Hudson, 1978, pg. 176.

4 Ibid. pg. 147.

5 Sjöö and Mor, pg. 276.

6 Mary Condren, The Serpent and the Goddess: Women, Religion, and Power in Celtic Ireland. New York: Harper & Row, 1989, pg. 9.

7 Ibid. pg. 9.

8 Leonard Shlain, The Alphabet Versus the Goddess: The Conflict between Word and Image. New York: Penquin/Compass. 1998, pg. 113.

9 James Hollis, Swamplands of the Soul: New Life in Dismal Places. Toronto: Inner City Books, 1996, pg. 31.

10 Riane Eisler, The Chalice and the Blade: Our History, Our future. San Francisco: Harper, 1987, 1995, pg. xv.

11 Ibid. pg. xv.

12 Ibid. pg. xvii.

13 Ibid. pg. xvii.

14 Ibid. pg. 64.

15 Elinor A. Gadon, The Once and Future Goddess; A Symbol for our Times. San Francisco: Harper & Rowe, 1989, pg. 188.

16 Ibid. pp. 167-168.

17 Ibid. p. 169.

18 Ibid. p. 169.

19 Ibid. p. 170.

20 Ibid. pg. 192.

21 Ibid. pg. 103.

22 Marina Warner, Alone of All Her Sex: The Myth and Cult of the Virgin Mary. New York: Vintage, 1976, pg. xx.

23 Ibid. pg. xxi.

24 Ibid. pg. xxv.

25 Ibid. pg. 48.

26 Ibid. pg. 48.

27 Ibid. pg. 59.

28 Ibid. pg. 60.

29 Ibid. pg. 78.

30 Gadon, pg. 195.

31 Ibid. pg. 196.

32 Ibid. pg. 198.

33 Ibid. pg. 199.

34 Ibid. pg. 199.

35 Ibid. pg. 223.

36 Sally Cunneen, In Search of Mary: The Woman and the Symbol. New York: Ballantine, 1996, pg. 272.

37 Joseph Campbell, The Hero with a Thousand Faces. Cleveland: Meridian Books, sixth printing, 1949, 1956, 1964, pg. 12.

38 Cunneen, pg. 338.

39 Ibid. pg. 338.

40 Ibid. pg. 339.

41 Eisler, pg. 214.

42 Ibid. pg. 21.

43 Cunneen, pg. 305.

44 Warner, pg. 269.

45 Ibid. pg. 269.

46 Barbara G. Walker, "Serpent Symbols," in Woman's Dictionary of Symbols and Sacred Objects. 13 November 2004 <http:// www.reptilianagenda.com/ research/r073101b.html>.

47 Lucia Chiavola Birnbaum, liberazione della donna: feminism in Italy: Connecticut: Wesleyan University Press, 1986, pg. 165.

Bibliography

Birnbaum, Lucia Chiavola. liberazione della donna: feminism in Italy. Connecticut: Wesleyan University Press, 1986.

Campbell, Joseph. The Hero with a Thousand Faces. Cleveland: Meridian Books, sixth printing, 1949, 1956, 1964.

Condren, Mary. The Serpent and the Goddess: Women, Religion, and Power in Celtic Ireland. New York: Harper & Row, 1989.

Cooper, J.C. An Illustrated Encyclopaedia of Traditional Symbols. London: Thames and Hudson, 1978.

Cunneen, Sally. In Search of Mary: The Woman and the Symbol. New York: Ballantine, 1996.

Eisler, Riane. The Chalice and the Blade: Our History, Our future. San Francisco: Harper, 1987, 1995.

Gadon, Elinor A. The Once and Future Goddess; A Symbol for our Times. San Francisco: Harper & Rowe, 1989.

Hollis, James. Swamplands of the Soul: New Life in Dismal Places. Toronto: Inner City Books, 1996.

The New American Bible. Nashville: Thomas Nelson Publishers, 1971.

Shlain, Leonard. The Alphabet Versus the Goddess: The Conflict between Word and Image. New York: Penquin/Compass. 1998.

Sjöö, Monica and Barbara Mor. The Great Cosmic Mother: Rediscovering the Religion of the Earth. New York: Harper, 1987, 1991.

Spretnak, Charlene. Missing Mary: The Queen of Heaven and Her Re-Emergence in the Modern Church, New York: Palgrave Macmillan, 2004.

Walker, Alice. "We Have a Beautiful Mother", found in Jennifer Berezan and Friends, Praises for the World, Albany, CA: Edge of Wonder Records, 2002.

Walker, Barbara G. Woman's Dictionary of Symbols and Sacred Objects. "Serpent Symbols." The Reptilian Agenda. 13 November 2004 <http.// www.reptilianagenda.com/ research/r073101b.html>

Warner, Marina. Alone of All Her Sex: The Myth and Cult of the Virgin Mary. New York: Vintage, 1976.

Mary in Islam

May Elawar

Introduction: Mary in Her Muslim Context

Visiting the main Marian shrine in Lebanon in the summer of 2003, it was interesting to note that nearly half of the people trekking up the steep spiral stairs to touch the statue of the Virgin were women covered by the traditional Muslim headscarf, the *hijab*. Islam holds Mary in honorable esteem both in sacred text and popular religious practice. In a religion devoid of imagery, Islam's distinctive Mariology, its stories and practice, is grounded in Islamic scripture.

Whenever the topic of Mary is approached, whether in the Christian tradition, or as in this case, in Islam, a quandary arises as scholars, theologians, historians, sociologists, feminists, and others attempt to define Mary's attributes and roles. In this paper, I present a narrative on the life of Mary from the Islamic sacred text (the *Qur'an* and the *Hadith*), highlighting two of the most hotly debated aspects of Mary within Muslim tradition: Mary as the "pure," and Mary as the "prophet." Towards this endeavor, I consult mainly the work of female scholars whose presentations include a broad spectrum of opinions regarding Mary. These women go beyond the customary androcentric traditional exegesis, to those opinions that portray the Virgin in her most exalted state in Islam. In particular, my paper is grounded in the work of Aliah Schleifer. *Mary the Blessed Virgin of Islam*; Yvonne Haddad and Jane Smith's "The Virgin Mary in Islamic Tradition" published in the *Muslim World Journal*; and, *Qur'an and Women: Rereading the Sacred Text from a Woman's Perspective* by Amina Wadud.

Any discussion of Mary in Islam directed towards a non-Muslim audience needs to address key theological aspects that affect the role and place of Mary within that tradition. It is essential to recognize that Islam accepts the two previous Abrahamic religions, placing Mary and her son Jesus in the lineage of ancient prophets that appear throughout the *Qur'an*. However, nothing distinguishes Christianity from Islam more than the different understanding of the person of Jesus. Belief in one God stands at the core of the teachings of the *Qur'an*, and those who view any creation as God's son, thereby honoring as divine something besides God, commit an act of treason against the faith.[1] Thus while the *Qur'an* gives Mary and Jesus a venerable place in the book, they are merely humans. The role of Mary as *Theotokos*, Mother of God, has no place in the Mariology of Islam. However, vehement denial of Jesus as the son of God makes him exclusively the son of Mary, who is held with the same if not more esteem as her son.[2]

Furthermore, any role for Mary in human redemption and atonement through the death of Jesus can never be resonant for Mary in her Muslim context. While in Christianity God descends into history out of infinite love, and sacrifices himself to save humankind from sin, in Islam, "the divine love conjoined with justice ensures that forgiveness is available to all who freely turn to God in penitence. The *Qur'an* represents a universal theophany which is not fallen, but merely forgotten and unread."[3] Thus Mary's role in Islam is more of one who bears witness to the presence of God who need not come into the world because he has never been absent from it.[4]

The concept of original sin also differs in the *Qur'an* from its Judeo-Christian predecessors in *Genesis*. While Mary in Christian tradition came to be viewed as the redeemer of the sins of Eve, this role is absent in the Muslim tradition as the story of creation implicates both male and female in the act of disobeying God. Thus insofar as the *Qur'an* in concerned, the negative implication that woman was the cause of evil and damnation does not exist. However, the ensuing traditions and narratives pick up the thread of the biblical Eve attributing the "defiling" character of menstruation squarely upon her shoulders,[5] and an aspect to be considered when contemplating Mary's state of purity and virginity.

Mary's Story in the Sacred Text of Islam

The *Qur'an*, the sacred text of Islam, is believed to be the word of God as revealed to the Prophet Mohammed. It is the basis of faith in the Muslim religion, and is considered as an extra-historical text, moral and transcendental in nature.[6] The *Qur'an* gives no indication of time and place regarding the life of Mary.

The other main texts that complete the narrative of Mary's story in Islam are the *Hadith* stories that together with the *Qur'an* constitute the Islamic *sunna* (the laws that shape Muslim values and ethics). Written over a period of 200 years following the death of the Prophet, by companions, wives, and acquaintances, this collection of narratives records in minute detail what the Prophet said and did.[7] Basically, the *Hadith* serve the role of filling in the historical and contextual gaps that the *Qur'an* left out.

There is no question that Mary is the female figure to whom the greatest attention is given in the *Qur'an*. Haddad and Smith provide a detailed statistical account of Mary in this text: "There are 70 verses that refer to her, and she is named specifically in 34 of these (24 in relation to Jesus son of Mary). Only three other persons, Moses, Abraham, and Noah are mentioned by name more frequently than Mary. She enjoys the special honor of having one of the *Qur'an's* 114 chapters titled after her (Maryam, sura 19)."[8]

A series of events in the third and nineteenth chapters of the *Qur'an* prepare Mary spiritually for her ultimate role in the annunciation. These events unfold with Mary's prenatal dedication to worship by her mother, and her establishment as part of the genealogy of ancient Israelite prophets through her father Imran.

Upon delivering Mary, her mother exclaims "My Lord I am delivered of a female" (3:36). Some translations differ slightly: "O Lord I have delivered **but** a girl,"[9] thus a whole different meaning grounded in pre-Islamic patriarchal Arabia conveys a sense of disappointment on the part of Mary's mother at having begotten a girl instead of a boy.[310] At that time, only boys were consecrated to the service of God at the temple, and other *Qur'anic* scholars regard this statement by Mary's mother as a request to God to excuse her from the vow she made.[11] Reading the Arabic myself, there is no sense of disappointment, it is just an informative statement that is followed by God stating "A boy could not be as that girls as," again emphasizing the special role awaiting Mary.

The next step in Mary's spiritual journey is a request made by her mother asking God "to preserve Mary and her children from Satan the ostracized." (3:36) God's fulfillment of this request is confirmed in an often cited *Hadith* that describes how every human is born with the touch of satan except for Mary and her son. Here, Mary is bestowed with one of her key attributes in Islam, that if inherent purity.

Following the casting of lots with quills to determine who would take care of Mary (3:44), we find her confined to a *mihrab* with Zachariah (John the Baptist's father) as her guardian. The *mihrab* which is translated as a chamber or sanctuary, in Arabic signifies a place accessible only through stairs, a place that is physically separated for the purpose of worship.[12] Thus rather than confinement, the word emphasizes a life of devotion. In later exegesis it is said that her location in this room also verifies that she had no access to men.[13]

In the *mihrab* Mary's unique relationship to the divine unfolds as she receives food miraculously from God (3:37). This act has been interpreted as a sign of her exceptional status, as proof of god's bounty, and his special approval of Mary.[14] In the *mihrab*, Mary is also visited by angels and it is here that she is told she is chosen and purified by god and enjoined to obedience and prayer (3:42). Traditions have arisen about the intensity of Mary's devotional practices as she is described standing in prayer until her ankles became swollen, prostrating until perspiration pours from her feet, emphasizing the fact that during this period of her life Mary existed solely for this purpose.[15]

The first mention of the annunciation (3:45) take place in the *mihrab* following the angel's entreatment of Mary into a life of prayer and obedience. The story of the annunciation is picked up in Mary's own chapter 19, with Mary's withdrawal into an "eastern place" that is secluded. She is then told by an angel that she would have a son who would speak to humankind while still in the cradle, and in manhood would be righteous with no faults. Mary demurred that she had never been unchaste, and was told that such a feat was easy for god who only has to decree what he wills. God then sent his spirit in the likeness of man, and at the sight of him, Mary sought refuge from god and questioned again how she a virgin could conceive. She was assured by the angel that all was possible with god. Mary's willingness to submit to god's will is seen as an equivalent act to Abraham's willingness to sacrifice his son in compliance to god.[16]

It is important to note here that Mary is not engaged or married in the *Qur'anic* version of the miraculous conception. Joseph does not surface until later exegetical traditions that are based in Christian sources.[17] The *Qur'an* repeatedly affirms that Jesus was born only to Mary by the pure will of god with no human father. Mary's chastity is unquestioned, and various explanations on the details of her conception all agree, to some extent, that the angel came in the form of a handsome man so Mary would not be repulsed by him, and he blew either into her pocket, her sleeve, or her mouth.[18]

Early commentators of the *Qur'an* (the first 300 years following the prophet's death) bestowed Mary with the title of *al-batul* to describe her chastity. This word implies more than her physical virginity. The root of the Arabic word *batul* is severance, the original meaning being a palm shoot which has separated itself from its mother tree.[19] Thus the phrase used to describe Mary as "*batul* among women" suggests a woman who has separated herself from men, having no desire or need for them.[20] While Muslim Arabs call Mary "Maryan *al-Batul*," Christian Arabs refer to her as the *al-adhra* which is the Arabic word for the physical state if virginity.

(Both Maryam and Batul are popular Moslem female names.)

Mary conceives and goes to a distant place. The *Qur'an* tells of labor pains driving Mary to the trunk of a date-palm tree and crying, "Would that I have died before this." A voice form beneath her reassured her and told her to shake the tree and eat and drink and "cool thine eyes." Next she was told to make a vow of fasting and silence (19:26). Following this, the narrative shifts into a testimonial about the special nature of Jesus. Mary returns to her people carrying her baby and when they accuse her of terrible wrongdoing, having taken a vow of silence, she points to Jesus. Despite the exclamations of the onlookers that a baby cannot talk, Jesus proceeds to affirm his own status as a prophet reaffirming his dutiful respect towards his mother (19:32)

Wishing for death when she was suffering from the pain of childbirth seems to be contrary to the submissive and devoted Mary. Her death wish has been given an altruistic interpretation as stemming from Mary's fear for her people who stand to suffer from slander associated to her alleged adultery.[21]

In the *Qur'an* Mary is mentioned alongside other prophets such as Noah, Moses and Aaron in Chapter 23, entitled True Believers. She is also mentioned with Zachariah, John, Ishmael, Enoch, Jonah, Job, Solomon, David, Noah, Isaac, Jacob, Lot, Abraham, Moses and Aaron in Chapter 21, entitled the Prophets.

Mary is also mentioned alongside other prophets in *Hadith* narratives. The "Prophet said: If I were to swear an oath that no one shall enter paradise before the early members of my *Umma* (community of Muslims), except a few, among whom are Abraham, Ishmael, Isaac, and Jacob, Moses and Jesus and Mary the daughter of Imran.[22] Another *Hadith* recounts Mohammad inquiring about radiant light she saw in his spiritual night journey to the Haram Mosque in Jerusalem. Gabriel told the Prophet: the one on the right is the *mihrab* of your brother David, and the one on your left is the grave of your sister Mary.[23]

Standing alone, without interpretation, without historical or geographical context, one can discern from the discussion above that the *Qur'an* presents Mary as one among the chosen, the pure, and the prophets. However, debates on the nature and role of the Virgin Mary in Islam were carried on in regions stretching from central Asia to Spain from the eighth century to the present.[24] In the following section, I will address some of the major controversy regarding Mary's stature in Islam: Is Mary to be considered merely an example, a role-model of devotion and submission to god, or so she to be considered as one among the prophets?

Commentary on Interpretations of Mary in *Qur'an*

Schleifer, Haddad, Smith, and Wadud present a broadly inclusive scope of scholars in their commentaries on the role of Mary in Islam. They combine traditional Islamic scholarship that emerged in the few centuries following the death of the Prophet with mystical Sufi writing that presents Mary as an exalted luminous light. They also include more contemporary *Qur'anic* scholarship that interprets Mary in the androcentric manner that has come to typify Islamic exegesis. Somewhere, in between these conflicting opinions, these female authors make the case for Mary as a spiritually pure prophet and luminary in Islam. In the following section I will discuss the debate surrounding Mary's highly debatable implications of purity, and prophethood.

Purity: Did Mary Menstruate?

In the third chapter of the *Qur'an*, the angels tell Mary "Indeed God has favored you and purified you and chosen you from all the women of the world" (3:42). A debate has arisen as to whether this signifies spiritual purity which connotes being purified from rebellious disbelief, or, physical purity which has been explained as purification from menstruation and the blood of childbirth.

Purity is a concept basic to Islam as a prerequisite for acts for worship. Blood, especially menstrual blood, has come to be understood as defiling of a state of purity.[25] According to feminist sociologist and *Qur'anic* scholar Fatima Mernissi, this might not always have been true. She describes stories of Aisha, the Prophet's wife, that were circulated by early Islamic scholars such as ibn Saad (840 CE). Aisha washed Mohammad's hair for his purification before prayer whiles she was menstruating.[26] Based on information from early Islamic sources, Mernissi explains that Aisha was concerned following the Prophet's death by the emerging beliefs on female purification that were rooted in pre-Islamic Arabia's superstitions about menstruating women as a source of pollution. Mohammad vehemently condemned superstitious beliefs and for this reason, early scholars that took part in the debate on the subject of menstruation, which is recorded at length in the religious literature, agreed with Aisha. A Prophet who tried by all means to struggle against superstition in all its forms, could not condone the superstitious belief that linked menstruation to pollution.[27]

The question of Mary's menstruation has become a key issue in the discussion about her purity. Early *Qur'anic* commentators seem to agree that Mary had menstruated twice before the annunciation.[28] It is not until after the nineteenth century that the trend seems to espouse the belief that Mary's purity must necessarily imply that she was free from menstruation throughout her life. Haddad and Smith write that contemporary scholars think it best to take purity in its broadest sense to include both purity of heart and body and to assume that god gave Mary the privilege of being pure from all bodily uncleanliness.[29]

Shifting the debate towards Mary's physical purity de-emphasizes the importance and significance of her spiritual purity. Schleifer writes, "Mary's purity is one of her key characteristics. It is the dimension of her being that made her a possible receptacle for the miraculous conception. And the purity of her spiritual striving is found as a symbolic goal for others, awakening them to a pristine vision of the meaning of devoutness, obedience, and worship."[30]

Was Mary a Prophet in Islam?

Perhaps the most contested role for Mary in Islam has been that of Prophet. This controversy over her precise spiritual status has been debated at large in the Muslim world through the medieval period and into contemporary times.

There is no human distinction above prophet in Islam.[31] The basic theme for contention over Mary as a Prophet, is whether any woman can be named a prophet in Islam. Various readings and interpretations of the **Qur'an** can make the case for or against ranking Mary among the prophets.

Presenting the case in favor of the title of Prophet for Mary, Schleifer, Haddad, and Smith all mention the work of Cordoban medieval *Qur'anic* scholars and writers, Qurtubu and ibn Hasm, who define the term prophethood/prophecy in Arabic as originating from the root which means "granting perception." Therefore, prophet consists of a message which comes from god in order to inform the recipient of something. Mary is a prophet as she receives revelation from god by means of an angel.[32]

The case can also be made for Mary's prophet-hood through her repeated appearance in the *Qur'an* and *Hadith* alongside male prophets. Writing on the social origins of Islam, social theorist Mohammed Bamyeh explains the pattern in the *Qur'an* of resurrecting the prophets of ancient history to link them through traditional tribal relations to Mohammed, in order to testify in one voice to their coming from the same divine source.[33] The divine revelation goes through Adam, Noah, Abraham, and Imran, and thus as the daughter of Imran, the *Qur'an* places Mary in the line of the great prophets. This perspective holds Mary as a symbol that brings together all revelation: as a descendent of the great Israelite prophets, the bearer of the word, the mother of Jesus, and as the *Qur'an's* chosen woman of all the worlds (3:42). She is the embodied symbolism of the *Qur'anic* message that revelation has not been confined to one particular people.[34]

Those contesting the status of Mary as prophet discount the discussion above by quoting a line form the *Qur'an* in which god tells Mohammed: "We sent not before thee save men" (12:109, 16:43, and 21:17) thus disqualifying Mary as female from having been considered a prophet. Yet, when it is extracted from its androcentric interpretations, this line does not preclude Mary from being a prophet. In this case, god is believed to be commenting on the role of Mohammed as messenger, not prophet.[35]The prophet is one who receives revelation, while the messenger is one who has been singled out to warn, guide or convey a divine message to a community. By making a distinction between these two roles, a distinction that is often ignored by those that would diminish Mary based solely on her gender, the aforementioned line from the *Qur'an* does not deny Mary the title of prophet.

I would like to end this section with what I believe to be one of the most accurate readings of Mary in the *Qur'an*. Sufi scholar Ruzbihan (1209) who acknowledges that Mary's great spiritual achievement preceded the miraculous conception of Jesus describes Mary not only as a mother of a prophet, "but as one who is chosen to be a spiritual luminary in her own right, through divine guidance, spiritual exercise, the awareness of blessings which drew her closer and closer into the reflection of the light of her lord, and the ability to act on such perception.[36]

Concluding Remarks

In this paper, I have approached the subject of Mary in Islam exclusively through a text based method. However, it is necessary to acknowledge that popular Islamic religious practice extends greatly beyond my presentation of Mary. Media reports describe Muslims flocking to Marian apparition sites and shrines. A tradition of identifying Fatima, the prophet's daughter, with Mary has emerged, in particular among Shiite Islam. I believe that the important question to ask at this point is whether Marian devotion can create a common ground between Islam and Christianity, given Islam's distinctly different approach towards Mary and Jesus as human luminaries and not the mother and son of god. One woman's journey to heal her mother opens a magical door into the underworld where she transforms through the teachings of the Black Madonna, the modern day embodiment of the Great Mother.

Notes

1 Martinson, Paul Varo, ed. Islam: An Introduction for Christians (Augsburg: Minneapolis, 1994) p. 188.
2 Schleifer, Aliah Mary the Blessed Virgin of Islam (Fons Vitae: Louisville, KY, 1997) p. 11
3 Ibid., p.11.
4 Ibid., p.11.
5 Haddad, Yvonne & Smith, Jane "The Virgin Mary in the Islamic Tradition and Commentary" in The Muslim World (Vol. LXXIX, nos. 3-4, July/October, 1989) p. 182.
6 Wadud, Amina Qur'an and Women: Reading the Sacred Text from a Woman's Perspective (Oxford University Press: NY, 1999) p. xxi.
7 Merniss, Fatima The Veil and the Male Elite: A Feminist Interpretation of Women's Rights in Islam (Perseus Books: Cambridge, MA, 1987) pp.42-48.
8 Haddad& Smith, op cit, p. 162.
9 Schleifer, op cit, p.24.
10 Ibid., p. 24.
11 Haddad & Smith, op cit, p. 164.
12 Schleifer, op cit, p. 26.
13 Ibid., p. 28.
14 Haddad & Smith, op cit, p. 165.
15 Schleifer, op cit, p.56.
16 Haddad & Smith, op cit, p. 168.
17 Schleifer, op cit, p. 21.
18 Haddad & Smith, op cit, p. 167.
19 Schleifer, op cit, p.66.
20 Ibid., p. 66.
21 Haddad & Smith, op cit, p. 170.
22 Schleifer, op cit, p. 43.
23 Ibid., p. 63.
24 Ibid., p. 18.

25 Haddad & Smith, op cit, p. 172.
26 Mernissi, op cit, p. 107.
27 Ibid., p. 173.
28 Schleifer, op cit, p. 29.
29 Haddad & Smith, op cit p. 174.
30 Schleifer, op cit, p. 72.
31 Ibid., p. 82.
32 Ibid., p. 82.
33 Bamyeh, Mohammed The Social Origins of Islam: Mind, Economy, Discourse (University of Minnesota Press: Minneapolis, 1999) p. 160.
34 Schleifer, op cit, p. 100.
35 Ibid., p. 74.
36 Ibid., p. 92.

When quoting from the Qur'an, the references are placed following the quote. The first figure denotes the number of the chapter in the Qur'an and the second figure denotes the line number in the chapter.

Bibliography

Bamyeh, Mohammed. The Social Origins of Islam: Mind, Economy, Discourse. Minneapolis: University of Minnesota Press, 1999.

Haddad, Yvonne & Smith, Jane, "The Virgin in Islamic Tradition and Commentary," in The Muslim World (vol. LXXIX, nos. 3-4, July–October 1989) pp. 161-187.

Martinson, Paul Varo. Islam: An Introduction for Christians. Minneapolis: Augsburg, 1989.

Mernissi, Fatima. The Veil and the Male Elite: A Feminist Interpretation of Women's Right's in Islam. Cambridge, MA: Perseus Books, 1987.

Schleifer, Aliah. Mary the Blessed Virgin of Islam. Louisville, KY: Fons Vitae, 1997.

Waddud, Amina. Qur'an and Women: Rereading the Sacred Text from a Woman's Perspective. NY: Oxford University Press, 1999.

Al Qur'an: A Contemporary translation by Ahmed Ali. Princeton: Princeton University Press, 1993.

Dancing in the Underworld:
the quest for wholeness

Naomi Lombardi, M.A.
Clinical Psychology

This is the story of my personal journey to the Black Madonna, a search towards wholeness, of how my ancestral grandmothers came to me in dreams, pulling me onto a path of no return that I later understood to be a crossing into the Underworld, a place where I would confront my deepest fears.

Over a twelve year period the golden thread of the ancient Mother Goddess wove me through an initiatory process opening my vision to an unseen realm. I discovered that my mother, grandmother and I are descendents of the Tarantata, the mad women that break free of the web of suffering through an ancient dance of purification. In my lineage when you are called you will be taken, as was my mother.

One of my greatest fears was wondering if I would ever regain the mother I had lost. Every year my mother was bitten by the mythical spider caught in a web of sorrow. Each year before Easter I witnessed her struggle with devastating depression. As a young child I watched in horror as she was taken away in the middle of the night by my father and uncle. Mythically, my mother was stolen away to the underworld like Persephone, Queen of the Underworld, who was kidnapped by Pluto and taken to Hades where she would relinquish all her attachments and become dismembered, stripped of all worldly possessions. The mythical journey of the Dark Goddess, Persephone, descended into unknown territory so she could know herself, become whole and complete. The journey was not without danger, the initiate must confront her death and dismemberment. When my mother returned two months later she did not recognize who we were, something was missing in her. I had lost my mother to her underworld journey and for this I was terribly sad.

She Is Everywhere Vol. 2

As a nine-year old child I did not understand the depression that would put my mother through so much suffering. Her journey to know herself had been interrupted with shock treatments and medication. From my vantage it appeared the journey was full of danger and perilous at every turn. I learned that one could get lost in those treacherous places.

Over the next five years I watched in bewilderment as my mother's and my spirit went into exile, hiding in underground caverns till it was safe to return. Just like the goddess whose spiritual consciousness floated in silent underground rivers, her melodious sweet song calling from the collective unconscious to free us from this web of sorrow.

Pilgrimage to the Black Madonna

Fearing my mother's spirit had been lost in the underworld I traced my lineage back to Southern Italy in search of clues that might be buried in the ruins and in the region where my Nona was born and raised. In the year of 2000, the Jubilee, I undertook my first pilgrimage to the Black Madonna in Southern Italy. Carrying prayers in my heart I crossed the Atlantic Ocean in search of wholeness, in search of my mother's spirit, in search of myself.

Through dreams, visions and waking states the Grandmothers led me on a mythical journey connecting with the Great Mother. Spanning back through time and history I went in search of the answer to the one question that had driven me my entire life. What would have helped my mother each year as she suffered with bouts of debilitating depression?

Watching with silent eyes as my mother struggled with grief, it would take years to understand the significance of her seasonal descent into these dark passages. No one told us of the ancient rites that existed in the lineage of women my mother was heir to and that would have helped her. My fervent prayer over the next thirty years would be to discover what would help my mother. She and I had been caught in a web of afflicted emotions, trapped in the labyrinth of the mind. I discovered I am Tarantata like my mother before me, and her mother before her and so on back through time. It was sacred psychology, a psycho-spiritual initiation of becoming whole and complete, a quest for wholeness. I began to see how my mother's descent to the underworld was a parallel growth process to that of the ancient goddess whose descent was ritualized and honored.

Descent as initiation within oneself to deepen, to acquire wisdom, to become fearless was a rite of passage for the women of ancient Southern Italy. Following the golden thread of the Great Mother the initiate journeyed to the underworld to break free of the labyrinth of the mind.

The initiate unraveled lifetimes of habituated patterns keeping her trapped in the web of suffering, legacies handed down from generation to generation. Through devotion to the Great Mother, Transcendent Wisdom, the initiate can break free of the cycle of suffering. One must be aware of the dangers that exist on the path. Getting caught in the web can bring illness, madness and death. Those that make it through the labyrinth are free of the fears that once consumed them and are empowered to lead others through the underworld. Tarantata dances in the veils of Her Grace having broken free of the cycle of afflicted emotions. Confronting their own madness they dance in the multidimensional realm of the goddess.

Beginning with the Black Madonna I traced history back to the 10th c.b.c. and uncovered a lost paradise weaving the golden thread of the ancient Mother through my heart. I discovered the magical dance performed in secret by Maenads, the ecstatic dancing priestesses. These wild women dancers worshipped Cybele, Rome's ancient Divine Mother. Over time and history these sacred dancers shape shifted into the Tarantati, women bit by the mythical spider caught in a web of madness, grief and loss. The only cure was an ecstatic dance of purification to break free of the cycle of suffering. This magical dance is still celebrated in small villages across southern Italy every August 15.

Walking in the footsteps of the ancestors I began to see how my beloved mother's journey was woven with a mythology of transformation and alchemy.

As I danced in my own underworld journey the grandmother's conjured up an alchemical cookbook with the secret recipe for sovereignty or wholeness. The Goddess was called Virgin, One unto Herself, whole and complete, in union with her true essence. I came to understand Virgin referred to purity of heart and mind. Through dreams and visions my mother and Nona revealed clues guiding me on the path to wholeness.

In July 1998 Nona and mom came in a dream bringing me to the holy feet of the "Underneath me is the ancient Mother of the Mediterranean, Cybele!" I went to the library and found volumes written on Rome's ancient divine couple, Cybele and Attis.

From 1998 to 2005 I went on a seven year quest to learn all I could about the Black Madonna and all the goddesses that preceded her. I was amazed to discover that for each goddess there was a mystical feast and festival and even a special recipe to propitiate the divine spiritual consciousness in each of us. In ancient Rome this was called venia or spiritual grace, the spiritual nectar of liberation from fear.

Search for the Transcendent Mother

Twelve years ago I began to write essays about my search for the transcendent Mother, it was a time when my own mother was dying. I knew I had a limited amount of time to be with her and wanted to heal my relationship with her. I began writing everything I understood my life to be as a result of my mother's life and her influence upon me. An infusion of the wisdom of the Grandmothers has taken place since my birth. All the lessons my mother learned in life, everything good, strong, courageous and loving has seeped into the fiber of my being, like healing waters, transforming me into the woman I am today. In all their splendor comes a legacy our Mothers carry and pass onto their daughters.

I am the embodiment of all the mothers that have gone before just as you are. Whether we are aware of it or not their dreams and legacies have been transmitted down through us. In my body I carry the sorrow and joy of all my Grandmothers. Their hopes, dreams and prayers are in my heart. By listening to the Grandmothers I learned how to reclaim my life by transmuting a painful legacy into an inexhaustible supply of blessings. The magical Land of La Cuccagna, a mythical paradise of abundance of the heart was revealed to me step by step.

Legacies hold the key to spiritual power, revealing what needs to be transformed, reclaimed and redeemed. Tapping into the collective unconscious legacies of the women in my lineage I discovered their struggles mirrored my own.

Siren's Enchanting Song

The year before my mother died I was coming to terms with my own unresolved issues. I was in a marriage that left me feeling empty and unfulfilled. Realizing my marriage was not going to make me happy I fell into a depression. I wanted so much to talk with my mother about my inner unrest but didn't want to burden her. I longed for the Transcendent Mother to comfort me, but didn't know how to find it within myself. A voice spoke to me, 'nothing outside yourself will make you happy.'

Archetypal images that once led the initiate to her sovereignty entered my life. Visions of the Mother Goddess, the Sorrowful Mother and the miraculous horse began emerging out of my consciousness. Visions of haunting images of the sorrowful mother were woven into the faces of my Nona, mother and aunts. The broken spirited mother filled me with unspeakable grief shape shifting into the Earth Mother and transforming into the warrioress that would eventually rise out of my consciousness. I was being seized by some collective unconscious grief that was funneled through my consciousness. I would have to stop whatever I was doing to sit down and let the feelings of sadness and giref pass through me. I was taken on a journey tapping into the collective unconscious legacies of the women in my ancestry. They were trying to tell me something. Their vast collective unconscious grief filled my vessel and I wept for all the women in my legacy whose dreams had vanished into darkness. Sad for them, sad for myself, I allowed their collective grief to seep into my being unafraid of the path they were leading me on. Allowing their untold sorrow to fill my body I invited in a transformative process.

Months passed and the visions kept coming. Ancestral voices called to me like the siren's song, irresistible and enchanting, taking me deeper into my unconscious back through history, back through time and space. I could hear my Grandmothers sing, "We are tired of Weeping and giving our lives away!" This song, an enchanting melody called me forward unraveling my heart with their mantra, "Dance in the joy and celebration of life!" They wanted me to hear their voices just as they wanted me to write their story. This was the beginning of giving it all up. The personal "I" began dissolving as I had one foot in my world and the other in my ancestor's. My life had been woven into the multi-dimensional realm of my ancestral grandmothers.

Wild Horses

My journey into the underworld would require access to a source of power I had not yet tapped. With no maps to chart my passage through these dimensions I listened intently to the whisperings of my ancestors weaving a tale of strength and power.

The spring before my mother died I began having visions of wild horses galloping toward me in the sky. As I was washing dishes in the middle of a sunny day I looked out the window and at the lead horse who communicated, "we must journey now." The horse captured my psyche galloping off into the distance and over the abyss until we disappeared into some other dimension. For months wild horses drug my psyche through a chasm of painful emotions, unfolding my inner mysteries leaving me breathless, my passion rising with the wind in search of the Great Mother. Whenever I heard their thundering hooves off in the distance I knew something painful was going to be revealed. Over time I learned to become fearless as I was taken to this unseen realm to confront my deepest fears. No longer afraid of what I would find I whistled for those wild horses exhilarated to be on the journey. My grandmother's filled me with the ecstasy of the union of grief and joy, the divine madness. What is madness if it isn't the search for the real self?

During this time childhood memories filled my mind pulling every ounce of the warrioress to the surface. Suddenly I was a child again galloping Dixie, a spirited mare, without a saddle or bridle holding on with wild abandon to her dark mane. I remembered falling off in full gallop laughing as I picked myself up, dusted myself off and tried again. I realized my ancestral mothers didn't want me to experience defeat any longer. From that point on I wove a radiant cloth with the golden thread of the goddess, draping my body in the healing power of the ancients, regenerating the mother inside of my heart.

That is when things began to change for me and my understanding of my spiritual grandmothers and the journey that I was on. I knew it wasn't just my journey. It was a collective journey of my mother, her mother and all the mothers that have gone before. That's when I realized my destiny was to serve. The personal 'I' was being dissolved so I could become an empty vessel to be poured out to the heart of humanity. I gave myself over to those wild horses gladly, willingly, fearlessly.

The miraculous and magical horse is legendary for traversing between worlds. Years later I became a student of a Tibetan Buddhist teacher, Tulku Thubten Rinpoche who said, "the miraculous horse will take you to your destination in an instant." What destination is this? I believe it is the liberation from all fear, in union with your true essence.

Horses have played a big part in taking Persephone (Greek) or the Roman Proserpina to the underworld. In museums across Southern Italy Pluto's winged horses carry her to the underworld in a chariot each spring so that she can dive deep into her mysteries in quest of her own wholeness. She must dive into the divine madness in order to know herself. The Queen of the Underworld transforms the darkness of faded dreams into love's pure light. This sacred drama was re-enacted in the sacred rites in ancient temples across outhern Italy.

In Locri, terra cotta plaques dating back to 650 b.c. have been found depicting Proserpina's descent to the underworld. In my travels to Italy I've spent days studying these artifacts. For each descent the goddess leaves something in the underworld and brings back a treasure.

Following in the Footsteps of my Ancestral Grandmothers

It's important to talk about the relationship that I had with my Nona. I never knew my Italian grandmother, Catarina, she died before I was born. There was only one photograph that I ever saw of her, a wedding picture.

Every time my mother spoke of Nona, she would break into tears. Her words trailed off into unfinished sentences and my arms quickly enfolded her. Her tears were like a prayer wheel invoking the most precious heart connection between she and I with grief, loss and sadness. My Nona's life was this great mystery waiting to be unraveled. A great longing was born inside my heart to know her.

She came to the United States at the turn of the century, married and had twelve children. She was gifted with being a healer, midwife, herbalist and was a very religious woman. People who knew her say she was a saint, a kind and compassionate wise woman.

Stories passed on by my aunts reveal a woman who had visions of the Holy Mother who would speak to her. When one of her children became ill a doctor told her there was no hope. She quickly ushered the doctor to the door and acted on a vision of the Virgin who told her to get a collection of money (alms) from the neighborhood and take it to the Catholic Church and make an offering of two statues of Santa Lucia. She did this and walked half the length of Spokane on her knees praying to Santa Lucia holding her beads reciting the rosary. Her small child miraculously recovered with full hearing and eyesight, something the doctors said he would never do.

Beginning about a month before my mother passed away in 1994, my grandmother came to me in a dream appearing as a young woman. She was climbing on a steep hill of vineyards or olive trees. It was dawn. She turned around to look at me. Her hair was wrapped up in those braids that only Italians can wear. She had on this interesting Italian frock and looked at me with enchanting eyes beckoning me to follow. She darted ahead of me then disappeared behind a tree. From that point on I had a relationship with my grandmother. It was as if the siren's irresistible song had captivated my attention calling me forward. In my family when grandma came in a dream it meant that someone was going to die. I was the one who received the visitation and in fact my mother died a month later.

After my mother's death I had a deep longing to find the transcendent mother and hold her in my heart. Over the next twelve years through my research and travels to Italy a rich spiritual heritage would be revealed to me of woman as prophetess. I became a historian tracing history back to the 10 c.b.c.. A melody was leading me on a spiritual adventure connecting with all the mothers. The best way to stay woven into my mother's heart was to carry on the lineage.

One of the ways I could do this was by fulfilling my mother's dream of becoming a writer and publishing a story about her life. She always wanted to write a book about the pearls of wisdom she learned. Just as soon as I made the decision to write a cookbook honoring my mother and Nona magical things began happening. Mother and Nona started coming in dreams and they were not alone. They brought a vision of the Black Madonna and various Greek and Roman Goddesses.

In the first dream, Elizabeth Ann Ventimigilo Plager, my beloved mother brought me through a passage, an ancient door revealing an underground cavern. Ducking my head I stepped through a portal into a vast stillness. She breathed into my being allowing me to flow in a gentle current carrying us into the luminous darkness. As I crossed the threshhold into another dimension my vision opened to something I had never experienced before. Statues of Black Madonnas and Roman and Greek goddesses covered the ground as far as the eye could see. Passing by several prayer stations ecstasy and bliss poured into me. I was brought before Nona sitting majestically near an olive green table my mother used to have in her house. Nona spoke, "I want you to know me. Through dreams I will reveal myself to you and the Italian heritage that is your birthright. We have selected you to tell our story as you are gifted. We are here to help you heal your pain."

The dream began and ended with a golden thread coming down from the shelf above my bed where pictures of my mother, Nona and the Black Madonna were set up in an altar, weaving and dreaming me into the realm of my ancestors.

What started out as simple Italian cookbook honoring both of these women turned out to be a much deeper process that would take seven years to complete. The more I listened the more I was woven into this unseen realm.

Underworld Stories

The winter of 1998 I was planted in front of my computer typing the stories my mother loved to tell. Stories of fierceness flowed onto the pages emerging out of my consciousness. Stories that make you laugh until you cry. Balanced on the other side of the stories were the depth of human experience few talk about, the deep dark secrets every family hides.

Since I was a small child I have been on a quest to understand my mother's perilous journey to the underworld. As a young child I saw my mother's first major depression. After giving birth to my little brother she had post-partum depression that turned into post partum psychosis. She stopped eating to get her shape back.

At nine years of age I watched in horror as my mother was dragged out of the house screaming in the middle of the night by my father and uncle. My young mind sifted through what I had done to cause this. The uncle, one of my mother's brothers, had been molesting me for the previous five years. He threatened to kill my mother, grandmother, my cat and me if I told. After he killed my cat at age five I vowed never to tell anyone. Devastated I thought he thought I told.

I felt a tremendous loss and emptiness as to who was going to take care of me, I pretty much learned that I was to take care of myself but most of all on some very deep level I felt that I caused her illness.

My mother's journey to know herself had become distorted, pathologizing the enchanting myths of the gods and goddesses in their search for wholeness. She and I were living out the mythology of Demeter and Persephone on a farm in eastern Washington. I watched as my mother, like Persephone, had been abducted by the dark lord Pluto, his horses leading her off into the horizon before disappearing into the abyss. Years later I found out my mother had visions of winged horses in the sky before her first breakdown. The doctors called it hallucinations.

Just before Easter my mother came home from the hospital after being gone for two months. A moment of bitter sweet. She walked into the kitchen without glancing up. She didn't seem her self. Hoping she'd forgiven me I baked a cake for her homecoming. Looking up at us with a blank stare she asked,"who are you?"

My mother's dangerous descent was interrupted with electro shock therapy and medication. Something was missing in my mother's life, she knew it but felt trapped by a society that didn't allow her to descend into this place on her own terms. She stopped dancing and her laughter disappeared into silent caverns.

I was in second grade. I remember stopping my tap dancing and ballet classes. Dancing in the sublime darkness of mother's psyche she and I were intricately woven into the dark mystery trapped in a web of suffering.

Over the next several years Easter, a time of celebration and renewal was experienced as foreboding and fearful. My longing for the mother continued over the next five years as she struggled each winter with devastating depression resulting in three sets of shock treatments with twelve in a series.

For the next thirty years I wanted to find out what would have saved my mother. Her journey to the underworld had become distorted, turning mythology into pathology. Years later I would come to my own understanding of what happened that sorrowful and joyful spring.

Just before her breakdown no one believed she was receiving obscene phone calls that upset her. Ten years later I told my father I was present when my mother received these upsetting phone calls. Astonished he said, "you mean she really did get those phone calls?" Handed down from Greek mythology is Cassandra, a prophetic priestess who had been given the gift of prophecy but was cursed with not being believed. My mother followed the legacy of Cassandra. She wanted to call her book, Listen to Me! Later in life my mother confided that she was way out there. My father responded in the best way he knew how.

My mother had begun her descent and I followed. As I grew older and went to college to study psychology, every book I bought for my classes I bought two. One for myself and one for my mother.

I learned how my mother's journey to the underworld, how my journey to the underworld and how all of your journeys to the underworld are a parallel growth process to that of the goddess. All of us must make this journey in the search for wholeness. Men must make this journey as well. Early in my journey I longed for some wise woman to guide me. But there was no one, only a voice and the irresistible song of my spiritual mother and grandmothers.

In ancient days there were guides called Sibyls, the prophetic priestesses skilled in taking initiates to the Underworld. Foreign dignitaries came from far and wide to have a meeting with the Sibyl. Rome's ancient writers quoted the Cumean Sibyl when she guided Aeneas to the Underworld to visit his dead father, "Summon your courage for you will need it! Have you spoken your vows? The great door will never open until you say your vows!"

The Sibyls knew how to transform a legacy of suffering in wisdom and into an inexhaustible supply of blessings.

Land of the Dead

In writing my mother's story I was to enter a realm few survive, the land of the dead. The goddess descended into the underworld to be dismembered with all worldly attachments stripped away and so had I. Illness, madness and death are the dangers on the path and all three knocked at my door. Perhaps the greatest enemy was within, one's own mind. The real demons are not outside oneself but hidden in our own ego where one lives out of the false self which only brings suffering.

I thought I had already faced my deepest fears. In the fifth year of writing my mother's story I experienced two head and neck injuries with several small strokes. Falling into a deep and almost unfathomable depression I became lost in the labyrinth of the mind unable to speak or think. I could not find my mind. I had no idea how hard I would have to fight for my life over the next three years.

The consciousness of death seeped into my bones and I came face to face with the Lord of Death. I remember in March 2003 laying down to sleep and out of my mouth came the death rattle. Death was swift and sudden as my body began shutting down. Every cell in my body became one cell and one consciousness. The portal opened and my ancestors appeared. I was happy to see them and thanked them for coming but was quick to tell them I wasn't ready to leave, that I hadn't accomplished what I was supposed to. I asked them to please tell me what they wanted me to know. I wasn't afraid of what would be revealed.

For three nights I danced in the Land of the Dead directly experiencing the consequences of all past harsh words and non-virtuous deeds. I saw the harm I had caused others with my negative actions. When I returned from this realm I cried for nine days from all the grief I felt for having caused so much pain. On the tenth day I sat at the foot of my Tibetan Teacher, Tulku Thubten Rinpoche. He said, "Leave this sorrow in the room with me, it doesn't belong to you."

Over the next three years I participated in a Dharma Apprenticeship Program working closely with my teacher and "practicing the Dharma like my hair was on fire." Tulku Thubten taught skillful means to transform all afflicted emotions into wisdom resulting in a never ending supply of blessings, always for the benefit of all beings.

Dancing through the veils of The Great Mother, Transcendent Wisdom, I learned how to transform all negativity into wisdom for the benefit of all beings.

As a tarantata I broke free of the web of suffering. My spiritual grandmothers poured Truth through my consciousness and guided me as I crossed the ocean of sorrow passing into the ocean of joy where blessings flow inexhaustively.

I had been liberated from the painful legacy that had been handed down to me and in doing so liberated my mother and Nona and all my ancestors. I emerged from the cycle of life, death and rebirth with the transcendent wisdom of the Black Madonna, the modern day embodiment of the Great Mother, pouring through my heart. May this story benefit all beings.

Naomi Lombardi, MA Clinical Psychology, author of *Dancing in the Underworld: the quest for wholeness*, lives in the San Francisco Bay Area offering individual consultations and is a Ritual Theater Performance Artist. She leads workshops called Dancing in the Underworld, a psycho-spiritual process, weaving archetypal psychology with ancient mystery rites.

Founder of Wisdom Traditions of the Dark Mother, A Mystery School, Naomi guides initiates in a process of becoming whole and complete.

Naomi leads tours to the sacred sites of Southern Italy pilgrimages to the Black Madonna. She is your guide and Sibyl using the tour as your personal journey towards wholeness.

For more information email: naomi_lombardi@yahoo.com. Call 510-601-6082.

Primordial Mothers in My Chinese Family

Pairin Jotisakulratana

My journey into women's spirituality began with a burning question, "How to live fully as a human being?" As a third generation Teochiu Chinese[1] immigrant in Thailand, I was the result of the anti-Chinese policy enforced by the Thai government. I grew up trying to hide my ethnic identity in order to assimilate into the Thai culture. I did not want to speak our Chinese dialect, instead I learned English because it was considered a "superior" language. I had never asked my parents about my ancestors' way of life or their beliefs.   In addition to that, being a Chinese woman is not considered something to be proud of either. There is a common saying among overseas Chinese in Thailand which says, "To have a daughter is like having a toilet in front of your house."   A toilet has no history. I was also left without any history of my people. Later, I realized that these feelings of shame and self-rejection had barred me from living life to its fullest.

In June 2004, I went to China with my mother in search for my people's history, the personal history of my family, as well as reclaim my fullness as a Chinese woman. My ancestors were peasants from a rural area populated by Teochius, generally known as Chaoshan in Guangdong province, Southeastern China. Swatow is a major city and port in this area. Teochius' religion blended in folk beliefs of Southeastern China, Taoism, Buddhism, and Confucianism. My father's side has been Catholic for more than a hundred years, so their spirituality was quite different. Their Catholic belief and practices were very much the result of the Western influence on China in the late 1800s.   As people of subaltern class, my ancestors on both sides suffered and struggled against the feudal system and patriarchal culture of China. Their history, everyday and celebratory rituals, and culture have blended into the resistance to the oppressive

349

systems. They had strong faith in female goddesses who were close to them like their own mothers. These mother goddesses are the embodiment of compassion as well as justice.

My mother took me back to her parent's village in China. There, I met my Chinese relatives. Some of them are still farmers, while some have become laborers in the new industrial system. My uncle, who had fought in the war with the Japanese, took me to the community temple to pay respects to our ancestor shrine. Stories of my grandmother's family that my mother had told me came back vividly.

My maternal grandmother was named Chua Neg E. She was born in a poor peasant family. She was the younger of two daughters born to my great grandmother Ung Sai Ngeg. After giving birth to Neg E, Sai Ngeg had to become a wet nurse to twin babies of one of her relatives, something only poor people did in China. Not long after my grandmother was born, her father passed away, leaving the family to experience real hardship.   My grandmother's family was the poorest one in the village, my mother said. The following story of our poverty has been passed on from my grandmother to my mother and to me.

There was a young boy who was my grandfather's cousin. We were so poor that he had nothing to eat. So this young boy ended up stealing food from other people all the time. People told him to stop but he did not. One day he was arrested by governmental officers. The officers wanted him to confess and repent, but he did not say anything. So they buried him alive. After they buried him and started walking away, they heard him say from the beneath the soil, "I am sorry."   But nobody went back to rescue him.

My mother broke into tears after telling me this story. She said, "You see how poor we were in China. Even our young boy had to be buried alive because we had nothing to eat." This was a story that my grandmother remembered all her life. Every time when she told this story, she, too, broke into tears. She told my mother that we would not be poor like that again and we would not let others look down on us. This is also what my mother has taught me since I was young.

My grandfather, who was a spiritual and kind man, also lost a brother in the war to protect the Chinese empire against the Japanese. I now see the big picture of the Chinese society during that time, and I understand that the social structure of an oppressive feudal system, together with the pressure from the Western powers, caused our poverty, hardship, and the death of our young boy. I also see that my ancestors' beliefs in women divinities gave them strength to face hardship.

While I walked around the village, I saw a shrine of the goddess

Tien Hau, the protector of sea travelers. My grandfather, who came from the same village as my grandmother, had faith in this goddess whom he intimately called "A-ma" or grandma. In Thailand, my mother recalled, grandfather always went to the shrine of Tien Hau to make offerings, which included food cooked by my grandmother, and to ask for her protection and guidance. I imagined that before he left for Thailand, he came to this shrine to ask Tien Hau to protect him on his journey and to keep his family safe.

The many stories of Tien Hau are an expression of the vernacular beliefs of the Chinese people. She is a folk deity who originated from the southern coastal province of China. Since she is a protector of seafarers, Chinese who traveled overseas brought their belief in the goddess with them all over the world. The legend of this goddess began in 960 C.E., the first year of the Song dynasty. At that time, a girl was born to a fisherfolk family on Meichow Island, Fujian. It is said that Kuan Yin, the Goddess of Compassion, came to witness the birth of this girl (Konantakiet, Thamnieb 62). Another legend tells how Kuan Yin aided in the conception of the girl by giving her parents a magic pill (Bosco and Ho 1).

The girl was totally silent during the first month of her life, so the family named her "Muk Neung," which means "quiet maiden." Muk Neung grew up to be a very wise girl. Her father treated her as an equal to her other brothers and gave her an education. She was also very spiritual and full of compassion. One source says that Muk Neung received teachings from a Taoist high priest and finally attained special spiritual powers (Yau 1). When she was 16 years old, the spirit of "an old well" came to gave her a magic charm, which enabled her to exercise magical power and travel outside her body (Bosco and Ho 1). Muk Neung used her supernatural power to heal the sick, predict weather, give warnings about dangers in the seas to fisherfolk, and rescue people from ship wrecks. Her miracles include saving the lives of her father and brothers. According to the story, once her father and brothers were out in the seas and got caught in a violent storm. While Muk Neung sat weaving on her loom, her spirit left her body and flew to help them. Some accounts say she failed to save her father because her mother woke her up from trance before she could do so.

Muk Neung did not get married as Chinese women typically do. She died at young age, either at 20 or 28. One source says that on the ninth day of the ninth lunar month, she passed away peacefully sitting upright on a hill (Yau 1). Another official source says that on the ninth day of the ninth lunar month, people were celebrating a festival by climbing up mountains for good luck. While they were celebrating, they heard celestial music and saw many gods arrive. Muk Neung stepped onto the clouds and ascended into heaven with all the gods (Bosco and Ho 4).

After her death, Muk Neung's spirit still came to help people who were in distress. She was famed for helping guide ships through dangerous waterways; assisting people in shipwrecks; ending drought, storms, and floods; protecting children; stopping epidemics by providing special well water or magic pills; etc. She is considered a protector of sea travelers and sometimes appears in the stormy sky as a shining light or a glowing fire that people can follow to their destinations safely (Thompson 58). She is a goddess who associates primarily with water and folk people (Bosco and Ho 3). Her veneration was not confined to folk people but Tien Hau also received titles in the official pantheon from emperors of China. However, local people know her simply as "A-ma" or "Matzu," which means "grandma." Through this endearing term, the goddess remains close to her people. I suggest that this folk belief reflects resistance against the governmental "take over" of the goddess.

An interesting submerged belief related to this goddess is reflected in the fact that her statues are often painted black or red. When I first saw her statue at her temple in San Francisco, I exclaimed, "She is a dark mother!" Through these colors, she may embody humanity's memory of the early human migration out of Africa in the Paleolithic age. As Lucia Birnbaum points out, "everyone's genetic 'beautiful mother' is african and dark, and that she is the oldest divinity we know" (dark mother xxv).

Some people suggest that Tien Hau's black color represents impartiality, the idea that she helps everyone who calls onto her without discrimination (Bosco and Ho 46).   This reminds me of Lucia Birnbaum's belief that the dark mother is the mother of us all. For me, Tien Hau's dark color represents the color of the subaltern class of southern Chinese people. As peasants and fisherfolk who work hard in the sun, our skin is darker than that of the ruling class from the north. This color represents our history of being considered by the dominant class as "barbarian," "outlawed," and "rebels."

The veneration of this goddess can also be seen as a counter-reaction to the patriarchal system influenced by state-promoted Confucianism. While girl babies were unwanted in Chinese society, according to the legend, Kuan Yin purposefully granted a baby girl to Muk Neung's parents. Instead of raising Muk Neung as a subordinated girl, her father raised her as someone of equal status with her brothers. He even gave her an education, which was considered a rare practice under Chinese patriarchy. Tien Hau's miraculous stories are full of symbols of the feminine, such as water, wells, ships, and the sea. Her legend associates her with Taoism, a religion that was blended into the folk belief of the south. I see her as a representative of the feminine force in Taoism. Her shining light in the midst of a dark storm can also be interpreted as the Taoist feminine principle that guides people out of the chaos of disruptive systems. She embodies the power that can save men's lives, even that of her own the father. Even though she was technically a "barbarian" woman from the south, the emperors, the supreme representatives of patriarchy and the ruling class, had to bow to her.

Another goddess associated with Tien Hau's legend is Kuan Yin, who is also a very important goddess in vernacular belief. Her name means "she who hears the cries of the world." This compassionate goddess is very important in my family, as well. My grandfather was a devotee of Kuan Yin. He made offerings and prayed to an image of Kuan Yin every day. Once my grandfather was very ill and the family had no money to take him to the doctor. My second aunt prayed to Kuan Yin, and in her meditation she saw Kaun Yin's whisk. She knew immediately that her father would be healed. Finally, my grandfather was recovered. He venerated Kuan Yin until the end of his life. A couple months before his death, the picture of Kuan Yin that he made offerings to everyday fell down without any cause and its glass frame broke. Another aunt of mine recalls that from that day on my grandfather prepared for his passing away. He knew that Kuan Yin had told him that his time was up. He burned that picture so that his children would not have to be responsible for making offerings to her.   One day he visited my aunt, said that he might not be able to come back again, and gave her some of his saving money. Shortly after that, my grandfather passed away.

My mother, who converted to Christianity after she married my father, still maintains her veneration to Kuan Yin. Normally, Kuan Yin's devotees do not eat beef. I think that this is related to farmers' beliefs. Because cows help them cultivate rice, farmers are grateful to them and do not eat them. As a devotee of Kuan Yin, my mother does not eat beef. My mother set up three Kuan Yin statues right in front of the door to our house. They are the first things people see upon entering. On the other hand, she puts statues of Jesus, Mary, Joseph, and the Christian cross on the second floor, where no guests see them. She tells everyone that she is Catholic, but I can see that her submerged belief is in Kuan Yin.

Kuan Yin is the most beloved deity of Chinese people. Historically, she was the Bodhisattva Avalokitesvara, the Buddha of Compassion, who was originally a Buddhist male deity in India. Buddhism first arrived in China during the first century C.E. Somkiet Lohpetcharat, a Thai art historian, believes that belief in Bodhisattva Avalokitesvara came later in 401 C.E.

and that this compassionate deity was well accepted by the Chinese. He says that the female form of this deity gradually developed through time. In particular, during the Tang dynasty (618-907), when Buddhism reached its peak, the images of Avalokitesvara became more feminine. During the Yuan dynasty (1271-1368), this male deity was totally transformed into a female goddess and people began to call her Kuan Yin. Lohpetcharat notes that the legend identifying Kuan Yin with an indigenous princess, Miao Shan, originated during this period, as well (50-55).

A legend my mother told me says that Miao Shan was born the princess of a cruel king. The king forced her to marry. Miao Shan wanted to walk on a spiritual path rather than have a worldly life, so she refused to marry. The king became very angry and wanted to kill her. Miao Shan escaped to a monastery to live her life as a nun. One day, the king got severely ill. His doctor said that only an arm and an eye could heal him. Nobody offered to sacrifice their body parts to the cruel king, except Miao Shan. She cut off her arm, and pulled out her eye, for the king, and he was healed. Because of this merit, the heavens gave Miao Shan a thousand arms and a thousand eyes. She became Kuan Yin, the Bodhisattva of compassion. The king repented and became a devoted Buddhist.

Like Tien Hau, Kuan Yin is a goddess who emerges in the midst of patriarchy and a cruel feudal system. As in Miao Shan's legend, Kuan Yin's father represents the aggression of the ruling class and the violence of men against women. Miao Shan represents the feminine force, which is full of compassion and endurance. This feminine force was recognized by heaven and finally won over the violent male ruler. Thus, women struggling under patriarchy often embrace her as their Mother goddess. Impoverished people also look to her because she is known to be the helper of the poor (Chantaronanon 131). Kuan Yin is also known to have the power to release prisoners from their chains (Storm 195).

Kuan Yins's mythology is also full of symbols of the divine feminine. She is said to live on a mountain or an island in the Eastern Sea, and to have given human beings rice, "which she makes wholesome by filling each kernel with her own milk" (Storm 194). Mountains and islands all over the world are believed to be the bodies and habitats of goddesses. Since ancient times, grains have also been associated with goddesses in many cultures. Kuan Yin is a goddess who nurses all humans with grains filled with her own milk. Her love is thus without any discrimination, because everyone, kings and peasants, sages and criminals, women and men, young and old, eat her rice.   Many statues depict Kuan Yin holding a baby, an image that reminds me of statues of the Black Madonna holding Jesus and Isis holding Horus. She is said to bless women with children and help all women and men who cry out to her. She is clearly an embodiment of universal motherhood. Andrew Harvey and Anne Baring suggest that the female form of Avalokitesvara was created from the fusion of Buddhism with Taoist belief in the divine feminine and the older image of the primordial Mother, which "was embedded deep within the soul of the Chinese people" (170-171).

A belief in the primordial Mother has persisted since the prehistoric period, long before the rise of patriarchy. Chinese archaeologists have unearthed Neolithic cultures that yield evidence of matriarchal clans. Jiao Tianlong reports that a 6,000-year-old Neolithic village named Banpo in Shaanxi province yields signs of a matrilineal society, that lacked a hierarchical disparity among its members (93).   Banpo belongs to the Yangshao culture, which has been found throughout the middle Yellow River area. Tian long also reports on another site from this culture named Yuanjunmiao in Shaanxi province. In this society, "woman played the leading role in production," and the "social position of females was generally higher than that of males, and that of girls higher than that of boys" (108). Neolithic goddess figurines, he continues, have been found in Liaoning, Hebei, and Inner Mongolia provinces. Furthermore, pottery used in sacrificial activities depicting women's features has been found in Gansu and Quinghai provinces (117-126). At present, the word for family name in Chinese has a character of a woman in it, depicting that once the family name was passed on through women.

In early Chinese mythology, the world is said to be created by Nu Wa, a mythic female who has the head of human and the body of a snake. Cai Junsheng, a senior research fellow of the Institute of Philosophy of the Chinese Academy of Social Sciences, states that "Nu wa is the most important and ancient mythological female figure handed down from the prehistoric age" (34). He notes that a written record dating to as early as the Warring States period (475-221 B.C.E.) mentions her name. An ancient dictionary of Chinese Characters states that Nu Wa is an "ancient goddess (shenshengnu) who gave birth to all living things on earth" (35). Junsheng also says that Nu Wa is not a specific individual but is rather "an archetype of the great feminine spirit of the matriarchal age that once prevailed across the Central Plain" (35). After the patriarchal system and monogamy became dominant, Nu Wa was paired with a mythic male figure, Fu Xi, in order to recreate humans (54). In modern times, sometimes Nu Wa is known as the "Dark Lady of the Ninth Heaven" (Storm 218). Here, she is associated with dark color, the color of the earth and the primordial dark mother.

Xi Wang Mu or Queen Mother of the West is another primordial

Mother. Her name was found on oracle bones of the Shang dynasty (1600-1100 B.C.E.) (Dashu 3). She is said to live in the immortal land on the Kunlun Mountains. In her garden, she grows the peaches of immortality, which bear fruit only once every 3,000 years. In the fourth century B.C.E., a text called Shan Hai Jing describes Xi Wang Mu as a human being who has "teeth resembling those of a tiger and a tail like that of a leopard" (Junsheng 55). Junsheng suggests that originally Xi Wang Mu might be the name of a female chief of the Kunlun area, and that her myth shows that people who lived there had a totem represented by a female and a matriarchal clan society (55).

Another goddess who has been venerated in my family is Mary. My father said that we had been Catholics for more than a century. One thing that I feel as a loss is the fact that as Catholics my relatives on my father's side do not practice any folk religion, not even ancestor worship. They tend to look down on folk practices as superstitious. This mentality definitely was introduced to the Chinese by Western missionaries who came to China with the racist ideas.

On the other hand, Christianity helped uplift the situation of women in China. Missionaries helped lessen the practices of footbinding and female infanticide. Catholic sisters established schools that provide equal educational opportunities for young girls and boys. My female ancestors who were converted to Christianity also received such benefits. My relatives in China who were adopted by my great grandfather's second wife (my grandfather was adopted by the first wife) told me a story about this second wife. After she was born, her parents believed that she would bring bad luck to the family so they left her on the street. A Catholic sister in our village found her and saved her. Hence, she grew up with the Catholic sister. If it were not for the Catholic sister, she would have died another victim of female infanticide.

While my mother maintains some of the folk practices, especially that of ancestor worship and the veneration of Kuan Yin, she also prays to Mary. Her name comes from the Latin *mare* which means the sea (Baring and Harvey 105). Just as my ancestors prayed to Tien Hau to protect their travel over the sea, my mother always recites the rosary, asking for protection and blessings for her daughters, especially when we travel. This divine mother is the only belief she can relate to in Western religion. I think this is because Mary is a mother goddess who resonates with the ancient goddesses of China.

My mother once told me a story of Mary's miracle in my family. My great grandmother (my paternal grandmother's mother) gave birth to a baby girl. Because girls are unwanted in Chinese tradition, she killed her baby. Thereafter, she was tormented by guilt. After my grandmother married and converted to Christianity, she tried to convince her mother to become a Christian, believing that her mother's sin would be forgiven by God. But her mother did not want to leave her traditional beliefs.

One night, when she was in her forties, my great grandmother had a dream. She saw Mary come to her carrying two babies. Mary said to her, "Do you want these babies?" "Yes, I do. But one is enough," she replied. "Which one do you want?" Mary asked. "The boy." Then Mary said, "The other one I will give to your cousin." That cousin was married but had not yet had a child.

My great grandmother did not believe this dream would come true. The next year, she got pregnant. She prayed that if this child were a son, she would become a Catholic. Finally, she gave birth to a son and both of them became Catholics. Her cousin also got pregnant and gave birth to a girl. The story was so unbelievable that when she told others, they thought she had made it up or was mentally ill, so she did not tell anybody outside the family. However, she became a very devoted Christian. After my great grandmother passed away, my grandmother continued her faith in Mary. When she was dying, we put a rosary in her hand. We stood around her bed and recited rosary.

From these stories, I can see that Mary acted like the compassionate Mother Kuan Yin, who is said to bless women with children. Mary is also like Xi Wang Mu, who is a giver of babies and a receiver of the dead. My great grandmother was released from the guilt of killing her girl baby with the help of Mary.

These are some of the stories I have reclaimed through my journey back to my ancestor's land. Stories after stories helped me see that despite thousands years of patriarchy and the oppressive feudal system, my Chinese people still maintain a belief in the compassion and justice of the feminine power. Her forms have changed through time, with various manifestations in different faiths. Yet all of her forms and manifestations are rooted in the power of the primordial mother, the Mother of all creatures.

Notes

1 Teochiu Chinese is a small group of Chinese living in a northeastern area of Guangdong province, a province in Southeastern China. Teochiu is the word we use to call ourselves. In Mandarin which is the official dialect of China, we are called "Chaozhou."

Bibliography

Baring, Anne, and Andrew Harvey. The Divine Feminine: Exploring the Feminine Face of God Around the World. Berkeley: Conari Press, 1996.

Birnbaum, Lucia Chiavola. dark mother: african origins and godmothers. San Jose: iUniverse, 2001.

Bosco, Joseph, and Puay-Peng Ho. Temples of the Empress of Heaven. Hong Kong: Oxford University Press, 1999.

Chantaronanon, Pornphun. Withijin. [The Way of the Chinese.] Bangkok: Prapantasan, 1994.

Dashu, Max. Streams of Wisdom. Oakland: Suppressed Histories Archives, 2000

Junsheng, Cai. "Myth and Reality: The Projection of Gender Relations in Prehistoric China." The Chalice and the Blade in Chinese Culture: Gender Relations and Social Models. Ed. Min Jiayin. Beijing: China Social Sciences Publishing House, 1995. 34-90.

Konantakiet, Jitra. Thamnieb Chao Mae and Phoo Wiset Khong Jin [Chinese Goddesses and Adepts.] Bangkok: Jitra, 2001.

Lohpetcharat, Somkiet. Kuan Si Im Po Suk. [Bodhisattva Kuan Yin.] Bangkok: Amarin Printing, 2004.

Storm, Rachel. Myths of the East: Dragons, Demons and Dybbuks: An Illustrated Encyclopedia of Eastern Mythology from Egypt to Asia. London: Southwater, 2002.

Tianlong, Jiao. "Gender Relations in Prehistoric Chinese Society: Archaeological Discoveries." The Chalice and the Blade in Chinese Culture: Gender Relations and Social Models. Ed. Min Jiayin. Beijing: China Social Sciences Publishing House, 1995. 91-126.

Thompson, Lawrence G. "Matsu – An Important Community Deity."
    The Chinese Way in Religion. Jordan Paper and Lawrence G.
    Thompson. Belmont, CA: Wadsworth Publishing, 1998. 54-59.

Yau, Timothy H.T. "Tien Hau the Goddess of Heaven." A Leaflet from
    Tien Hau Temple in San Francisco.

Sita: Perfect Wife or Glorified Sex Object in K. R. Srinivasa Iyengar's Sitayana

An Essay

Rainbow Mooon

In all ages and in all places men have conceived of a
Great Mother These Great Mothers whose worship have
dominated the religious thoughts of peoples far removed
from each other in time, space and culture, have an essential
similarity which cannot but amaze us.[1]
Erich Neumann

The story preserved in Vālmīki's Sanskrit epic, the *Rāmāyaṇa*, is little known to the general public in this country though over large parts of Asia the names of Sītā, wife of Rāma, of the vulture Jatāyus, the monkey Hanuman, and the monstrous King Rāvaṇa are as familiar to the Asian people as are to us the names and characters in the Judaeo-Christian nativity myth, the *Odyssey*, Aesop's fables, *Romeo and Juliet*, or even *Star Wars*. There are those who say that this is a story that combines adventure and aphorism, romance and religion, fantasy and philosophy; a story that makes young children marvel, burly men weep, and old women dream.[2] For two and a half millennia the characters in the *Rāmāyaṇa* have been kept alive and thriving by generations of painters, dramatists, sculptors and story-tellers in India, Burma, Malaya, Java, Bali, Siam, Tibet and in China.[3]

The details of the story have undergone countless modifications and many additional episodes have been added as each writer revived it and tinged it with the color of his own social period and gender-based environmental expectations. The Vālmīki *Rāmāyaṇa* is considered the original, but should not necessarily be taken as a fixed text and the others necessarily as variants as the latter usually contextualized the differing worldviews of particular segments of Indian society.[4] Each variant is best seen in its own specific context without necessarily needing to be juxtaposed with the 'authoritative' version; there is, however, a need to recognize that a range of social groups have adapted the story or at least fragments of the story to express their multivariate worldviews.[5]

There are so many viewpoints one could take in understanding and interpreting the *Rāmāyana* epic that it would be mind-boggling to attempt an exhaustive investigation into the various meanings of Sītā, Rāma, and Rāvaṇa, the Titan. There are literally so many variants on the *Rāmāyana* epic Paula Richman has been able to produce two volumes[6] of scholarly comments on the various themes of the epic with significant discussions on the numerous types and styles.[7] This suggests that I am not the only one questioning the ethics of the tale. Usha Nilsson tells us that there is a "differently imagined world in India where women unfold the story of Rāma and Sītā according to their social location and worldview, creating sites of resistance; where lower-caste and higher-cast tellings contain both convergences and dissociation."[8] Sally Goldman points out that Sītā is given a voice in the original epic written by Vālmīki in which the muffled voice of traditional upper-class women of the 'epic age' can be heard: "How wretched to be under the power of another,"[9] and later when she voices her disaffection with her world.[10]

Iyengar suggests that the way Vālmīki himself visualized the *Rāmāyana* was as a mingled yarn of "the sky-blue heroic story of Rāma, Prince of Ayodhya, and the gold-sheened Sītā story, the epic of the Earth-born, merging with the dark-hued blood-smeared tale of Ravana the Titan ending with his death; with Sītā's tragic history fatefully linking the Rāma and Rāvaṇa stories."[11] This suggests that Vālmīki was not intending a standard for a culture to adopt as an Ideal.

With so many scholars already discussing this epic Indian saga including the serialized Indian television version of *Rāmāyana* produced by Ramanand Sagar on Doordarshan, India's government-owned television network in 1987-89,[12] why, you may ask, is Sītā of any significance to us in the West? Initially, I was looking for what I thought was the way Indian women were able to live a spiritual life within their secular lives. I was expecting to see an example of the 'perfect husband' and how he loved his 'ideal wife'. I wanted to find a way to use the epic as a story worthy of sharing in the West since our romantic tales seem so wanting. I mean, when I think of the romantic tendency of the young women in the West, I think of the Barbie doll and Marilyn Monroe even though both are/were 'unmarried'. I remember that growing up my role models were the Beaver's mom and Harriett Nelson, Ricky's mom. My daughters had the perfect spousal model in Bill Cosby's seriously idealized television career wife who also had time to be the loving mother of his four or five children.

When Madhu Kishwar interviewed young Indian women of the 21st century about their feelings on the image of Sītā as a relevant Ideal she was told "that the example Sītā sets will always remain relevant, even though they themselves may not be able to completely live up to it." Most women added that they do try to live up to the Sītā ideal to the best of their ability while making adjustments in light of present-day circumstances.[13] I also remember listening to a sixteen year old girl living in an impoverished Black American neighborhood talking about the "diamond ring her man was going to get her when he finally found a job" irregardless of the fact that 'her man' was a high school dropout and they were sleeping together without protection. After reading the epic, I was concerned that this tale gave permission to spousal abuse, to upper and lower class and caste women being actively beaten by their imperfect husbands. This was an unexpected twist to my research. What could I learn from the various forms this saga has taken; what new ideas could I form from understanding Sītā's story of life on earth as told by Iyengar?

For forty centuries the lack of feminine symbolism in the theistic and anthropomorphic symbol system of Western religions has stressed the personal dimension of their symbols of the *ultimate*, and stressed that the *ultimate* should be conceived of and related to as if it were a Personal Being in relationship with other Persons. The problem is that this personal god is always symbolized and addressed as a Man in the three major religions of the West, and the white male forms of symbolization and address are adamantly maintained, especially, it seems for Women of Color. It is undeniable that the male symbolism of deity has been a major contributor to the exclusion of women from positions of respect and authority in Western society and religion,[14] and thereby doubling the exclusion of Women of Color.

So, for the last 4,000 years, the feminine principle, which manifests in mythological history as the Goddess and in cultural history as the values placed upon spontaneity, feeling, instinct and intuition, has been lost as a valid expression of the sanctity and unity of life. Unfortunately, in Judaeo-Christian mythology there is formally no feminine dimension of the Divine because our culture is structured in the image of a masculine god who is beyond creation. He just orders it from without; he is not within creation as were the ancient Mother Goddesses which results inevitably in an imbalance of the masculine and feminine principles thus funding fundamental implications for how we create our world and live in it.[15] In India the deity at least always is expected to incarnate into a mortal form as male *and* female when the world is in dire need of them. This suggests one reason why the story of Sītā is popularly fortified with so many variations; the people revisit the saga whenever there is political and or social unrest. In this way the women can reassess their most practical functions socially and collectively.

Most of the variations of the epic do not give emphasis on the 'age' of the principal characters; in Iyengar's time-scheme, Rāma and Sītā marry when they are 16 and 14, and they spend less than a year together in Ayodhya before they are exiled to Dandaka for 14 years. They return to Ayodhya when they are 31 and 29. Another year and Sītā is exiled again. Then, twelve years later they meet in the Aswamedha Pavilion in Naimisa Forest; finally, as Sītā returns to her Earth-Mother she is 42 and Rama is 44.[16] This covers a significant span of life; a time span similar to a normal life of marriage, you think?

We begin Iyengar's tale with a child who is the incarnation of Śri-Lakṣmī, born to the King of a State in which everyone knows of her birth; and who at fourteen is being wooed by every available prince from countries far and wide. Sita literally grew up to be beyond beautiful; but she was also physically strong enough to play with Śiva's bow, a sacred weapon that few men could lift.[17] So we have a self-confident, beautiful, well-educated and talented, appealing young teenager who is instantly smitten by the most beautiful prince to quest for her hand in marriage and the only one of hundreds who undertook the challenge of stringing Śiva's bow to actually do so. In our story, sixteen-year old Rāma is the pride of his king father and queen mother and hope of his three brothers and therefore a mite egotistical. But he is also depicted as outrageously charming and spiritually just.

The shining couple is married in grand splendor and begins 'apprenticeship in Kingcraft' until about one year later when the throne is snatched from them and Rāma is to be exiled for fourteen years. Sītā chooses going into exile with her husband over staying in the palace without him for that period of time. Go figure. And because she so surprised the royalty and the population with her choice it was decreed that she would not have to wear bark-cloth like the ascetics and beggars who lived in the forest but was instead given regal clothes to last for the full fourteen years. So off she goes with the Prince of Ayodhya and his brother, Laksmana, to live the life of abstinent hermits. There is no question that Sītā is from the moment of her birth being righteously taken care of; she wants for absolutely nothing from anyone, least of all her new husband who worships her. This should be a prerequisite for being the 'perfect wife' in my humble opinion.

There is an episode in which Sītā admonishes Rāma quite lovingly but firmly about his random slaughtering of innocent animals for sport. It is one thing to have fun slaying demons, but quite another to kill just for the fun of killing. Interestingly, Rāma is amazingly contrite and vows to be more respectful of life in all of its forms. He honors the fact that the role of the wife is to bring the power of Grace and Wisdom into the partnership and he bows before her admonishment. Another prerequisite then for fostering the perfect wife is a husband who respects her thoughts, feelings, and counsel.

Throughout Iyengar's story we see both Rāma and Sītā respecting one another as equals; reflecting on the mistakes they make along their wilderness journeying; two teenagers growing up in Nature roaming from one ashram to the next, whiling away the years in meditation and deeply probing conversations about their Dharma, studying philosophy and social politics while meeting and studying with various saints and yogis. But the glorious three are not immune to the challenges of life; though the trio was blessed to have premonitions of doom; a doom realized after Śūrpanakhā, the Rakshasi, was sent howling back to Rāvaṇa, the King of the Demons. Śūrpanakhā was the demon sister of Rāvaṇa, who while flying over the happy trio one day in the forest, was "stricken with instant infatuation for the bewitching brothers." Being too aggressive in her lust for one or the other she was promptly spurned by both brothers. "Marking the strange mixture of amusement and rejection in their looks, the jealous Rakshasi with blood-shot eyes, leapt on terrified Sītā."[18] Not a good move with two mighty protectors standing at her side, for Lakshmana sprang up first in Sītā's defense and cut off the Śūrpanakhā's nose and ears.

Of course Rāma knew there was now going to be a mighty battle. Sītā is sent off to a cave to hide with Lakshmana to guard her safety while Rāma single-handedly slays an army of fourteen thousand Rakshasa sent to avenge the mutilation of Śūrpanakhā. But the bloody revenge does not end here. The sole survivor of the holocaust rushes to tell Rāvaṇa of the grim annihilation of the armored forces but warns against any frontal attack on Rāma. He instead suggests that Rāma's weakness is his wife, Sītā. "Rāma dotes on his chaste young wife, Sītā, a beauty without a peer; and were she carried away by deceit, he would shrivel up and die."[19] Śūrpanakhā also does a complete sales pitch to Rāvaṇa for the seizure of Sītā.

This Sītā isn't like the routinely fair you've oft collected before: Sītā, even like her handsome Rāma, signifies the Ultimate. Her light-glancing steps make the earth feel blest by the soft tread of her feet; the music of many sylvan voices merges in her native speech. Her rich flowing tresses are bewitching, cloud-like dark, and rain-like too; she's a visitant here from far heaven, a rare phantom of allure. Her face has the sweet charm of the lotus; her eyes, deeper than the sea; her breast, like twin cups of gold, body forth the rapture of paradise. How can I describe, O royal Brother, what defies analysis? Her beauty beyonds the categories and strikes one both blind and dumb! This unearthly marvel of a woman who teases you out of thought may be savored only by possession – arise, and claim your guerdon! [232:491-496]

This is very telling as not many enemies speak so lavishly about a hated foe. Sītā as the perfect wife was called "the angel fair, chaste and holy, the Light of the wide world's Life: *therefore*[20] the temptation, *therefore* the fall, the succumbing to evil!"[21] Women striving to be perfect wives, beware. Because Sītā is perfect she is believed to *cause* others to want to defile her. "All Asuric nature feels allergic to spiritual beauty, and breeds an irresistible desire to enact desecration. Goodness is a pure gemlike tongue of flame that blazons forth its challenge and invites the denizens of the Dark to a suicidal race."[22]

So it seems, as the perfect wife Sītā unconsciously is susceptible (unavoidably?) to being kidnapped by Rāvaṇa who because of her 'knowing' has to trick her into gaining entrance into the hermitage in the cave where she's hidden but left alone. What is most amazing about this abduction is that the mighty king of all the demons, the king who is racing to his own doom out of sheer lust and a dark desire for revenge, the king who has abducted thousands of women for his own sport, this demon king is unable or unwilling to risk actually raping Sītā. And though Sītā screams for help only to be defended unsuccessfully by the King of the Vultures, Jatāyu, she is never fearful of actually being violated as she is sure of her own chastity. She easily manages to keep Rāvaṇa at bay with a massive verbalization of insults.

Sītā's calm inner confidence and resolve is the real key to the happenings in her life. Though the story is not without major histrionics, Sītā is always the one to insure a calm, focused centering on her Dharma throughout the tale. This is especially recognized after Rāma slays Rāvaṇa and is being reunited with Sītā. The about-face that occurs in his demeanor can perhaps only be understood by another arrogant man: "I've killed Ravana in battle, thereby avenging the injury and insult he caused me by carrying you away in my absence. Not for your sake, woman, this war was fought;

'twas to redeem my honor: but I can't take you back, for your sight hurts as light pains a diseased eye. When you had perforce to live in his place, Rāvaṇa couldn't have left you undefiled, since you are so beautiful and hence so desirable."[23]

He then told her to feel free to go with one of his brothers or pick someone else, but he couldn't be the husband of damaged goods. O'Flaherty tells that the basis of his boastful rejection of Sītā is that he, a mortal man, has accomplished such prodigies in battle for the sake of his illustrious (mortal) family, and that he cares more about appearances and public opinion than about the happiness of himself and his wife[24] – all totally undercut and dwarfed by the revelation that he is *not* a mortal at all. So are we left with believing that Rāma, as an incarnation of the God Viṣṇu, is a spousal brute?

Wounded to the core, Sītā doesn't break down but instead admonishes Rāma once again on his poor judgment and stubborn blindness. "Why do you talk to me like that, oh Hero, like a common man talking to an ordinary woman?....You, lion among men, by giving way to wrath and passing premature judgment on a woman, have acted like a worthless man."[25] ..."At this grim moment when I'm perched near the abyss, it's not my present shame and suffering that I take to heart so much, but rather the certainty that by this one squeak of aberration you [Rāma] will be held up to opprobrium for all the ages to come. Obscuring your countless acts of valor and uncanny righteousness, this cardinal and cruel rejection of your lawful loyal wife will in all future time set the pattern of vulgar, selfish, prideful, one-sided, pitiless desecration of supportless womankind."[26] This is a pronouncement of things that came to be, or so it seems to me.

She then demanded a funeral pyre be built since life could no longer be worth living; but the god of fire, Agni, would not accept her death as she was clearly innocent. The miracle was not that Sītā was untouched by the flames, the miracle was "as Rāma, unable to bear the sight so poignant and so ghastly, closed his self-accusing eyes, his inner eye burst open, and he SAW! Rāma saw the blameless stainless Sītā rise out of the glowing fire, her limbs and raiment wholly unimpaired, and her grace more gracious still. Like one awakened from sleep, he let slip the darkened past as one drops the memory of nightmares, and advanced to take his God-given wife."[27]

Sadly, it was only a matter of time before Rāma returned to his deep sleep-state. It seems that it would be a lot easier to be the perfect wife if you had the perfect husband; but Sītā was taught and teaches that even the most divine men are not always awake and thus can be assailants. "Woman's love---a mother's, wife's, sister's, or a daughter's, any woman's---

by its own law fosters and sustains life, but the male always assails with his pride, ambition, self-righteousness, and the woman pays, hapless mankind pays, the entire commonwealth pays; but woman pays most of all."[28] By helping men live life well, women guarantee a better life for everyone and apparently Sītā's Dharma was to live as an example of such love for a husband. But her exemplary life is not over yet.

After fourteen years of wandering, after the slaughter of Rāvaṇa and the genocide of a whole race of Beings, the couple returns to Ayodhya for their coronation and reunion with family and friends. About a year after their return, Rāma hears that folks are talking about them; about his taking back a wife who'd spent twelve months under the roof of the Demon King. So Rāma banishes Sītā from the capital and sends her to an ashram to live for a while or until the gossip dies down. This he did knowing she was pregnant at the time; it was twelve years before Sītā saw Rāma again. Sītā, the perfect wife is again unbelievably wounded but accepts her fate and leaves quietly. She births twin boys and happily raises them with the help of Muni Valmiki (the author of the *Rāmāyana*) to become twin rhapsodists who roam the countryside singing hymns of divinities and chanting legends quite the way we watch television and go to movies and concerts today.

Mind you, during the twelve years of Sītā's exile Rāma is said to miss her so much that he had a life-size golden statute made to sit with him on the throne. And yet when he accidentally hears his sons, whom he immediately recognized as his, and though he was overjoyed to learn that Sītā was well and thriving, Rama still could only accept her back as queen if she would publicly reenact the baptism by fire so that the population could also witness proof of her original innocence. It is not difficult to see how this story correlates to the practice of *sati*, the act of a widow immolated on her husband's funeral pyre, as understood to be a key marker of the woman's character as purity and extreme devotion to her husband.[29] We as Westerners may not understand *sati*, but a huge number of wives in the West understand and allow domestic terrorism. In this final affront, Sītā is not at a loss.

This was a major event, but Sītā "shows a healthy sense of her own worth, even at a moment of such crushing injury;"[30] she realized that a woman's lot is only suffering and that one woman can only do so much. She'd lived an exemplary life, raised her two sons virtually alone, spent fourteen years wandering the wilderness with her husband and brother-in-law, had been kidnapped and held hostage for a year by a demon king, been exiled another twelve years because of her supposed defilement and was now being asked to prove her fidelity for a second time via a repeat performance of trial by fire. Sītā was fourteen years old when she met and married Rāma; she was now 42 years old.

When Rāma, for the second time needs Sītā to prove her innocence, when he says he believes she's innocent but she needs to prove it to the people, "Sītā, clothed in the brown bark dress of a forest dweller, folded her palms and looking downwards said, 'If I have loved and served none but Rāma and Rāma alone; if I have never strayed from the path of virtue and if these my words are wholly true, may Mother Earth open a cleft for me to take shelter in.' Immediately the earth before her opened with a tremendous roar. A divine throne, wondrous in splendor, appeared, held aloft on the heads of mighty serpents. The throne was studded with precious jewels. On it sat Mother Earth reaching out to Sītā with both her arms. She and her retinue welcomed Sītā warmly. Then slowly the throne sank below the earth and the fissure closed. Flowers were showered by the gods from the sky."[31]

Now this is indeed an appropriate response to and for an ungrateful husband, royal or otherwise. But it also suggests death, or a form of death as the only way out of a bad marriage; and Sita's marriage would not be what I would actually call "a bad" marriage. At least what we can interpret here is that if a husband *cannot* be perfect or even civil but still insists that he have the perfect wife, it is obviously up to the wife to say when enough crap is enough. Sītā is a perfect example of this. Though Sītā is valorized for her love and loyalty it should also be noted for men who abuse the gift of Grace, feminists in the East and the West are radically challenging the Sītā saga of life as misery; and as scholars dig deeper and listen more inclusively we continue to find evidence of feminist revision, subversion and protest in disparate social, ethnic, and economic groups.

Clearly, the circumstances of Sītā's birth and death amply prove that she was no ordinary mortal.[32] In Iyengar's tale, Sītā was found by her childless father as he was ploughing his field. King Janaka had "dug a deep furrow and as he stepped back in satisfaction to look at the narrow, deep gap, he noticed an extremely beautiful little baby girl lying peacefully inside it."[33] This birth connects her to the Earth Mother offering a symbolic connection to Demeter and Persephone, Isis and Osiris, and even Maat. It is said that as the consort of Rāma, Sītā is Nature; she is primordial power, the embodiment of divine splendor; the joy of consciousness. "She shines like pale gold; has two arms and is adorned with heavenly jewels. In her hand she holds a lotus.[34] Sītā is the Heaven attained through penance, the nature of the universe, conscious and unconscious; "that which knows and that which does not know."[35] "Sītā is Fortune (Lakṣmī)"; he "the Pervader"; she is the fair Pārvatī and Rāma the Lord-of-Sleep (Śiva).[36]

Rāma, who is usually depicted as of dark hue carrying a bow and arrow, is believed to have been Viṣṇu incarnated in mortal form to save the world from the oppressions of the demon Rāvaṇa. To his devotees Rāma combines the ideals of the gentle, faithful husband, the leader brave in hardship, and the just and benevolent king.[37] Having read the story it is clear to see why male devotees would perceive Rāma as sensitive and just, but in *Sitayana* he was also prone to hysterics, cruelty, and insensitive political blindness. Basham suggests it is perhaps significant that Rāma became nationally popular after the Muslim invasion of India.[38]

The Goddess Śri, who is also commonly known by the name Lakṣmī, has been known in the Hindu tradition since pre-Buddhist times. She is one of the most poplar goddesses in the Hindu pantheon. She has a considerable body of mythology and is widely worshiped by Hindus of all castes throughout India to this day. Since the late epic period (ca. A.D. 400) she has been particularly associated with the god Viṣṇu as his wife or consort. In this role she plays the part of a model Hindu wife, obediently serving her husband as lord. Throughout her history Śri has been associated with prosperity, well-being, royal power, and illustriousness. In many respects she is the embodiment of these qualities, and it is commonly understood that when these qualities are evident, Śri herself is present or reveals herself.[39] Śri-Lakṣmī's presence ensures a king more than ruling power: a female earth goddess with a male sky/rain god/king is an example of a divine pair in reciprocal roles of generating and sustaining life.[40] The point being made here is that Sītā, as a mortal princess and wife of Rāma, was believed to be one of the incarnations of Śri-Lakṣmī.[341] In addition to being the Great Goddess Fortune (Śri-Lakṣmī), in several late versions of the *Rāmāyana* Sītā assumes the form of Kālī. "On his return from Laṅkā, where he had just vanquished the mighty ten-headed Rāvaṇa, Rāma is confronted with an even more terrifying foe – a thousand-headed Rāvaṇa. When Rāma is unable to defeat this monster, Sītā, as Kālī handily slays the new menace.[42] So we have many ways we can understand the saga of Sītā and her actions (nay Dharma) with her not so perfect husband.

In bringing our review of Sītā to a close, we recognize that Sītā is indeed supposed to be a role model for the perfect wife as well as another submerged symbol of the patriarchal takeover of the matriarchal way of living. Let us suppose that Sītā is not a role model of the wifely perfection; but is rather a representation of the real anthropomorphic symbolism that was sexually motivated by the patriarchy, for it seems to me that this epic tale is more about 'sex as an object' for possession than about the Love and Loyalty of one woman for her fickle, self-centered, arrogant royal husband versus the lust-driven demon who for twelve months kept her prisoner, threatened to cook and eat her, but never touched her.

I believe that Sītā, in her final response to once again prove her chastity, her individual self-containment, her mental, emotional and psychological innocence, left a primitive feminist message for all of us who have fallen under the spell of the 'perfect wife' syndrome to ruminate on and digest slowly. I believe she was clear that the real issue she suffered for was related more to a significant religious metaphor with sexist overtures and terms of genderized persecution. If western wives and Women of Color globally continue to give in to the constructed institutions of sexual supremacy on a spiritual, mental, emotional and psychological basis, we can only blame ourselves for the physical, mental, emotional, and psychological abuse spawned by male-assertive sovereignty. We must collectively reject the male ideals of femininity by continuously deconstruct their concocted interests for love and loyalty while needing pure possession as proof. All young women dreaming that one day your Prince will come, I say unto you; Rama was a fine example of what can be expected from the 'perfect Prince-Charming;' and think hard about what Sleeping Beauty and Cinderella had to go through for their supposed perfect princes. Sītā, on the other hand, was certainly NOT the perfect obedient wife many variants of the Ramayana would have her made out to be; but it takes reading the story for yourself and gleaning what it is your Dharma to receive for you to understand my perspective, perhaps.

Notes

1 Engelsman: 19

2 Blank: ix

3 Collis: vii

4 Richman: vii

5 Richman: Romila Thapar's Foreword, ix

6 Many Rāmāyaṇas: The Diversity of a Narrative Tradition in South Asia [1991] and Questioning Ramayanas: A South Asian Tradition [2001]

7 Richman: Thapar's Foreword, vi

8 Nilsson, Usha; "Grinding Millet but Singing of Sita" Power and Domination in Awadhi and Bhojpuri Women's Songs, Richman: 137

9 "dhig astu paravaśyatām"

10 Sally J. Sutherland Goldman; "The Voice of Sītā in Valmiki's Sundarakāṇda", Richman: 223

11 Ivengar: viii

12 Hess: 1

13 Madhu Kishwar; "Yes to Sita, No to Ram: The Continuing Hold of Sītā on Popular Imagination in India", Richman: 285

14 Gross: 217

15 Baring: xii

16 Iyengar: x

17 Pattanaik: 60

18 Iyengar: 225 [426]

19 Iyengar: 230 [473]

20 Italics are my emphasis.

21 Iyengar: 232 [489]

22 Iyengar: 231 [488]

23 Iyengar: 490 [141, 145-46]

24 O'Flaherty: 198

25 Hess: 6

26 Iyengar: 492-93 [168-71]

27 Iyengar: 494-95 [186, 194-95]

28 Iyengar: 498 [217-18]

29 Hess: 7

30 Hess: 6

31 Bhattacharji: 102

32 Bhattacharji: 82

33 Bhattacharji: 84

34 Daniélou: 175

35 Daniélou: 173

36 Daniélou: 173-74

37 Basham: 303

38 Basham: 303

39 Kinsley, 1988: 19

40 Kinsley, 1988: 25

41 Basham: 316

42 Kinsley, 1996: 85 [fn8]

Bibliography

Baring, Anne and Jules Cashford; The Myth of the Goddess: Evolution of an Image, Arkana Penguin Books, London, England, 1991

Basham, A.L.; The Wonder That Was India: A Survey of the Culture of the Indian Sub-Continent Before the Coming of the Muslims, Grove Press, NY, 1959 (1954)

Bhattacharji, Sukumari; Legends of Devi, Orient Longman Ltd., Calcutta, India, 1995

Blank, Jonah; Arrow of the Blue-Skinned God: Retracing the Ramayana through India,

Houghton Mifflin Company, New York 1992

Collis, Maurice; Quest for Sita, The John Day Company, New York, 1947

Daniélou, Alain; Hindu Polytheism, Bollingen Series LXXIII, Pantheon Books, New York, 1964

Engelsman, Joan Chambelain; The Feminine Dimension of the Divine, Chiron Publications, Wilmette, Illinois, 1995 (1987, 1994)

Gross, Rita M.; "Hindu Female Deities as a Resource for the Contemporary Rediscovery of the   Goddess", The Book of the Goddess Past and Present: An Introduction to Her Religion,   Carl   Olson, Editor, Crossroad Publishers, New York, 1990

Hess, Linda; "Rejecting Sita: Indian Responses to the Ideal Man's Cruel Treatment of His Ideal Wife", Journal of the American Academy of Religion, March 1999, Vol 67, No.1 Issn: 002-7189

Iyengar, K.R. Srinivasa; Sitayana: Epic of the Earth-born, Samata Books, Madras, India, 1987

Kinsley, David R.; "Kālī: Blood and Death Out of Place", Devi: Goddesses of India, John Stratton Hawley and Donna Marie Wulff, editors; University of California Press, Berkeley, California, 1996

Kinsley, David R.; Hindu Goddesses: Visions of the Divine Feminine in the Hindu Religious Tradition, University of California Press, Berkeley, California, 1988 (1986)

O'Flaherty, Wendy Doniger; Hindu Myths, Penguin Books, London, England, 1975

Richman, Paula; Questioning Ramayanas: A South Asian Tradition, University of California Press, Berkeley, California, 2001

Pattanaik, Devdutt; Devi: The Mother-Goddess, An Introduction, Vakils, Feffer and Simons Ltd. Mumbai, India, 2000

La Madre Nera

Tommi Avicolli Mecca

c 2004

These genes have been on an incredible journey

born in Africa hundreds of thousands of years ago

they migrated through the Middle East to Asia

then back across Europe

over the Bering Strait to the Americas

that weren't called the Americas

they climbed mountains

slept in caves

built pyramids and towers of babel

farmed and made art

crossed oceans

endured ice   heat

earthquakes

floods

these genes have been indestructible

clever fellows

they re-shaped eyes and nose

straightened hair

lightened skin

to adapt to new climates

new diets

Still they carried the memory of the first mother

you call her Eve

you say she had 33 daughters

who became the mothers of us all

tribe of Eve

never losing her maternal gene

as they spread to every shore

populated the length, width and breath

of an already ancient planet

Black mother

in the heart of Africa

holding a black child at her dark nipple

nourishing civilization on her fleshy tits

black as the night

black as the depths of the ocean

black as the earth

weeping black tears when her children left

to explore the places beyond

perhaps driven by legends of a land of milk and honey

perhaps needing only to sever the umbilicul

perhaps needing to find the point where the

night turned back into day

defiant children rebelling against their fathers

but never forgetting their mother

they would rename her earth

sky madonna

goddess art science medicine

but she's still the same Eve

black as the Africa

she called home

"Beyond the Symbol" series by Tricia Grame
Oil, acrylic, and mixed media.
These pieces are from a series inspired by my research in Italy and Malta, where prehistoric images of the female were discovered.

"Beyond the Symbol" series by Tricia Grame
Oil, acrylic, and mixed media.

"Beyond the Symbol" series by Tricia Grame
Oil, acrylic, and mixed media.

The Symbol: A Source of Empowerment

Tricia Grame, Ph.D.

Controversies about art and its meaning are not new. Some of the most shockingly. infamous art of recent decades created an outrage within the art world. The works exhibited became debatable and were removed from the muscum because of their startling symbolism, presentation of human bodies and reference to religious beliefs. [1]

Eighteenth century philosophers David Hume (1711-1776), and his successor, Immanuel Kant (1724-1804), were instrumental in forming the basis of our modern aesthetic theory. Both scholars struggled with the term "taste, one's ability to perceive quality in an art work".[2] For many, the discussion continues today. How can we prove that one's judgment or taste is superior and how does that person come to understand the essence of the art without the artist's interpretation. Hence, the inquisition continues, what is the purpose of art, what does it mean, is it art, why do we value it and what really is art? Although these crucial questions and answers are often formulated by the thriving art market and exclusive galleries, the erosion of art and its credibility remains an issue.

In order to respond to these questions, I will first begin by defining the word symbol and how the symbol was vital in prehistoric art and is imperative in contemporary art. I will discuss the work of European archeologist Marija Gimbutas whose ground-breaking research changed history. I will include the transformative effects the feminine element in prehistory and contemporary art has upon my work. I will then discuss two contemporary renowned women artists, Louise Bourgeois and Eva Hesse who I believe created and manifested symbols of the female in their provocative body of work. To further my theory about the symbol, a source of empowerment in art, I will describe the ancient sacred images and temples discovered on the island of Malta and how their symbols continue to influence contemporary artists while acknowledging the similarities and recurrent themes that appear in the work of various artists from different cultures and times. Most extraordinary and often unacknowledged by artists, unknown to one another and without prior communication or shared life influences, women have continually created art that speaks of female spirit. Concluding, that it has always been the artist who creates symbols as visual language. Thus, it is the symbol of the female that continues to have the most profound effect upon my work, other contemporary artists and our audience. These symbols have contributed to our understanding of past and present conditions.

Webster's New Dictionary defines the symbol as, "an authoritative summary of faith or doctrine, an object used to represent something abstract, as an arbitrary or conventional sign standing for a quality, process, relation, a mark or letter". [3]

Symbols are not mute, they speak a language that has been used by artists from Paleolithic times to our contemporary artists. These artists were unavoidably inspired to create and recreate the language of symbols. They were not created accidentally but within an organized system of rituals, mythic contexts and selected activities. As it was in prehistoric mythology and religion, the symbol has always been and continually endures as a primary source for understanding.

In the 1950's Marija Gimbutas, a professor of European archaeology at UCLA was the first to investigate and unearth the hidden, prehistoric symbols of Western Civilization. Gimbutas offered an alternative to androcentric theories and patriarchal conditioning for Western women whose traditions excluded the deity in female forms. She stressed the multiple functions and associations of these prehistoric symbols and images, which were often found to have anthropomorphic and zoomorphic forms. By systematically examining thousands of symbols, Gimbutas concluded that civilization during the Paleolithic and Neolithic periods, roughly 30,000 B.C.E. to 2,500 B.C.E., celebrated the female, placing her in a harmonious matrifocal position with divine reverence. Her exaggerated form conveyed and evoked her powerful presence and human significance for life and creativity. She was often symbolized as a bird, a woman with breasts and protruding buttocks, triangles, meanders, spirals and vulva contours and lines. Gimbutas stated that the symbol of the female depicted a source of empowerment, she was first portrayed as birth-giver, protectress and nurturer, known as the Earth Goddess. These symbols can be traced back to the period when the first sculptures of bone, ivory or stone appeared around 30,000 B.C.E., an undocumented era. Gimbutas defined the symbol as a script, a primary source for understanding language, beliefs, religion and dreams, that are able to infuse, inspire and transform.

The symbols of ancient art are the sacred remains of the silent forms and images that tell the story of life before ours. Gimbutas gave these female symbols all the title of Goddess.[4]

By incorporating scholarship from ethnology, religion, mythology, linguistics, and anthropology with continued archaeological discoveries of prehistoric symbols, Gimbutas brought a new understanding and vision for the arts into modern Western consciousness. Many scholars and artists have done much to preserve and advance Gimbutas's work, as well as to reverse the endless amount of distorted history exhibiting that many women have struggled for acceptance. Although ancient traditions have been passed down, many lost or forgotten, they somehow resurface in the obscured or subconscious memories of the contemporary artist. These symbols are our archetypes, achieving legitimacy through the roots of tradition, which results in a coherent organized picture about our history.

Carl Jung believed that the symbols in art are the archetypes, the true essence of art and the root of the imagination. They can be highly numinous and provide the content for the unconscious to enter the conscious. Jung claimed that symbols have the ability to shape beliefs, values and self-image.[5] The archetypal symbol is powerful, it continues to serve as a vehicle for the artist to express what has often been silent.

The birth of the symbol for the artist is possible through the creative process, which then enables the spiritual expression for the symbol to surface. It evokes a kind of magical experience, a sensation of excitation to discover what lies within this inward emotional language. It is not about representing a realistic human form. Certain symbols often imply something more than their obvious and immediate meaning. In order to understand the symbol, the art and soul of creativity, one must attempt to bridge the gap in distinguishing those variables that have formed the core of modernity and are what influenced the modern world from its prehistory. Although art does not do or say the same thing epoch after epoch, function varies from one society to another. There is always a correlation between society's values, directions, motives and the art it produces. But whether we agree or not, traditions have histories that weave together with other histories, ideas and inner visions. The paint and materials incorporated into the art are secondary to the language, the symbol.

Some critiques believe that today's art is radically new and different from our history. There are controversies about art, morality and aesthetic taste. Many believe that the content of the art and the standards from the past are irrelevant, with little connection or use to us. Is there no tradition sufficiently enduring, are we in an era of pluralism with limits to what we can image and create? Unfortunately, this results in very few people who have any real understanding of what art is about, it's purpose rather than style or aesthetic appeal.[6] Therefore, it is the symbols in art that need to be understood in order to comprehend the meaning of what is art and who is it for. It is those symbols that are created by the artist whose true sense of integrity can teach us what art is about. Those special, courageous individuals who are able to rise above and whose non-acquiescence of authenticity result in conscious, historical and independent moral innovations. Therefore, art must never be deprived of purpose and ability to provoke, interrogate, challenge and to push things to their limits. The artist is that avant-garde individual, who has the resolution to insist that art has a message and goes against the tide even when it is unfashionable to do so.

For me, feminine symbols have a quality that has the ability to bring back a fragmented part of life. Consciously exploring and interpreting my art has been an innovative, daunting and challenging experience. My objective is to find connections in my symbolism and to make myself and my work understood. I examine the circumstances surrounding the appearance of my symbols from my unconscious and their significance in my conscious life as a woman, as an expression of my psychological condition. Carl Jung's psychological theories have enabled me to explore the archetypal components of the female psyche and to recognize and understand the power of those symbols in my work. My subject matter includes prehistoric images and how they manifest themselves in contemporary art. The images and symbols that continue to reappear in my art and which have an enduring psychological effect upon me have held significance from the earliest aesthetic expressions by humans to the present day. They offer ways of transforming oneself while simultaneously exploring the elements of the origins of art. My attempt to reveal the symbols beneath the surface and to surrender to what happens spontaneously without preordination or intention has given me some answers to who I am.

My work as a curator has encouraged me to travel to different countries, where I have connected and dialogued with other artists. I have investigated the history of the female symbol created by other artists who worked thousands of years ago. Artistic associations and similarities between the symbols contributes to the visual evidence that the female symbol, in her different forms, expresses the essential language that communicates the primal power of women. Our internal links remain grounded as prehistoric and contemporary art harmoniously and significantly meet. A woman's relation to her feminine principle, is something which controls her from deep within. There is a mystery about the past, a passion for ancient sites and images that continues. My opinion, supported by my research, is that the most effective contemporary artists working with ancient images and ideas are those who are most aware of their origins.

Conscious recognition and appreciation of ones critical relationship to the past enables one to make art viable as social commentary in the present world. Thus, these symbols are still very much alive in women artist's consciousness. However, nothing will evolve or change as long as we refuse to question and remain unconscious of the fundamental forces, which shape the symbols in art. For only in this examination can art find its justification and the creative powers of real depth. Exploring different symbols created through time will enable us to understand the development of consciousness. Focusing on the elements of the origins of art and how they manifest themselves in contemporary art has enabled me to translate the symbols into what I believe has transformed my life into art and my art into life. My passion for my work stirs up memories and unanswered questions, forcing me to turn inward where I search for symbolic meaning. The symbols that I paint and sculpt provide an insight into a search for a deeper understanding, in its purest form, the soul of my creativity.

Artists who restore the iconography of the female symbol in contemporary culture are reacting to the position of human experience. Two renowned contemporary women artists that have created provocative symbols in their work are Louise Bourgeois (1911, French and Eva Hesse (1936-1970, German). Both portrayed a kind of innate and rhythmical poetry for the materials they used, the properties and the symbols that make up the richness of their physically symbolic images. Their work has a magical and pure sensitivity. They are tactile and the visual aspects of their sculptures relate to one another in a remarkable way, enabling one to feel the quality of the art. For me, their art depicts an abstract, manifestation of female forms. The nature of their infinite spirit becomes a reality through the materials used, wood, fibers, clay and stone mediums. There appears to be a sexual anthropomorphic meaning in their work, on an unconscious level.

Bourgeois's monolithic, goddess like sculptures appear austere with unrefined, imperfections and an ability to evoke the nostalgic world. Her work consists of coarse pieces of wood, biomorphic and geometric shapes that appear to be organically and emotionally charged. She creates a sort of unpolished, sacred simplicity that echoes the primeval origins of art.[7] Her titles have archetypical names, such as, *Cell, (Arch of Hysteria)*.

Hess created skin-like, ephemeral symbols. The texture and sensuality of her sculptures evoke a visceral reaction. She used fragile and deteriorating materials such as latex and fiberglass, successfully fusing past and present. Hess pushed a given medium to its limits by repeating a process that appeared to express emotional obsessiveness.[8]   She successfully portrayed abstract, primal female forms.

Both artists portray multi-layered symbols that are associated with archeological objects, fetishes and magical objects symbolizing a feminine spirit. It is apparent that these two women artists have been influenced and inspired by prehistoric female images. The personal subterranean layers of these artist's inner depths in which their sublime desire to create the symbol in art is unquestionably a projection of their unconscious journey. It is the symbol, in that embodied space, that links the transformation of life into art and art into life. For it is the artist who is capable of creating vibrations that move the soul. They open one's vision and ideals. They make the effort to regain the pure dignity of art. Bourgeois's and Hess's female sculptures are boundless, free from any restraints. Their simplicity and inspiration symbolizes their respect for the nature of materials, enabling them to perfect harmony between form, content and symbol. When the life of the art, the content, can pulsate forcefully, the spirit can be felt and the symbol will be heard. The image of the woman, is a force which can move the human spirit forward and upward, it must be released and revered.

My passion for the sculpted female symbol took me to the island of Malta where hundreds of sculptures and etchings have been found depicting full-bodied and or pregnant women. My curiosity was inspired for this small island, sun bleached in golden, orange, pink and copper hues, that contains the oldest and most well preserved temples in the world. The plethoric ancient female symbols discovered in Malta are an excellent example of a place that created a language through the art of symbol making. It also presents a path whereby one could return to a time when the symbol of the woman was celebrated as sacred. Figures with pronounced breasts and incised pubic triangles standing or in birth-giving positions are chiseled and carved into limestone or modeled in clay. Her temples of stone with magical, intense energy evoke female power. The ancient temples symbolizing female presence or for some a Goddess having symbolic significance. They manifest forgotten images and meanings, which can be awakened by the artist.

Malta's ancient symbols, images and temples are marked with repeated pitting, dots, spiral, snakes and lozenge motifs on their walls and altars. Red ochre stains the walls of the caves and temples, appearing to have been rubbed onto some of the sculptures. Art historians have suggested that the spiral may represent the force and energy of the feminine in nature. For thousands of years spirals were used as an element in spiritual pictorial language. Traces of the snake and fish iconography have also been discovered and are believed to reveal a connection to the mystery of birth, fertility and the cycle of life. The same symbols are seen on pottery vessels and bowls.

Some scholars believe that rituals of regeneration, healing and dream centers may have been first held in underground cave sanctuaries where many female looking sculptures and symbols have been discovered. The three-level subterranean Hal Saflieni Hypogeum, with its many egg-shaped chambers, appears to have been used for these purposes for many thousands of years. A small exquisitely formed, clay sculpture, the Sleeping Goddess, was found in a deep shaft in the Hypogeum. It depicts a reclining, possibly pregnant female, thought to be a priestess, sleeping and presumably dreaming. Perhaps this sculpture was used as a votive offering in conjunction with performing the act of dream incubation. It has been dated in the range from 3000 to 3600 B.C.E.

The Oracle Room in the Hypogeum is another example of a place that depicts the power of the feminine symbol in art. The walls and ceilings were painted with red ochre in designs and symbols of fruit resembling pomegranates and curvilinear spirals. The spiraling symbols on the ceiling are complex, a mass of curves, tendrils and a variety of branches all interwoven, connected, reaching, extending to create a harmonious and balanced composition. Art historians have suggested that the spiral symbol may represent the female force and energy of nature and her circling movements of atmosphere and earth currents.

The temples above ground, are believed to have been deliberately constructed to symbolize the body of the Goddess, most especially so in those cases where the architecture itself forms the shape of female bodies such as the Ggantija and Tarzien temples. More than thirty stone sculptures of female figures with enlarged breasts and swollen vulvas indicative of pregnancy have been found in various temples areas, including Mnajdra, Sorba, Hagar Qim, Ggantija and Tarzien. The largest one, the bottom half of a female form found at Tarzien, is pejoratively known as *The Fat Lady*. This fragment, one meter in height, consists of round, exceptionally large legs with tiny feet, clothed in a skirt to the mid-calf. The corpulent body is believed to symbolize a goddess of giving birth, and its hidden mysteries. The figure stands erect on a pedestal with a design of alternating egg shapes and columns.

Other important sculptures are the *Venus of Malta*, a female symbol standing boldly erect, with her left hand on her abdomen and the other on her large breasts. *The Double Goddess* was most recently discovered, during 1991 excavations at Brochtorff Circle on farmland outside Zaghra, Gozo. This small sculpture, painted with red ochre, depicts two seated women dressed in skirts decorated with U-forms. One holds a pot. Various speculations on the symbolic meaning of these figures have been made, including a priestess, a hieratical goddess of life and rebirth, perhaps a mother and daughter or sisters. It is suggested that each female sculpture's skirt design symbolizes the vulva and the pot signifies life and death.[9]

Malta's prehistoric temples, sculptures and symbols are evidence of a culture that appears to have celebrated the female as a symbol of the divine. This Mediterranean island, with its megalithic stones, offers a reservoir of essential spiritual images, a powerful resurgence of sacred symbols, a reminder of deep feminine connections.[10] The surviving iconography and the prevailing rounded, organic and sensuous symbols discovered in Malta, as well as other countries throughout the world, have always motivated artists to create art. The contemporary artist's multimedia, often abstract techniques and forms frequently leaves the viewers searching for hidden secrets, mysteries and messages about these exquisite female symbols.

Erich Neumann describes this process of the creative power as, unplanned. It seizes and evolves from the unconscious of the individual, with force and takes possession of her. The artist is an instrument of the transpersonal, and cannot escape.[11]

The evidence supports the research that the female images and symbols in all forms are related and very much alive in women artist's consciousness. This phenomenon enables us to interpret and appreciate myths, history, religious beliefs, social needs and personal experiences. The many female symbols discovered throughout the world provides us with direction for discovering truths and values necessary to reclaim our heritage and beliefs as women and as artists. These symbols continue to express an essential visual language, communicating the strength, courage and primal power innate in women. Thus, it is the artist who attempts to reveal the symbols beneath the surface. These images and symbols that continue to reappear in art have enduring psychological effects and hold significance from the earliest aesthetic expression by humans to the present day. They are a catalyst for future knowledge. They offer ways of translating iconography of the symbols of life while simultaneously exploring the elements of the origins of art.

When I work alone in my studio I am in a sacred place that I call home. It is a retreat where I can participate in the world's mystery, discover my innermost self and communicate in a language of visual symbols. The female symbol found her place on my canvas as she unveiled from beneath the layers of pigment. Her symbol weaves together with other symbols and inner visions that dance onto the canvas. Artistic creations can be symbols of something eternal and innate. These symbols have meaning, although meaning is formless, non-tangible and non-existent. Symbols have existence, shape and are tangible; they are connected and derive their significance from meaning. Therefore, meaning manifests itself from the symbol, the female symbol and the nature of its spirit are no exception.

The paramount possibilities of art, where the archetypes of our individual and personal lives are nourished and remain fertile can be apprehended by us. Therefore, we must learn to interpret the language of our symbols and to then release our souls to our unconscious world–this is where the drama in art lies. Ultimately, there is a silence beyond words that the creation of a symbol can provoke. In conclusion, it is my belief that the purpose of art, its value and meaning is to be found in the language, the soul of the symbol. As it was in prehistoric times, the symbol is the primary source for understanding. The mystery of modern art is not all that different from ancient artists giving spirit to the symbol. Like ancient artists abstracting from pure nature, we too transcend our individual experiences to communicate our emotions, concerns and needs through art and the power of the symbol as we embrace and link art and life. Thus, it is the artist, that creative person who has a passionate need for expression and who intensely continues to reveal an eternal truth derived from the symbol.

Notes

1 Cynthia Freeland. *But is it Art?* New York, Oxford University Press, 2001, p. 27

2 Ibid., p. 9

3 Webster New World Dictionary, New York, Simon & Schuster, Inc., 1996, p. 623

4 Marija Gimbutas. *The Language of the Goddess.* San Francisco, Harper Collins, Publishers, 1989

5 Desmaris S. Wehr. *Jung and Feminism: Liberating Archetypes.* Boston, Beacon Press, 1987, p. 104

6 Suzi Gablik. *Has Modernism Failed?* New York, Thames & Hudson, 1987, p. 16, 17

7 Josep Helfenstein. *The Early Work: Louise Bourgeois.* Illinois, University of Washington Press, 2002, p. 31

8 *Eva Hesse*, edited by Elisabeth Sussman, San Francisco, Ca., Museum of Modern Art, 2002, p. 79-86

9 Veronica Veen, *Female Images of Malta, Goddess, Giantess, Farmeress,* Holland, Fia, 1994, pp. 9-15

10 Marija Gimbutas, *The Living Goddesses,* Berkeley, University of California Press, 1989, pp. 93-98

11 Erich Neumann. *Art and the Creative Unconscious.* Princeton University Press, 1959, p. 98

Bibliography

Albright, Thomas. *Art in the San Francisco Bay Area 1945-1980*.

Berkeley: University of California Press, 1985.

Alloway, Laurence. *"Carolee Schneenman: The Body as Object and Instrument."* *Art in America*, March, 1980.

Chadwick, Whitney. *Women, Art, and Society*. London: Thames and Hudson, 1990.

Chicago, Judy. *The Dinner Party: A Symbol of Our Heritage*. Garden City, New York: Anchor Press, 1982.

_____. *Through the Flower: My Struggle as a Woman Artist*. Garden City, New York: Anchor Press, 1982.

Flack, Audrey. *Art and Soul: Notes on Creating*. New York: Penguin Books, 1986.

Hooks, Bell. *Art on My Mind: Visual Politics*. New York: Norton, 1995.

Hughes, Robert. *Shock of the New*. New York: Alfred A. Knopf, Inc., 1980.

Kandinsky, Wassily. *Concerning The Spiritual in Art*. New York: Dover Publication, 1977.

King, Ursula. *Women & Spiritually: Voices of Protest and Promise*. Pennsylvania: Pennsylvania State University Press, 1993

Lederer, Wolfgang, M.D. *The Fear of Women*. New York: Grune & Stratton, 1968.

Lippard, Lucy. *Eva Hess*. New York: University Press, 1976.

_____. *From the Center: Feminist Essays in Women's Art*. New York: E.P. Dutton & Co., Inc., 1976.

_____. *GET THE MESSAGE. A Decade of Art For Social Change*. New York: E.P. Dutton. Inc., 1984.

_____. *Mixed Blessings*. New York: Pantheon Books, 1990.

_____. *Overlay: Contemporary Art and the Art of Prehistory*. New York: Pantheon, 1983.

Lisle, Laurie. *Portrait of an Artist: A biography of Georgia O'Keefe*. New York: Seaview Books. 1980

McGrath, Lynette. "Anne Sexton's Poetic Connections: Death, God and Form." In *Original Essays on the Poetry of Anne Sexton*. Frances Bixler, ed. University of Central Arkansas Press: 1988

Owl painted by Stella Kimura
Japanese/American ninety-year old grandmother: "The owl means we
should be kind to one another."
Photographed by Wallace Birnbaum

In honor...in remembrance....of Love's Voice

Victoria M. Batraski

She remembers a time when....
The truth of a woman lived. When her stories were told, and her voice was held as sacred.

This truth haunts and lives in my bones
    It screams to be heard from the inside of my pores
I am not able to close my eyes and rest for I am shown my truths in dreams, if I am not willing to look at them while waking
    When one shuts down another's truth by speaking their own
    The time when women honored each other as sisters is gone

How can our light, our flickering flame, which has been suppressed and taken from us directly or indirectly, survive, while desperately fighting for the right in our own communities, to give and receive each others voice. The drum was the voice of the people of Africa and many other traditions. They fought for their voice, their connection to their tradition, culture, themselves and Spirit.

My truth has been and felt intuitively shut down the last six months in community, where I am most aware and present to it's reoccurrence more so than anywhere else. Yet through this I bump up against my own face of inner truth by who and what I am, or not. The mirror speaks loudly. I now have the opportunity and strength to reclaim my voice and the voice of my sisters, whose voices I will remember as my own. While giving a class presentation, another sister walked out of the room when the drum was played, as she took responsibility for herself and left the room. I now understood this to have been a selfless and honoring act. She was allowing for the expression of another sisters voice, while honoring her own. Recently, a woman asked for the drum to be stopped, during a ritual

I was leading, as an enactment of a moon lodge from ancient times was being created, in essence tearing the thread and layers of the web that was being birthed.

When one woman is the focus of violence, and the response is one of blame, how can other women, believe they have the right and space to speak their truths. How can we support truth to be spoken as opposed to continuing the suppression of inner spirit song and voice of women right here in our own communities. The calling of your inner voice comes in whispers and will continue knocking harder until there is pain, in the form of emotional or physical dis-ease, in your mind and body; for your own Spirit is calling you to honor her, to express her, to pay heed and attention, for that is her food, the food of the soul. By waking to our soul calling, we honor the light within us, the breath and divinity, of our temple within.

For all of the people in Trinidad who were forbidden to play the drum, whose spirit was expressed and cultivated by the drum, it was torn from their arms, as a baby nursing it torn from the breast, their nourishment, the soul food, was taken from the people to control them.

As the bullfrogs have come out to sing their song in the rain, and keep me up until the wee hours of the night listening, trying to make sense of their croaking, I listen to how their collective voice, may teach me. My initial reaction was, get the frogs out, as they do not make the sound of nightingales, singing comforting and smooth ballads. They shriek throughout the night, as if there were an earthquake coming. This is their way of communicating earthquakes and celebrations, to each other, warning all around them of the burning in their hearts, coming in the form others may not think is pleasant, or in their language. Although we must awaken to the right and need all sounds and languages must be made heard. A safe space if begging to be created, especially, in an educational setting where diversity of voice is the Goddess speaking through all of us.

Now is the time to remember to speak your truth, and honor those who have the courage to do so, in such a way for other sisters to be held in theirs. This is a charge to all of us to remain true to our inner spirit, and to honor love's voice.

When voice and space for authentic self expression are taken away, we lose our knowledge of and sense of self. The true self disappears and is replaced by another's concept or idea of who we are and how we should be. The soulprint inside of the seed is not allowed to reveal itself, it is lambasted with sauce of a different flavor, one that is not our own. We then become the roasted chicken who has been killed for the sake of another's appetite, filling their own hunger needs. Whether of ego or of physical nourishment, this is not the way of the tiger.

She remember a time when…

Masculine and feminine were honored and revered as such, and when bodies were holy and sacred vessels and were viewed as such.

The depth of a woman resides in the earth, where earth meets breath, and voice meets sound, sacred sounding…grounding.

Entering the pulsating wombspace, the earth awaits your return to her….as you lie in her arms, allow yourself to sink into her depths, soaking inside of her womb, you begin to remember……

Love's Voice.

Perhaps I'll Find Her?

Willow LaMonte

Dedicated to Sid Reger, and to the thousands of orange trees throughout
Valrico, Florida – all clear cut in the last two years for suburban sprawl

If I found Her again at the center of my map
could my life be treasured once more?
But first can you tell me:
If Her long ago dismembered parts
were lovingly reassembled anew,
could I heal and release this fresh aching
along with the ancient sorrow?
And if I cried quietly alone in my room at night
could I loudly hear Her ceremonies resounding once more,
processing and singing in full view of a warm sunlit sky?
Then, if I found Her stones and shells on my altar
could I track my path back following rock and feather?
If I walk past Her oak trees and ghost of orange grove,
could I chart song footprints embedded in mud,
detect sandalprints whispered along tops of sand dunes?
If I picked white sage, marjoram, and rosemary from my garden,
could I find Her basket filled with woodland acorns, amanita,
but also red-orange blossoms of Mexican tithonia?
If I heard Her laughter coming from that sparkle place,
could navigate through the glints of facets of deep delight?
If I let Her roiling waters spill over neatly placed sandbags,
could I ride this rush of emotion returning to Her core?
Oh, now can you please tell me this:
If I found Her statue cupped in her beautiful hands,
would I discover even more revealed across the map,
fashioned of terracotta, limestone, granite and bone

adorned with red ocher, inspired by black carbon
incised, chevroned, and engraved?
If I found Her priestess placing statues along the perimeter,
would I be able to beacon my way back to Her precious land?
And by then could I at last declare myself:
In love with such heritage, smitten by this legacy,
devoted to a future search of knowing my way home?
Oh, then could I find Her undenied at the center of my map?
Well maybe,
perhaps maybe
but not
quite just
Yet ...
– © *Summer, 2003 Willow LaMonte*

Inspired in part by the "Daughters of the Ancient Goddess" workshop
presented by Sid Reger at Womongathering 2003. I had never before seen
Goddess figures to scale, spanning tens of thousands of years, physically placed
geographically down on the map representing a few thousand square miles. That
experience was profoundly transforming, and the tectonic plate shifts of my inner
landscape are still unfolding.

Contemporary sculpture that recalls
the ancient African black mother and child
Toulouse, France
Photograph by Wallace Birnbaum 2005

Biographies

Annette Williams, M.A. has her degree in psychology with an emphasis in Jungian and archetypal approaches. Currently she is a doctoral student in Philosophy and Religion with an emphasis in Women's Spirituality at the California Institute of Integral Studies as well as being a student of the Yoruba Ifa tradition. An admirer of hermetic tradition, she is a professional astrologer as well as a certified Sivananda yoga instructor. She assisted Lucia Birnbaum and Karen Villanueva in gathering the essays for this volume.

Arisika Razak, RN, CNM, MPH, has been a midwife healer and spiritual dancer for over thirty years. She has provided full scope midwifery care to indigent women, and women of color in inner city of Oakland for over twenty years, serving as a home and hospital birth attendant, hospital based CNM, health care administrator and health educator. She currently directs the Integrative Health Studies Program at the California Institute of Integral Studies, San Francisco, CA where she is also an Associate Professor of Women's Spirituality. Arisika has led spiritual and healing workshops for women for over two decades, and her dance celebrates the physical body of woman and the blood mysteries of childbirth, menstruation, sexuality and menopause. She is a contributor to several books, and presents at numerous conferences on the subjects of multiculturalism and diversity, women's health and healing, and embodied spirituality and movement.

Chandra Alexandre is a scholar, activist and devotee of Maa Kali. She received initation to women's mysteries from her maternal grandmother and *diksha* (spiritual initiation) in Puri (1998) and Kamakhya (2003). Chandra is the founder and Executive Director of SHARANYA (www. sharanya.org), a *devi mandir* (goddess temple) in San Francico. She is also adjunct faculty at the Institute for Transpersonal Psychology in Palo Alto teaching classes on Goddess and Dark Goddess.

China Galland, M.A., is the author of *The Bond Between Women, A Journey to Fierce Compassion; Longing for Darkness, Tara and the Black Madonna;* and the forthcoming, *The Keepers of Love* (HarperSanFrancisco, 2007). Galland is a Professor-in-Residence at C.A.R.E., the Center for the Arts, Religion, and Education at the Graduate Theological Union and the founder and Director of Images of Divinity under the sponsorship of C.A.R.E. Galland is featured in a documentary on the BBC/Opus Arte's DVD, *Stabat Mater*. Her book, *Longing for Darkness*, was the first book on the Black Madonna published in the United States (1990). *The Bond Between Women* was a finalist for the annual "Best Spiritual Book Published" for the year of publication. Galland lectures and teaches at colleges and universities around the country, leads periodic retreats and pilgrimages, and facilitates the Black Madonna Circle and the Circles of Love. Website: www.imagesofdivinity.org

Claudia von Werlhof, born in 1943 in Berlin, Germany, mother of a son, Prof. for Political Sciences and Women´s Studies, University of Innsbruck, Austria. Master in Economics, PhD in Sociology, University of Cologne, Habilitation in Political Sciences, University of Frankfurt. Empirical research in Central America and Venezuela. Co-founder of the international women´s (studies) movement. Activist against neo-liberalism and globalization. Theoretical work on a feminist theory of society, patriarchy, matriarchy and alternatives to western civilization. Last book together with Veronika Bennholdt-Thomsen and Nicholas Faraclas: There is an Alternative. Subsistence and Worldwide Resistance to Corporate Globalization, London, zedpress, 2001.

Deborah J. Grenn, Ph.D., is founder and director of The Lilith Institute and Voice of the Spirit, a mobile women's spirituality/study group and lecture series. She has hosted *Honoring The Sacred Feminine* on KVON Radio, Napa, and co-created the annual Women's Rites of Spring Festival (Napa) with Leilani Birely, now in its third year. Dr. Grenn is co-director and core faculty in the Institute of Transpersonal Psychology's Women's Spirituality MA Program. She also teaches at Napa Valley College and California Institute of Integral Studies. Her dissertation, *For She Is A Tree of Life: Shared Roots Connecting Women to Deity,* focuses on identities, beliefs & practices among the Lemba of South Africa & European-American Jewish women. She wrote *Lilith's Fire: Reclaiming Our Sacred Lifeforce* (Grenn-Scott, Universal Publishers, 2000); her most recent article, *Connecting With Deity Through a Feminist Metaformic Thealogy,* appears in the first issue of Metaformia: A Journal of Menstruation and Culture (www.metaformia.com,) an online academic journal launched in 2005 by cultural theorist Judy Grahn.

Dianne E. Jenett, Ph.D is core faculty and co-director of the Women's Spirituality Masters Program at New College of California and research faculty at California Institute of Integral Studies and the Institute of Transpersonal Psychology. Her research interests are community and women's rituals to the Goddess in South India, women's psycho-spiritual development, and qualitative research methods. Her research has been published in the US, Europe and India. Dianne returns to Kerala each year to cook pongala for the Goddess.

Elinor Gadon is a cultural historian whose research interests and publications are focused on the analysis of myth and image in their cultural context as they affect issues of gender. Her academic training, teaching and publication are both interdisciplinary – in art history, history of religions and cultural anthropology – as well as multi-cultural. Her specialty is the art and culture of the Indian subcontinent. Her major publication, "The Once and Future Goddess; A Symbol for Our Time," is a visual chronicle of the history of the sacred female and her re-emergence in the cultural mythology of our time. She is currently working on two projects for publication – the completion of a comprehensive study of the mythology of the masculine in American culture. The second is a socio-cultural analysis of the village goddess in India based on five seasons of fieldwork in Orissa. She has taught at the Harvard Divinity School, Tufts University, University of California, Santa Barbara and Mills College where she was an Associate Scholar in the Women's Leadership Program. She developed and directed an M.A. and Ph.D. in Women's Spirituality at the California Institute of Integral Studies in San Francisco.

Francesca Roccaforte is Southern Italian American, born and raised in NYC. She currently lives and works in the SF Bay area. Inspired by her rich culture, she has used words, images, video, film and multimedia to express divine feminity in women's spirituality, culture and ritual. She is an award winning poet, photographer, digital documentary producer/ director, and producer of video and film festivals. She can be reached at rocknfranny@mindspring.com website   rocknfranny.com 510 417-1332. She has a Masters Degree in Visual Communications from California University East Bay. Her Thesis and published articiles focus on Italian American Women's culture and sexual gender roles and lesbianism (Articles poems photos and oral herstories published: Hey Paesan, Curaggia, Voices of Italain American, Milvia Street Journal)

Genevieve Vaughan author of *For-Giving, a Feminist Criticism of Exchange,* activist , social change philanthropist, and founder of the feminist Austin, Texas-based Foundation for a Compassionate Society 1988-1998 , is originator of a perspective which uses gift giving as the basis for an analysis of Patriarchal Capitalism and reveals the possibility of an alternative economy and culture based on women. Recently Genevieve and the staff of the Center for the Study of the Gift Economy organized and sponsored two international women's conferences:in 2004 A Radically Different WorldView is Possible; the Gift Economy Inside and Outside Patriarchal Capitalism; and in 2005 Societies of Peace: 2nd World Congress on Matriarchal Studies, directed by German philosopher Heide Goettner Abendroth. Genevieve is the editor of an issue of the Italian journal *Athanor* titled *Il Dono/the Gift, a feminist perspective* (2004)and author of a children's book, *Mother Nature's Children* (1999), and has produced a cd of her *Songs for the Tree of Life.* Her books, many articles and the dvds of the gift conference are available on her website www.gift-economy.com. She lives part time in Italy.

Heide Goettner-Abendroth is a woman philosopher and researcher in culture and society, focused on matriarchal studies. In 1973 she earned her Ph.D. in philosophy at the University of Munich, where she taught philosophy for ten years (from 1973-1983). She published various books on matriarchal society and culture and has become the founding mother of Modern Matriarchal Studies. In 1986 she founded the International Academy HAGIA. "Academy for Matriarchal Studies and Matriarchal Spirituality" in Germany. In the year 2003, she organised and guided the "First World Congress on Matriarchal Studies: SOCIETIES IN BALANCE" in Luxembourg/Europe and in the year 2005, the "Second World Congress on Matriarchal Studies: SOCIETIES OF PEACE" in San Marcos, Texas/USA.
www.goettner-abendroth.de
INTERNATIONAL ACADEMY HAGIA
Weghof 2, D-94577 Winzer - Germany
www.hagia.de

Jamie Logsdon Kuehnl, M.A., is an eco-feminist and a scholar of women's literature and spirituality who lives and writes in "God's and Goddess' Country" — the Upper Peninsula of Michigan. It is along the shores of

Lake Superior that she raises her two children: Jessee David and Jasmine Victoria. She attained her Master's degree in Literature from Northern Michigan University and is currently a Ph.D. student in the Women's Spirituality program at the California Institute of Integral Studies.

Being a lifetime science fiction aficionado, it is not surprising that Jan Marijaq did her doctoral dissertation on science fiction themes found in the work of Sheri S. Tepper, especially since her Ph.D. concentration at the California Institute of Integral Studies was in Women's Spirituality. An experienced technical writer, a part-time technical trainer, and a mastered librarian, Dr. Marijaq has had a checkered career so far. Her major intellectual interests are political change, respectful globalization, and the religions and cultures of the world. But her fun is with her daughter Susie and son-in-law Chris, her grandchildren Moira and Gavin, her cats, and with sharing ideas with friends. And nothing beats staying in bed for no reason reading mysteries and science fiction, or walking someplace beautiful in the sunshine.

Jayne DeMente received a Masters degree in Religion and Philosophy from the California Institute of Integral Studies, with a specialty in Women's Spirituality. It was here that she developed a theory about Mary's contribution to the mythology of spirituality in her paper "Trinity of the Hebrew Goddess". She attended Antioch University as an undergraduate - the emphasis of her research was on gender balanced ethics curriculum. She spent her youth in the field of entertainment and is the daughter of evangelist, William Thomas DeMente. She is also the founder/director of Women's Heritage Project and Endowment, which gives grants and scholarships to women.

Jen Miller-Hogg is a Ph.D. student in the Women's Spirituality Studies at the California Institute of Integral Studies in San Francisco, California. She received her master at New York University in education and her bachelor's at the University of Southern California in English. Jen lives with her husband, Marcus, and their three cats, Fiona, Bobette, and Bobo in the East Bay of San Francisco.

Joan Beth Clair, M.A., M.Div., is the author of Wind-of-Fire, The Story of an Untouchable. A graduate of The Pacific School of Religion, Berkeley, California, her M.A. thesis, Creature Rites: Towards a Life Affirming Liturgy has been acknowledged as the first work of its kind in the world. Her art work Alive in Her: She Who is Perfectly Empty and Perfectly Full was recently reproduced in the book <u>Mary Magdalene, Bride in Exile</u> by Margaret Starbird. A version of the work as a wall hanging may also be found at Martin de Porres House of Hospitality and Safehouse for Women Leaving Prostitution in San Francisco as well as other places in the Bay Area of California that work with the homeless. A lifelong poet, many of her poems in recent years have been published in <u>Street Spirit</u>.

Jodi MacMillan is an ordained priestess and has been a professional clairvoyant and trance medium healer since 1992. She is the founder and executive director of Belladonna, a non-profit organization for women's ancient and contemporary spiritual traditions in Berkeley, California.

Karen Nelson Villanueva is a Philosophy & Religion doctoral student with a specialization in Women's Spirituality at the California Institute of Integral Studies in San Francisco. She holds Masters degrees in Public Administration from George Washington University and Culture & Spirituality from Holy Names College. A native of Detroit, she attended the University of Michigan as an undergraduate. Karen currently lives in San Francisco with her husband Max, a recreation director for the City, writes, teaches, and helped gather the essays for this volume with Annette Williams and Lucia Birnbaum.

Kim Bella is a therapist, teacher, artist, and researcher based in Sonoma County, California. Her research interests focus on investigating the human phenomenon through art-based methodologies, as well as bridging the personal, the artistic, and the spiritual. She is passionate about animal rights, women's spirituality, and political and spiritual activism. A certified yoga teacher, yoga therapist, and psychospiritual facilitator, she believes the wisdom of the body-mind connection is accessible to everyone. She is currently in the process of completing her PhD studies in the field of East/West Psychology at the California Institute of Integral Studies.

Lucia Chiavola Birnbaum, Ph.D. is a feminist cultural historian and Professor of Philosophy and Religion in the Women's Spirituality program of the California Institute of Integral Studies in San Francisco; she and her husband, Dr. Wallace Birnbaum, live in Berkeley close to their jewish/ sicilian/multicultural family. Lucia's books include *Liberazione della donna. Feminism in Italy* (Middletown, Ct., Wesleyan University Press, 1986, American Book Award from the Before Columbus Foundation, 1987; *Black Madonnas. Feminism, religion and politics in Italy* (Boston, Ma., Northeastern University Press, 1993); italian edition, *Black Madonnas.*

Femminismo, religione e politica in Italia (Bari, Italia, Palomar Editrice, 1997), Premio Internazionale di Saggistica (Salerno, Italia, 1998), and republished iUniverse (Loc. Cit.) reprint edition. *Dark mother. African origins and godmothers* (New York, Chicago, Lincoln and Shanghai, iUniverse, 2001); Enheduanna Award for Excellence in Woman-Centered Literature, 2002, italian edition, *la madre o-scura* (Cosenza, Italia, MEDiterranea MEDia, 2004); french/european/african/caribbean edition, *La mere noire* (Paris and Cameroun, Menaibuc Editions, March 2007). Among other publications she gathered the essays for volume one, *She is Everywhere! Writings in womanist/feminist spirituality* (New York, et al., iUniverse, 2005) and, with Annette Williams and Karen Villanueva, gathered essays for volume two, *She is Everywhere!* (Loc. Cit., iUniverse, 2008).

Lydia Ruyle is an artist scholar on the Visual Arts faculty of the University of Northern Colorado in Greeley, Colorado. She has a Bachelor of Arts degree from the University of Colorado at Boulder, a Master of Art from UNC and has studied with Syracuse University in Italy, France, Spain, and with the Art Institute of Chicago in Indonesia. She works regularly at Santa Reparata International School of Art in Florence, Italy and Columbia College Center for Book and Paper in Chicago. Her research into sacred images of women has taken her around the globe. For seven years, Ruyle led women's pilgrimage journeys to sacred places. Ruyle creates and exhibits her art and does workshops throughout the U.S. and internationally. Her Goddess Icon Spirit Banners made their debut in 1995 at the Celsus Library in Ephesus, Turkey. Since then they have flown in Australia, Canada, Britain, France, Luxembourg, Italy, Greece, Serbia, Bulgaria, Germany, the Czech Republic, Hungary, Poland, Russia, Turkey, Ghana, Kenya, Brazil, Mexico, Peru, Japan, New Zealand, Nepal, Bhutan, Tibet, China and the U.S. spreading their divine feminine energies. A book about her work, *Goddess Icons Spirit Banners of the Divine Feminine*, was published in 2002. *Turkey Goddess Icons Spirit Banners of the Divine Feminine* was published in Istanbul in 2005.

Małgorzata (Margaret) Kruszewska – Born in Poland and immigrating with my family of three sisters at a young age, I grew up in Bridgeport, Connecticut where my parents worked in factories.   I am currently completing my doctoral studies in Asian and Comparative Studies and write about and research female spiritual practices of ancient India and Africa. I am also a theater playwright/director having had my plays, *MotherGhost*, *MarX' Daughter* and *Daddy meets Durga* produced in New York and Los Angeles.

Mary Ann Robinson has studied at the California Institute of Integral Studies in San Francisco and is currently enrolled at the Jesuit School of Theology at Berkeley at the Graduate Theological Union. She holds a M.A. in theology from the Washington Theological Union in Washington, D.C. Married with two grown daughters, she lives in Oakland, California, where carries on her research on the impact the figures of Eve and Mary continue to have in our lives.

May Elawar is a student at the California Institute of Integral Studies working towards a PhD in Women's Spirituality. She is of Middle Eastern background and is interested in bringing this area into the rapidly growing pool of women's spirituality research. May holds a BA in International Relations from Webster University in Geneva, Switzerland, and an MA in International Communication from the American University in Washington, D.C.

Pairin Jotisakulratana is a graduate student in Women's Spirituality program at California Institute of Integral Studies, San Francisco. In Thailand, she works as a social change trainer.

Rainbow Mooon began teaching astrology in 1978 at the School of Metaphysics in Kansas City, Missouri. She began practicing shamanic forms of healing in 1988 after she returned from Vision Quest in southern Florida. Always a seeker of various forms of knowledge and methods of understanding, Rainbow returned to the academy to receive her undergraduate degree in Sociology from the University of Kansas City in Missouri. She and her cat drove her Honda from Missouri to California where she received her graduate degree in Social and Cultural Anthropology from the California Institute of Integral Studies where she is now working on her doctoral degree in Asian and Comparative Studies. Women's issues and parenting are her spiritual and academic focus.

"Beyond the Symbol" series by Tricia Grame
Painting is oil, acrylic, and mixed media. Sculptures are terra cotta, lime, cement, copper, and pigment. These pieces are from a series inspired by my research in Italy and Malta, where prehistoric images of the female were discovered.

"It is possible to show by now when this project known as globalization will necessarily come to and end, at the latest when the non-renewable resources of the planet have been used up...that Western lifestyles are utterly impossible to impose on a global scale. Ecological collapse would be the immediate result."
-- Claudia von Werlhof

"Experiences of insight are all metaphors for understanding the longing of the soul to have liberation and peace... my insights led me to understand the feminine part of the spiritual story and it gives me peace."
-- Jayne DeMente

"Gypsies are as real psychologically as they are literally and understanding our own inner gypsyhood can go a long way into integrating the "dark other" as ourselves."
-- Kim Bella

"Since a belief in the sacredness and interconnectedness of all things may be one of the foundational elements necessary to save our planet, it follows that we should also conduct **research** as if it were sacred."

-- Dianne E. Jenett

"Her African features do not represent the physical features of Her worshipers-what stories then have upheld her strong presence in Poland-what issues of race and divine female powers are being sustained through the people who adore Her?"

-- Malgorzata Kruszewska